OKL

AN INTRODUCTION
Fourth Edition

Edited by

Brett S. Sharp
University of Central Oklahoma

and

Christopher L. Markwood
University of Wisconsin-Superior

KENDALL/HUNT PUBLISHING COMPANY
4050 Westmark Drive   Dubuque, Iowa   52002

Original cover design by Jon Toney.
Cover redesign by Craig Beuchaw.

Copyright © 1998, 2000 by Christopher L. Markwood
Copyright © 2005, 2007 by Brett S. Sharp and Christopher L. Markwood

ISBN 978-0-7575-4626-6

Kendall/Hunt Publishing Company has the exclusive rights to reproduce this work, to prepare derivative works from this work, to publicly distribute this work, to publicly perform this work and to publicly display this work.

All rights reserved. No part of this publication may be reproduced, stored in a retrieval system, or transmitted, in any form or by any means, electronic, mechanical, photocopying, recording, or otherwise, without the prior written permission of Kendall/Hunt Publishing Company.

Printed in the United States of America
10 9 8 7 6 5 4 3 2 1

To our students

CONTENTS

List of Tables vii
List of Figures viii
List of Leadership Profiles ix
Foreword by Governor Brad Henry xi
Acknowledgments xiii

CHAPTER 1	Federalism and Oklahoma .... 1 Christopher L. Markwood	
CHAPTER 2	The Constitutional and Cultural Context of Oklahoma Government .... 17 Christopher L. Markwood	
CHAPTER 3	The Political Economy of Oklahoma: An Overview .... 37 Loren C. Gatch	
CHAPTER 4	The Oklahoma Legislature .... 59 Jan C. Hardt	
CHAPTER 5	Oklahoma's Governor and Elected Executives .... 95 Timothy W. Faltyn and Kenneth Kickham	
CHAPTER 6	Public Administration in Oklahoma .... 111 Brett S. Sharp	
CHAPTER 7	The Judicial System of Oklahoma .... 127 Keith R. Eakins	
CHAPTER 8	Oklahoma and the Supreme Court .... 155 Danny M. Adkison	
CHAPTER 9	Parties, Elections, and Political Participation in Oklahoma .... 167 Jan C. Hardt	
CHAPTER 10	Interest Groups and Campaign Finance in Oklahoma .... 195 Jan C. Hardt	
CHAPTER 11	The Oklahoma Tax System .... 233 Loren C. Gatch	

CHAPTER 12	**Municipal and County Government in Oklahoma**	253
	Deborah D. Ferrell-Lynn	
CHAPTER 13	**Public Policy in Oklahoma**	277
	Markus S. Smith and Dana K. Glencross	
CHAPTER 14	**Oklahoma Environmental Policy: Conflict and Complexity in a Traditionalist State**	287
	John R. Wood	
Bibliography	301	

LIST OF TABLES

1–1	Selective Incorporation and the Bill of Rights	6
2–1	A Comparison of State Constitutions	25
2–2	Comparison of State and Federal Constitutional Provisions	30
3–1	Output (Gross Product) by Industry in Percent, U.S. vs. Oklahoma 2005	51
4–1	Differences Between the Oklahoma House and Senate	63
4–2	House and Senate Leadership Turnover	66
4–3	Compensation/Expenses Comparison between the Oklahoma, Texas, and California Legislatures, Current as of May 1, 2007	70
4–4	Education, Age, and Tenure of the Members of the 2004 Legislature	72
4–5	House and Senate Leadership Positions as of 2004	80
4–6	How an Idea Becomes a Law	86
5–1	Compensation for the Oklahoma Governor	98
5–2	Elected Executives and Their Agencies	108
6–1	State Government Workforce Representation 2007 (Excluding Higher Education)	116
6–2	The Governor's Cabinet as of May 2007	119
7–1	Summary of District Court Cases Filed July 1, 1003–June 30, 1994	150
9–1	The Democratic and Republican Parties in Oklahoma	170
9–2	Changes in Oklahoma Congressional and State Seats	190
10–1	Percentage of Oklahoma Lobbyists in Five Categories, in 1986, 2003, and 2007	197
10–2	Average Money Spent by Type of Seat Sought for the 1998, 2002, and 2006 Elections	210
10–3	2002 and 2006 Top Recipients/Spenders in Oklahoma State Legislative Races	213
10–4	Top 10 PAC Contributors in Oklahoma State Legislative Races, 2002 and 2006	214
10–5	2002 and 2006 Top 10 PACs by Total Amount Donated	216
10–6	2006 AVG PAC Contributions—By House and Senate	219
10–7	Average PAC $, Average Number of PAC Donations, Average PAC Donation Amount, Average Receipts and Average Expenditures to All State Legislative Candidates in the 2006 Elections	221
10–8	2002 vs. 2006 Elections—Type of PAC—Which Ones Give the Most and Least?	222

List of Tables

10–9	2006 Election PAC Contributions by Type of PAC, Divided by House and Senate	224
10–10	2006 Election PAC Contributions by Type of PAC, divided by Democrats and Republicans	225
10–11	2006 Election PAC Contributions by Type of PAC, Divided by Winners and Losers	226
10–12	2006 Election PAC Contributions by Type of PAC, divided by Incumbent, Challenger, and Open Seat	227
11–1	Major Exemptions to the Sales Tax	238
11–2	Oklahoma State Taxes and Collections, Amount and as a Percentage of All Revenues, by Major Sources, FY 2006	240
11–3	State and Local Taxes as a Percentage of Personal Income and Per Capita, Oklahoma, Neighboring States, and the National Average, FY 2002 (National Rank Out of 50 States, 1 = Highest)	242
11–4	Property, Sales, and Income Taxes as Percentage of Personal Income and Per Capita, FY 2002 (National Rank Out of 50 States, 1 = Highest)	243
11–5	Property, Sales, and Income Taxes as a Percentage of the Three-Tax Revenue Total, Oklahoma and Neighboring States FY 2002 (National Rank Out of 50 States, 1 = Highest)	244
11–6	Share of State and Local Tax Collection By State Governments, Oklahoma and Neighboring States FY 2002 (National Rank Out of 50 States, 1 = Highest)	244
11–7	State and Local Intergovernmental Revenue Per Capita and as a Percent of State and Local General Revenue: Oklahoma and Neighboring States FY 2002 (National Rank Out of 50 States, 1 = Highest)	245
11–8	Major Revenue Sources as a Share of State and Local Own-Source General Revenue, Oklahoma vs. Neighboring States, FY 2002	246
11–9	"Tax Freedom Day"	248
12–1	Ten Largest Cities in Oklahoma and Land Area	257
12–2	City of Norman Select Departments and Functions	262
14–1	Oklahoma State Environmental Agencies	288

LIST OF FIGURES

2–1	The Twin Territories	19
4–1	Oklahoma House Districts 2002–2010 Elections	77
5–1	Administrative Structure	99
6–1	Number of Executive Branch State Employees in Oklahoma by Fiscal Year	121
6–2	Oklahoma State Employees Current Average in Pay Band 2007	124

List of Tables

9–2	Oklahoma Congressional Districts 2002–2019 Elections	180
12–1	FY 2003–2004 City of Oklahoma City Operating Expenditures by Function	263
12–2	The City of Oklahoma City FY 2004–2005 Operating Expenditures by Category	264
12–3	City of Edmond General Fund Revenue by Source FY 2001–2002 (by Percent)	265
13–1	Policy Making Process	279

LIST OF LEADERSHIP PROFILES

Tom Cole, Member of Congress, 4th District–Oklahoma 10
Wilma Mankiller, Former Principal Chief of the Cherokee Nation 21
Enoch Kelly Haney, Chief of the Seminole Nation 34
Julie Knutson, President and CEO of Oklahoma Academy for
  State Goals 43
Amy Polonchek, Executive Director, Oklahoma Department of
  Commerce 54
Judy Eason McIntyre, Member of the Oklahoma State
  Senate–District 11 73
Governor Brad Henry, 26th Governor of the State of Oklahoma 97
Jari Askins, Lieutenant Governor 107
Bill Citty, Chief of Police, City of Oklahoma City 112
James D. Couch, City Manager, City of Oklahoma City 115
Oscar B. Jackson, Jr., Cabinet Secretary of Human Resources and
  Administration 123
Marian Opala, Vice-Chief Justice, Oklahoma Supreme Court 133
Michael C. Turpen, Attorney and Counselor at Law 162
Gary Jones, Chairman and Executive Director, Oklahoma
  Republican Party 172
Mary Fallin, Member of Congress, 5th District–Oklahoma 176
Saundra Naifeh, Executive Director, Oklahoma Association of
  Optometric Physicians 217
Scott Meacham, Oklahoma State Treasurer 237
Cindy Simon-Rosenthal, Mayor, City of Norman, Oklahoma 260
John Smaligo, Jr., Tulsa County Commissioner for District #1 270
Jeanette M. Nance, Agency Liaison and Public Policy Specialist,
  Office of the Governor 282
W. A. "Drew" Edmondson, Attorney General of Oklahoma 296

FOREWORD

Governor Brad Henry

The pioneers who took part in the first land run of 1889 were drawn to the prospect of simple things: some property and a home in a land that seemed as vast and limitless as the magnificent skies that stretched along its horizon. From such unbridled hope and optimism emerged Oklahoma.

The obstacles met by these early settlers helped shape a citizenry renowned for resilience. Oklahomans are a strong people. We have endured more than our share of economic challenges, from the Dust Bowl of the 1930s to the farming crisis and oil bust of the 1980s. We have persevered in the face of deadly calamity. In the wake of the 1995 Oklahoma City federal building bombing and deadly tornadoes that roared through central Oklahoma in May of 1999, the people of our state revealed a determination and purposefulness that came to be known as "the Oklahoma Standard."

Our political landscape, however, has been decidedly more complicated. Like the twisters that sweep through this region each spring, the beginnings of Oklahoma state government proved unwieldy and often tumultuous. The framers of the state constitution, guided by staunch Populism, hammered out a document of astounding complexity and length.

Despite the march of time, remnants of that Populist spirit remain evident today. The scope of the governor has been significantly limited, while the state constitution invested greater authority in the legislative branch. Oklahomans elect a number of statewide officeholders who are typically appointed in other U.S. states. Unlike the process of many states, Oklahoma's governor and lieutenant governor do not campaign for election as a team. Seventy-seven counties and nearly 550 public school districts attest to the singular pride of Oklahoma's many communities.

And along the way, we have witnessed our share of interesting personalities. The first woman elected by Oklahoma to the U.S. Congress, Alice Mary Robertson, ran on a platform of opposing women's right to vote. Undoubtedly the most colorful governor in state history was William H. "Alfalfa Bill" Murray, who served as president of the state's constitutional convention and later became Oklahoma's governor during the Great Depression. An avowed segregationist who went on to an unsuccessful campaign for the presidency, Murray dispatched the National Guard 34 times, declaring martial law to manipulate oil prices and even square off against Texas Rangers over a toll road controversy. Of course, the annals of Oklahoma history are also filled with leaders of toughness, integrity, and vision: J. Howard Edmondson, Robert S. Kerr, Carl Albert, Henry Bellmon, and David Boren, to name but a few.

The diversity of Oklahoma politics mirrors the state's rich cultural tapestry, from its American Indian heritage—39 tribes are headquartered in our state—to the more than 50 all-Black townships that sprang up following the Civil War. The state has a significant Hispanic tradition that dates back to the 1500s, when Coronado led an expedition through what is now the Oklahoman Panhandle. Oklahoma City boasts one of the larger Vietnamese populations in the nation. More languages are spoken within the borders of Oklahoma than in all of Europe.

I commend Professors Christopher Markwood and Brett Sharp, as well as their contributors, for this informative, comprehensive and scholarly examination of Oklahoma state and local government. An effective government is reliant on its people to be knowledgeable and involved. That is why efforts such as this book are so vital to our democracy. My late uncle, Lloyd Henry, used to say that public service was "the rent you pay for the space you occupy." That sentiment, I believe, also applies to being informed about the workings of public service.

You have before you a valuable owner's manual. Read it closely. A lot is at stake.

ACKNOWLEDGMENTS

Fourth Edition

This book is a collaboration of efforts. We are indebted to many people for their assistance on this revision. First, we want to thank the contributors to the fourth edition. The efforts of Danny Adkison, Keith Eakins, Tim Faltyn, Deb Ferrell-Lynn, Loren Gatch, Dana Glencross, Ken Kickham, Markus Smith, and John Wood. And deserving of extraordinary recognition is Jan Hardt who not only contributes three different chapters, but hers are also some of the most difficult ones to keep up-to-date. Her work helps to keep this book the standard reference on Oklahoma politics.

Second, we are grateful for contributions to previous editions of this book by Sharon Carney, George Humphreys, Stephen Jenks, and Phil Simpson. Their pathbreaking work continues to serve as models for our own efforts.

Third, we appreciate the able assistance of our students: Jeffrey Sheldon, who worked tirelessly gathering and organizing data for several chapters; and Tiffany Palmer, Kristy Roberts, and Michelle Stricklin who contributed leadership profiles. Also, thanks to Tom Patt, Everett Slavik, and others at the Oklahoma Office of Personnel Management for their quick response to our queries.

Finally, the graphic arts skills of Craig Beuchaw, Jon Toney, Keith Bowden, and James Barrow deserve special recognition for their assistance in designing the cover and developing many of the figures and illustrations.

CHAPTER ONE

FEDERALISM AND OKLAHOMA

Christopher L. Markwood

The question of the relation of the States to the federal government is the cardinal question of our constitutional system . . . It cannot . . . be settled by the opinion of any one generation, because it is a question of growth, and every successive stage of our political and economic development gives it a new aspect, makes it a new question.

Woodrow Wilson, *Constitutional Government in the United States* (1908), 173.

I. INTRODUCTION

Understanding the politics and government of Oklahoma requires a basic understanding and appreciation of the American system of federalism. **Federalism** in the United States can be defined as "a system of government in which power is divided between national and subnational governments with both exercising separate and autonomous authority, both electing their own officials, and both taxing their own citizens for the provision of public services" (Dye 1997). This chapter will 1) examine American federalism and how powers are divided between the national and state governments, 2) analyze the evolution of power as it relates to the national and state governments, 3) discuss the responsibilities of both the national government and the states, and 4) explore the interstate relationships of Oklahoma and the other states in the Union.

II. DIVIDING THE POWERS OF GOVERNMENT

Almost all nations have some type of local government and thus a distribution of power among the levels of government. While there are a number of ways to compare various forms and types of government, one way to classify and compare governments is by the formal distribution of power among the various governmental actors. Political scientists identify three general forms of government based on the distribution of power: confederal, unitary, and federal. All three types are very different from each other but at one time or another, the United States has operated under each one.[1]

Types of Governments

Governmental systems with a central government dependent upon the unit governments for authority or power can be referred to as **confederal systems**. While the unit governments can join together for common purposes, each unit retains its independence and grants only limited authority to the central government. As a result, the central government may be weak and ineffectual. After the American Revolution (1781–1789), the Articles of Confederation was the constitutional arrangement by which the nation was governed. Under this system, the national government had very little power and relied upon the states for both administrative and financial assistance. The national government could not tax, regulate interstate commerce, or effectively enforce its laws. These weaknesses led to the constitutional convention and ultimately the adoption of a new system of government in the Constitution of 1789.

Many countries, including England, Sweden, and France, have a **unitary system** of government, which exercises centralized control over all other governmental and political subdivisions. Whether referred to as a province, republic, village, territory, or state, local and regional subdivisions in a unitary system owe their very existence to the central or national government. Each subdivision may only exercise the authority given to it by the central or national government. As a result, subdivisions tend to be administrative divisions of the central government with little power to act on their own. Prior to the American Revolution, the Colonies were subject to a unitary system under England. Today, Oklahoma, like other states, has a unitary governmental structure as it relates to its political subdivisions, known as counties. However, in Oklahoma there is an interesting variation to this structure. Since the Indian nations have been given constitutional sanction and are not "local" governments, they are not subject to the unitary structural arrangement that exists between the state and local governments in Oklahoma. As a result, many areas including some issues involving taxes, gaming, and property rights fall outside the traditional unitary structural arrangement thus limiting Oklahoma's governmental authority.

In a **federal system**, both the national government and governmental subdivisions gradually derive their authority from the people. As a system of shared powers, each level of government has authority to make some decisions free from the external control of the other. Responsibilities can be divided between the national government and subdivisions, or responsibilities can be shared. Each level of government has spheres of authority and each has limitations. The American Constitution of 1789 created a federal system of government and divided powers between the national and state governments. These powers can be classified into five categories: delegated, implied, reserved, prohibited, and concurrent.

Types of Powers

The United States federal government is strengthened by several grants of power. Sometimes referred to as "enumerated" or "expressed" powers,

delegated powers are those powers specifically granted to the federal government in the U.S. Constitution. For example, Article I, Section 8, of the U.S. Constitution specifically gives Congress the power to establish a post office, levy and collect taxes, regulate interstate commerce, declare war, and coin money; Article II, Section 2, specifically gives the president the power to negotiate treaties, make appointments, and serve as commander in chief of the armed forces and state militias; and Article III, Section 2, specifically gives the Supreme Court the power to resolve disputes between states.

Implied powers are not specifically mentioned in the U.S. Constitution, but can be inferred from those that are specifically mentioned. Implied powers expand the scope of delegated powers. Article I, Section 8.18 gives Congress the power "To make all Laws which shall be necessary and proper for carrying into Execution the forgoing Powers." The Supreme Court defined and justified implied powers in the case of *McCulluch v. Maryland (1819)*, reasoning that since Article I specifically gives Congress the power to coin money, regulate its value, collect taxes, and borrow money, it can be implied that Congress needs a bank even though the U.S. Constitution does not expressly give Congress the power to create one. The "necessary and proper" clause has given the national government a tremendous amount of elasticity in carrying out its powers and has allowed the federal government to expand its role.

Despite this rather broad bestowal of power, the 10th Amendment to the U.S. Constitution provides that "The powers not delegated to the United States by the Constitution, nor prohibited by it to the States, are reserved to the States respectively or to the people." These powers are referred to as **reserved powers.** While an exhaustive list has yet to be compiled and agreed upon by legal scholars or policy makers, it is generally recognized that state governments, including Oklahoma, retain extensive control and responsibility for regulating most domestic matters, including: the operation of public schools; maintaining public services such as transportation, hospitals, and parks; conducting most criminal and civil trials; and, administering the election process.

Powers that are denied to the national government, state governments, or both are referred to as **prohibited powers.** For example, both the federal government and the states are prohibited from passing **ex post facto laws** (a retroactive criminal law imposing punishment after an act has been committed). Article I, Section 9, of the U.S. Constitution specifically prohibits the national government from giving preference to one state over another and granting titles of nobility, while Article I, Section 10, prohibits state governments from entering into a treaty or alliance with a foreign country, coining money, or interfering with the obligation of contracts.

Concurrent or **shared powers** are those possessed by both the national and state governments. For example, while the national government has the power to tax, build roads, pass legislation, establish courts, and regulate corporations, the state of Oklahoma has these powers, too. As a result, people in Oklahoma can be taxed by both the national and state government, drive on federal interstates and state highways, and be requested to appear in federal courts for violations of federal law and state courts for violations of state law. While these powers do overlap, state laws are not allowed to conflict with federal laws.

Supremacy of National Law

Occasionally, state laws are thought to be in conflict with federal law or the U.S. Constitution. The result can be a legal battle. Article VI, Section 2, of the U.S. Constitution states:

> This Constitution, and the Laws of the United States which shall be made in Pursuance thereof, and all Treaties made or which shall be made under the Authority of the United States shall be the supreme Law of the land; and the Judges in every State shall be bound thereby, any Thing in the Constitution or Laws of any State to the Contrary not withstanding.

This clause is known as the **National Supremacy Clause.** When conflicts arise between the laws of Oklahoma and federal laws, this constitutional provision requires that federal law take precedence. Several times, Oklahoma laws have been challenged as inconsistent with federal law. The result has been a challenge to the United States Supreme Court. The cases of *Sipuel v. University of Oklahoma* (1948) and *McLaurin v. Oklahoma State Regents for Higher Education* (1950) are illustrative.[2]

Until 1949, African American students were not allowed to attend graduate or professional school in Oklahoma. While students could purse an undergraduate education at Langston, a black college established prior to statehood, Oklahoma statutes required "separate but equal" education. Ada Lois Sipuel-Fisher was denied admission to the University of Oklahoma Law School in 1946 because she was African American. In an appeal to the United States Supreme Court, the Justices found Oklahoma in violation of the "separate but equal" doctrine because there was no option for African Americans who wanted to pursue law school. In *Sipuel v. University of Oklahoma,* the Supreme Court ordered Oklahoma to either admit Sipuel-Fisher to the University of Oklahoma or create a separate law school where she could attend. Rather than admit her to the University of Oklahoma Law School, the state of Oklahoma opted to create a separate law school for blacks at Langston. Ada Lois Sipuel-Fisher refused to attend the separate law school and reapplied for admission to the University of Oklahoma, where she was again denied admission.

In 1948, the University of Oklahoma denied admission to six African Americans to the graduate school. George McLaurin, one of the students denied admission, reapplied and was again denied admission. The Federal District Court for Western Oklahoma soon ordered his admission. However, McLaurin was still subject to blatant discrimination. He was forced to study at a separate table in the library and was separated from the other students in classrooms.

In 1949, the University of Oklahoma admitted a number of African Americans to graduate school and Ada Lois Sipuel-Fisher to law school. However, students were still segregated in classrooms, the library, and the cafeteria. In an attempt to stop this type of discrimination, McLaurin took his case to the United States Supreme Court. In *McLaurin v. Oklahoma Regents for Higher Education* (1950), the Court ruled in favor of McLaurin and banned all forms of segregation in graduate programs.

Shortly thereafter, the United States Supreme Court decided *Brown v. Board of Education of Topeka* (1954), where the justices unanimously agreed that "separate but equal" education was unconstitutional. Although slow in some areas, Oklahoma responded by obeying the Supreme Court's order to desegregate with "all deliberate speed."

III. The Ebb and Flow of Federal Power

American federalism expects that both the national government as well as state governments will affect each other's development. What the national government does will impact Oklahoma—what Oklahoma does will impact the national government. The relationship between the national government and the states has changed over the years with the national government generally seen as gaining power and influence over the states. This increase in the national government's power is in part the result of the incorporation of the Bill of Rights, the regulation of interstate commerce, and the use of financial incentives.

Incorporation of the Bill of Rights

During the debates surrounding the adoption of the U.S. Constitution, opponents (anti-federalists) argued that there were no protections for individual rights and liberties from the national government. As a result, after the adoption of the new U.S. Constitution, the first ten amendments were proposed and ratified. These amendments became known as the Bill of Rights and guarantee such liberties as freedom of speech, press, religion, and the right to counsel. However, the founders were primarily fearful of the national government. As a result, the wording of the new guarantees was such that the amendments only protected citizens from the national government—not the states. Indeed, the First Amendment provides "Congress shall pass no law. . ." The Supreme Court made it clear in *Barron v. Baltimore* (1833) that if the founders had intended the restrictions on government actions to apply to states they would have said so.

After the Civil War and the ratification of the 14th Amendment in 1868, this interpretation began to change. The Fourteenth Amendment provides:

> *No State shall make or enforce any law which shall abridge the privileges or immunities of citizens of the United States; nor shall any State deprive any person of life, liberty, or property, without due*

Table 1–1
Selective Incorporation and the Bill of Rights

Amendment	Right	Case	Date
I	Free Exercise of Religion	*Cantwell v Connecticut*	1940
	Establishment of Religion	*Everson v Board of Education*	1947
	Speech	*Gitlow v New York*	1925
	Press	*Near v Minnesota*	1937
II	Keep and Bear Arms	Not Incorporated	
III	No Quartering of Soldiers in Peacetime	Not Incorporated	
IV	No Unreasonable Searches and Seizures	*Wolf v Colorado*	1949
V	Just Compensation	*Chicago, B&O RR. Co. v Chicago*	1897
	Self-Incrimination	*Malloy v Hogan*	1964
	Double Jeopardy	*Benton v Maryland*	1969
	Indictment by Grand Jury	Not Incorporated	
VI	Public Trial	*In re Oliver*	1948
	Right to Counsel	*Gideon v Wainwright*	1963
	Speedy Trial	*Klopher v North Carolina*	1967
	Jury Trial	*Duncan v Louisiana*	1968
VII	Jury Trial in Civil Cases	Not Incorporated	
VIII	No Cruel and Unusual Punishment	*Robinson v California*	1962
	No Excessive Bail or Fines	Not Incorporated	

process of law; nor deny to any person within its jurisdiction the equal protection of the laws.

The Supreme Court slowly utilized this amendment to apply protections found in the Bill of Rights to the States. Through a process known as **"selective incorporation,"** the Supreme Court has identified sections of the Bill of Rights that are essential to "ordered liberty" and has extended individual protection from state governments as well as the national government. As a result, as shown in Table 1–1, most protections found in the Bill of Rights not only keep the national government from infringing upon our rights, but keep the Oklahoma government from violating our rights as well.

Regulation of Interstate Commerce

A second way the national government has increased power is through an expansive interpretation of interstate commerce. In response to the economic growth and problems experienced as a result of the Industrial Revolution, Congress gradually began asserting power over various aspects of the economy. While Article I, Section 8, provides "Congress shall have power . . . to regulate Commerce . . . among the several States," the U.S. Constitution does not specifically detail what is meant by the term "interstate commerce." In a series of court cases over a number of years, the Supreme Court gradually expanded the definition of interstate commerce, thus expanding the ability of Congress to regulate commercial activity. Some critics of increased national power thought that the Court had defined interstate commerce so broadly that Congress could regulate virtually all commercial and economic activity, even activities once thought to be under the authority of state governments.

Recently, the Supreme Court found that Congress went too far in using their power to regulate interstate commerce. In *US v. Lopez* (1995), the Supreme Court decided that Congress exceeded its constitutional authority to regulate interstate commerce when it enacted a 1990 law banning the possession of guns on or near school property. The majority found that mere possession of a gun had "nothing to do with 'commerce' or any sort of economic enterprise, however broadly one might define those terms." This can be viewed as a significant departure from the Court's past practice. While the Supreme Court has generally upheld the power of Congress to regulate what legislators felt to be interstate commerce, even if the connection between commerce and the issue in question was distant, the Court now seems to require at least a minimum connection with commerce.

Financial Incentives

A third way the national government has increased power and influence over the states is through the use of financial incentives and powers. The national government has utilized tax credits, grants-in-aid, and the threat of withholding federal funds to encourage and coerce states into adopting or changing certain policies.

Tax credits are used by the national government to, among other things, encourage states to adopt particular policies. For example, in 1935 Congress passed the Social Security Act. In an effort to encourage states to develop unemployment compensation programs, the Social Security Act imposed a tax on all employers. However, the act granted employers a 90 percent tax credit for contributions they made to a state program. Since few states had such programs, it was employers who encouraged state legislatures to begin unemployment compensation programs. Soon after the adoption of this law, Oklahoma, along with other states, developed an unemployment compensation program.

Grants-in-aid are transfers of money from one level of government to another, to be spent on specified programs. Grants-in-aid generally come with standards and/or requirements. Many grants are operated on a matching basis where the state government must contribute a certain percentage. Grants can be classified into two general types: categorical grants and block grants.

Categorical grants are targeted for specific purposes and generally have conditions and restrictions on their use. Thus, state and local governments have little discretion in selecting where they will spend the money. **Block grants** are generally awarded for general purposes and are awarded directly to states as opposed to local governments. Block grants allow states considerably more discretion in allocating money to individual programs. For example, while a categorical grant may provide funds for Native American Studies in state high schools, a block grant may make funds available for educational programs. A state may choose to fund Native American Studies with block grant funds, but may also choose to fund other educational programs. Comparing the amount of money that flows from Oklahoma into the federal treasury through taxes and fees and the amount of money that Oklahoma receives from federal grants and programs, Oklahoma is one of a number of states that receives more money than it contributes.

After years of receiving federal funds, many states have become dependent upon that money. As a result, the national government has been able to require cooperation and uniformity in certain policy areas by withholding, or threatening to withhold, funds. Several examples in which federal money is tied to changing state laws or enforcing federal rules include: the speed limits, the 21 year-old drinking age, the use of seat belts, and the Americans with Disabilities Act (ADA). In most cases, all that is necessary to gain compliance from states is the threat of losing a portion of federal funds. In recent years, Oklahoma has changed its laws regarding speed limits, the use of seatbelts, the drinking age, as well as compliance and enforcement of ADA to remain eligible for federal funds.

In many areas, the federal government has imposed rules and regulations to address specific problems but has not provided the funds to meet the stated objectives. These requirements are commonly called unfunded mandates. **Unfunded mandates** are laws or regulations that require state or local governments to comply with federal rules under the threat of civil or criminal penalty or as a condition of receiving any federal grants. Examples of unfunded mandates include regulations regarding national clean air standards, drinking water standards, as well as the treatment and disposal of hazardous waste. By 1994, as much as 30 percent of local government expenditures was in response to unfunded federal mandates. Increased competition among the states for state and local funds, a growing opposition to such government mandates as well as new Republican majorities in both the United States House of Representatives and the United States Senate, led Congress to pass the Unfunded Mandates Act in 1995, restricting the national government's ability to require state and local governments to shoulder the costs of implementing federal rules and regulations (O'Connor and Sabato 1997).

IV. Responsibilities and Obligations

Maintaining a working federalism relationship means that the federal government and the states must work with each other. The U.S. Constitution prescribes a number of obligations on the federal government's relations with the states and requires states to participate in the government process.[3]

National Responsibilities and State Governments

The national government has a number of responsibilities to the states. These responsibilities include the guarantee of territorial integrity, a republican form of government, and protection from both invasion and domestic violence.

The U.S. Constitution provides guidelines for the admission of new states into the union and a guarantee of territorial integrity. Article IV, Section 3, provides:

> New States may be admitted by the Congress into this Union; but no new State shall be formed or erected within the Jurisdiction of any other State; nor any State be formed by the Junction of two or more States, or Parts of States, without the Consent of the Legislatures of the States concerned as well as of the Congress.

Several states were once a part of other states. These states include Kentucky, Tennessee, Maine, Vermont, Virginia, and West Virginia. While some questions exist with regard to the separation of West Virginia (sympathetic to the North) from Virginia (member of the Confederacy) in 1863 during the Civil War, the other states appear to have followed constitutional procedure. Prior to statehood, the Oklahoma panhandle was once part of Texas.

Few scholars seem to know exactly what the founders meant when they wrote in Article IV, Section 4, "The United States shall guarantee to every State in this Union a Republican Form of Government." Some define republican government as a type of democracy where people select representatives to make decisions. According to the U.S. Constitution, Congress is responsible for judging the elections of its members. The Supreme Court, it appears, seems willing to assume that if Congress allows a state's congressional delegation to take its seats in Congress, then the United States has certified that state to have a republican form of government.

Referring to the states, Article IV, Section 4, provides "the United States shall . . . protect each of them against Invasion; and on Application of the Legislature, or of the Executive (when the Legislature cannot be convened), against domestic Violence." If a state asks for assistance in repelling an invasion or putting down domestic violence, the national government is obligated to help. But this does not mean that the national government must always wait for invitation. If the enforcement of national law, personnel, or property is in danger, the national government may utilize

Chapter One

LEADERSHIP PROFILE

TOM COLE
Member of Congress, 4th District-Oklahoma

TOM COLE was elected as the Representative for Oklahoma's Fourth Congressional District on November 6, 2002. During his tenure, he has been an advocate for a strong national defense, a defender of the interests of small business and taxpayers, a proponent of education at all levels, and a leader on issues dealing with Native Americans and tribal governments. Cole was named as one of "Five Freshmen to Watch" by *Roll Call* at the outset of his congressional career.

Congressman Cole is a member on the House Armed Services Committee to which he was appointed in 2002 as well as the Committee on Natural Resources. Cole serves as a Deputy Whip in the U.S. House. In this role, he helps line up the votes needed to pass the legislative agenda of the President and the House Republican Conference. Cole also serves as Chairman of the National Republican Congressional Committee, making him a member of the House GOP Leadership.

Cole has a significant background of service to his home state of Oklahoma. He has served as a District Director for former Congressman Mickey Edwards, a member of the Oklahoma State Senate, and as Oklahoma's Secretary of State. In this capacity he served as former Governor Frank Keating's chief legislative strategist and liaison to the state's federal delegation. Keating tapped Cole to lead Oklahoma's successful effort to secure federal funds to assist in the rebuilding of Oklahoma City in the wake of the bombing of the Alfred P. Murrah Federal Building on April 19, 1995.

Cole is a founding partner and past president of CHS & Associates, a nationally recognized consulting and survey research firm based in Oklahoma City. The firm has been named one of the top twenty in its field in America and has literally dozens of past and current clients scattered across the country.

A former college instructor in history and politics, Cole holds a B.A. from Grinnell College, an M.A. from Yale University, and a Ph.D.

> from the University of Oklahoma. Cole has been a Thomas Watson Fellow affiliated with the Institute of Historical Research in London and a Fulbright Fellow at the University of London. He currently serves on the National Board of the Fulbright Association. He also serves on the board of the Aspen Institute.
>
> Tom Cole is a fifth generation Oklahoman and an enrolled member of the Chickasaw Nation. He is currently the only Native American serving in Congress and was inducted in the Chickasaw Hall of Fame in 2004. His late mother, Helen, is also a member of the Chickasaw Hall of Fame and served as a state representative, state senator, and Mayor of Moore in her native state of Oklahoma. Cole's late father, John, served twenty years in the United States Air Force and worked an additional two decades as a civilian federal employee at Tinker Air Force Base. Tom and his wife Ellen have one son, Mason, and reside in Moore, Oklahoma.

whatever force is necessary to eliminate the threat. In addition, the orders of federal courts may also be enforced by federal authorities within state boundaries.

State Responsibilities and the National Government

State governments also have responsibilities and obligations to the national government. Among those are the election of federal officials and the consideration of constitutional amendments.

The federal government does not hold elections for federal officers. Instead, it is the responsibility of states to operate and maintain election machinery, elect members to the United States House of Representatives and the United States Senate, as well as provide support for the electoral college. Article I, Section 4, of the U.S. Constitution requires state governments to provide the election machinery for national elections. As a result, state governments have been relatively free to regulate voter registration, control absentee ballots, supervise voting, prevent voter fraud, count ballots, and publish returns. However in 1993, Congress passed the **National Voter Registration Act** (more commonly known as the "motor voter" law) which requires states to make registration available at certain government agencies as well as make voter registration available by mail. Oklahoma adopted its own motor voter act (HB 1088) in 1993 shortly before Congress passed the national law. The National Motor Voter law went into effect in 1995.

State governments are also called upon to conduct elections for their respective congressional delegations. Today, the United States Senate is composed of 100 members, with each state responsible for electing two senators, and the United States House of Representatives is composed of

435 members apportioned to the states by population. After the 1990 census, Oklahoma's population guaranteed it six members in the House of Representatives. This was the same number that the state had after the 1980 census. Unfortunately, because Oklahoma's population growth has not kept up with growth in other states, Oklahoma lost a seat in the House of Representatives after the 2000 census.

The national government also relies on states to provide electors to the electoral college. Contrary to what many Americans may think, the people do not vote directly for the president and vice president of the United States. Rather, Article II, Section 1, as amended by the 12th and 23rd Amendments, provides that each state is guaranteed electoral college representation equal to the number of senators and representatives it has in Congress, and that the electoral college has the responsibility to formally elect the president and vice president. As a result, Oklahoma has seven electoral votes. (The District of Columbia has three votes by virtue of the 23rd Amendment). According to Article II, Section I, the U.S. Constitution leaves the actual selection method to each state. Some states select electors by conventions, some use primaries, and some use committees. In Oklahoma, political parties use their statewide conventions to select their presidential electors.

States are also responsible for the consideration of constitutional amendments. Article V of the U.S. Constitution states that amendments may be proposed by one of two methods: by a two-thirds vote in both houses of Congress or by a constitutional convention if two-thirds of the states petition Congress and ask for one. Amendments may also be ratified in one of two ways: by three-fourths of state legislatures, or by specially called ratifying conventions in three-fourths of the states. All constitutional amendments to date were originally proposed by Congress; the convention system has never been used, although we have come close several times. State legislatures have been used to ratify all but the 21st Amendment. Congress submitted the repeal of prohibition to state conventions for fear that state legislatures (dominated by rural interests) would be less favorable to repealing prohibition. In recent years, the Oklahoma legislature has deliberated on several proposed U.S. constitutional amendments. The Oklahoma legislature has considered two amendments to the U.S. Constitution in recent decades. In 1982, the legislature voted against ratifying the proposed Equal Rights Amendment, and in 1985, the legislature voted in favor of ratifying the 27th Amendment to the U.S. Constitution which prevents congressional pay raises from taking effect until after an election.

V. Interstate Relations

The U.S. Constitution also details the relationships that are to exist among the states. States are to grant each other's public acts and records full faith and credit, extend privileges and immunities to citizens of other states, return people who are fleeing from justice in another state, and consult Congress before entering interstate compacts.

Full Faith and Credit

Article IV, Section 1, provides that "Full Faith and Credit shall be given in each State to the public Acts, Records, and judicial Proceedings of every other State." In an increasingly mobile society, it has become very important that state governments recognize the public acts, records, and judicial proceedings of other states. This means that documents such as wills, mortgages, birth certificates, and contracts, as well as acts such as adoption, marriages, and divorces granted or issued in Oklahoma, must be recognized and enforced by other states. One of the growing problems in interstate relations is the reluctance of states to meet their obligations under the **Full Faith and Credit Clause,** particularly in the area of domestic relations. It is often very difficult for a former spouse to collect alimony and child support from a spouse or parent who has moved out of state. A future question under the Full Faith and Credit Clause that may be decided by the U.S. Supreme Court involves the issue of same-sex marriages. If a state recognizes same-sex marriages as legal, and requires state officials to issue marriage certificates to same-sex couples, will Oklahoma have to recognize that marriage? In an attempt to define the position of the federal government, Congress passed the Defense of Marriage Act (DOMA) in 1996 and provided that states are not required to recognize same-sex marriages from other states, but did not prevent them from doing so if they wanted (Kersch 1997).

Extradition

Article IV, Section 2, provides "a person ... who shall flee from Justice, and be found in another State, shall on Demand of the executive Authority of the State from which he fled, be delivered up, to be removed to the State having jurisdiction of the Crime." Oklahoma, and all other states, have adopted the Uniform Criminal Extradition Act which unifies the procedures for requesting the return of an accused criminal. However, the U.S. Supreme Court has not always required states to return individuals fleeing the justice system of another state. In *Kentucky v. Dennison* (1861), the Supreme Court ruled that Ohio's Governor Dennison was not forced to return a black man to Kentucky, a slave state, where he was accused of helping slaves escape. The Supreme Court stated governors were under a moral duty to return accused individuals, but not a legal duty.

In 1987, the Supreme Court reversed its Civil War era ruling. In the case of *Puerto Rico v. Branstad,* the Court ruled that Iowa's Governor Branstad had a legal duty to return an individual to Puerto Rico for a manslaughter trial, regardless of whether or not the governor thought the individual could get a fair trial. In effect, the court changed its mind and said that honoring an extradition request was a legal duty, not just a moral duty. In 2004, the state of Oklahoma entertained 91 formal extradition requests from other states and made 96 formal requests for accused criminals to be returned to Oklahoma.

Privileges and Immunities

Article IV, Section 2, provides "The Citizens of each State shall be entitled to all **Privilege and Immunities** of Citizens in the several States." This means that states are not supposed to discriminate against citizens of another state or give favorable treatment to their own citizens. The Supreme Court has ruled that citizens of any state may travel freely in other states, may purchase property in other states, may use the court system in other states, must be guaranteed equal protection of the law, and may take up residence in another state. There are, however, several exceptions where states are allowed to treat residents differently. First, states are allowed to establish reasonable residency requirements of those holding public office. Second, states are also allowed to charge nonresidents more for services such as fishing and gaming licenses and for state institutions of higher education. Third, states are allowed to require individuals to obtain state licenses before practicing professions such as law and education. As such, in Oklahoma, the governor must have been a qualified voter for 10 years prior to taking office, out-of-state tuition is often double what an in-state student pays, and those wishing to be teachers, lawyers, social workers, and numerous others must be licensed or certified by the state of Oklahoma.

Interstate Compacts

Article I, Section 10, of the U.S. Constitution provides "No State shall, without the Consent of Congress . . . enter into any Agreement or Compact with another State . . ." **Interstate compacts** are formal binding agreements between two or more states. Today, there are over one hundred interstate compacts on issues including: flood control, wildlife, interstate toll highways, coordination of welfare programs, supervision of parolees, traffic enforcement, disaster assistance, child placement, and waste disposal. Oklahoma has joined a number of interstate compacts, including the Interstate Oil Compact, which attempts to monitor and coordinate the conditions and price of the oil industry (Morgan et al. 1991). While the U.S. Constitution requires congressional consent for interstate compacts, there is no mention as to when or how this consent is to be given. Indeed, Congress provides little supervision in the development of interstate compacts and the Supreme Court has never ruled an interstate compact unconstitutional (Hardy et al. 1995).

Suits between States

Occasionally, conflicts between two or more states cannot be settled among those involved. When that occurs, the Supreme Court has original jurisdiction and the power to resolve the dispute. As a result, the case can be heard immediately by the Supreme Court without having to begin in lower federal courts. The Supreme Court has heard and settled disputes between states that have involved issues of borders, water rights, and the disposal of garbage. Oklahoma's "Red River rivalry" with Texas has resulted in numerous law suits including *Texas v Oklahoma* 457 US 172 (1982), a dispute over the Red River boundary.

Strengths and Weaknesses of Federalism

The American system of federalism has both strengths and weaknesses. As a system that seeks to decentralize powers, American federalism is a mix of national and state powers that helps manage political conflict by dispersing political power among governments. With both the national government and state governments seeking to solve many of the same problems, federalism encourages policy innovation by having many different governmental actors developing ideas and strategies. Federalism can also provide greater responsiveness by allowing state and local governments to address problems directly rather then relying on one central agency to administer the solution.

However, a federal system also has weaknesses. Decentralization and diversity creates a lack of uniformity and considerable duplication. State and local governments have different laws with regard to traffic, what constitutes a crime and the penalty associated with crime, educational requirements, and even marriage and divorce rules. These different laws and rules can cause confusion. National, state, and local governments often provide duplicate services. This overlapping of functions can be both inefficient and confusing.

VI. Conclusion

Intergovernmental relations in our federal system are important and dynamic. Federalism affects virtually every aspect of policymaking and governing. The federal government and the states must work together and the states must develop cooperative working relationships with each other. Yet, like all relationships, American federalism has experienced change. While the federal government has increased its powers over the course of two centuries, recently, it has been Congress asserting that states should shoulder a larger burden of the development, oversight, and financing of policies and programs. Whether this shift is the result of a "conservative" shift in American political ideology, an abdication by the federal government of its leadership role, or the result of fewer federal dollars for state programs, state governments, including Oklahoma, are having more expected of them. As a result, states have become leaders in policy innovation in such areas as welfare reform, tax reform, health care, corrections, affirmative action, and in the case of Oklahoma, term limits.

To understand government and politics in Oklahoma, one must understand the system within which it operates. Oklahoma is only one of 50 states that have come together to form the federal system we have today. However, Oklahoma brings to American federalism a unique perspective on governing, which affects its relationships both with the federal government and with other states. In addition, Oklahoma brings to the federalism relationship a distinctive history which affects its own internal governmental structure as well as public policy.

NOTES

1. For additional discussions on federalism and how it has changed, see Hardy 1995: 5–20; O'Connor and Sabato 1997: 79–100; Lorch 2001: 21–48; Dye 1997: 55–90.
2. This discussion about segregation in Oklahoma is largely drawn from Gibson 1981, 237–239 and Morgan et al. 1991: 27.
3. For a more detailed discussion, see Lorch 2001: 42–44.

CHAPTER TWO

THE CONSTITUTIONAL AND CULTURAL CONTEXT OF OKLAHOMA GOVERNMENT

Christopher L. Markwood

Invoking the guidance of Almighty God, in order to secure and perpetuate the blessing of liberty; to secure just and rightful government; to promote our mutual welfare and happiness, we, the people of the State Oklahoma do ordain and establish this Constitution (Preamble).

I. INTRODUCTION

State and local governments play important and powerful roles in every citizen's life. But state and local governments are not without their limitations. Two important constraints on state and local government power are state constitutions and political culture. State constitutions are formal documents that detail the powers and limitations of government, as well as the rights and liberties of its citizens. **Political culture** is more of an informal limitation on government and can be defined as the attitudes, beliefs, and expectations people have toward government and toward what government should do. These two constraints are very much related. As pioneers settled America in different areas, they brought with them from their homelands goals, ideals, and traditions regarding how government should operate and what government should and should not do. As these settlers migrated west, they encountered new problems and new environments. These experiences, traditions, and cultural traits all influenced the development of governing documents (Elazar 1982). In this chapter we will: 1) explore the distinctive historical background of Oklahoma; 2) examine the constitutional framework for Oklahoma government; and 3) discuss the impact political cultural values have on Oklahoma government and politics.

II. HISTORICAL BACKGROUND

An understanding of Oklahoma's Constitution requires a brief review of Oklahoma's historical beginning.[1] The land that would become Oklahoma was originally part of the 1803 Louisiana Purchase. While territories and states were quickly formed all around Oklahoma, the quest for Oklahoma statehood would take a unique route.

Pre-Civil War Era

Concern over Indian presence and land possession in the Southeastern part of the United States led Congress to pass the **Removal Act in 1830**. This act called for the Cherokee, Choctaw, Seminole, Chickasaw, and Creek tribes (often referred to by historians as the **Five Civilized Tribes** because of their social and political development) to be moved west. The removal process of all of these tribes has been symbolized as a "Trail of Tears." Historians estimate over 70,000 Native Americans were forced off their land and resettled to Oklahoma with an estimated one-fourth dying en route.

In large part, the removal and relocation of the Five Civilized Tribes was complete by 1840. Treaties were signed with the tribes thereby dividing Oklahoma, or what was then called Indian Territory, among them. The federal government established military forts to protect the tribes, and the tribes established constitutions and developed local governments. In what has been called the "golden years" of the Five Civilized tribes, school systems, agriculture, commerce, and self-government flourished.

Civil War Era

Although initially pursuing a policy of neutrality during the Civil War, the Five Civilized Tribes ultimately signed treaties with the Confederacy in 1861. In the treaties, the Confederacy promised to provide material and military support, and Native American regiments were organized to defend against Union invasion. After the Civil War and the defeat of the Confederacy, the Five Civilized Tribes were forced to accept terms which included the abolition of slavery and the surrender of much of Central and Western Oklahoma for resettlement of other tribes. Caddoe, Delaware, Kickapoo, Modoc, Osage, Comanche, Shawnee, and other tribes were soon relocated from Kansas and other parts of the United States to Western Oklahoma.

Although forbidden to live in Indian Territory without a permit from the tribes, white settlers continued to push into Oklahoma. By 1889 the federal government was ready to open the "unassigned" lands in Central Oklahoma to homestead settlers. Knowing that there were more people interested in homesteading than land available, the government utilized **land runs,** whereby individuals were lined up on the border of a region of land and allowed to run for a piece of it. By the 1890s, Oklahoma was divided into two separate areas known as the twin territories—Oklahoma Territory and Indian Territory. **Oklahoma Territory,** to the west, had been opened to non-Native American people. **Indian Territory,** to the east, remained set aside for the Five Civilized Tribes.

FIGURE 2-1 The Twin Territories

SOURCE: Adapted from *Oklahoma Politics in State and Nations*, 16.

The Drive for Statehood

While Native Americans were largely opposed to statehood for Indian Territory, almost immediately efforts were under way to seek statehood for Oklahoma Territory; however, several problems existed.[2] First, much of the land was temporarily not taxable because of homestead exemptions, thus making the issue of raising revenue problematic. Second, compared to other recently formed states, the geographical composition of Oklahoma Territory was significantly smaller than other Western states. Third, partisan politics contributed to the delay in statehood. National Republicans enjoyed being able to make appointments in the territory and hoped that Republican strength, if given time, would grow, thus producing a Republican state in the traditionally Democratic Southwest. Democrats, confident of maintaining a majority in the territory, pushed for statehood. Fourth, questions regarding statehood for Oklahoma Territory necessarily raised questions regarding the future of Indian Territory and the Five Civilized Tribes.

Discussions of the future of the twin territories generally centered around four possible plans. First, Oklahoma Territory could be joined with Indian Territory to form one state. Proponents of single or joint statehood argued that a single state would have economic and geographic advantages and that, in the not-so-distant past, the two territories were previously joined. Second, the two territories could be admitted as separate states. Fearing the possibility of Oklahoma Territory politicians and interests dominating in a single state scenario, leaders of the Five Civilized Tribes favored the separate state proposal if statehood was unavoidable. In addition, some Democrats, who supported separate statehood, envied the possibility of two Democratic senators from Indian Territory and two Democratic senators from Oklahoma Territory. Third, some favored what was called "piecemeal absorption." This process would allow immediate statehood for Oklahoma Territory and allow the various Indian nations to be absorbed into Oklahoma as they were ready. The fourth option was to allow Oklahoma Territory to enter as a state, and leave Indian Territory and the Five Civilized Tribes to remain as they were.

Although the leaders of Indian Territory were opposed to joining with Oklahoma Territory for fear of being discriminated against in a state where whites would dominate, their opposition was easily overcome. In a series of congressional acts during the 1890s, Congress reduced, and ultimately eliminated, Native American governmental and tribal court authority over Indian Territory and abolished communal land ownership. The transfer of land from tribal ownership to individual ownership was overseen by the **Dawes Commission,** which was created by Congress in 1893. Only after Congress gave the Dawes Commission the authority to make individual land allotments to the tribe members without tribal consent in 1896 did leaders of the Five Civilized Tribes begin to accept the inevitability of individual allotment. By 1901, the Dawes Commission and Congress had overcome resistance to the individual allotment. All persons whose name appeared on tribal rolls were granted an allotment of land despite the importance of communal land ownership in tribal culture. The remainder of land in Indian Territory was for designated townsites, schools, as well as coal and timber land, much of which was sold by sealed bid with proceeds credited to the tribes holding the land. Unlike Oklahoma Territory, there was no surplus land for homesteading.

The Sequoyah Convention

As the prospect of joint statehood with Oklahoma Territory grew stronger, some of the leaders of the Five Civilized Tribes, and a number of non-Native American and individuals with only nominal tribal ties, called for a statehood convention for Indian Territory to meet in Muskogee in August of 1905.

While many individuals had personal political goals, the stated goal of this convention was to produce a constitution for a new Native American state to be called **Sequoyah.** Delegates were selected from across Indian Territory and work began on the proposed constitution. Despite the proposed constitution's similarity to other state constitutions, as well as the national constitution, in that the document began with a preamble and created three separate branches of government and despite a lopsided ratification vote in Indian Territory in favor of the new constitution, Congress was not interested and quickly rejected it.

As a movement to propel separate statehood, the Sequoyah movement was unsuccessful. However, the movement was significant for several reasons. First, the failure of the Sequoyah Constitution effectively ended the drive for separate statehood. As a result, the members of the Five Civilized Tribes were forced to accept the inevitability of joint statehood with Oklahoma Territory. Second, the Sequoyah movement forced federal officials to

LEADERSHIP PROFILE

WILMA MANKILLER
Former Principal Chief of the Cherokee Nation

THE CHEROKEES have a rich history of women serving in leadership positions however, with European contact that tradition nearly came to an end. When Wilma Pearl Mankiller became Deputy Chief, and then Principal Chief of the Cherokee Nation, the historic leadership role of women was revitalized.

Mankiller was born in 1945 in Tahlequah, Oklahoma. When she was ten, her family moved to San Francisco through a federal relocation program designed to remove Indians from their rural homelands to large urban areas.

In 1966, when American Indian activists occupied Alcatraz Island to dramatize the injustices their people had suffered, Mankiller experienced an awakening that changed her life. Besides participating in the struggle, she did volunteer work among Native Americans in California. By the mid 1970s, she had returned to Oklahoma. Mankiller's initial work for the Cherokee Nation included recruitment of young Native Americans into university training in environmental science. In 1979, she completed her college degree and began commuting to the University of Arkansas for graduate study.

In 1981, Mankiller became the founding director of the Cherokee Nation Community Development Department, using the Cherokee's *gadugi* tradition of working collectively to help build a 16-mile water pipeline and homes in Bell, Oklahoma. Two years later, Principal Chief Ross Swimmer asked her to serve as his running mate for tribal office, and on August 14, 1983, Mankiller became the first woman Deputy Chief in Cherokee history. Later, she became the Principal Chief after Swimmer's resignation and then successfully won election to her own term of office.

After leaving office in 1995, Mankiller co-authored *Mankiller: A Chief and Her People*, which included the story of the Cherokee nation, one of the country's largest tribal groups. Her latest book, *Every Day is a Good Day: Reflections of Contemporary Indigenous Women*, has been

> featured on *Native America Calling*, the favorite national radio talk show in Indian Country.
>
> She is a recipient of the Presidential Medal of Freedom, and in 2007 she won the first annual Oklahoma Humanities Award.

speed up action on statehood. Within five months of the rejection of the Sequoyah Constitution, Congress passed, and President Theodore Roosevelt signed, the **Enabling Act**, which provided for the unification of the two territories and for a convention to develop a constitution for a new state. Third, the Sequoyah Convention gave its leaders, like William H. Murray, an Indian citizen by marriage, the opportunity and platform to push for progressive reform. While suffrage was still limited, the Sequoyah Constitution provided for corporate regulation, mine safety, consumer protection, and social guarantees for women, workers, and children. The proposed constitution also instituted prohibition and created a strong corporation commission with regulatory responsibility. Indeed, had the Sequoyah Constitution been approved by Congress and a new state formed, its constitution would have been one of the most progressive state constitutions in America (Goble 1980).

The Constitutional Convention in Guthrie

The Enabling Act of 1906 cleared the way for Indian and Oklahoma Territories to join and become the 46th state in the union. The act called for the election of delegates to a constitutional convention that was to meet in Guthrie with 55 delegates from Indian Territory, 55 delegates from Oklahoma Territory, and two delegates from the Osage Nation. While Republicans hoped to elect enough delegates to control the convention, when the election of delegates was complete, Republicans only had 12 of the 112 delegates. As a result, the Democrats were able to organize and control the convention, often ignoring their Republican opponents. In electing delegates to the convention, voters chose a very different type of representative. Few of the delegates had formal educations and most were newcomers to politics. Some scholars note the absence of most of the prominent Democrats and Republicans from this gathering (Goble 1980). However, given the defeat of Republicans in Oklahoma Territory and the general inexperience of many would-be Democratic leaders in Indian Territory, that most of the delegates were new to politics is not surprising.

The Guthrie Convention existed in a political and social climate that sought change. The economic depression of the 1890s exposed many Americans to the reality of the unequal distribution of wealth that was associated with industrialization and economic progress. Fears of urbanization, explosive population growth, machine politics, ethnic differences, and corporate power gave fuel to populist and progressive reform movements across the country (Morgan & Morgan 1977).

Populism developed as a potent political and social force in the 1880s out of the West, South, and Midwest. Favoring agrarian policies and fearing corporate monopolies, reformers sought social, political, and economic changes, including agrarian reform, a graduated income tax, regulation of corporations, and an expanded supply of paper money. While the Populist Party failed to become one of the two major political parties, many populist ideas were adopted by the Democratic Party in 1896 when William Jennings Bryan ran both as the nominee of the Democrats, as well as the nominee of the Populist Party.[3]

Fearful of large political machines and special interests, **progressives** in the early 1900s believed in the "goodness and wisdom of individual citizens" (Janda et al. 1997). Progressive reformers urged the adoption of primary elections that would give citizens the ability to choose party candidates for office, the initiative and referendum as means to propose and pass laws, and the recall to remove elected officials from office.

From the beginning, it was clear that delegates to the constitutional convention were reform-oriented. The delegates began by electing William H. Murray as convention president. His experience as an advocate for reform, and the experiences of the other members of the Guthrie Convention who had served in the Sequoyah Convention, helped establish Murray as one of the undisputed leaders of the convention.

While most of the Democrats pledged their support to a reform oriented constitution, the issues of where to place county seats, woman's suffrage, and prohibition all carried the possibility of splitting the convention apart and required careful management. Murray used his considerable influence in the placement of county seats to extract loyalty and support from convention delegates, and secured the proposal of a reform-oriented constitution.

Ratification

Democrats orchestrated an effective campaign for ratification, arguing the necessity of the proposed constitution. Campaigning against the corruption of corporations, individual candidates for state and local offices ran campaigns associating themselves with the constitution's reforms. William Jennings Bryan, the popular reformer, even journeyed to Oklahoma to urge adoption of the constitution and the election of Democrats. Republicans opposed the constitution and many of its reforms. William Howard Taft, then Secretary of War, campaigned in Oklahoma and warned that the constitution was "flavored with Socialism" and contained too many provisions that should be decided by the legislature (Goble 1980: 224–225).

Oklahomans ratified the constitution on September 17, 1907, with 71 percent approval and with majority support in every county. In addition, Democrats swept the executive, legislative, and judicial races, as well as four out of five congressional races. Senators were still selected by state legislatures and the new legislature would be overwhelmingly Democratic with 93 Democrats and only 16 Republicans. The election set the stage for decades of Democratic dominance of state politics (Goble 1980: 225).

III. Significant Features of the Oklahoma Constitution

The proposed constitution was a model for populist reformers and was even championed by William Jennings Bryan himself. The framers designed a government that divided powers among three equal branches (legislative, executive, and judicial) but also limited the powers of the branches of government. The proposed constitution revealed the faith the framers had in the people, by providing avenues of direct democracy, and revealed the scepticism and distrust the framers had of government and special interests. As one of the nation's longest state constitutions, the Oklahoma Constitution lays out the powers and responsibilities of state and local government as well as the protections and rights of the people.

Length LOS

One of the major differences between the federal and Oklahoma Constitution is the length of Oklahoma's document. In general, constitutions can be thought of as a set of founding principles and guidelines. Much of the detail work of government is usually done by the legislature in the form of statutory law. However, the framers were largely distrustful of legislatures and were developing this constitution during a period of time in which current political, social, and economic ideas were being challenged. As a result, the framers sought to place as much as possible outside the legislative arm of state government. One of the practical effects of this strategy was the creation of one of the nation's longest state constitutions. By comparison, the United States Constitution is only about 8,700 words and the average state constitution has about 30,000 words. The Oklahoma Constitution contains over 79,000 words and ranks third behind Alabama, with 220,000 words, and Texas, with almost 81,000 words (see Table 2–1). Coinciding with length is extensive detail. Because the framers were distrustful of government but believed that government, if properly regulated, could be beneficial to the people, they sought to be specific and detailed. As a result, today's Oklahoma Constitution contains provisions specifically declaring the flash test for kerosene to be 115 degrees Fahrenheit, specifically listing maximum dollar levels of indebtedness for capital improvements for buildings and institutions, as well as providing a thorough description of what the state seal must look like.

Rule by the People LOS

The Oklahoma framers joined a small number of other states and provided several avenues for direct democracy, placing some legislative authority directly in the hands of the people. The Oklahoma Constitution provides for the referendum and the initiative.

Table 2-1
A Comparison of State Constitutions

State	Number of Constitutions	Dates of Adoption	Estimated Length	Number of Amendments Adopted
Alabama	6	1819, 1861, 1865, 1868, 1875, 1901	340,136 (a)(b)	746 (c)
Alaska	1	1956	15,988 (b)	28
Arizona	1	1911	28,876	133
Arkansas	5	1836, 1861, 1864, 1868, 1874	59,500 (b)	89 (d)
California	2	1849, 1879	54,645	507
Colorado	1	1876	74,522 (b)	143
Connecticut	4	1818 (f), 1965	17,256 (b)	29
Delaware	4	1776, 1792, 1831, 1897	19,000	136
Florida	6	1839, 1861, 1865, 1868, 1886, 1968	51,456 (b)	96
Georgia	10	1777, 1789, 1798, 1861, 1865, 1868, 1877, 1945, 1976, 1982	39,526 (b)	61 (g)
Hawaii	1 (h)	1950	20,774 (b)	100
Idaho	1	1889	24,232 (b)	117
Illinois	4	1818, 1848, 1870, 1970	16,510 (b)	11
Indiana	2	1816, 1851	10,379 (b)	43
Iowa	2	1846, 1857	12,616 (b)	52 (i)
Kansas	1	1859	12,296 (b)	92 (i)
Kentucky	4	1792, 1799, 1850, 1891	23,911 (b)	40
Louisiana	11	1812, 1845, 1852, 1861, 1864, 1868, 1879, 1898, 1913, 1921, 1974	54,112 (b)	124
Maine	1	1819	16,276 (b)	169 (j)
Maryland	4	1776, 1851, 1864, 1867	46,600 (b)	218 (k)
Massachusetts	1	1780	36,700 (l)	120
Michigan	4	1835, 1850, 1908, 1963	34,659 (b)	23
Minnesota	1	1857	11,547 (b)	118
Missouri	4	1820, 1865, 1875, 1945	42,600 (b)	103
Montana	2	1889, 1972	13,145 (b)	27
Nebraska	2	1866, 1875	20,048	219 (m)
Nevada	1	1864	31,377 (b)	131
New Hampshire	2	1776, 1784	9,200	143
New Jersey	3	1776, 1844, 1947	22,956 (b)	36
New Mexico	1	1911	27,200	148
New York	4	1777, 1822, 1846, 1894	51,700	216
North Carolina	3	1776, 1868, 1970	16,532 (b)	31
North Dakota	1	1889	19,130 (b)	144 (o)
Ohio	2	1802, 1851	48,521 (b)	160
Oklahoma	1	1907	74,075 (b)	165 (p)
Oregon	1	1857	54,083 (b)	235 (q)
Pennsylvania	5	1776, 1790, 1838, 1873, 1968 (r)	27,711 (b)	30 (r)
Rhode Island	3	1842 (f), 1986 (s)	10,908 (b)	7 (s)
South Carolina	7	1776, 1778, 1790, 1861, 1865, 1868, 1895	22,300	484 (f)
South Dakota	1	1889	27,675 (b)	112
Tennessee	3	1796, 1835, 1870	13,300	36
Texas	5 (u)	1845, 1861, 1866, 1869, 1876	80,000	432
Utah	1	1895	11,000	103
Vermont	3	1777, 1786, 1793	10,286 (b)	53
Virginia	6	1776, 1830, 1851, 1869, 1902, 1970	21,319 (b)	38
Washington	1	1889	33,564 (b)	95
West Virginia	2	1863, 1872	26,000	70
Wisconsin	1	1848	14,392 (b)	133 (j)
Wyoming	1	1889	31,800	91

Continued

TABLE 2-1 CONTINUED

SOURCE: Adapted from *Book of the States*, Volume 36, 2004:10–11. Survey conducted by Janice May, The University of Texas at Austin, January 2004.

NOTES

*The constitutions referred to in this table include those Civil War documents customarily listed by the individual states.

(a) The Alabama constitution includes numerous local amendments that apply to only one county. An estimated 70 percent of all amendments are local. A 1982 amendment provides that after proposal by the legislature to which special procedures apply, only a local vote (with exceptions) is necessary to add them to the constitution.

(b) Computer word count.

(c) The total number of amendments adopted, 746 includes one usually overlooked.

(d) Eight of the approved amendments have been superseded and are not printed in the current edition of the constitution. The total adopted does not include five amendments proposed and adopted since statehood.

(e) Proposed amendments are not submitted to the voters in Delaware.

(f) Colonial charters with some alterations served as the first constitutions in Connecticut (1638, 1662) and in Rhode Island (1663).

(g) The Georgia constitution requires amendments to be of "general and uniform application throughout the state," thus eliminating local amendments that accounted for most of the amendments before 1982.

(h) As a kingdom and republic, Hawaii had five constitutions.

(i) The figure does not include one amendment approved by the voters and later nullified by the state supreme court in Iowa (three), Kansas (one), Nevada (six) and Wisconsin (two).

(j) The figure does not include one amendment approved by the voters in 1967 that is inoperative until implemented by legislation.

(k) Two sets of identical amendments were on the ballot and adopted in the 1992 Maryland election. The four amendments are counted as two in the table.

(l) The printed constitution includes many provisions that have been annulled. The length of effective provisions is an estimated 24,122 words (12,400 annulled in Massachusetts, and in Rhode Island before the "rewrite" of the constitution in 1986, it was 11,399 words (7,627 annulled).

(m) The 1998 and 2000 Nebraska ballots allowed the voters to vote separately on "parts" of propositions. In 1998, 10 of 18 separate propositions were adopted; in 2000, 6 of 9.

(n) The constitution of 1784 was extensively revised in 1792. Figure shows proposals and adoptions since the constitution was adopted in 1784.

(o) The figures do not include submission and approval of the constitution of 1889 itself and of Article XX; these are constitutional questions included in some counts of constitutional amendments and would add two to the figure in each column.

(p) The figures include five amendments submitted to and approved by the voters that were, by decisions of the Oklahoma or U.S. Supreme Courts, rendered inoperative or ruled invalid, unconstitutional, or illegally submitted.

(q) One Oregon amendment on the 2000 ballot was not counted as approved because canvassing was enjoined by the courts.

(r) Certain sections of the constitution were revised by the limited convention of 1967–68. Amendments proposed and adopted are since 1968.

(s) Following approval of the eight amendments are a "rewrite" of the Rhode Island Constitution in 1986, the constitution has been called the 1986 Constitution. Amendments since 1986 total seven proposed and seven adopted. Otherwise, the total is 105 proposals and 59 adopted.

(t) In 1981 approximately two-thirds of 626 proposed and four-fifths of the adopted amendments were local. Since then the amendments have been statewide propositions.

(u) The Constitution of the Republic of Texas preceded five state constitutions.

(v) The number of proposed amendments to the Texas Constitution excludes three proposed by the legislature but not placed on the ballot.

The **referendum** can be required by 5 percent of the legal voters or by an absolute majority of the legislature to allow the people to vote on a piece of legislation previously passed by the legislature. The **initiative** process allows citizens to circulate a petition and gather signatures to place an issue on the ballot. To propose a law through the initiative process requires 8 percent of the legal voters to sign the petition requesting an issue be placed on the ballot. To propose a constitutional amendment, 15 percent of the legal voters must sign a petition requesting an amendment to the constitution be placed on the ballot. If the required number of valid signatures are gathered, the issue will appear on the ballot, and the people may vote on it directly. These procedures put legislative authority in the hands of the people and take it away from the legislature. Oklahomans have used the initiative process to limit taxes, impose term limits on legislators, and legalize parimutuel betting.

Legislature

Article V of the Oklahoma Constitution establishes the legislative authority in state government. The Constitution provides for a **bicameral legislature,** with a House of Representatives and a Senate. The House of Representatives consists of 101 members. State representatives are elected for a two-year term, with the entire House membership up for election at the same time. The Senate consists of 48 members. State senators are elected for four-year terms with half of the Senate membership elected every two years. What is most notable about this provision is the inclusion of the initiative and referendum. Section 1 states:

> The Legislative authority of the state shall be vested in a Legislature, consisting of a Senate and a House of Representatives; but the people reserve to themselves the power to propose laws and amendments to the Constitution and to enact or reject the same at the polls independent of the Legislature, and also reserve power at their own option to approve or reject at the polls any act of the Legislature.

The provision of the initiative and referendum as means for allowing citizens to propose and vote on legislation or constitutional amendments is a clear expression of the distrust the Oklahoma framers had in legislative power. Believing that government had to be restrained in order for good government to work, the framers placed a number of other restrictions on the state legislature as well. These restrictions include a limitation on the length of legislative sessions, a prohibition on passing revenue bills during the last five days of the legislative session, and a requirement that laws be passed by an absolute majority of members rather than a majority of those present and voting.

The Executive

Expressing their distrust of strong governmental officials, governors were to be elected for four-year terms and were not allowed to succeed themselves. Like other states that had a similar provision, this restriction has now been modified to allow a governor to succeed himself/herself once. Further reducing the powers of the governor, the framers vested executive authority not only in the governor, but also in a number of other executive officers, each elected by the people. Today, the Lieutenant Governor, Attorney General, Superintendent of Public Instruction, State Auditor and Inspector, State Treasurer, three Corporation Commissioners, Commissioner of Insurance, and Commissioner of Labor are all elected separately and independently of the Governor. As a result, they may pursue policies and agendas that may or may not be consistent with those of the governor.

Like other governors, the Oklahoma governor has the power to veto acts of the legislature. This power includes the line-item veto for appropriations. While this is the only real power the governor has over the legislature, the state legislature may override the governor's vote by a two-thirds majority in both houses.

The Oklahoma governor may also grant pardons, paroles, and reprieves to those convicted of crimes in Oklahoma. As discussed in Chapter Five, while the governor once enjoyed exclusive power to make these decisions, this power has been limited by a constitutional amendment that created the State Pardon and Parol Board.

Judiciary

Like other state constitutions, the Oklahoma Constitution proposed a hierarchical system of courts. The lowest level of courts would be trial courts and the highest level of courts would hear cases on appeal. However, unlike most other state court systems, the Oklahoma framers proposed a separated appellate court system with a **Court of Criminal Appeals** and a **Supreme Court.** The Court of Criminal Appeals was to be the highest court for criminal cases and the Supreme Court was to be the highest court for civil cases. Only one other state, Texas, has two courts of last resort. Other provisions dealing with the judiciary include the methods of selection. Rather than executive appointment, the framers decided to have judges elected. As with other positions, the justification was to keep public officials responsible to the people. However, as discussed in Chapter Five, problems with inefficiency and corruption led Oklahoma to change its judicial selection method.

Constitutional Change

Article XXIV of the Oklahoma Constitution provides a number of methods for amending the constitution. As with the national constitution, there are two steps: 1) proposal of a constitutional amendment and 2) ratification of a proposed constitutional amendment.

Proposal of a constitutional amendment in Oklahoma can be accomplished in one of three ways. First, the state legislature may propose an amendment to the constitution by a majority vote in both houses of state legislature. Second, the people may propose a constitutional amendment through the initiative petition. Oklahoma was the second state to allow amendments to be proposed by this method. To propose a constitutional amendment using this method, supporters must get the signatures of 15 percent of the voters. Third, a constitutional convention, approved by the voters, may propose amendments to the constitution. Article XXIV, Section 2 also requires that a question of whether or not to have a constitutional convention be put to the voters at least once every 20 years. Oklahoma voters have voted against calling a constitutional convention in 1926, 1950, and 1970. Interestingly, neither the legislature nor the Secretary of State has placed the issue on the ballot since 1970.

The second step in the process of formally amending Oklahoma's constitution is **ratification.** All three methods of proposing a constitutional amendment require the same method of ratification. All proposed amendments must be approved by a majority of those voting in a regular or specially called election. Until 1974, the constitution required that to ratify an amendment proposed by the initiative process, the proposal had to receive a majority of all votes in the election, not just on the proposed amendment. This allowed a proposed amendment to be defeated even if it received a majority of the votes on the amendment, because of what has been termed the **silent vote**—those participating in the election, but not voting on the amendment.

The Liquor Question

The Enabling Act Required that alcohol be banned in Indian Territory for 21 years after ratification. However there were no restrictions on alcohol for the rest of the state. Constitutional Convention President Murray had supported prohibition at the Sequoyah Convention and was supported by the Anti-Saloon League in his bid for the position of president of the Guthrie Convention. While most delegates were "dry," fear that the liquor issue might cause otherwise supportive citizens to vote against the proposed constitution led Murray to propose placing the liquor question in the form of an amendment on a separate ballot to be decided at the same time the people voted on the ratification of the proposed constitution. While the feelings on both sides were strong, the amendment passed and inaugurated prohibition throughout the entire state (Bryant 1968). Oklahoma has since loosened the restrictions on the sale of alcohol including allowing the sale of 3.2 beer in 1933 and allowing county option for liquor by the drink in 1986.

Individual Rights and Liberties

The utilization of state constitutions to itemize or list specific rights is not unique. Thus, Article II of the Oklahoma Constitution is similar to other state constitutions in that it provides individual protections and freedoms for Oklahomans. Many of the rights protected in this article are also protected by the federal constitution. For example, Section 30, which protects inhabitants against unreasonable searches and seizures, is almost identical to the Fourth Amendment of the United States Constitution. However, what is more noticeable is that many of the guarantees found in

Table 2–2
Comparison of State and Federal Constitutional Provisions

	U.S. CONSTITUTION	OKLAHOMA CONSTITUTION
Freedom from Unreasonable Search and Seizure	The right of the people to be secure in their persons, houses, papers, and effects, against unreasonable searches and seizures shall not be violated, and no Warrants shall issue, but upon probable cause, supported by Oath or affirmation, and particularly describing the place to be searched, and the persons or things to be seized. *U.S. Const. Amend. IV*	The right of the people to be secure in their persons, houses, papers, and effects against unreasonable searches or seizures shall not be violated; and no warrant shall issue but upon probable cause supported by oath or affirmation, describing as particularly as may be the place to be searched and the person or thing to be seized. *Okla. Const. Art. II sec. 30*
Freedom of Religion	Congress shall make no law respecting an establishment of religion, or prohibiting the free exercise thereof . . . *U.S. Const. Amend. I*	No public money or property shall ever be appropriated, applied, donated, or used, directly or indirectly, for the use, benefit, or support of any sect, church, denomination, or system of religion, or for the use, benefit, or support of any priest, preacher, minister, or other religious teacher or dignitary, or sectarian institution as such. *Okla. Const. Art. II sec. 5*
Freedom of Speech	Congress shall pass no law . . . abridging the freedom of speech, or of the press . . . *U.S. Const. Amend. I*	Every person may freely speak, write, or publish his sentiments on all subjects, being responsible for the abuse of that right; and no law shall be passed to restrain or abridge the liberty of speech or of the press . . . *Okla. Const. Art. II sec. 22.*

the Oklahoma Bill of Rights go further and are more specific than the federal constitution. For example, as Table 2–2 details, the protection against government establishment of religion and the guarantee of freedom of speech are much more detailed and specific than the establishment and free speech clauses of the U.S. Constitution's First Amendment.

The framers of the Oklahoma Constitution wanted to limit government's authority. As such, they gave individuals specific and often detailed protections. That the framers were fearful of government's ability to protect individual freedoms could be due in part to the fact that at the time the Oklahoma Constitution was being developed, many of the protections found in the United States' Bill of Rights had not yet been incorporated and applied to the states.

As a result of the framers' concerns about government power, in an effort to prevent state government from abusing power and restricting individual rights and liberties, the Oklahoma Constitution, like most other state constitutions, provided protections independent of the United States Constitution. The Oklahoma framers were skeptical of government power and sought to put constitutional restraints on government.

Women's Suffrage

While the Oklahoma Constitution was reform-oriented, one major reform failed to make it through the convention. Article III of the Oklahoma Constitution did not allow women the right to vote. Women's groups had been very active in promoting suffrage in the territories and had come very close to persuading the Oklahoma territorial legislature to adopt women's suffrage. Prior to statehood, women were allowed to vote in school board elections. Proponents of women's suffrage viewed the constitutional convention as the best opportunity to settle the question for the entire state (Goble 1980).

The issue of suffrage faced strong opponents. Organized by William H. Murray, opponents feared women would vote out of emotion rather than reason. At a critical moment, the issue was linked to race. Opponents claimed that allowing women to vote would increase African American political power. Opponents pointed to a February 5, 1907, Guthrie school board election to make their point. Out of all the ballots cast, 751 African American women voted and only seven white women voted. Murray quickly called a vote on the suffrage question. Delegates from areas with large African American populations generally voted against suffrage for women, and delegates from areas with small African American populations generally voted for women's suffrage. With the exception of school board elections, women's suffrage was defeated (Goble 1980).

Corporate Regulation

Some of the most aggressive reform proposals were those that dealt with corporations and regulation.[4] Perhaps intentionally drawing on the Sequoyah Constitution, the framers detailed provisions designed to end the influence of special interests and establish the public interest as supreme.

The constitution created a Pure Food Commission, allowed for municipal ownership of utilities, prohibited corporate ownership of land, prohibited corporate contributions and influences on campaigns, and gave the state expansive taxing authority. In addition, the constitution created a powerful Corporation Commission given the responsibility of "supervising, regulating, and controlling all transportation and transmission companies doing business in this state" (section 18). This three-member, elected commission was given investigative and enforcement authority for the state.

IV. Cultural Context of Oklahoma Government

State government is not only formally shaped and restricted by constitutions, but also informally shaped by political culture. **Political culture** can be defined as the attitudes, beliefs, and expectations people have about what government should and should not do. These attitudes and beliefs are derived from experiences and give individuals expectations about who should participate in politics and what rules should govern group behavior. Political culture has gained a great deal of attention in political science, in part, as an explanation for how various geographical areas have developed different political systems. Perhaps the leading scholar on political culture is Daniel Elazar. His work, *American Federalism: A View from the States*, argues that political culture has its roots in the historical experience of individuals. This in turn has an effect on the way individuals view government. He suggests that even though states have lost power to the national government, they are still important political systems. Elazar suggests that within the United States, there are three dominant subcultures, each with distinctive characteristics. These subcultures are traditionalistic, individualistic, and moralistic.[5]

Traditionalistic Political Culture

The **traditionalistic political culture** emphasizes the maintenance of the current social order. Government generally does not initiate a large number of new programs unless the new program benefits the ruling elite. Political parties are generally not as important as social or family ties. Bureaucracies are generally viewed negatively in that they tend to depersonalize government. Active participation in politics is generally limited to a small group of elites.

Individualistic Political Culture

The **individualistic political culture** emphasizes minimal government and views politics as a marketplace. Government is responsible for regulating the marketplace to guarantee everyone the chance to pursue their own self-interest. Government also exists to distribute favors to those who support the current regime and to help politicians get ahead. The individualistic culture looks favorably on large bureaucracies because of the patronage jobs that are available for political workers and the services that can be provided to voters. Beyond voting, political participation by the general public is not expected. Corruption in government and politics is tolerated.

Moralistic Political Culture

The **moralistic political culture** views government as a positive force for achieving social goals in the public interest. As a result, government has a much larger role. Government often initiates programs without public pressure and justifies the activity as being in the public's interest. Bureaucracies are looked upon as useful in achieving desired ends through neutral and detached processes. Unlike the individualistic political culture, which uses patronage in the staffing of bureaucracy, moralistic political cultures rely on merit-based employment practices where people are hired based upon what they know, not who they know. Active political participation by the public is encouraged, and public officials are expected to live up to high ethical standards. Corruption is not tolerated.

Impact of Political Culture

The question remains as to the impact political culture has on government, politics, and policies in different states. There appears to be a regional aspect to political subcultures in the United States. Traditionalist subcultures are generally found throughout the South, while the individualistic subculture is found throughout the middle states. The moralistic subculture is found primarily in the Northern states, although now there is a strong moralistic presence in the Rocky Mountain and Southwestern states.

There are a number of other generalizations that can be made as well. First, political participation is higher in moralistic states and lowest in traditionalistic states. Second, states with a moralistic political culture generally spend more money on welfare, produce more innovative government programs, have more lenient divorce laws, and are more likely to have ratified the Equal Rights Amendment. Third, not as many public officials are convicted of corrupt behavior in moralistic states as they are in individualistic and traditionalistic states. Fourth, political culture appeared to play a role in the defeat of the Equal Rights Amendment. Moralistic states were more likely to have ratified the ERA and traditionalistic states were the least likely to have approved the ERA.

Oklahoma's Political Culture

Oklahoma is part of a cluster of Southwestern states with a predominantly traditionalist culture, but with strong individualist tendencies. Reflecting much of what Elazar generalized and what other scholars have found, Oklahoma's classification appears accurate. Historians and political scientists point out that in Oklahoma: 1) change comes slowly; 2) state and local governments often act primarily as caretakers rather than innovators; 3) state and local politics have been dominated by one political party; 4) taking care of constituents back home has been more important than party unity; 5) corruption has played a prevalent role throughout the state's history; 6) funding for many public services is below the national

Chapter Two

LEADERSHIP PROFILE

ENOCH KELLY HANEY
Principal Chief of the Seminole Nation of Oklahoma

ENOCH KELLY HANEY was born to a Seminole father and a Creek mother, and was the grandson of the Seminole tribal chief in the 1940s. When a young Indian couple in Seminole, Oklahoma gave birth to a baby boy on November 12, 1940, little did they know that this infant would someday leave an indelible mark on not just his tribe, but the state of Oklahoma and the entire country. Haney spent his childhood in that small Oklahoma town, making small sculptures in the Oklahoma clay, but was destined to become a very prominent fixture in Oklahoma art, politics, and history.

Haney went on to college and received a bachelor's degree in fine art from Oklahoma City University. He went into the career that called to him as a boy and began creating pieces of art on a professional level. As he developed his skill as an artist it became evident that his heart was with his people. His work became well known and in 1975 he was designated as a Master Artist of the Five Civilized Tribes. He has continually been recognized for his work in Native American art. His paintings and sculptures have been shown all over the United States, and throughout the world. Today, he owns and operates an art studio in his hometown. In a December 2000 interview, he stated, "I believe this about my life: I don't have a choice about being an artist. I just am" (Hamilton, p. 41A). It was this same spirit that led him into politics.

For twenty years, Haney served in Oklahoma politics. He went to work serving citizens of his home district in both the Oklahoma State House for three terms and then he was elected to the State Senate. While serving in the Senate he was Chairman of the Appropriations Committee. He has said about his service that he also felt like he did not have a choice. He saw that a job needed to be done, and he thought he could do it well. In addition to his time with the Oklahoma legislature, he has served his tribe in various leadership roles on councils and in the business community. He even ran for governor in 2002. However prominent he has

> been in politics, he is likely to be most remembered for his first love—art.
>
> In 2002, the Oklahoma State Capitol had construction completed on its new dome. Before its completion, a contest was held to select a statue to sit on the apex as the crowning glory of this new architectural triumph. Along with many other distinguished Oklahoma artists, Haney entered the contest. The judges made their choice without knowing which artist had entered pieces and in the end, they chose Haney's sculpture unanimously. "The Guardian," a seventeen-foot statue of a Native American man, was placed on top of the Capitol Dome on June 7, 2002, and the dome was dedicated in November of that year. This beautiful piece of art now looks over Oklahoma City and the entire state.
>
> Today, after years as an artist, legislator, and history maker, Haney has returned to serve his tribe. He is currently the Principal Chief of the Seminole Nation of Oklahoma, following the footsteps of his grandfather before him. With a life of service like his, the future holds unlimited possibilities for those that his life will touch. He is a living example of a Renaissance man who follows his heart with a sense of truth and integrity mixed with great artistry.
>
> Kristy Roberts

average (Morgan et al. 1991: 9); and , 7) the legislature voted not to ratify the Equal Rights Amendment (Kincaid 1982: 20).

Oklahoma's political culture has been shaped by many forces. These forces include the traditions brought by those, both Native Americans and others, who settled the area, the unique history that influenced territorial development, and the nature and use of natural resources as well as the social and political reform movement of populist and progressivism that surrounded the development of its social and political institutions. However, political culture is not bound by the past. As Oklahoma's economic base and demographic characteristics continue to evolve, the traditions and institutions of the past will face growing pressure to change. The tradition of a one-party state, a reluctance to fund public services, and an acceptance of political corruption may change as well.

NOTES

1. The historical account is largely drawn from Gibson 1981 and Goble 1980: 202–227.
2. This account of the development of the Oklahoma Constitution is largely drawn from Gibson 1981: 196–97; Morgan and Morgan 1977: 72–79; and Goble 1980: 187–227.

3. For a detailed description of the populist movement, see Hicks 1959.
4. For other discussions of the corporate regulation in the Oklahoma Constitution, see Goble 1980, 214–218; Morgan et al. 1991, 72–74.
5. This discussion of political culture is drawn from Elazar 1982.

CHAPTER THREE

THE POLITICAL ECONOMY OF OKLAHOMA

Loren C. Gatch

This would be a great world to dance in if we didn't have to pay the fiddler.

Will Rogers.

I. INTRODUCTION

The study of political economy focuses upon the links between political and economic life. Governments affect the economy in two important ways. First, they redistribute wealth through the tax system. Second, they set the rules of the game by which people pursue their economic interests. For example, modern governments control the quantity and quality of money, and thus peoples' access to credit and capital. Through the tax system, governments take wealth away from some people and give it to others, thus influencing peoples' well-being, as well as their incentives to work and to take risks. Through bureaucratic regulation, governments have asserted control over such issues as economic development, workplace safety, environmental pollution, and healthcare. In sum, economic life never takes place in a vacuum; it occurs within a legal and political environment that both channels economic activity and, to some extent, makes that activity possible in the first place.

In this chapter, we will focus on the political economy of Oklahoma. As one of fifty states within a federal system, Oklahoma's political economy has been shaped by the common national experience of a constitutionally-imposed separation of powers. Since the 1980s, great changes have been taking place in national–state relations that have important consequences for Oklahoma. After considering briefly the consequences of federalism, we will turn to the political and economic history of Oklahoma, highlighting those experiences that have influenced the state's present-day political and economic relationships. The most important intersection of the economy and the polity occurs through the tax system, which is treated in Chapter 11. Finally, we will step back to consider the contemporary challenges that Oklahoma faces in the twenty-first century.

Chapter Three

The Evolution of a National Political Economy

As with other states comprising the national union, the political economy of Oklahoma has been shaped in basic ways by the evolving pattern of shared powers under federalism. **Federalism means that political power is shared between the national and state governments; the result is often called a system of "dual sovereignty."** At the time of America's founding, the Constitution limited the economic power of the individual states, thus closing off certain avenues of state regulatory development. The Constitution reserved interstate commerce, tariff, and treaty-making powers to the national government (Article I, Sections. 8 and 10). As a result, individual states could not cut deals with foreign governments. Nor could states tax or otherwise restrict the flow of goods and services across state borders. In this way, each state was compelled to be an economic market for all the other states.

In a similar vein, the Constitution deprived states of the ability to "coin Money, and emit Bills of Credit," leaving monetary policy (but not banking regulation) in the hands of the national government (Article I, Section 8). During colonial times, the states were notorious for printing paper currency ("bills of credit") of uncertain value. The Constitution put a stop to this practice. In addition to this vertical limitation, the Constitution enforced an important horizontal limitation upon state powers through the "Full Faith and Credit" and "Privileges and Immunities" clauses of Article IV. Essentially, these clauses required each state to respect certain laws of all the other states, and to treat the citizens of other states as fairly as they treated their own citizens.

Standing above all these rules was the authority of the Constitution itself. The Constitution authorized the Supreme Court to rule on legal disputes that emerged between states. Ultimately, the Constitution was the "Supreme Law of the Land," meaning that in the event of a disagreement between state and national Constitutions, the national law had the last word (Articles III and VI). Yet this supremacy was of a limited sort. It was bounded by how the founders understood the powers of the national government. The national government was a government of *delegated* powers. Essentially, the national government was allowed to do things only if the Constitution explicitly granted it the powers to do so. Otherwise, according to the Tenth Amendment, any powers not given to the national government were automatically reserved for the states and the people. In contrast, state governments were organized according to the reverse principle: any power that was not specifically denied to the states was assumed to be available to them. As a result, while the national constitution confined itself to laying out the basic structure and principles ("the rules of the game") by which the national government would operate, state-level constitutions accumulated a lot of legislative detail. Over time, state constitutions grew much longer than the national one, as they sought to spell out what state governments could and could not do with their powers (Elazar, 1982).

From these beginnings, the division of labor imposed by American federalism assumed a basic pattern that lasted for nearly 150 years until the New Deal era (1933–1939). Congress assured the quality of the money supply, imposed tariffs on imported goods, fought the Indians, and otherwise sponsored "internal improvements" such as new roads, canals, and railroads. Through these means, the national government carried out its basic mandate to create a nationwide economic market and promote commerce. Very little regulation in the modern sense was undertaken at the national level. Most government spending served the interest of patronage politics; what was good for the nation was also frequently good for the Democratic or Republican Party.

Under this federal system, each state gave up its ability to control any commerce that crossed its borders. Nonetheless, individual states retained extensive powers to regulate economic and social behavior within their borders. This division of powers was reinforced by important Supreme Court rulings that defined "interstate commerce" in a limited way (*Gibbons v. Ogden, 1824*), and that recognized the claims of state over national citizenship (*Barron v. Baltimore, 1833*). In this fashion, the federal system kept the national government from intervening in most areas of economic life. Indeed, for most practical purposes, it was the extensive "police powers" of the several states and not any activity of the distant national government that mattered most to the average American citizen during the nineteenth century. This practical dominance by the state governments was reflected in the tendency of the states, throughout the nineteenth century, to revise, rewrite, and lengthen their constitutions as if these documents were ordinary tools of legislation rather than frameworks of governing principles. In contrast, the national Constitution has been revised relatively infrequently. By and large, changes to its contents have come about by changes in its *interpretation*, not changes in its *wording* (Sturm, 1982; Keller, 1987).

Eroded somewhat by the passage of the Fourteenth Amendment (1868) and the regulatory innovations of the Progressive Era (ca. 1890–1920), the balance of power between the states and the national government shifted decisively in favor of the latter during the New Deal. In order to combat the Great Depression, the national government assumed greater authority to tax, spend, and regulate economic life. People got into the habit of looking to the national government to solve their problems. After initially resisting this new trend, the Supreme Court gave in. By enlarging its interpretation of "interstate commerce" to include practically all economic activity, the Supreme Court's rulings in *NLRB v. Jones & Laughlin Steel Co.* and *Stewart Machine Co. v. Davis* (both 1937) cleared the way for expanded regulatory power at the national level, and for the establishment of the modern welfare state.

Accompanying these changes was a shift in the balance of power between the states and the national government. No longer the chief political presence in the average person's life, state governments lost prestige, authority, and power from the 1930s to the 1980s. Economic planners assumed that states were too incompetent or corrupt to deal with the problems of a modern economy. The national government intervened first in the economy and then extended its reach into political and social life at both the state and local level. The Supreme Court's ruling in *Baker v. Carr* (1962) forced states, including Oklahoma, to reform their electoral systems in order to better represent their new urban majorities. The civil rights revolution was largely imposed by the national government on the unwilling states; in particular, the term "states' rights" became a euphemism for racist resistance to progress by people of color. But above all, the expansion of the national government's tax base enabled it to literally buy the states' cooperation in many policy areas by simply offering them grants-in-aid to finance various policy initiatives. States followed the national government's lead in public policy because, to paraphrase Willie Sutton, that's where the money was.

This state of affairs began to change in the 1970s, as the national government sought to renegotiate its relations with the states. In the past several years, the United States has shifted a good deal of responsibility for social policy back to the state level. In particular, state governments are now the sites of important new experiments in such policy areas as welfare and public education. Homeland security efforts to combat terrorism are yet another burden assumed by the states. This shift in power known as **devolution** has different causes. In part, devolution has occurred because of a growing conservative political climate that viewed government itself as a problem, not necessarily as a solution. This new climate has encouraged the transfer of responsibilities back to state governments. In addition, reinforcing these changing attitudes are new fiscal realities. The recent era of budget surpluses has given way to a return to budget deficits. The funding demands of Iraq war, as well as the long-term fiscal problems facing Social Security and Medicare mean that the money is simply not there for new programs. Conversely, devolution has challenged states like Oklahoma to take on responsibilities that the national government is no longer willing or able to bear (Nathan, 1996).

II. Oklahoma in American Political Development

One of the most important insights of political economy holds that *how* an economy develops depends in great part upon *when* it begins to develop (Gerschenkron, 1962). Thus, within the evolving pattern of American federalism, the timing of Oklahoma's path to statehood accounts for basic features of its early political and economic life. While a long part of the nation's history, Oklahoma as the forty-sixth state is itself relatively young. At its birth, Oklahoma had the experiences and mistakes of the previous forty-five states to learn from and to repeat! As the Oklahoma historian Angie Debo wrote nearly a half-century ago, "In Oklahoma all the experiences that went into making the nation have been speeded up. Here all the American traits have been intensified. The one who can interpret Oklahoma can grasp the meaning of America in the modern world" (Debo, 1987).

What are these traits? From its beginnings, the character of the American nation was shaped by the triumphs and hardships of subjugating an unknown and unexploited world. Beckoning with the twin attractions of political freedom and untold wealth, the unconquered land rewarded restless, acquisitive individuals who were capable of breaking old ties and embarking upon new adventures. The focus of these adventures was the American frontier, as it spread westward upon waves of settlement. The settlement of Oklahoma itself marked the final disappearance of the continental American frontier. Yet as a part of American history, Oklahoma has a far older significance. As a piece of the original Louisiana Purchase, the territory fits into the new nation's land and Indian policies by serving from the 1820s onward as the destination for the forced relocation of Indian tribes. In particular, after 1840 the Five Civilized Tribes established a degree of political independence that lasted until the Civil War when the Tribes' support of the Confederacy earned them the hostility of the Union. After the war, the national government retaliated by depriving the Indians of their land in central and western Oklahoma and reducing the Five Civilized Tribes' control over their remaining eastern territories. In their weakened condition, the Tribes were ill equipped to resist incursions by land-hungry whites and railroad speculators. As the dimensions of Oklahoma's natural wealth became clearer, Native-Americans were systematically cheated of their land allotments.

In its early organization, Oklahoma repeated the larger American pattern of frontier settlement, but at a vastly accelerated pace. Energized by the spectacular land run of 1889 and the subsequent discovery of vast petroleum reserves, Oklahoma became a laboratory for rapid economic development under fluid social and political conditions. According to Debo, this early period of Oklahoma's history witnessed "the quick and ruthless exploitation of natural resources, the freedom from restraint, and the meteoric rise of individuals" (Debo, 1987). From the start, the Oklahoma economy developed in two ways. In the southeast portion of the state comprising the former Indian Territory, where the rain was good but the soil poor, small-scale agriculture prevailed. Descendants of immigrants from the old South—small landholders worshipped a Baptist god and favored the Democratic Party. In contrast, white immigrants from the Northern Plains states had settled in the west and northwest lands of the former Oklahoma Territory. There they farmed wheat and raised cattle, prayed for wet weather and dry saloons, and voted Republican (Hale, 1982; Goble, 1982; Warner, 1995a). Finally, the beginnings of an urban economy sprung up along the main railroad lines, first on a north–south axis through Oklahoma City and Guthrie, and then, in the wake of the oil boom of the early twentieth century, east from Oklahoma City through Tulsa and Joplin.

Oklahoma's political system reflected its historical circumstances. The frenzy, first over land settlement and then over mineral rights intersected with two national political movements of the time—Populism and Progressivism—to determine the content and character of the Oklahoma Constitution of 1907. As a national force, **Populism** emerged in the 1880s throughout the American South and West as an agrarian rebellion against low agricultural prices and monopolistic abuses by the railroads. Populists distrusted experts and other elites. Instead, they upheld the virtues of the farmer and an idealized life of agrarian simplicity against the education and wealth of the eastern cities (Hicks, 1931).

For its part, **Progressivism** drew more from urban, middle-class roots in the municipal reform movements and "muckraking" journalism of the early twentieth century. Convinced of the corrupting effect of business on politics, the Progressive movement attacked patronage and machine politics in the name of an apolitical ideal of civic management. Far from distrusting expertise, Progressives worshipped the expert; Progressives believed that by separating business interests from politics, politics could be cleaned up and made rational and more efficient. Ultimately, they fantasized that the messy practice of politics could be reduced to a science. Ironically, even though they feared the corrupting effects of business interests, they thought they could borrow from business management methods that would make politics work as smoothly as a business. Unlike the Populists, Progressives tended to be more skeptical about the abilities of the average person, even though they claimed to be acting on his or her behalf. Progressives distrusted representative government and favored a stronger executive branch versus the legislature (McCormick, 1986).

Despite their different origins, both movements influenced the Oklahoma Constitution. Populism and Progressivism joined forces in a common farmer–labor hostility to outside concentrations of corporate wealth and power. This hostility was compounded by a dim view of legislators' ability to withstand the corrupting effects of money. In the context of Oklahoma's spectacular settlement and explosive economic development, these sentiments reinforced an overarching desire to keep land and mineral rights out of the hands of the large corporations and under the control of local entrepreneurs.

Reflecting these sentiments, the spirit (and sheer length) of the 1907 Constitution testified to the reformist agenda and suspicions of the time. The document resembled other state constitutions produced in the early twentieth century in its incorporation of detailed measures to fight public corruption by business interests (Sturm, 1982). For example, Article IX sought to control nearly every conceivable aspect of corporate life. It established a Corporation Commission empowered to regulate the activity of private corporations, especially railroads. Otherwise, no consideration was too great or small for the Constitution. It addressed everything from the safety of railroad crossings and the flash point of kerosene to the prohibition of monopolies. In addition, the Constitution gave the state

LEADERSHIP PROFILE

JULIE KNUTSON
President and Chief Executive Officer, Oklahoma Academy for State Goals

JULIE KNUTSON, twenty years ago, made a simple but offbeat request that launched her career in a completely new direction. While working as a counseling director and assistant principal for the Norman public schools, she requested that her superintendent send her to a local conference on economic expansion in Oklahoma. She had always felt that educators—especially at the common school levels—were not keenly aware of how the economic growth of a community or a state affected education. Moreover, there was little understanding of how education affected economic growth. Her superintendent asked her why in the world she would want to attend. The very question exemplified her thought process. She promised to come back from the conference and give a workshop for her fellow educators. Her superintendent set aside any misgivings and let her go.

It was the first major conference sponsored by the Oklahoma Academy for State Goals. The organization was still in its early stages of development and this conference held at the University of Oklahoma was quite ambitious. Knutson went up to the conference leaders and complimented them on a fine program. She explained why she had come and what she intended to do with the information she had gathered. A few weeks passed and she received a letter informing her that the Oklahoma Academy was looking for an executive director. They had never had one before and were conducting a nationwide search. From an initial 250 applicants, the search committee had narrowed the field. Knutson was one of the three finalists. She believes that she was ultimately selected because of her experience in psychology. She knew it was not going to be an easy job, especially "juggling all those chiefs." In addition, she had some experience at the national level chairing a group of people from the Midwest Region of the American Counseling Association.

For the past two decades, Knutson has employed her skillful leadership to steer a statewide, citizen-based nonpartisan organization to improve the public policy of Oklahoma. Her patience has paid great dividends. "We're ultimately changing cultural thinking—that's the bottom line of what we're doing and that's never a quick process," she says. Each year, more and more people become involved in the process and become aware of the Oklahoma Academy's wonderful work in getting diverse groups of people to work collectively on major state issues. The recommendations issued by the Oklahoma Academy are given serious attention by state policymakers.

As politics has become more polarized, the Oklahoma Academy has become something of an antidote to bite-sized campaigning. Through Knutson's leadership, the Academy has earned a wonderful reputation for credibility on both sides of the political aisle. She says, "Some years we may look like we're heading more to the right or to the left, but ultimately we get to those recommendations through an incredibly collaborative process that result in the best solution for the greater good of the state." She is the first to point out that the organization is not really run by one person, but rather an executive committee of about 25 people. Other states are now looking at the Oklahoma Academy as a model for what is possible.

In what little is left of her free time, she loves to spend in the great outdoors—gardening or riding her bicycle. She likes to read for pleasure, especially mysteries and works that inspire creativity like the Harry Potter series. She has even been known to volunteer her services to help teach elementary students how to read.

She was recently recognized by *The Journal Record* as the "Woman of the Year." Knutson offers this advice for young people: "I think that if you are going into any career that's public service oriented, it's one of the most rewarding things you can do, and you'll learn more than you think you can. It's an excellent way to help make a difference."

Brett S. Sharp

---

itself permission to engage in any business, apart from agriculture. It specified the length of the working day and banned child labor. Corporations were restricted in their ability to deal in land, while foreigners were outright prohibited from its purchase. Article V provided for the more typical Progressive aim of direct democracy via initiative and referendum. Yet, even as it reflected Progressive ideals, the Oklahoma constitution also codified Populist suspicions of a strong executive. Article VI dispersed the governor's authority by limiting his power to hire and fire officials within the executive branch.

Produced by a Democrat-controlled convention, the Constitution also inaugurated a tradition of Democratic domination of the state. Henceforth, state politics was not only Populist and Progressive, they were Southern and Democrat too. In Southern style, Democratic rule was quickly solidified by the disfranchisement of African–Americans, who at the time supported the Republican Party. Oklahoma politics quickly began to acquire something of the conservative, states'-rights outlook, typical of the Old Confederacy. Attacks upon the rights of African–Americans were followed by similar actions against third-party challengers. While it may amaze the present-day observer, in the years before World War I, the Socialist Party briefly emerged as a strong third-party contender in state politics. Nurtured by local conditions of farm poverty and hardship, as well as factional splits within the Progressive movement, this rural socialism merely carried forward the Populist–Progressive agenda into the arena of state politics. At its peak in 1914, the party garnered over 20% of the vote for its gubernatorial candidate, Fred Holt. Yet by 1920, the Democrats had taken advantage of the patriotic hysteria of World War I to forcibly suppress their Socialist rivals.

Although controlled at the outset by the Democratic Party, Oklahoma has never entirely been a Southern state. Its Populist–Progressive constitutional inheritance assured that the role of the state in the economy would differ from that found elsewhere in the South; except, perhaps, for Louisiana where a strong Populist tradition also persisted. Indeed, the momentum created by Oklahoma's statehood carried forward during the early years into further enactments of the reformist agenda, including the passage of corporate and income taxes; a system of bank deposit insurance; labor codes; compulsory school attendance; and mineral conservation. Much of this agenda anticipated by twenty-five years were key features of New Deal legislation—even though, ironically, two of Oklahoma's three New Deal-era governors (Murray and Phillips) proved largely hostile to New Deal programs.

By the early twentieth century, then, the basic elements of the Oklahoma political economy had fallen into place. Heavily, agricultural (smallholdings in the East, cotton in the South, wheat and cattle in the west) and blessed with promising reserves of petroleum and natural gas concentrated in the center of the state, the Oklahoma economy initially prospered as a producer of natural resources. However, its exploitation of this natural wealth was both spectacular and wasteful. This waste reflected not just basic human greed, but the structure of property rights. Farmers tended to overuse the land with a single crop because the typical homesteading farm was too small for sustainable agriculture in a semi-arid climate. Farmers went into debt to produce, and produced to get out of debt. One tragic result of these farming practices was the **Dust Bowl** conditions of the 1930s. Similarly, oil producers overpumped their wells because no one could say who owned the vast pools of oil that lay beneath the land; if one person stopped pumping, another person would take his share (Hale, 1982; Debo, 1987). While the state was poor relative to the more settled parts of the country, Oklahoma nonetheless made rapid progress despite the weak farm prices that plagued the agricultural sector throughout the 1920s. In fact, until the development of Texas fields, Oklahoma remained the nation's largest producer of oil and gas. By 1916, state oil production represented a good third of the national total.

Oklahoma's Populist–Progressive legacy dovetailed with traditions of Southern Democratic dominance to shape how the state's abundant natural resources would influence political life in the 1920s and 1930s. Like its economy, Oklahoma's politics was also wild: the 1920s alone saw two governors impeached, and a period of martial law. The state's overwhelmingly rural constituencies responded to authoritarian and charismatic political leaders—"Our Jack" Walton, "Alfalfa Bill" Murray—who embodied the compassion and contradictions of Populism. Tax revenues from agricultural and mining activity reinforced a traditionalistic politics of patronage that sustained a level of social welfare spending which distinguished Oklahoma from other states. Governments spent in a Populist fashion, but for Progressive purposes. In fact, the sheer notion that state employees ought to be hired on the basis of merit rather than party patronage did not receive legislative sanction until the governorship of J. Howard Edmondson (1959–1963).

Nonetheless, true to the state's inveterate distrust of political power, the revenue streams from various sources were to a great extent "earmarked" for predetermined purposes in an effort to protect the state's resources from unscrupulous politicians. Article X, Section 19 decreed that "Every act . . . levying a tax shall specify distinctly the purpose of which said tax is levied, and no tax levied and collected for one purpose shall ever be devoted to another purpose." This sentiment was duly incorporated into subsequent Oklahoma statutes. For example, from 1933 to 1987 Oklahoma's traditionally-generous social welfare policies rested upon the earmarking of sales tax revenues for public assistance programs. Thanks to this earmarking, by the early 1960s Oklahoma emerged as the leading state in per capita spending for public assistance, even though the state otherwise ranked among the lowest third of all states in per capita income terms (Klos, 1965).

At the same time, Oklahoma's political traditions have emphasized grassroots control over spending. Article V of the Constitution, like its national counterpart, places the authority to originate revenue bills with the House of Representatives; moreover, no revenue bill may be passed during the last five days of a given session in order to avoid a gubernatorial veto. A 1933 amendment to the Constitution took the power to tax property out of the state governments' hands and left it with the localities (Article X, Section 9). By 1937, the hard times of the Depression era led to chronic state indebtedness and an overhang of "warrants," or short-term borrowing that was extended year after year. Thus, for good measure, voters added to the constitution an amendment in 1941 mandating a balanced budget (Article X, Section 23). In 1985, the constitution was again amended to limit budget appropriations to 95% of the estimate of a given year's revenues. Most recently, the passage in 1992 of State Question 640 amended Article V to require that any tax increase either be approved by a popular referendum or be voted in by a three-fourths majority of both sides of the legislature. Only one other state in the Union—Arkansas—places such severe constitutional restrictions on the ability of the government to raise taxes.

In sum, Oklahoma's revenue practices as they have been embodied in its constitution reveal a great deal about the character and priorities of the state. Wary of both outside corporate interests and its own politicians, the Oklahoman political culture has sought to live up to its Progressive ideals of social welfare and economic regulation, even while its Populist suspicions have led it to maintain strict controls over the use (and misuse) of public funds. State government operates with considerable constitutional restrictions upon how much money it can spend, and how it can raise those funds.

The Changing Structure of the Oklahoma Economy: From Depression to Oil Boom

If, in political terms, Oklahoma entered statehood with a progressive constitution ahead of the times, in economic terms it lagged well behind them. True, along with the rest of the nation Oklahoma was growing more urban and industrial. By 1929, Oklahoma's income per capita reached nearly 65% of the national average, although this figure masked sections of extreme poverty in the southeastern part of the state. Agriculture, mining, and internal trade (wholesale and retail) together comprised over 57% of the source of this income, versus a mere third for the country as a whole. Compared to the rest of the country, relatively few Oklahomans made their living producing manufactured goods. This meant that on the cusp of the Great Depression, Oklahoma remained industrially underdeveloped (Klein, 1963). This underdevelopment and lack of economic diversification exposed Oklahoma to "boom and bust" cycles in commodity prices, which were far more volatile than non-farm wages and retail prices, and left the state vulnerable to downturns in the national economy as a whole.

The shock of the Great Depression and the tragedy of the Dust Bowl are well known. During the years 1929–33, when national per capita income dropped 30%, Oklahoma's fell significantly further. The state government responded fitfully and incompetently to the tragedy, hobbled by its divisive politics and patronage instincts (Goble and Scales, 1983). Families left the state in large numbers to escape the ecological and economic disaster. The resulting outmigrations drained away nearly 400,000 people, or one-sixth of the population by 1945. Thereafter, the population count turned up, albeit more slowly than the national growth rate, and did not return to its 1930 figure until three decades later. Relative per capita income rebounded more quickly (thanks in part to the departure of poorer residents), regaining its pre-Depression proportion by 1938 and ascending to a plateau of somewhat over 80% of the national average by the 1960s (Klein, 1963). This per capita income gap between Oklahoma and the rest of the country has persisted to the present day.

Economic recovery in Oklahoma meant in a real way simply becoming more like the rest of the country. Although wheat, cattle and cotton remained the state's three single largest areas of farm production, the proportion of Oklahoma's employment and income derived from agriculture and mining declined steadily since 1929 as the state moved towards a more manufacturing- and service-based economy. As in other rural states, Oklahoma's agriculture itself took on industrial characteristics. The number of farms fell but their average size grew as farming became more capital-intensive. Corporate hog farms are only the latest and most fragrant example of this trend. Again, the situation varied across the state. In the "Little Dixie" area of southeastern Oklahoma, farms remained smaller and less mechanized, while productivity and incomes stagnated. In contrast, wheat and cattle farming to the west and in the Panhandle adapted more successfully to modern conditions and methods (Klein, 1963; Lage et al., 1977).

The oil and gas industries form a special case, since Oklahoma was blessed with resources that other states lacked. Characteristic of these industries is that while their wages are above the average, they contribute only a small percentage of the state's employment total. By the late 1920s, energy and mining activity except for natural gas turned downward, both as a proportion of national production and relative to the state's other economic sectors. While the physical volume of petroleum production recovered somewhat after the Second World War, oil made a decreasingly significant contribution to the state's output until the oil "shocks" of 1973 and 1979. Of longer-term significance, estimated reserves reached a high in 1955, which pointed towards the inevitable depletion of this once-bountiful source of wealth. Production peaked in 1969 at 225 million barrels a year, and annual production has since declined to about one-fourth of that amount. Nonetheless, oil and gas did and still do make a meaningful contribution to the Oklahoma economy (Klein, 1963; Lage et al., 1977; Dauffenbach, 2005).

After the Second World War, manufacturing, services, and government began replacing the agricultural and mining sectors as drivers of the Oklahoma economy. These shifts were paralleled by the rapid growth of the Oklahoma City, Tulsa, and (more recently) Lawton metropolitan areas. In contrast, the population of rural Oklahoma continued to decline. To a large extent, Oklahoma only experienced during the postwar period the same large-scale economic transformations that the nation as a whole had undergone. And even then, demographic recovery from the disaster of the 1930s occurred hesitantly; only by late 1950s did population growth consistently offset outmigration. Nonetheless, throughout the promising 1950s and 1960s, Oklahoma's growth in per capita income consistently outstripped that of the nation.

Despite these trends towards better days, Oklahoma's economic structure continued to differ from the nation's at large. Not only did agriculture and mining loom large in the state's fortunes, but also government activity made outsized contributions to Oklahoma's income. The combined state and national government contribution to Oklahoma's economy exceeded that of the average state. This reflected, in part, the New Deal extension of federal responsibilities and the growth of revenue sharing. In addition, however, Oklahoma congressmen succeeded in placing federal installations and their payrolls (Tinker, Fort Sill, the FAA Aeronautical Center) in the state. Such patriotic devotion to federal largess has not prevented state politicians from campaigning locally on anti-tax platforms. Furthermore, compared to the average state, Oklahoma has relied more on the national government as a percentage of its revenues. This revenue pattern is discussed in the chapter on the Oklahoma tax system. In its aggregate economic impact, however, government activity during the 1960s and 1970s made a higher than average contribution to Oklahoma's employment and income. On the state and local level alone, the expansion of government payrolls continued apace throughout the 1960s and into the 1970s, even as growth in federal employment tailed off.

By the early 1970s, on the eve of the second oil boom, agriculture, mining, and government were still large sectors in terms of state employment and income compared to their relative importance within the U.S. economy. Economic diversification had taken place, but the state still remained behind the rest of the nation. An expanding government sector had helped stabilize the Oklahoma economy since the 1930s, but there was no guarantee that federal spending would continue. By the same token, agriculture relied upon federal price supports that shielded farmers from the worst fluctuations in commodity prices. Yet, the deregulatory movement beginning in the late 1970s has eroded even these supports. Most ominously, in view of the inexorable decline in oil production, Oklahoma has been running a long-term race against time: can the economy develop alternative sources of income quickly enough to escape its reliance on uncertain or even depleting natural endowments? While the goals of economic development and diversification may have changed over the years—first manufacturing, then services, and now the high-tech industries—Oklahoma has faced this same underlying problem for decades.

For a while, however, the old boom times seemed to get a new lease on life. Beginning in 1973, the Organization of Petroleum Exporting Countries (OPEC) began to assert its market power by restricting the world supply of crude oil, imposing export embargoes upon selected countries, and setting ever-higher prices on the international oil market. Followed by the Iranian revolution and the second oil "shock" of 1979, OPEC pushed oil prices to levels ten times higher than those of the 1960s.

For America generally, gas lines and "stagflation" were the miserable results. For Oklahoma in particular, misery for the nation meant a windfall for the state's economy. Between 1975 and 1982, employment in Oklahoma's mining sector (which includes oil and gas) doubled; by 1982, over 20% of the state's economic output came from this sector, compared with barely 5% nationally (ODOC, 2006a). In the wake of this sudden prosperity, wages and property values rose, and taxes fell even as state revenues bulged with the proceeds of oil and gas severance taxes. The beauty of these severance taxes lay in the fact that outsiders paid this tax, not Oklahomans. For a brief moment, per capita income even reached the national average.

The good times were not to last. The success of the OPEC cartel was its own undoing. By the mid-1980s, the price of a barrel of oil had fallen by nearly half from its peak, and Oklahoma was faced with the prospect of painful economic retrenchment. Not only did the mining sector collapse, but even the state's population declined. After growing fast during the 1960s and 1970s, state output now stagnated for the next decade. Thus, in a reversal of the 1970s, by the 1980s what was good for America proved very bad for Oklahoma. Cursed with temporary good fortune, Oklahoma lost precious time in its longer-term goal of developing a truly modern and diversified economy.

While these troubles were not Oklahoma's fault, its response to good fortune highlighted the state's economic vulnerabilities. Unlike Texas or Colorado, two states with similar economic roots in natural resource extraction, Oklahoma has not moved its economy as far away from natural resources and towards manufacturing and services. Oklahoma was late to enter the computer age, and much of its technology employment was concentrated in support industries for oil and gas extraction (*Economics of High Technology in Oklahoma*, 1985). Despite some success in catching up with the high-tech boom of the 1990s, a variety of studies have suggested that Oklahoma's economy is still less high-tech oriented than the economies of other states (Warner and Dauffenbach, 2002). It is important to understand that high-tech jobs are not confined to computer hardware or software companies, but are spread out across a number of industries, where scientists, mathematicians, and engineers might be employed. According to the Oklahoma Department of Commerce (ODOC), by 2005, the state's share of high-tech employment, understood broadly, still lagged the national average, both in terms of the numbers of employees and the concentration of high-tech employees throughout industry (ODOC, 2006b).

Oklahoma in a New Century

In the words of two observers, "the last two decades of the twentieth century will probably not go down in the history books as the greatest period of economic growth in the state of Oklahoma" (Snead and Ireland, 2002: 9). Nonetheless, by the early 1990s, an era of sustained economic growth returned. Not only has Oklahoma's performance outpaced the

Table 3-1
Output (Gross Product) by Industry in %, U.S. vs. Oklahoma 2005

Industry	United States (%)	Oklahoma (%)
Natural Resources and Mining	2.7	14.6
Construction	4.9	3.6
Manufacturing (a)	12.1	9.7
Trade	12.6	12.1
Transportation and Utilities	4.8	5.9
Services (b)	51.2	37.9
Government	11.9	15.9

SOURCE: U.S. BEA, *Survey of Current Business* (2007). Percentages do not add up to 100, due to rounding.

NOTES

(a) Includes durable and nondurable goods.

(b) Includes: information; financial activities; professional and business services; education and health services; leisure and hospitality; and other.

nation's growth rate, but its unemployment rate has also remained consistently below the nationwide level. By 2006, per capita income reached 88% of the national average, and perhaps higher when adjusted for regional cost of living differences (Snead, 2007; ODOC, 2007). Despite these gains, the state lags comparatively. For example, Oklahoma's per capita personal income in 2006 ranked 37th, or among the bottom fourth, of the fifty states (*U.S. Bureau of Economic Analysis*, 2007). Although Oklahoma's industrial structure continues to converge with that of the nation, noticeable differences remain. Table 3-1 contrasts Oklahoma and the United States in terms of the distribution of output across economic sectors.

This contrast illustrates both Oklahoma's progress compared to previous decades and the persistent legacy of Oklahoma's political and economic history. Stimulated by the surge in energy prices since 2004, the Natural Resources and Mining sector continues to make an outsized contribution to the state's economy. The importance of Government activity as a contributor to output is also reflected in the state's high ranking (7th in the nation for 2005) in terms of public employment as a percentage of total employment (Hovey and Hovey, 2006). In contrast, the state remains average or lags in other areas. Diversification away from its traditional sources of livelihood remains a long-term goal for Oklahoma's economic development. Yet, as this diversification takes place, the chronic income gap between Oklahoma and the rest of the nation becomes an ever-more puzzling problem.

Chapter Three

III. Oklahoma in The Global Economy

Despite its inland location away from major trade centers, Oklahoma has always been closely tied to world markets. The prices of its raw material exports were traditionally determined in distant places like Chicago, Liverpool, and London. In contrast, Oklahoma's manufacturing has been less attuned to foreign markets than the nation's at large (Jadlow and Lage, 1992). Yet, whether or not Oklahoma produces for a world market, its own economic fortunes will be increasingly influenced by what happens there, especially if the state's petroleum resources dwindle at their present rate. Accordingly, analysts and policymakers have looked to this market for solutions to the riddle of Oklahoma's income gap. At the very least, as Oklahoma's employment pattern and industrial structure converge with those of the nation, the most plausible explanation for the state's low per capita income appears to be the *type* of jobs created in Oklahoma, and not necessarily the *industry sector* in which those jobs are created. In particular, the Oklahoma economy trails the nation in creating high-paying occupations of the professional and managerial type (Ireland, Snead, and Miller, 2006).

Traditionally, Oklahoma has advertised itself to prospective business as a low-cost, low-wage, low-tax, non-union state (ODOC, 2007). According to *Congressional Quarterly*, compared to other states, Oklahoma's cost of living in 2005 ranked near the lowest (47th) in the nation. In 2004, the average annual pay of Oklahomans ranked 43rd. The state's per capita state and local tax burden in 2002 placed Oklahoma 42nd in the nation. Labor union membership in 2005 amounted to a mere 5.4% of the work force, versus 12.5% nationwide (Hovey and Hovey, 2006; *Statistical Abstract of the United States 2007*, Table 647). The perennial debates about workers' compensation costs as well as the state's passage in 2001 of a "right-to-work" (antiunion) referendum emerge from the same mindset. While individual homeowners might feel otherwise, Oklahoma has been spared the distorting effects of the housing bubble that, in other parts of the country, has put affordable housing beyond the reach of the middle class (Dauffenbach, 2006a). Yet, while low costs may attract a certain sort of labor-intensive manufacturing and service mix, low wages now do not necessarily lead to higher incomes later. Indeed, it is precisely these industries that are most likely to be "outsourced" to even cheaper locations outside of the country. Thus, policymakers increasingly recognize the importance of nurturing Oklahoma's high-tech manufacturing and service sectors. After the last oil bust, the legislature passed House Bill 1444, also known as the Oklahoma Economic Development Act of 1987. Broadly speaking, the Act has sought to encourage economic development of a sort that did not engage the state in the traditional competition with other states for so-called "smokestack" industries.

Towards this end, the Act put into effect a number of measures that reflected two basic approaches to economic development. First, it created the Oklahoma Center for the Advancement of Science and Technology (OCAST) to encourage basic and applied research, as well as the commercialization of promising technology. Through a variety of programs, OCAST attempts to leverage modest state appropriations by attracting matching funds from federal and private sources. Most recently, the state has also sought to strengthen the links between academic research and commercialization by making it easier for universities and researchers to exploit their discoveries. Since the passage of State Questions 680 and 681 in 1998, Oklahoma colleges and universities and their faculty are now legally able to own equity in start-up firms.

Secondly, HB 1444 sought to expand the supply of investment capital by enlarging the state's role in financing high-tech startups and other small businesses whose exports would bring wealth into the state. Led by the Oklahoma Development Finance Authority (ODFA), this effort makes use of the state's credit to underwrite promising investments. By selling its own bonds in the capital market, the ODFA can in turn lend to borrowers that meet the agency's criteria. Alternately, the ODFA can enhance the credit, and thus lower the capital costs, of worthy borrowers by guaranteeing the interest and principal of their loans with private lenders. Through its investment affiliate, the Oklahoma Capital Investment Board (OCIB), the ODFA even has the authority to extend its guarantees to equity financing of startup industries. In effect, the OCIB involves the state as a stakeholder in venture capitalism. Finally, through a separate project the state has established a Linked Deposit Program to lower the borrowing costs for farmers and small businesses. In exchange for accepting below-market rates of interest on its own deposits, the state enables banks to make low-interest loans to qualified borrowers (Murray, 1988; Warner and Smith, 1991).

In sum, the two approaches incorporated into HB 1444 have aimed at increasing both the human and financial capital that Oklahoma has at its disposal. More recently, the passage of SB 1391 in 2002 updated the provisions of HB 1444 by establishing the Oklahoma Science and Technology Research and Development Board to oversee OCAST, and stimulate in particular information and biotechnology industries (Warner, 2002). In 2006, OCAST was given the additional responsibility of administering Governor Brad Henry's Economic Development Generating Excellence (EDGE) endowment that will fund directly research into cutting-edge technologies (Brainard 2006).

A second major program approved by the legislature in 1993, the Oklahoma Quality Jobs Program, focuses not upon augmenting the state's resources, but upon the direct creation of jobs through the reduction of employer costs. The Quality Jobs Program encourages the hiring of new workers by offering participating companies cash rebates of up to 5% of payrolls of new employees. Targeted at manufacturing and service firms that make most of their sales out of state, this program amounts to an employment subsidy to encourage certain kinds of desirable industry to

Chapter Three

LEADERSHIP PROFILE

AMY POLONCHEK
Executive Director for the Oklahoma Department of Commerce

AMY POLONCHEK is the Executive Director for the Oklahoma Department of Commerce. She provides strategic direction and oversight to the agency's economic and community development activities. She has expertise and experience in economic and policy research, performance measurement, process improvement, strategic planning, finance, and government relations.

Previously, Polonchek was the principal of a consulting group, specializing in management and policy analysis for public and private sector clients. She has also served as Executive Director of the Oklahoma Institute, Project Manager for TekSystems, and served on the management team at the Oklahoma Department of Career and Technology Education.

Polonchek has published a variety of articles and papers, and served as Visiting Assistant Professor for Strategic Management at Oklahoma State University. She holds a Bachelor of Science in Economics from Michigan State University and a Master of Science in Economics from Oklahoma State University.

---

expand in Oklahoma. Companies that do not sign up with the Quality Jobs Program can still make use of a variety of tax credits, exemptions and refunds (ODOC, 2007a, b).

As with the R&D initiatives created by HB 1444, the Quality Jobs Program aims to make Oklahoma an attractive place to do business without necessarily selling the state as a source of cheap, docile labor. Both initiatives aim to cultivate the kind of high-tech, high-wage industries that hitherto have been underrepresented in the Oklahoma economy. Both initiatives are also politically attractive in that they do not involve any great upfront expenses to the state. Apart from the seed money provided by OCAST, the ODFA and OCIB merely require the state to make use of its credit standing with the financial markets to underwrite and otherwise guarantee private initiatives. As long as these initiatives are profitable, the state spends nothing and may even earn a return. While the Quality Jobs Program does require direct state payments, these payments have been rationalized by appealing to the sales and income tax revenues that these new jobs produce. As long as the state is encouraging hiring that otherwise would not take place, then in a certain sense the Quality Jobs Program can be said to pay for itself.

Do these various development initiatives work? It is far too early to tell. Some aspects, especially those concerned with education, research and development, will show results only in the long term, in the form of increased high-tech employment and business startups. OCAST estimates that, since 1987, investments of $138 million in state money has leveraged $2.4 billion in funding from federal and private sources for various Oklahoma technology initiatives (OCAST, 2007). The fruits of venture capital investment are likewise a long way off. According to the Oklahoma Department of Commerce, the Quality Jobs Program has enrolled some 450 companies to which have been credited $445 million in wage rebates (ODOC, 2007b). Yet as OCAST itself notes, Oklahoma averages only one-seventh of national average for industry-funded R&D per capita. The state also continues to lag behind the national average in the percentage and number of business startups that are technology-intensive (ranked 35th and 32nd respectively), as well as in the percentage of business payrolls in such industries (OCAST, 2004). By various measures of technology intensiveness, the structure of the Oklahoma economy as of 2003 was generally neither more nor less high tech than the early 1990s (Warner and Dauffenbach, 2006). Against this backdrop, even if the net benefits of such programs are less than obvious, a small state like Oklahoma that foregoes such development incentives puts itself at a competitive disadvantage vis-à-vis its neighbors (Warner and Dauffenbach, 2004a, 2004b).

The great uncertainty underlying all such investment and employment projections is the question of the counterfactual: would this activity have taken place anyway in the absence of these various incentive programs? The more basic these incentives are, the more confident one can be that their expense generates a net benefit. For example, a well-educated and trained workforce is a better investment incentive than a tax break, since that workforce will attract more than one industry. All things being equal, capitalists invest in those industries, locales, and markets which promise the highest rate of risk-adjusted return. This prospective rate of return depends upon many variables, some of which are beyond Oklahoma's control. If in the real world all things are not equal, then what it is about Oklahoma that discourages investment for high-wage growth?

Two types of answers have been given. The first claims that, contrary to prevailing beliefs, the tax burden imposed by Oklahoma's government, when adjusted for the low cost of living in the state, is among the top third in the nation. According to this argument, a high tax burden both reduces per capita income and discourages investment (Jones and McClure, 1997).

The second answer blames Oklahoma's educational system for not teaching its students the cognitive skills necessary to succeed in the information age. Increases in per capita income are strongly associated with increases in the percentage of the workforce that has college degrees (Dauffenbach, 2006b). Angie Debo may have exaggerated when she claimed that "Oklahomans do not read." However, other commentators do point out that Oklahoma is not exactly a hotbed of research and scholarship—that its colleges and universities have specialized in "emphasizing quantity over quality"—and that educational resources are spread too thinly over too many politically-protected schools (Debo, 1987: 250; Morgan, 1991: 180). Based upon ACT test results, Oklahoma lags behind comparable states, and the trend is not auspicious. As one recent analysis put it, in educational terms "if the United States is a 'Nation at Risk', Oklahoma qualifies as a 'State at Risk'" (Moomaw, 2006: 67). At the highest levels of education, Oklahoma produces only two-thirds of the national average of Ph.D. scientists per 10,000 population, and has garnered less than half of the national average for federally-funded university R&D expenditures per capita (OCAST, 2004). While the absolute amount of Oklahoma's academic R&D expenditures per capita has increased between 1990 and 2003, in relative terms these expenditures are barely 60% of the national average (Warner and Dauffenbach, 2006b).

If this portrait illustrates anything, it is that there are no easy solutions to the problem of Oklahoma's per capita income gap. Moreover, any solution will necessarily have a political as well as an economic dimension. This alone represents grounds for caution when proposing any reforms. Certainly, politicians do not worry about counterfactuals when justifying their favorite program or defending their local college. In the long run, there is no free lunch in economic development: sooner or later, a bill comes due—be it in the form of increased education costs, guaranteed loan defaults that must be made good, or tax increases that must compensate for funds paid out in employment subsidies. So far, many of these costs remain implicit. Indeed, what has made these current business finance programs politically palatable in the first place is precisely their lack of upfront costs! The offloading of borrowing and guaranteeing authority onto independent agencies both avoids political conflict over resources and reduces responsible political oversight over these agencies' activities. In this regard, Oklahoma is unfortunately quite up to date with national practices.

IV. Conclusion

This survey of the political economy of the Sooner State has sought to draw links between history, politics, and economic development in order to explain certain features of present-day Oklahoma. If Angie Debo is at all correct, then a study of the Oklahoma experience teaches us something about the nature and soul of the United States. The overarching theme of this account has been the long-term convergence of Oklahoma's economic fortunes with those of the larger nation. Variations on this theme include the legacies of Oklahoma's Populist–Progressive heritage, especially as they are embodied in its constitution. In addition, Oklahoma's experiences of economic bonanza and catastrophe highlight its precarious reliance upon natural resources as a significant source of its wealth. All of these factors suggest why Oklahoma remains both different from, and instructive to, the rest of the nation.

A final word should be added about constitutional reform. While this topic is not directly related to political economy, in Oklahoma's case some remarks can be made about the economic consequences of the early enthusiasms of Oklahoma's reformist past. While many of its statutes are obsolete in practical terms, such mainstays as Article IX remain a manifesto of anti-business sentiment. Article X limits the state's ability to exercise its borrowing authority (thus indirectly encouraging the device of independent agencies), while Article VI disperses gubernatorial authority that could otherwise be used to manage more effectively the executive branch (Clark, 1988; Warner, 1990). One report even contends that the constitution discourages investment from out of state, and that the notorious Article IX in particular "fairly bristles with hostility toward business and its presumably wicked ways." This report calls for the outright repeal of Articles IX and X (Constitution Revision Study Commission, 1991).

While some of these reform suggestions would have a largely symbolic impact, others would attempt to clear the constitution off the thickets of legislation that have grown up within it. Again, thoughtful people will always disagree about how much economic and social regulation a government should impose. Ideally, a constitution establishes the framework of law, while legislatures grapple with the details of political life. Keeping these two enterprises separate would be good for business as well as for the state. At the same time, who knows what surprises might emerge from a second constitutional convention?

CHAPTER FOUR

THE OKLAHOMA LEGISLATURE

Jan C. Hardt

> In Oklahoma, legislative leaders have been very effective in reforming the institutional capacity of the Legislature. Operations are more accessible, a stronger staffing component has been implemented, state agencies have been made more accountable for their activities to the Legislature, and a more professional public image has been developed. As a result, the Oklahoma Legislature performs an independent role in the democratic system of checks and balances as authors of the Oklahoma Constitution intended.
>
> Lloyd Benson, former Speaker of the Oklahoma House of Representative

I. INTRODUCTION

So how does that old baseball song go?—"Buy me some peanuts and Cracker Jack. I don't care if I never get back." Well, at least in Oklahoma, that may be a thing of the past—at least in Oklahoma public schools, as the legislature made the effort to try to eliminate junk food from the public schools and offer a more healthy diet to its youngest citizens. But the effort to remove junk food from the public schools experienced some tremendous hurdles and it also provided great insight into how the Oklahoma legislature and Oklahoma politics work.

It started in 2004 when Senator Bernest Cain, D-Oklahoma City, introduced Senate Bill (SB) 1425, which attempted to limit the amount of junk food and soft drinks that could be offered in vending machines by the state's public schools. As originally written, SB 1425 would have forced schools to replace non-nutritional beverages and snacks completely with more healthy items. This bill involved multiple interests in Oklahoma. It was sponsored by the Oklahoma Fit Kids Coalition as one of its initiatives to deal with obesity in Oklahoma's children. Oklahoma typically rates in the bottom ten of all fifty states in the number of obese children, as well as adults. It was also supported by numerous parents who wrote letters to various newspaper editors throughout the state. Oklahoma's effort to pass this legislation was part of a nationwide trend among various states, including Texas and Indiana, which considered or passed measures to deal with child obesity. Yet, the opponents of SB 1425 were vocal as well. Numerous school districts and their superintendents worried about the consequences of banning junk food from vending machines in their schools. Many school districts have multi-year contracts with soft drink and junk food manufacturers, which can supply needed revenue for those school districts. The Oklahoma City Public School District in 2004, for example, received fifty-five cents for every dollar spent on junk food in the schools which provided the district with about $275,000 in revenue that year. Not surprisingly, the bill was also opposed by manufacturers of the products that would have been banned, including the Oklahoma Soft Drink Association.

The 2004 Junk Food Bill, as it became known in the legislature, also showed that legislation needed to go through numerous hurdles before it became law. The bill was successful in its first phase; the Oklahoma Fit Kids Coalition was able to get Senator Cain to agree to author the bill, a must in the Oklahoma legislature. The bill also passed through its Senate Committee. But it ran into trouble when it arrived on the Senate floor. Numerous amendments were added to the bill. The most controversial eliminated the complete ban on junk food, and instead said that nutritional and non-nutritional fare could be offered at the same time. Supporters of the Junk Food bill argued that this would certainly weaken the intent of the bill, because most children are probably inclined to choose junk food over healthy food when given the choice. Another amendment dealt with the issue of pre-existing contracts that school districts had with the junk food and soft drink companies.

As a result, the final vote in the Senate was 18–26, meaning that the bill failed because twenty-five votes were needed for passage. Even then the Junk Food bill was not dead. Two days after its defeat, Senator Cain made the motion to reconsider the bill, which would have meant revisiting the issue. But that motion also failed. Then, the bill ran up against a final rule, which ultimately doomed the bill for good—all legislation in the Oklahoma legislature must begin in each house by a certain date. For the Senate, the date was March 11, 2004, which meant that the Junk Food bill died in the 2004 Oklahoma legislature. Even if it had passed the Senate, the bill still would have had to pass the House, in the same form as passed in the Senate, or else there would have been a conference committee. The Governor would also have had to approve the bill.

Yet, the bill was revived in the 2005 Oklahoma Legislature as Senate Bill 265, which required school board members to create tiered access to foods with "minimal nutritional value." Again, Senator Cain, D-Oklahoma City, sponsored the legislation in the Senate, while Representative Susan Winchester, R-Chickasha, sponsored it on the House side. In elementary schools, access to foods of minimal nutritional value would be restricted except on special occasions. Middle school students would only have such access after school, at evening events, and on special occasions. For the high schools, the school districts were mandated "to provide students with incentives meant to encourage healthy food choices as options." This measure was passed into law on April 14, 2005, and was signed by Governor Henry, but it faces one last hurdle; despite its passage in spring 2005, it will not take effect until July 1, 2007, so it will be in place for the 2007–2008 school year.

The extensive lobbying activity by parents, school superintendents, and various interested parties, along with the heavy press coverage of this bill all reflect the populist attitude that Oklahomans sometimes have toward their legislature. Oklahomans tend to prefer that the people, not the lawmakers, have a greater say in the decision making process. Not coincidentally, one of the leading arguments against this bill was that this sort of school decision should be made by the schools at the local level, and not by the state legislators. Ultimately, it was that particular argument that killed the bill initially. This same populist attitude can be seen in how the Oklahoma legislature is structured, how it gets its lawmakers, and how those lawmakers perform once in office.

II. How the Oklahoma Legislature Is Structured

Annual Sessions

Prior to the passage of a state question in 1966, Article V of the Constitution specified that the Oklahoma legislature would meet biennially, or every other year. Today, the legislature meets annually in regular session. Annual legislatures are thought to have numerous advantages: more legislation can get passed, significant state issues can be addressed in a more timely fashion, lawmakers have more time to consider legislation, and the legislature is strengthened as an institution compared to the executive branch. The passage of a 1989 State Question shortened the sessions of the Oklahoma legislature. It still meets in annual sessions, but those sessions must start by noon on the first Monday in February and must adjourn on or before 5:00 p.m. on the last Friday in May of each year. There is an additional half-day organizational session in odd-numbered years on the first Tuesday of the first Monday in January. Most current legislative sessions last sixty-six legislative days. In odd-numbered years, the regular session will also include one extra day in January. Because of the short session, the last few days of May are very busy for both the legislature and the governor, as typically there is a logjam of bills that must be passed and signed into law.

Numbering and Types of Sessions

To make it easier to identify a particular session, each legislative session has been numbered. Two annual legislative sessions make up a legislature and are identified by consecutive numbers. Thus, the 2007 session was called the first session of the 51st legislature, with the 2008 session being called the second session of the 51st legislature. Between annual sessions, the Oklahoma legislature meets in an **interim session**. During this time, the legislative branch is without lawmaking authority. Public hearings, committee work, bill preparations, and investigations take place during the interim period. With the passage of a 1980 State Question, Oklahoma lawmakers can call themselves into a **special session** if an emergency develops during an interim session. Prior to 1980, only the governor could call a special session. As found in the Oklahoma Constitution (Article V, Section 27), a special session does have lawmaking authority and can take place after agreement by two-thirds of the members of both houses or after a call by the Governor. This special session called by the legislature gives the legislature added power by allowing lawmakers to maintain their influence while not in regular session. There are no time limits on special sessions, but lawmakers can only discuss the issues set out when the Governor called the session. As of 2007, the last special session was called in June 2006 when state legislators met to discuss the FY 2007 budget, which had not been passed in the 2006 regular session, but needed to pass by July 1, 2006, to avoid a state government shutdown. The Oklahoma legislature made it; on the last day of the June 2006 special session, lawmakers approved the $7.1 billion budget, the largest in the state's history.

A Bicameral Legislature

Article V of the Oklahoma Constitution created a legislature that is **bicameral**, or composed of two houses. In Oklahoma, these two houses are called the House of Representatives and the Senate. All fifty states except Nebraska have a bicameral legislature. A bicameral legislature offers many advantages. In a bicameral legislature, legislation needs to be passed by two different houses. Although this can cause delays, legislation is less likely to be passed hastily. Moreover, a bicameral legislature usually is more representative because typically most states follow the federal model, with the lower house having shorter terms and members representing smaller districts, and the upper house having longer terms, with larger districts.

The Size of the Legislature

One of the major differences in selecting legislators is determined by the size of each house. Senate districts usually comprise several House districts, and are larger in size. The overall size of the senates ranges from sixty-seven members in Minnesota to twenty members in Alaska, while the lower houses nationwide range from a high of 400 representatives in New Hampshire to a low of forty in Alaska. Nationwide, the averages are

TABLE 4-1
Differences between the Oklahoma House and Senate

	HOUSE	SENATE
Size of Legislative Body	101 Representatives	48 Senators
Qualifications for Office	Minimum age of 21	Minimum age of 25
Terms of Office	Two-year terms	Four-year staggered terms
Rules	More restricted rules and procedures	Less organized rules
Style of Debate	Less collegial atmosphere	More debate-style atmosphere

39.4 senators and 110.4 representatives for each state so Oklahoma's legislature with its 101 House members and forty-eight Senators is about average in terms of its size (National Conference on State Legislatures, 2007). The Citizens Conference of State Legislators concluded that the Oklahoma legislature was just about the right size for its population (Morgan, England, and Humphreys, 1991). Because of their different sizes, the Oklahoma House and Senate operate very differently, as shown in Table 4-1. Each house is allowed by the Constitution in Article V, Section 30, to create its own internal rules and judge the elections of its own members. The larger size of the House means that it tends to have more restrictive rules to make it easier to control the great number of members. The Senate, on the other hand, tends to have more a collegial atmosphere, with fewer rules that tend to encourage longer debates.

Qualifications for Office

The members of the Oklahoma House and Senate are also different in terms of their qualifications. Representatives must only be twenty-one or older when elected, while Senators must have reached the minimum age of twenty-five. Both need to be qualified electors in their respective counties or districts and must reside there during their terms of office, according to Section 17 of the Constitution. Article V, Section 18 of the Constitution also prevents current United States or state government officers, as well as those persons convicted of a felony, and state legislators expelled for corruption from serving in the Oklahoma legislature. Members of both houses must take office within fifteen days after the General Election in which they were elected. Moreover, Article V, Section 23 of the Constitution says that lawmakers "shall, except for treason, felony, or breach of the peace, be privileged from arrest during the session of the legislature, and in going to and returning from the same."[1] This protection is only available to lawmakers while performing their official duties in office. Lawmakers also cannot be appointed by the governor, or legislature, or to a state office during their legislative terms. Lawmakers also must disclose any personal or private interest in any bill before the legislature as per Section 24 of the Constitution and are subject to a variety of ethics rules promulgated by the State Ethics Commission.

Terms of Office

State senators usually have longer terms than those of representatives. Such is the case in Oklahoma and thirty-three other states where senators serve four-year terms and the representatives serve two-year terms (Council of State Governments, 1996). In Oklahoma, representatives are elected in even-numbered years. Senators, on the other hand, are elected for four-year terms, with half of the senators elected every two years. Senators in odd-numbered districts were elected or re-elected in 2006, while senators in even-numbered districts will be elected in 2008. In five other states, all members serve four-year terms. With the remaining eleven states, all lawmakers serve only two-year terms. The length of a legislative term is important. With shorter terms, members of the House are up for re-election often so they are more likely to be responsive to the demands and needs of their constituents. With the longer terms, however, senators can think more about the long-term goals of the state.

Term Limits for Legislators

In 1990, Oklahoma became the first state in the country to vote for limits on legislative incumbency, by placing **term limits** on the terms that members could serve in office. Oklahoma voters through a 1990 initiative limited state legislators to a twelve-year maximum combined terms of House and Senate service starting with the November 1992 elections. The move by Oklahomans to create term limits for state legislators attracted a great deal of attention. Not only was Oklahoma the first state to adopt legislative term limits, but after Oklahoma, twenty other states quickly adopted their own term limits, creating a national precedent. Many of these other states, including California, moved more quickly to enact their term limits, and as a result, while Oklahoma was the first state to create term limits for its legislators, it was not the first state to enact them. This is because the Oklahoma term limit law allowed those members serving on January 1, 1991, to finish their term before their twelve years began to accumulate toward the limit. Since legislative terms start in November, those elected in 1990 were allowed to finish that entire term before being elected. Thus, Oklahoma's term limit law did not begin affecting state legislators until 2004. Today, only fifteen states, including Oklahoma, still have term limit laws, as the supreme courts in Massachusetts, Washington, Oregon, and Wyoming have ruled term limits in those states unconstitutional, and the state legislatures of Idaho and Utah repealed term limits in 2002 and 2003, respectively (National Conference of State Legislatures, 2007).

Many scholars, however, have speculated about the consequences of term limits. On the positive side, term limits might make state legislators more responsive to constituents because these lawmakers know that they will only be in office for twelve years. Therefore, term limits may increase the ability of voters to make their legislators more accountable. Yet, term limits may have some negative consequences as well. Term limits may increase the power of executives, lobbyists, and staff relative to members (Fowler, 1992). Term limits may also not have the desired effect on state legislators because they tend to have shorter tenures than their counterparts in the U.S. Congress (Gray and Eisinger, 1997; Harrigan and Nice, 2004). Critics of term limits also point to the loss of experience, institutional memory, and continuity that may result if term limits are enacted (Benjamin and Malbin, 1992; Copeland and Rausch, 1993).

As expected, term limits in Oklahoma have had four immediate consequences. First, the average length of service of each representative and senator has decreased significantly, as one would expect. Prior to term limits in 2003, the average length of service was 8.8 years in the House and 10.5 years in the Senate. In 2007, those numbers are 2.96 and 3.3 years, respectively. Second, there has been a subsequent increase in the percentage of junior members, defined before term limits took effect as representatives with less than three terms of service (six years) in the House and less than two terms (eight years) in the Senate. The percentage of junior members in the House was only 40.4% in 2002 before term limits took effect while in 2007 it was 64.3%. For the Senate, there is a similar story with only 28.6% junior members in 2003, but 56.25% in 2007. Third, with less seniority, it might be expected that the members are also younger in age, since now members cannot serve twenty or thirty-year terms as they did in the past. That is indeed the case. The average age of representatives and senators was 54.1 and 54.6, respectively, in 2003 before term limits. Today, in 2007, those average ages are 48.6 for the House and 50.2 for the Senate (all author's calculations of data sourced from www.lsb.state.gov). Lastly, there has been substantial turnover in the leadership of both the House and the Senate. As Table 4–2 shows, there are many new members serving in the leadership, with the greatest impact occurring in the Senate. Prior to term limits, there were about two to three members who left the Senate leadership every year. For 2007–2008, twenty-nine out of forty House leaders are new, as are nine out of seventeen Senate leaders.

TABLE 4-2
Oklahoma Legislature Leadership Turnover

	NUMBER OF NEW LEADERS	
YEAR	HOUSE	SENATE
1989–1990	12 of 21	6 of 11
1991–1992	12 of 20	2 of 9
1993–1994	9 of 21	2 of 9
1995–1996	12 of 23	5 of 10
1997–1998	13 of 24	2 of 10
1999–2000	13 of 27	2 of 10
2001–2002	14 of 26	2 of 11
2003–2004	15 of 26	6 of 14
2005–2006	18 of 28	9 of 15
2007–2008	29 of 40	9 of 17

NOTES: Table compiled from House and Senate directories by Travis Covey and Rick Farmer, Committee Staff Division, Oklahoma House of Representatives, 5/21/07. See http://www.okhouse.gov/Research/LeadershipTurnover.doc.

III. WHO ARE THE MEMBERS OF THE OKLAHOMA LEGISLATURE?

Membership in the Legislature

With any state legislature, it is important to look at its demographic characteristics. How many of the legislators are women? How many are African–Americans? What are the most common occupations? These questions are important because they raise issues of **representation**. Can a legislature be truly representative if it does not resemble the population as a whole? While it may be impossible, and perhaps not desirable, for the legislature to match the population perfectly, the demographic characteristics of a legislator can make a difference because studies have found that certain groups vote differently. African–American female legislators, for example, are more interested in education, minority issues, and healthcare reform (Kirksey and Wright, 1992; Barrett, 1995; Button and Hedge, 1996). Women in general are more likely to help constituents than male legislators (Richardson and Freeman, 1995). Women are also more predisposed to see women's concerns (Githens, Norris, and Lovenduski, 1994;

but see Dolan and Ford, 1995) and perceive the causes of crime differently (Kathlene, 1995).

Across the country, the most dominant profile in state legislatures is that of a middle-aged white male who is a business owner or an attorney. In fact, nationwide the state legislators are about 88% white and 77.4% male with an average age of fifty-three. The percentage of lawyers, however, has fallen from a high of 25% in the mid 1970s to about 15% today (National Conference of State Legislatures, 2007). In fact, most of the legislators in the 1970s fit this profile, because there were few, if any racial-ethnic minorities in the state legislature nationwide and few women. However, there have been some changes in state legislative membership. There has been a substantial increase in the percentage of female legislators, with 180% more female state legislators in the last twenty years; in 1996, this meant that women represented 20% of all state legislators nationwide (Dresang and Gosling, 1996) and in 2002, it was 22% (Bowman and Kearney, 2002). Since 1969, the number of women serving in legislatures has increased substantially from several hundred to 1,667, or 26% of the 7,382 seats. An even more significant sign of the greater representation of women in the state legislatures can be gleaned by looking at the percentage of the legislature that is female. Nationwide, about 51% of the United States population is female, but as of 2002, only six of the fifty state legislatures were more than 30% female. As of 2007, that number is now eleven, with Maryland, Delaware, Nevada, Vermont, and Washington having some of the highest percentages.

In looking at African–Americans and Latinos, it is instructive to compare the percentage of legislators with their percentages in the U.S. population. As of the 2000 census, the percentages of Americans reporting Hispanic or African–American was roughly equal, about 12.5% each, but only 2.9% of legislators are Latino, while 8.1% are African–American (National Council of State Legislators, 2007). In fact, the percentage of African–American legislators, has fluctuated over the years, with only 2% in 1970 to almost 9% in 1993, but dropped back to 7% in 2002 (Bowman and Kearney, 2002) and then increasing to 8.1% in 2003 (National Council of State Legislators, 2007). For Latinos, not only is the nationwide percentage of legislators small at 2.9%, but the picture becomes even more clear when the states of the legislators are examined. Most of the Latino legislators come from a limited number of states, including Arizona, California, Colorado, New Mexico, and Texas, with thirty-four states having no Latino legislators (National Council of State Legislators, 2007).

Oklahoma has also experienced increases in the number of its female, Latino, and African–American legislators, although on a much smaller scale. In 2004, Oklahoma was ranked 49th, or second from last in terms of the percentage of women legislators nationwide, as it had only nineteen female legislators out of 149, with seven in the state Senate, and twelve in the state House. Thus, 12.7% of the state legislators in Oklahoma were women, as compared with 22% nationwide. As of 2006, Oklahoma had increased its female membership to some extent. With fourteen female legislators in the House and eight in Senate, for a total of twenty-two, the Oklahoma legislature now ranks 45th with its 14.8% female legislators. In terms of African–American and Latino legislators, however, the Oklahoma legislature ranks far below the national averages, with no Latino legislators and only 3% African–American legislators as of 2007 (National Council of State Legislators, 2007).

Compensation of Oklahoma Legislators

Compensation is always a controversial issue with the members of the public because they often believe that politicians are overpaid. With the state legislature, salaries are particularly problematic, because with the lifting of constitutional restrictions on legislative compensation in all but four states in 2000, most state legislators are in the curious predicament of setting their own salaries (Bowman and Kearney, 2002). It is also difficult to determine the exact yearly salaries of state legislators because of differences across the nation in how the legislators are paid. In eight states, including Alabama, Kansas, Kentucky, Nevada, North Dakota, and Wyoming, among others, the state legislators are paid by the days worked. For states that use this compensation system, the pay ranges from $10 per day in Alabama to $170.10 per day in Kentucky with a nationwide average of $108.01 per day. One state, Michigan, pays its state legislators by the week, giving them $589 per week, while in two others, New Hampshire and South Dakota, state legislators get paid for the two-year term, at $200 and $12,000, respectively. All of the remaining states pay by the year, including not only Oklahoma, but many of Oklahoma's neighboring states such as Arkansas, Arizona, Missouri, and Texas, but not Kansas. The yearly compensation varies tremendously, with state legislators in California earning $110,880 per year, and Texas pay $7,200 per year, with a nationwide average of $35,352.82.

Complicating the math in computing salaries is the fact that most states pay a per diem, either by the day or month, for when the legislature is in session. These per diem amounts can range as low as $10 per day to $200 per day, and can vary depending on whether the distance traveled by the legislator, whether lodging is required, and whether or not the per diem is tied to the federal per diem rate. It should be noted, however, that one state, New Mexico, was left out of the salary calculations because it does not offer any compensation to its state legislators, but does pay a per diem rate of $146 per day (National Conference of State Legislators, 2007).

In Oklahoma's case, the Constitution set legislative compensation until 1968 at $1,200 per year plus $15 per day for up to seventy-five legislative days during the biennial session. In 1968, Oklahoma did away with that constitutional limitation after a state question was passed creating a Legislative Compensation Board (LCB). Now, salaries are determined by a nine-member board appointed by the Governor, the President Pro Tempore, and the Speaker of the House of Representatives, according to Article V, Section 21, of the Constitution. Almost half of the other states also recognized the salary dilemma creating similar commissions (Bowman and

Kearney, 2002). Once the commission makes a decision, it then takes effect fifteen days after the next general election.

In 1989–1990, this salary was raised to $20,000, or eighth best in the nation. In 1997, the salary of legislators was $32,000, or tenth in the nation. The last pay increase for Oklahoma legislators came from the Board of Legislative Compensation at its 1997 meeting. The Board gave Oklahoma legislators a pay increase of $6,400, making their salaries $38,400 effective November 18, 1998, and legislators were still at that same pay as of Summer 2007. This salary now makes Oklahoma legislators rank 15th highest nationwide (National Conference of State Legislatures, 2007). Moreover, the House Speaker and Senate President Pro Tempore received an additional compensation of $17,932 per year, while other leaders as shown in the Table 4–3 received an additional $12,364 per year. With the pay increase of November 1998, for the first time the chairs of the House and Senate Appropriation Committees also received $12,364 as additional compensation. Furthermore, in 1997, every member of the Oklahoma legislature received a monthly allowance to purchase various insurance benefits ($262.19 per month), mileage benefits, a voluntary retirement package, a per diem for those unable to commute from home during the session, expenses for meetings, and expenses for office supplies (Council of State Governments, 1998).

A comparison of Oklahoma's compensation package with two other states, Texas and California, is shown in Table 4–3. An important fact to consider, however, when examining compensation levels is that the Oklahoma legislature meets only from February to May of each year. Most of the states with higher salaries, such as California and New York at $110,880 and $79,500, respectively, are year-round legislatures. Thus, the Oklahoma legislature has one of the highest compensation rates for the number of days it is in session. Several reasons are suggested for these higher salaries. Today, legislators face more complex problems than they ever have before. Oklahoma legislators are also facing more demands from constituents, thus requiring them to work more during the interim session.

Occupations of Legislators

Most Oklahoma legislators hold other jobs and are considered part-time legislators. As a result, the National Conference of State Legislatures classifies Oklahoma as **a transitional legislature**, or a legislature moving from amateur to professional status. The most common second occupations among Oklahoma lawmakers are business owners, educators, attorneys, and farmers. Nationwide, lawyers are the largest occupational group among legislators, but they are an increasingly smaller percentage. In the 1970s, about 25% of state legislators were attorneys, compared to today's 15% (National Conference of State Legislatures, 2007). Oklahoma has been fairly close to the national average. In the 2007 Oklahoma legislature, only 9.9% of House members but 31.3% of Senators were attorneys. This compares to figures of 14.1% and 20.8%, respectively for the 2004 Oklahoma legislature.

TABLE 4-3
Compensation/Expenses Comparison between the Oklahoma, Texas, and California Legislatures, as of May 1, 2007

TYPE OF EXPENSE	THE OKLAHOMA LEGISLATURE WHICH MEETS IN ANNUAL SESSION FROM FEBRUARY TO MAY.	THE TEXAS LEGISLATURE WHICH MEETS IN 140-CALENDAR-DAY BIENNIAL SESSIONS.	THE CALIFORNIA LEGISLATURE WHICH MEETS FULL-TIME IN ANNUAL SESSIONS.
Salary	$38,400 per year	$7,200 per year	$110,880 per year
Additional Compensation	$17,932 for Pro Tempore and House Speaker; $12,364 for House and Senate Majority and Minority Leaders (4), for the Senate Assistant Majority Leader, and for the chairs of both Appropriation Committees.	$7,200 per year for the Speaker.	$14,850 per year for the Senate President Pro Tempore and House Speaker; $7,425 per year for the Senate and House Majority and Minority Leaders (4).
Travel Allowance	31 cents per mile.	28 cents per mile.	18 cents per mile.
Per Diem for Those Unable to Reside at Home	$116 per day (unvouchered) tied to the federal rate.	$128 per day unvouchered set by Ethics Commission.	$138.00 per day for each day they are in session.
Office Supplies	$350 per year for unvouchered office supplies plus 8 rolls of stamps.	$25,000 per month staffing allowance includes secretarial and other staff and interstate travel for the members' staff.	Both the Senate and House Assembly have an allowance to cover District offices; the House also has an allowance to cover capital offices.
Retirement Expenses	After age 60 and 6 years of service, a contribution rate of 4.5%–10%.	After age 60 and 8 years of service or after age 50 and 12 years of service, a contribution rate of 12%.	CA Proposition 140 terminated participation by legislators elected after January 1, 1991.

SOURCE: www.ncsl.org/programs/legismgt/about/05salary.htm, www.senate.state.tx.us/75r/senate/members/dist25.

Across the country, the percentage of full-time legislators grew from 3% in 1976 to 15% in 1993 (Dresang and Gosling, 1996). Today, Oklahoma lawmakers are finding that maintaining a full-time job while being a legislator is increasingly difficult. Political scientists suggest that both full-time legislatures and part-time legislatures have their advantages. With a full-time legislature, lawmakers can be more responsive to their constituents, answering phone calls and passing legislation on a daily basis. Greater demands on the legislature, particularly in terms of budgeting and oversight, may now require year-round attention. The fiscal year (FY) for a budget, for example, goes from July 1 to June 30, yet the legislature is only in session from February to May. Government agencies need to be watched year-round to make sure that they are performing their proper functions. Those in favor of a part-time legislature, however, point out that full-time legislators can be more detached from the real world. Legislators can get an "inside the Capitol" mentality that may put them out of touch with the real problems and needs of working people. These seem to be the sentiments of most people in Oklahoma, given the prevailing culture of populism.

Education and Age

Members of the 2007 Oklahoma legislature are very educated as shown in Table 4-4. In the House, 65.5% have a college degree or better, while in the Senate 79.6% of the members have a college degree or better. As expected, given the minimum ages for Representative and Senators at twenty-one and twenty-five, respectively, members of the House on average are a little younger than their Senate colleagues. The average age in the 2007 Oklahoma legislature for Representatives is 48.6, while the average age for Senators is 50.2. It is worth noting, however, that just as recently as 2004, the average age for the House was 54.1 and for the Senate, 54.6, so today's Oklahoma legislators are younger. One of the possible explanations for this is term limits. Oklahoma's term limits took effect completely in 2004, making the 2006 election class only the second class after term limits have taken effect. Term limits should produce younger members in a legislature because by serving fewer terms it is limiting the number of legislators that will serve in their old age. One of the youngest Oklahoma legislators ever was Kenneth Corn (D-Howe) when he was elected in 2000 to serve in the House at the age of twenty-two. Today, he is called Senator Corn, because he was elected in 2002 to serve the Fourth Senate District in Oklahoma. At thirty years of age, he is currently the youngest Senator and was the youngest Senator in Oklahoma state history when he was elected in 2002. The youngest House member in the 2007 legislature is Eric Proctor (D-East Tulsa) who is twenty-five. The oldest members in the 2007 legislature are both female, Representative Sue Tibbs (R-Tulsa) who is seventy-three, and Senator Mary Easley (D-Wagoner) who is seventy-one.

Table 4-4
Education, Age, and Tenure of the Members of the 2007 Legislature

	House	Senate
% of Members with College Degree or Better	65.5%	79.6%
Average Age of Members	48.6	50.2
Youngest Member	Eric Proctor (D), 25	Kenneth Corn (D), 30
Oldest Member	Sue Tibbs (R), 73	Mary Easley (D), 71
Oldest Tenure (continuous years) –all term limited in 2008)	David Braddock (D) James Covey (D) Darrell Gilbert (D) Terry Ingmire (R) Al Lindley (D) Ray McCarter (D) Dale Turner (D)	Mike Morgan (D) Owen Laughlin (R) Jeff Rabon (D) Kathleen Wilcoxson (R) James Williamson (R)
Average Tenure of Members	2.96 years	3.3 years
Junior Members (served three terms or less in the House, two terms or less in the Senate)	64.3%	56.25%
The percentage of current legislators who are term-limited in 2008.	6.9%	10.4%

Source: Author's calculations taken in April 2004 from the Oklahoma State House and Senate websites, see www.lsb.state.ok.us.

Tenure in Office

Tenure in office is currently one of the most important issues facing today's Oklahoma legislature. That is because of the term limit law that took effect in 2004. All members of the legislature after that date were limited to twelve years of service, dating from 1992. Thus, in recent years, the Oklahoma legislature has experienced tremendous turnover, particularly the Senate in the past few years. This is because as shown in Table 4–4, the Senate had not only the longer average length of service (10.5 years vs. 8.8 in the House), but it had fewer junior members (28.6 vs. 40.4% in the House), and more senior members who were subject to term limits in 2004 (40.8 vs. 21.2% in the House). The effects of term limits are already having an impact on the Oklahoma legislature, as can be seen in the large number of retirements and open seats for both the 2004 and 2006 elections. In the 2006 elections alone, twenty-seven new House freshmen were elected, and thus 26.7% of the members in the 2007 legislature are serving their first year in office. Even more startling is the tenure of the entire house. Of the 101 House seats, sixty

LEADERSHIP PROFILE

JUDY EASON MCINTYRE

Member of the Oklahoma State Senate—District 11

JUDY EASON MCINTYRE, as an African–American student in the sixties, grew up during the time of segregated schools in Tulsa, Oklahoma. Her parents had met each other at Langston University, and placed a high value on education. They were very protective, and shielded their daughter, the eldest of four children, from the worst instances of racism. When her mom would go into a department store to buy clothes, she bribed the children with ice cream to stay in the car. That way, Judy and her siblings would not see that their mother was not allowed to try on the clothes.

At age eighteen, Eason McIntyre was invited by a local minister to get on a bus and travel to the March on Washington in 1963. She listened to the stirring words of Martin Luther King, Jr. But it was not until later when she went to the University of Oklahoma as one of only a handful of African–American students that she was exposed to overt racism for the first time. One professor would regularly recognize Eason McIntyre only with a pejorative term. She and the other black students were separated from the white students in the dorm. She still remembers signs posted around Norman that told blacks to get out of town after dark. The signs said to them, "If you can read this, run. If you can't read, run anyway." She went from innocence to anger and got caught up with the broader civil rights movement for the first time.

She graduated OU with a Bachelor of Science in Social Work and used her degree to get a job with the Oklahoma Department of Human Services. She became active in protests and was even involved with the Black Panther Party for a short time. At the time, she had no goals but anger and rage. When the Black Panthers began distributing guns, Eason McIntyre got out.

Her husband at the time became involved in politics and went on to be elected to the Oklahoma House of Representatives and State

> Senate. She learned to get along with people and how to move in political circles. Being a political wife, she learned to work within the system. She ran successfully for school board president. Eason McIntyre continued her career in social work. Finally, in 1996, she retired from both positions.
>
> Her retirement did not last long. Leaders within the Democratic Party approached her to run for a seat in the House of Representatives vacated due to term limits. She had to think long and hard, but ultimately she agreed to contend. After her electoral victory, she was the first freshman to get on the leadership team.
>
> Then the same people came to her to run for Senate. Now after her electoral victory, she serves in the Senate on the Judiciary, Rules, and Tourism and Wildlife Committees and is the Co-Chair of the Education Committee. Late in 2006, Eason McIntyre successfully battled against breast cancer. She now uses her varied life experiences from her political activism, social work career, and health challenges to make a difference. Despite her hard work and wonderful successes, Senator McIntyre has often been upstaged by her able canine assistant, a little terrier aptly named Harry "Give 'Em Hell" Truman.
>
> Brett S. Sharp

members, or 59.4% of the House, have served two years or less, since many of these additional members were elected in the 2004 elections. In the Senate, the consequences have been just as significant. As of 2007, 56.25%, or just over half the Senate, had served two terms or less, making both the House and the Senate less senior indeed. Thus, in the future, nobody will be able to match the tenure of former Senator Gene Stipe (D-Tahlequah) who has the distinction of being the longest serving member in the history of Oklahoma. He served in the House of Representatives from 1949 to 1954 and in the Senate from 1975 to 2003. But in 2003, he resigned from office after facing federal charges relating to campaign fundraising in 1998.

IV. HOW OKLAHOMA LEGISLATORS GET INTO OFFICE

Elections and Turnover

Elections are watched carefully by members of the legislature in both parties because the elections decide which party has majority control of the legislature. The party that controls the legislature has several major advantages. The most obvious advantage is that the majority party has more votes, and thus is more likely to prevail on major policy decisions. But beyond that, the entire legislature is structured by party. Members of the majority party get more staff, more seats on the various committees, better offices, etc. With the exception of 1921, 1922, and most recently 2004 and 2006, this has favored the Democrats. The Oklahoma Legislature has been consistently majority Democrat since statehood. Republicans continue to hope that someday they too will control both houses of the legislature, and they are getting closer and closer to achieving their goal. In 1999, the House had sixty-one Democrats and forty Republicans; today, after the election in 2006, Republicans are the majority, holding fifty-seven seats while the Democrats only have forty-four. In the Senate, however, the elections of 2006 were much more interesting. The 2006 elections created a Senate with twenty-four Democrats and twenty-four Republicans. Thus, the Democrats have lost seats recently, as they held twenty-eight in 2004, and thirty-three after the 1998 elections. Despite the Republican advantage in the House, there will still be many close battles to come in the legislature. With tax legislation, the legislature needs a three-fourths vote, or else that legislation will have to be voted on by the people. Even with non-emergency legislation, if the governor should enact a veto, a two-thirds vote of both houses would be needed to override the veto. Either the Republicans or the Democrats would have trouble reaching both of these extraordinary majorities.

Comparing the partisanship of the Oklahoma legislature to other state legislatures nationwide, the Oklahoma House is more Republican and the Senate is closer to the nationwide average. In 2007, Oklahoma's House with sixty-seven Republicans and thirty-four Democrats was 56.43% Republican. Nationwide, only twenty of the legislatures are Republican, representing 40% of the seats, and twenty-nine of the legislatures are Democrat, representing 58% seats. The remaining 2% of the seats are held by Independents or are vacant. One state, Nebraska, is not included in these totals because it has a unicameral, bipartisan legislature. Oklahoma's Senate, though, is much closer to the nationwide averages, with the twenty-four to twenty-four split, because nationwide twenty-five of the forty-nine state senates are majority Republican and twenty-two are Democrat. With two split Senates (Oklahoma and Tennessee) and Nebraska having a unicameral legislature, this meant that 51% of the state senates were majority Republican, and only 44% were majority Democrat (National Conference of State Legislators, 2007).

Elections are also noteworthy because sometimes they produce **divided government**, or where the different seats in government are controlled by different parties. In recent years Oklahomans have typically voted Republican for many state-level offices but have created a Democratic legislature. Thus, while the current governor, Brad Henry, serving his second term in 2007 is a Democrat, the former governor was a Republican, Frank Keating, who was elected in 1994 and held office until 2002. The 2006 elections seemed to reverse this trend somewhat. While the Oklahoma House is Republican and the Oklahoma Senate is split twenty-four to twenty-four, eight of the nine statewide offices, went to the Democrats, with an average margin of victory of 13.7%. But half of the races won by Democrats in 2006, including those for Governor, Attorney General, Superintendent of Public Instruction, and the Commissioner of Labor, were not even close with an average margin of victory of 24.8%. The most competitive races were for Labor Commissioner where Republican Brenda Reneau lost her incumbent seat to Democrat Lloyd Fields by .3%, and even more importantly as far as the state legislature is concerned, the Lieutenant Governor's race won by Democrat Jari Askins over Republican Todd Hiett with a margin of 2.63% of the vote. This race was watched extra closely by the state legislators, because the Lieutenant Governor with the even split in the Senate could break potential ties. Yet four of the five seats in Congress, both U.S. Senators, and the Corporation Commissioner (the lone statewide race won by Republicans in 2006) are all Republican. This can happen in Oklahoma because the governor and the legislature are selected separately. Although Oklahoma has a straight-party ballot, fewer voters are using that option and instead are voting to **split their ticket**, voting different parties for different offices on the same ballot.

Reapportionment

Of all the factors that govern elections, **reapportionment** probably had the most impact on the Oklahoma legislature. Before 1964 legislative districts could be unequal in size because there was no law to prevent it. Thus, in the same state, one representative for the U.S. Congress could represent 800,000 people, while another could represent 150,000. A combination of Supreme Court decisions successfully remedied this problem, placing sharp limits on the states' ability to control their own elections. Most important, *Baker v. Carr* (1962) gave the national government and the courts the right to rule on legislative districting. It established the "one person, one vote" principle, thereby making each legislative district roughly equal in size. In the second decision, *Reynolds v. Sims* (1964), the Court ruled that state legislative seats must be apportioned substantially on population.

Today, most legislative districts within a given state are of roughly equal size based on population. In fact, many districts do not follow traditional county boundaries, economic boundaries, or ethnic boundaries, but are rather artificial creations based on political concerns. These two decisions had a tremendous impact on Oklahoma. Prior to these decisions, Oklahoma was one of the nation's worst-apportioned assemblies. Many of the legislative districts were hopelessly unequal and favored the state's most rural counties. As a result of these decisions, the Oklahoma legislature lost some of its rural domination while the more populated areas (Oklahoma City, Tulsa, and Lawton) gained seats.

The time period after the 2000 elections was a very important one for Oklahoma because of **reapportionment,** or the resizing of districts, both in the U.S. Congress and in the state legislature, to accommodate changes in population. It is the job of the state legislature in every state to redraw the district lines, or **redistricting**, after a census. A national census is taken every ten years in the United States. This very short, usually one-page, form is sent to all households in the United States and its goal is to count the population within each city, county, and state. Because U.S. Congressional districts must be roughly equal in population size, when a state loses population, it can be in danger of losing one or more congressional seats. Oklahoma lost one congressional seat in 2002 as predicted, because of its declining population relative to other states. As a result, the Oklahoma state legislature had to fulfill one of its major responsibilities—the drawing of both the state legislative as well as congressional districts. These lines were redrawn in 2002 and the end result for the Oklahoma House of Representatives are shown in Figure 4–1.

Ethics

In 1990, Oklahomans passed State Question 627 with a two-to-one vote, adding an Ethics Commission to the Constitution. The Ethics Commission, formerly called the Oklahoma Council on Campaign Compliance and Ethical Standards, is composed of five members appointed by the Governor, President Pro Tempore of the Senate, Speaker of the House, Chief Justice of the Supreme Court, and the Attorney General. To make sure that the commission is balanced, no more than three of the commissioners can come from the same party and congressional districts can only be represented once. The purpose of the Ethics Commission is to regulate

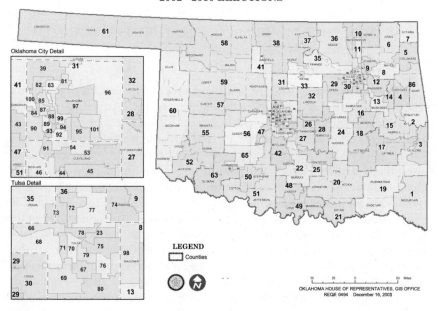

FIGURE 4–1

the political and campaign activities of state officeholders, lobbyists, and others engaged with the state government. In recent years, the ethics laws have been substantially strengthened and as a result, Oklahoma's ethics laws are stronger than those of many states.

The Ethics Commission imposes specific limitations on Oklahoma lawmakers. Lawmakers must file financial disclosure statements. Although these statements are not a complete report on legislative personal wealth or income, they must disclose individual income sources that exceed $1000 annually. Also, lawmakers can neither engage in activities nor have interests that conflict with their legislative duties. Section 24 in Article V of the Constitution requires members to refrain from voting on bills where they have a conflict of interest. Generally, these are bills that would benefit a particular interest and not a larger group.

Individual lawmakers can only receive contributions of $1,000 annually from individuals and $5,000 annually from labor organizations or Political Action Committees (PACs). Oklahoma ethics laws prohibit corporations from contributing directly to candidates and no public funds can be used to fund campaigns. Lawmakers are also required to file quarterly reports, with additional reports required as an election approaches. Moreover, lawmakers cannot receive contributions from state highway patrol members and supernumerary tax consultants. Candidates may not use their campaign funds to defray personal expenses, but rather only those expenses associated with the campaign or their duties as public officeholders. Candidates, including powerful legislative leaders, cannot give campaign funds to other candidates. Finally, individuals can receive a $100 state tax deduction for donating to state candidates.

V. How the Oklahoma Legislature Is Organized

Leadership

In the Oklahoma legislature, a distinction can be drawn among formal leadership positions, committee leadership, and the leadership team. The formal leadership positions include the Speaker, President Pro Tempore, and various other House and Senate majority and minority party leaders. These leaders are either elected by their respective **party caucus** or appointed by other leaders. The committee leadership includes those who chair the various committees. The third leadership component is relatively rare for state legislatures and exists only in the house. The leadership team consists of an informal brain trust selected by the speaker of the House. These legislators are his/her inner circle or kitchen-cabinet and often function as a sounding board for the speaker. Compared to the other more established leadership positions, membership in the brain trust is fluid, with members moving in and out of the circle.

As is already apparent, the Oklahoma legislature has numerous leadership positions. Looking just at the leadership positions listed by the

Council of State Governments, 1999, Oklahoma has more formal leadership positions than any other state legislature. The 2007 Oklahoma Senate has seventeen legislators in leadership positions in both parties, while the House has a whopping twenty-four Republican leadership positions and seventeen Democratic leadership positions. Thus, forty-one of the members of the House, or 40.6% are in leadership positions. The leadership in both houses is organized first by party. The most prestigious positions for both houses with the current leaders as of 2007 are indicated in Table 4–5. The number of seats held by a political party will determine whether that party is in the majority or the minority for that house. This got more interesting after the 2006 elections as Republicans continued to have the majority in the House, but there is split control in the Senate, with each party having twenty-four seats. Thus, the Senate created co-leader positions for the first time.

In the Oklahoma House, the most important position is called the Speaker of the House, while the Senate's leader is called the President Pro Tempore (also called Senate Pro Tem). The Lieutenant Governor is the President of the Senate, but this has been largely a ceremonial position that calls for the person holding the post to preside over joint sessions and to cast the very rare tie-breaking vote in the Senate. Yet with split control of the Senate after the 2006 elections, this position will probably have much greater significance. These two leaders get their powers from several sources: 1) the Oklahoma Constitution in Article V gives these leaders substantial power over legislative agenda setting and they both control the flow of legislation within their respective chambers; and 2) these leaders have the authority to make key legislative leadership, staff, and committee assignments for their colleagues. In many state legislatures, these leaders are also the most senior members, meaning that they have the most tenure of any member in that house. However, this is not usually the case in Oklahoma, and with term limits is even less likely to be so.

The Oklahoma House Speaker works with other leaders in the majority, including the Speaker Pro Tem, the Majority Floor Leader, Assistant Majority Floor Leader, and the Majority Whip. Only the Speaker and the Speaker Pro Tem are elected by all the members of the House. The Speaker is given additional power because not only does he/she appoint the floor leader and whip positions but he/she also has substantial control over the **party caucus** which selects all the other majority party positions. The party caucus is the meeting of all lawmakers of a party in a particular house. The Speaker of the House has substantial duties in addition to making these appointments. The Speaker presides over each day's session, assigns bills to their appropriate committees, appoints the membership of standing and special committees in the House, including the chairs, and is the chief representative of the House when working with the Senate, the Governor, and state agencies. By tradition, the Speaker and Speaker Pro Tem are also ex-officio members of all standing committees.

Table 4-5
House and Senate Leadership Positions as of 2007

House Leadership Positions	Senate Leadership Positions
Speaker of the House—Lance Cargill (R)	President—Jari Askins (also Lt. Governor) (D)
Speaker Pro Tempore—Gus Blackwell (R)	President Pro Tempore—Mike Morgan (D)
Majority Floor Leader—Gregg Piatt (R)	Co-Floor Leader—Charlie Laster (D)
Assistant Majority Floor Leaders—Lee Denney, Terry Ingmire, Mike Jackson, Daniel Sullivan, and Randy Terrill (all R)	Co-Assistant Floor Leaders—Jay Paul Gumm and Jeff Rabon (both D)
Majority Caucus Chair—John Wright (R)	Democratic Whip—Susan Paddack (D)
Majority Caucus Vice-Chair—Lisa J. Billy (R)	Democratic Whip—Nancy Riley and Charlie Wyrick (both D)
Majority Whip—Rob Johnson (R)	Democratic Caucus Chair—Kenneth Corn (D)
Deputy Majority Whips—Don Armes, Lisa J. Billy, Jeffrey W. Hickman, and Mike Thompson (all R)	Co-President Pro Tempore—Glenn Coffee (R)
Assistant Majority Whips—Marian Cooksey, Fred Jordan, Scott Martin, Steve Martin, Skye McNeil, Phil Richardson, Colby Schwartz, and T.W. Shannon (all R)	Republican Leader Emeritus—James A. Williamson (R)
Majority Caucus Secretary—Ann Coody (R)	Co-Floor Leader—Owen Laughlin (R)
Minority Leader—Danny Morgan (D)	Assistant Co-Floor Leaders—Mike Mazzei and Randy Brogdon (both R)
Minority Floor Leader—James Covey (D).	Republican Whips—Kathleen Wilcoxson, Cliff Branan, and Clark Jolley (all R)
Deputy Minority Floor Leaders—David Braddock, Ben Sherrer, and Dale Turner (all D)	Republican Caucus Chair—Todd Lamb (R)
Assistant Minority Floor Leaders—Mike Brown, Wallace Collins, Joe Dorman, Rebecca Hamilton, Wes Hilliard, Jerry McPeak, Wade Rousselot, and Jabar Shumate (all D)	
Minority Whip—Terry Harrison (D)	
Minority Caucus Chairman—Ryan McMullen (D)	
Minority Caucus Secretary—Eric Proctor (D)	

SOURCE: see www.lsb.state.ok.us.

Perhaps because of this immense power, the Democratic Caucus in the past had limited the Speaker to three terms of service as Speaker. With term limits operative in the Oklahoma legislature today, this will probably be continued with the House Republicans now in the majority.

Comparatively speaking, legislative leaders in the Oklahoma Senate have less power. First, because the membership of the House is larger, the House is more centralized, thereby making it easier for the Speaker to have control. With only forty-eight Senators, such centralization is less necessary, the debates and rules are more informal, and therefore, the President Pro Tem has less power. Second, the Lieutenant Governor, with the exception of breaking ties, is given much less of a role in the Oklahoma Senate. In many states, including Texas, the Lieutenant Governor is called the President of the Senate and has substantial responsibilities, including managing the floor debate, controlling legislation, and other such powers. Although the Oklahoma Lieutenant Governor is President of the Senate, the Lieutenant Governor does not have these same powers, and instead functions much like the Vice-President of the United States does for the Congress—acting only when there is a tie in the Senate or presiding over a Joint Session. Third, unlike the House Speaker, the Senate Pro Tem has much less control over committee assignments and leadership selection. Committee assignments in the Senate are determined by a special committee, while the leaders are selected by the party caucus. Finally, the President Pro Tem is also limited in power because the Senate has the tradition of electing the future President Pro Tem during the terms of a sitting Pro Tem, thereby fracturing power in the Senate. No President Pro Tem has served more than three terms in Oklahoma (Oklahoma Department of Libraries, 1997). Yet, the major leaders in the Oklahoma Senate still have power. Like their counterparts in the House, the Senate Pro Tem and the Assistant Majority leader are ex-officio members of all Senate standing committees, giving them immense power. A major source of power for both the Speaker and President Pro Tempore is that of appointing members to conference committees where the fate of important legislation is decided.

Committees

Committees are the workhorses of the Oklahoma legislature. Committees formulate legislation, hold hearings, and modify proposed legislation. Committees also are beneficial because most unimportant legislation is eliminated here and the public truly gets the greatest chance to understand the legislature through formal hearings.

Like the formal leadership, the committees have a hierarchical structure. There are four different types of committees. First, each house has **permanent or standing committees**, where most legislation is handled. In 2007, the Senate had sixteen standing committees, while the House had ten for a total of twenty-six. The number of committees in the Oklahoma legislature has sharply reduced since 2004 and especially since 1967. In 2004, there were thirty standing committees in the House and seventeen, in the Senate for a total of forty-seven. In 1967, each house had thirty-six committees, for a total of seventy-two (Morgan, England, and Humphreys, 1991). The number of committees is important because while it may make the legislature more representative, it can also lead to duplication and a larger workload for lawmakers. Second, the Oklahoma Legislature has **joint committees**, composed of the members of both houses. In some states like Connecticut, Maine, and Massachusetts, these committees are used exclusively, giving the leadership more control. Examples of joint committees in Oklahoma include committees to study accountability in government, federal funds, and state–tribal relations. The third type of committee is the **special committee**. These are created by the presiding officers of each house. Special committees are distinguished by their short tenure. Oklahoma in 2007 had a Joint Special Committee on International Development. Finally, there are **conference committees.** Conference committees are actually joint committees with a special purpose. They exist solely to resolve the differences between the House and Senate versions of a bill. Three members typically from each house are appointed by their presiding officers for each bill under consideration. There are some exceptions, such as the General Conference Committee on Appropriations (GCCA) where the state budget is written.

Certain committees are more important to legislators than others. Legislators usually try to pick committees that will be beneficial to their constituents and that will meet their own goals. In both houses, legislators submit requests for their desired assignments after a general election. The leaders of both houses do try to accommodate members' committee requests (Harrigan and Nice, 2004). Many lawmakers usually elect to continue their existing committee assignments, both to build up seniority and expertise on that committee. House members will typically serve on four to six committees, while many Senators have five committee assignments. The most important committee is Appropriations, because this committee makes most of the budgetary decisions for the legislature. Other committees that are considered noteworthy include Education, Revenue and Taxation, Judiciary, and Transportation. The House Speaker usually tries to give each lawmaker one major committee assignment, in addition to minor committee assignments.

A hierarchy also exists within each committee. Both the Education and Appropriation Committees are subdivided into separate subcommittees. These subcommittees are very specialized and serve to divide the work of the various committees. The leaders for both the committees and subcommittees are called the chair and vice-chair. Senate chairs are appointed by the President Pro Tem, while House chairs are appointed by the Speaker. In the Senate, the Minority Leader appoints minority members to standing committees. This is a typical pattern in most state legislatures. The chairs schedule legislation for their committees, preside over committee meetings, and keep track of all changes to the legislation. **Seniority**, or the length of tenure, is also an important factor on each of these committees. Not only are the most senior members typically given the "best" committee assignments, but seniority also serves to distinguish members on individual committees.

Staff

Much of the work of both the legislative committees and the leadership could not be done without the legislative staff. The staff helps members with their research and constituents, gets the bills ready for distribution, and performs many other important functions in the legislature. Thus, it is no surprise that legislative staffs have increased. From 1979 to 2003, there has been an increase in the number of permanent staff nationwide from an average of 338.6 permanent staffers per legislature in 1979 to 561.3 in 2003. Legislatures, however, have reduced their session-only staff, with 201.5. session-only staffers on average in 1979, and only 138.2 on average in 2003.

The large number of bills combined with a shortened annual legislature makes a legislative staff almost imperative in Oklahoma. For the Oklahoma legislature, the staff experienced an increase from 326 staff (1979) to 394 (1988) to 415 (1996) and 433 in 2003. This represents an increase of about one-third during the past twenty-five years, but it is comparable with the increase in legislative staff across the nation. In 2007, the Oklahoma legislature had only 408 staffers, with 182 in the House, and 226 in the Senate. Oklahoma has consistently been only one of two states, the other being Massachusetts, to use very few session-only staffers. In 2007, the Oklahoma legislature listed thirteen session-only staffers, all in the Senate, on its website, while the House had forty-two session-only staffers (staff information from interview with Dave Bond, Communication Specialist, Oklahoma House of Representatives, April 17, 2007).

Four major changes in the last two decades have influenced Oklahoma staff. First, prior to 1981, the Oklahoma legislature used centralized staff support called the Oklahoma Legislative Council. This council staffed both houses and all committees. Second, in 1981, the legislature abolished this centralized staff and replaced it with separate professional staffs for both houses. A smaller centralized staff agency now exists to perform functions that are common to both houses: copy services and the sharing of computer technology. Third, Senate leader Stratton Taylor in 1995 allowed every senator to have a full-time secretary/assistant instead of just a skeleton crew of secretaries who worked during the interval between legislative sessions. All but six of the forty-eight senators opted for a full-time secretary. Consequently, with one decision the Senate's full-time secretarial staff increased from seventeen to forty-eight, expanding the Senate's annual payroll by $500,000. House leaders, however, did not make the same decision; twenty-eight full-time secretaries handle the work for 101 representatives. Today, in 2007, there are fifty-five executive assistants serving forty-eight Senators (Mike Morgan has five), and fifty permanent legislative assistants serving 101 Representatives (Interview with David Bond, Oklahoma House Communication Specialist, 2007). Fourth, there has been a trend nationwide toward the greater use of full-time staff rather than part-time staff, because of the greater complexity of legislation and the need to conduct business year-round. Oklahoma has definitely been a part of this trend. Compared to the 101 permanent staffers, and 225 who worked only during the session in 1979, today there three times as many permanent staffers (353), and the number of session-only employees has dropped to 55.

VI. THE WORK OF THE OKLAHOMA LEGISLATURE

Legislative Roles

One of the greatest demands upon legislators is the constant tension that exists between their two primary duties: lawmaking and representation. The **lawmaking function** demands that lawmakers pass laws that are best for both their state and their constituents. Not only may these demands conflict, but time spent as a lawmaker can detract from the other function, representation. The **representation function** demands that legislators spend as much time as possible with their constituents, listening to their needs, responding to their concerns, and visiting the constituents in their homes. This causes a tremendous conflict because it is much more difficult to pass laws when visiting the district than working in the Capitol. One way of looking at this representation problem is to look at **role orientations**. The three most common role orientations are trustee, delegate, and politico. **Trustees** believe that their constituents trust them to do the right thing. They believe that their constituents have given them great leeway to make the best possible decision. A second role orientation is a delegate. **Delegates** believe that they are in office to satisfy the demands of their constituents. It is very common for delegates to poll, either formally or informally, their constituents to see what decisions they should make in the upcoming legislative session. The final role orientation is a politico. Politicos are a combination of the trustee and delegate orientations. **Politicos** believe that they are in office for their constituents, but also recognize that some decisions may have to go beyond the wishes of those constituents. These lawmakers tend to think about what is good for the state (Eulau et al., 1959).

Role Orientation in Oklahoma

Samuel Kirkpatrick in his exhaustive study of Oklahoma legislators found that most legislators tended to be trustees, with 45.8% of the Senate, and 50% of the House indicating they were trustees. The least common role orientation was delegate, with only 12.5% of the Senate and 10% of the House suggesting they were delegates (Kirkpatrick, 1978). Malcolm

Jewell, a political scientist and the author of numerous works on state legislatures, however, suggests that this idea of role orientation may be more appropriate for Congress, and less appropriate for state legislatures (Jewell, 1982). As a result, others have examined the tension between the lawmaking and representation functions differently. One of the common ways to do this is to ask lawmakers what makes the most difference in their voting decisions. A 1986 survey of Oklahoma legislators found that if lawmakers could choose between voting for the district (constituents) and a legislator's conscience, most (56%) would vote for the district, while 26% said their conscience. The choice becomes much clearer, however, when a political party is considered. Of those legislators, 80% would choose the district, while the rest would vote with their political party if there was a tension between the two (Morgan, England and Humphreys, 1991). What both of these methods of role orientation seem to suggest is that Oklahoma legislators, whether in 1978 or 2007, pay close attention to the demands of their constituents when making a decision. That is not surprising since it is those constituents that decide whether or not to keep a lawmaker in office.

Lawmaking

What keeps lawmakers in office is their ability to pass the laws that will meet the needs of their constituents and the state. While this can conflict with the representation function, it still remains the most important responsibility of any lawmaker. Because of the Oklahoma legislature's short session, many lawmakers develop their legislation during the period from September through January. There are four different measures that can be passed by the Oklahoma legislature. The first is a **bill**, the most common form of legislation. A bill may be introduced in either house and must be signed into law by the governor after being passed by both houses. The second measure is a **joint resolution.** It still must be passed by both houses and signed by the governor, but is used when the measure has short-term applicability or frequently for state questions requiring voter approval. The third type of measure is a **concurrent resolution.** This type of resolution must be passed by both chambers, but does not have the force of law and will not be signed by the governor. It is often used when the legislature wants to express the opinion of both chambers. Finally, legislators can also adopt **simple resolutions** which can memorialize a prominent Oklahoman, affect the internal workings of just one chamber, express the particular sentiments of a chamber, or congratulate a person or group of persons.

The process of passing laws starts with the **formal introduction** of bills to the legislature. A chart of how this process works in the Oklahoma legislature is fully described in Table 4–6. Bills can only be introduced by members in either house prior to the start of the legislative session unless there is a two-thirds vote of the legislature to extend the time limit. The formal introduction includes two formal **readings** of the legislation on the floor of one house. There has been some concern about the large increases

TABLE 4–6
How an Idea Becomes a Law

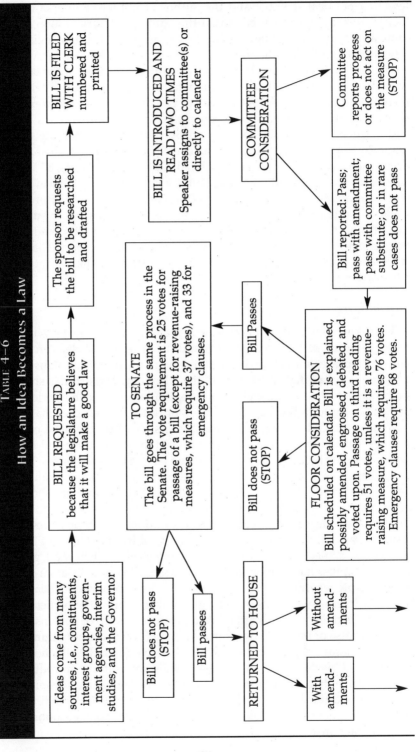

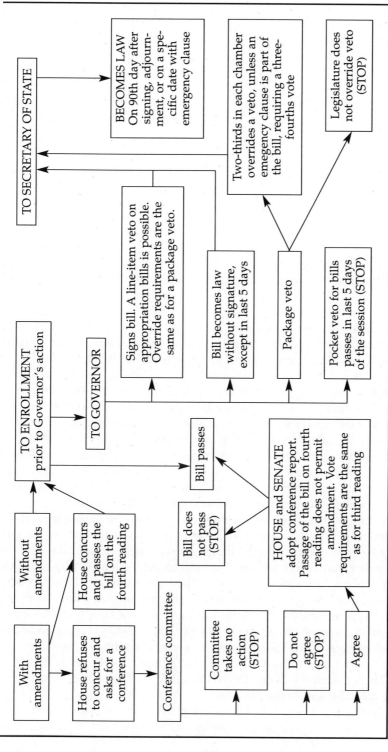

Adapted from the Oklahoma House of Representatives, http://www.lsb.state.ok.us/house/idea.gif by James M. Barrow.

in legislation in recent years. While the 1991 and 1992 sessions considered 2,656 bills and joint resolutions, and enacted 783 of them, the 1997–1998 sessions produced 3,930 measures and 872 enactments. To counter the trend, the Oklahoma House imposed an eight-bill limit on its members which was largely responsible for a drop in House bills and resolutions introduced from 1,257 in 1997 to 865 in 1999. Yet this trend did not continue. In 2006, Oklahoma lawmakers filed 2,700 measures, and in 2007, there were 2,316 measures filed, with 1,195 in the House and 1,121 in the Senate. These totals do not include concurrent and simple resolutions, which do not have the effect of law. Once a bill has been introduced, it is referred to a particular committee. This **referral** is made by the presiding officer of either house, either the Speaker or the Senate President Pro Tem. Bill referral gives these leaders tremendous power because there are often times where the jurisdiction of a bill may overlap several committees. The U.S. Congress solves this problem by occasionally referring a bill to more than one committee in the same house.

Once a bill has been introduced and referred, the real work begins in committee. As stated previously, most of the heated debates over legislation will probably occur in committee, because this is where the public hearings are held and where most changes are made to the legislation. If a committee votes favorably on a bill, it will send a report to the particular house. In the Senate, there is a recorded **roll call vote** and each committee makes a recommendation to the full Senate, while in the House bills may be reported out by **voice vote** or by signing a written **majority report**. If unhappy with the outcome of the committee work, members of a House committee can file a **minority report** (a rare action) opposing the position of the committee's majority. This report must be filed within one legislative day after the majority report is filed. The full House of Representatives can then debate and accept or reject this report. By making a motion to **report progress**, the committees of either house can indefinitely delay making a recommendation on a bill or resolution (Ferguson, 1989).

Bills passed by committees are then sent directly to the House or Senate floor. In the House of Representatives, the **consent calendar** holds all bills assigned to that calendar by a committee or the speaker. These bills cannot be amended or debated and must stay there for four days. A single member may object and send the bill to the **General Order**, which is a docket of all bills considered before the House that legislative session. Bills, however, do not need to be considered in chronological order; rather, the order is determined by the leadership of both houses. Once a bill is called up from the general order docket, it is subject to amendment. After disposing of amendments, there is a third reading of the bill on the floor followed by a debate on the legislation and a vote on its final passage. The legislation will need to be passed by both the House and Senate before it can be sent to the governor.

In the event a measure has been amended in the opposite chamber or it was "crippled" in the house of origin by striking the title of the bill, it will return to the originating house. Thus, the amendments can be accepted, which cause a fourth reading of the bill and a vote, or the amendments will be rejected, causing a measure to be sent to a conference committee. If a measure is reported out by a conference committee, the measure cannot be amended in any way (except that failure to receive a two-thirds majority in either chamber on an emergency clause will cause it to be debated.)

The passed bill is then submitted to the governor who has five working days to sign. The governor can also choose to reject the entire bill (**veto**) or just reject parts of the bill (**a line-item veto**). The line-item veto, however, is only used for appropriation measures. At the end of the session, the legislature adjourns *sine dine* and the Governor has fifteen working days to sign or veto a bill; the lack of action constitutes a **pocket veto** of the legislation. With a vetoed bill, both houses must seek to override the veto with a two-thirds vote in both houses or a three-fourths vote if the measure has an emergency clause. Bills will ordinarily become law ninety days after the session adjourns or five days after a session if the governor vetoes.

The Oklahoma legislature has one additional unique feature. Traditionally, a large percentage of the bills have **emergency clauses.** Emergency clauses are different from ordinary bills because they require a tw-thirds vote of the legislature and become law immediately upon the Governor's signature (or a veto override). Today, Oklahoma state agencies are usually funded at the same level as last year. Budget bills will then appropriate new money and hence, the emergency clause is not used very often. If the Governor vetoes an emergency clause, a three-fourths vote in both houses is required to override.

Recent Oklahoma Legislatures and Lawmaking

One of the recent trends in the Oklahoma legislature is the **backlog** of bills that tends to develop at the end of a legislative session. Usually, a large number of measures must be signed into law by the Governor during the last few days of the session. For example, on the penultimate day of the 1997 session, Governor Frank Keating took action on forty-three bills, ranging the legislative gambit from education funding to more beds for violent juvenile offenders. A second trend that has developed during the last few years is the large number of **vetoes.** While the number of vetoes from 1991 to 1994 averaged about seventeen per legislative session; from 1995 to 1998 the governor vetoed 203 bills. Just as important, while the legislature managed to override an average of five bills from 1991 to 1994, there were no successful overrides during 1995 and 1996.[3] In 2003, Governor Brad Henry in his first year in office approved 488 pieces of legislation and issued twelve vetoes and one line-item veto, none which were overridden by the Legislature. Those numbers for 2005 and 2006 were 479 signed and ten vetoed in 2005 and 419 signed and seven vetoed in 2006 (see www.governor.state.ok.us). Governors now play an even larger role in shaping legislation. Not only does the Governor make a State of the State address indicating his/her policy wish list, but the Governor also proposes a budget and a set of budget recommendations. These create the main blueprint for the legislature's budgetary decisions during a given session.

With the crush of bills at the end of a session, the Governor tends to play an important role. This was particularly true in May 2006, as it appeared that the Oklahoma legislature might not be able to finish funding the state government for FY 2007 before the 5:00 p.m. May 26, 2006 deadline. There was a major fight in the Oklahoma legislature over the issue of tax cuts, including state income and inheritance taxes, as well as spending issues. Yet, a budget needed to be passed by July 1, the start of FY 2007, in order to avoid a state government shutdown. Thus, even before the 2006 regular session ended, both the leaders and Henry pledged that the Oklahoma legislature would have a special session in June. Governor Henry also offered two weeks before the session ended a compromise proposal that served as the model for the eventual compromise reached during the special session. On the third and final day of the special session held in June 2006, the lawmakers approved a $7.1 billion budget, which included the largest tax cut in state history. The budget would eliminate the inheritance tax in three years and reduced the state income tax from 6.25 to 5.25% within four years, changing the state income tax structure. The budget also phased in revision of the state's standard deduction, which according to lawmakers would mean that 45,000 low and moderate-income families would not have to pay state income tax. Other highlights in the budget included a $3,000 pay raise for Oklahoma teachers, a $130 million boost for higher education, $15 million for the State Emergency Fund, and a 5% pay raise for state employees. As a result, Oklahoma ended up with the second largest revenue growth in the country in FY 2006 (Mock, 2006).

Budgeting

One area of government control available to the Oklahoma legislature is the **appropriation process.** In the 1970s, the legislature's ability to determine the overall state budget was comparatively limited. Almost two-thirds of the budget was outside the legislature's appropriation process because of federal and earmarked state fees. Thus, the legislature only controlled one-third of appropriations. This was typical of most state legislatures. Today, the Oklahoma legislature has become much more of an equal partner with the governor in creating the budget. First, all revenue raising measures must start within the House, according to Article V, Section 33. Second, despite the fact that lawmakers raised taxes three times during the 1980s and again in 1990, Oklahoma remains a low-tax state. Third, and most important, Oklahoma voters passed State Question 640 in 1992 which prevents the legislature from raising taxes unless there is either a vote of the people or a three-fourths vote of the legislature. This sharply limits the amount of money legislators can use to fund state programs. Legislators raised those taxes because they found that export taxes, particularly the Oklahoma severance tax on oil and gas, was not enough to pay for the state's education system and other government programs.

In Oklahoma's budgeting process, the **FY** begins July 1 and ends on June 30, so FY 2007 is the period from July 1, 2006 through June 30, 2007. All state budgets must also be balanced, according to the Oklahoma Constitution. With the FY beginning on July 1, Oklahoma's 123 state agencies must submit their budget requests, including how they plan to spend the money and how they have performed as an agency, by September of the prior year. On the first day of the legislative session, the governor proposes an executive budget recommendation. By the beginning of the session, the State Equalization Board also determines how much revenue the state has to spend that year and informs the legislature. Because the budget must be balanced, the Oklahoma Constitution in Article V states that the legislature cannot spend beyond 95% of expected revenues.

The real decision-making process, however, does not begin in earnest until April when the General Conference Committee on Appropriations (GCCA) composed of both houses, is appointed by the Speaker and President Pro Tempore. The legislature reaches an agreement on how much will be spent on each broad area, such as education or roads. These are called **subcommittee allocations.** Once these allocations have been determined, the GCCA subcommittees can then decide how much each government program will receive. The budgets for about six agencies are then formulated into the appropriation bill which needs to be passed by a two-thirds vote of both houses (in order for the emergency clauses to be attached). The passed bill is then submitted to the governor who has five working days to sign. The governor can also choose to reject the entire bill (**veto**) or just reject parts of the bill (**a line-item veto**). As expected, Oklahoma appropriations have increased in recent years, although the growth has been somewhat limited. In FY 1997, the legislature appropriated $4.1 billion, while in FY 1999 the amount was $4.7 billion.[4] As stated previously, the amount for FY 2007 was $7.1 billion, the largest budget in state history.

Oversight

Ironically, one of the jobs that students studying the legislature most overlook is oversight. Most states (41) including Oklahoma have some sort of **oversight**, whereby the legislature reviews the actions of the executive branch. The Oklahoma legislature has full responsibility for examining not only the governor, but also the 123 state government agencies. This is an enormous task because rules passed by state agencies have the force of law, yet must be monitored by the legislature. The question for state legislatures is how to supervise those agencies. Only twenty-five states including Oklahoma, have given the legislature the authority to veto, suspend, or modify agency rules. In Oklahoma, the House of Representatives has a standing committee that reviews both proposed and existing rules. The membership of this committee is appointed by the

House and Senate leadership. Generally, the Oklahoma legislature has thirty legislative days to approve or disapprove a rule. The lack of objection constitutes an approval of a proposed rule. The courts have ruled against one-house vetoes in several states, including Oklahoma, acting by themselves on behalf of the legislature.[5]

The Oklahoma legislature has two other tools that it can use to conduct oversight—sunset legislation and the appointment process. These tools are not available in all states.[6] First, the Oklahoma legislature can enact **sunset legislation.** According to the Sunset act, state agencies are forced periodically to justify their existence and demonstrate that they have done their proper jobs. The life of an agency subject to sunset review is six years, but there is a phase-out period of one year (Council on State Governments, 1996). Sunset laws across the country have rarely accomplished much of substance. Instead, they primarily serve a symbolic function in the twenty-five states that have such an act (Dresang and Gosling, 1996). Of the two tools, almost all states allow the legislature to oversee the **appointment process.** Although the state agencies and commissions are part of the executive branch, the Oklahoma Senate confirms the appointments of certain agency directors and many members of state boards and commissions. The state senators control county election board secretaries, and they also choose the heads of the motor vehicle tag agencies (Morgan, England, and Humphreys, 1991).

VII. THE FUTURE OF THE OKLAHOMA LEGISLATURE

Professionalization of the Legislature

One of the current trends among state legislatures is the move toward professionalization. Legislatures are considered professional when they meet several of the following characteristics: higher salaries, legislative careerism, longer sessions, more rules, fragmentation of power in the legislature, and politicization of the legislative process. This move toward becoming professional has been bolstered by several recent studies of state legislatures, including that done by the Citizens Conference on State Legislatures, who found that professional legislatures when structured properly tend to be both more representative and efficient. The Oklahoma Legislature has become more professional over the years. With its longer sessions, higher salaries, and extensive committee structure, the Oklahoma legislature is clearly moving in that direction. Yet, there are several scholars of state legislatures who suggest that this may not be a good thing. Professor Alan Rosenthal of Rutgers University, one of the leading scholars on state legislatures, indicated that state legislatures when becoming professional may act more like the U.S. Congress, with its extensive delays and internal politicking.

This move toward professionalization may also contradict the wishes of the people of Oklahoma. A strong populist movement in the state of Oklahoma seems to develop whenever Oklahoma politicians seem to veer too far away from the wishes of the people. According to a lengthy study of Oklahoma politics, "almost all Sooner legislators see themselves as part-time citizen legislators." (Morgan, England, and Humphreys, 1991). This attitude is bolstered by two recent and important actions taken in the state of Oklahoma. First, the increase in legislative salaries in 1989–1990 came only with a subsequent decrease in the length of the sessions. This somewhat contradictory move was supported not only by the legislators, but also by the Republican Governor at the time, Henry Bellmon.

Conclusion

Overall, the Oklahoma legislature seems to be in a period of transition. During both the 1980s and 1990s, the Oklahoma legislature made substantial changes in how it conducts business. First, not only are there more permanent staff, but the legislature also has more control of the budgeting process. Second, the number of committees has been sharply reduced, as the Citizens Conference on State legislatures suggested. Third, the Oklahoma legislature has also greatly increased its information capacity. More of its activities are computerized, including the legislature's World Wide Web site. Fourth, members of the legislature earn higher salaries, but face tougher ethics limits on the amounts they raise and spend during their campaigns. Fifth, the Oklahoma legislature has made some progress in becoming more representative, with more women and minorities getting elected. Redistricting decisions forced the legislature to reallocate more of its districts to the urban areas of Oklahoma. It should be noted, however, that the Oklahoma legislature still could be far more representative. It is far under the national averages for percentages of women and minorities. Further, the drawing of legislative districts to benefit incumbents and rural interests has denied metropolitan areas greater representation in the legislature.

Most of these changes have thus made the legislature more responsive to the people. Now, the people can contact the legislature during the interim session and the staff can respond more easily. This fits in perfectly with the populist tradition in Oklahoma. The legislature is still limited, with shortened sessions and sharp restrictions on passing appropriations and taxation legislation. Yet, it can still meet the demands of the people.

What does the future hold for the Oklahoma legislature? Hopefully, there will be better reporting of committee information, particularly greater details about the hearings, meetings, and votes that are scheduled. Computerizing the legislature's activities and the World Wide Web site are excellent steps in the right direction. In 2004, the Oklahoma legislature's current lawmakers were subject to term limits. This has already had an impact on the Oklahoma legislature, with sixty of the Oklahoma House members out of 101, having served two years or less after the 2006 elections. Whether term limits will have a positive or negative effect in terms of the legislation that gets passed remains to be seen. Certainly, though, the Oklahoma legislature will be an interesting one for years to come!

WWW RESOURCES

For information, including full text of legislation, bill statutes, and links to the Oklahoma House of Representatives and the Senate, visit the web site at:

www.lsb.state.ok.us

The Oklahoma State Government Information Server has information and links to many areas of Oklahoma government:

www.okla.state.ok.us

For information on state legislatures throughout the United States, see:

www.ncsl.org

The Oklahoma Ethics Commission is charged with promulgating rules of ethical conduct for state officers and employees, campaigns for state elective office, and campaigns for state initiatives and referenda. See the Oklahoma Ethics Commission site at:

www.state.ok.us/~ethics

NOTES

1. See Article V, *Oklahoma Constitution*.
2. The states with over 30% female legislative membership are Arizona, California, Colorado, Delaware, Hawaii, Kansas, Maryland, Nevada, New Mexico, Vermont, and Washington (National Conference of State Legislatures, 2007).
3. For further information on the vetoes, see the Oklahoma legislature's web site at: http://www.lsb.state.ok.us. These statistics includes measures that were line-item vetoed, but not concurrent or simple resolutions or measures filed during any of the special sessions.
4. See the Oklahoma legislature's web site at: http://www.lsb.state.ok.us.
5. The other states include Alaska, Missouri, Montana, and North Carolina where the courts ruled against legislative committees acting alone on federal funds.
6. A legislative veto has been found by the courts to violate the state constitutions in some states, including Arkansas, Connecticut, Montana, New Hampshire, New Jersey, and West Virginia.

CHAPTER FIVE

OKLAHOMA'S GOVERNOR AND ELECTED EXECUTIVES

Timothy W. Faltyn and Kenneth Kickham

A feeble Executive implies a feeble execution of the government. A feeble execution is but another phrase for a bad execution; and a government ill executed, whatever it may be in theory, must be, in practice, a bad government.

Alexander Hamilton, The Federalist, no. 70

Since the Civil War the training ground for successful presidents has been the gubernatorial office in the states, where they seem to serve an incomparable executive apprenticeship.

Historian Wilfred E. Brinkley

I. INTRODUCTION

It has been said that politics is show business for ugly people. On Oklahoma's political stage, leaders of the executive branch are woven into the state's history. They shoulder the responsibility of playing the lead role in the story of Oklahoma. From our first governor, Charles N. Haskall, to our current governor, Brad Henry, Oklahoma's governors stand as solitary figures in the limelight of time passed (Oklahoma Almanac, 2004). However, the governor's direct impact on the state's governmental process is a bit less dramatic.

The populist roots of our great state are reflected in the Oklahoma executive branch. Populism by definition requires direct accountability to the electorate. While some might argue the strengths and weaknesses of populism as a philosophy, the actual application of it in Oklahoma has produced a very distinctive political dynamic. The Oklahoma executive branch is responsible for initiating, implementing, and enforcing effective policies. These responsibilities must be accomplished within a uniquely **pluralistic system** that dilutes the powers of Oklahoma's governor by granting many of the powers to govern to other elected executives.

Traditionally, state government textbooks draw a direct comparison between the powers of the President of the United States and the powers of a governor of a state. However, such comparisons are not so simple when examining the Oklahoma executive branch. Unlike a president, who has power to appoint executive branch administrators, an Oklahoma governor's power to direct the activities of the executive branch is diluted by the activities of the ten other separately elected executives (Council of State Governments, 2003). The writers of the Oklahoma constitution feared the concentration of power, so they held as many officials responsible to the people as possible. As a result, Oklahomans initially elected seventeen members of the executive branch. Today, that number has been reduced to a total of eleven, but still includes the Lieutenant Governor, attorney general, superintendent of public instruction, state auditor and inspector, state treasurer, three corporation commissioners, commissioner of insurance, and commissioner of labor. This seemingly simple difference in structure has a significant impact on the governor's power to govern. Since these other executive branch officials are separately elected, they can belong to different political parties, and have different political philosophies, agendas and power bases than the governor. Political conflicts between the governor and one or more of the separately elected executives are likely.

Theoretically, a president can ensure a cohesive governing strategy when all of the administrators are required to follow the president's agenda. In Oklahoma, the other elected administrators are accountable to the Oklahoma electorate, creating a situation that is not always likely to produce a cohesive governing strategy within the executive branch. Oklahoma's pluralistic system drastically weakens the governor's power to initiate, implement, and enforce effective policies. On the other hand, this approach assures that the large bureaucracy controlled by the executive branch is held more directly responsible to the people.

II. THE GOVERNOR

Within the existing pluralistic structure, the primary goal of an Oklahoma governor is to be the leader of the state. To be the governor of Oklahoma, one must be a citizen of the United States, at least thirty-one years-of-age, and a qualified voter in the state for ten years prior to holding office (Council of State Governments, 2003). Once elected, the governor serves a four-year term in office with a limit of two consecutive terms. As indicated in Table 5–1, Oklahoma governors are compensated with a salary, transportation (including a driver and pilot), a travel allowance, and an official residence located near the capital complex in Oklahoma City. The governor is provided with an approximately forty-member staff to fulfill the responsibilities of the office and make an effort to accomplish the objectives set for the administration (Council of State

LEADERSHIP PROFILE

GOVERNOR BRAD HENRY
Twenty Sixth Governor of the State of Oklahoma

BRAD HENRY, a third generation Oklahoman and Oklahoma Governor, was born in Shawnee, Oklahoma, where he attended public schools and graduated from Shawnee High School. The governor attended the University of Oklahoma as a President's Leadership Scholar and earned a bachelor's degree in Economics in 1985. In 1988, he was awarded his Law degree from the University of Oklahoma College of Law, where he served as Managing Editor of the Law Review.

Governor Henry returned to Shawnee to practice law with his father, Charles, and start a family. He married the former Kim Blain, a Shawnee schoolteacher, and they have three lovely daughters, Leah, Laynie, and Baylee.

Before his election as governor, Brad Henry served ten years in the Oklahoma State Senate, chairing the Senate Judiciary Committee and serving as Vice-Chairman of the Senate Economic Development Committee. As a gubernatorial candidate in 2002, his campaign themes focused on strengthening education, providing quality healthcare, and ensuring greater economic opportunities. His refreshing approach connected with voters, and Brad Henry won the election in November 2002. He was officially sworn in as Oklahoma's twenty sixth governor on January 13, 2003.

Governor Henry took office in the midst of the worst budget crisis in state history, but forged a historic bipartisan agreement among legislative leaders that shielded education and healthcare from massive cuts. He also successfully fought to let voters decide whether to establish an education lottery to benefit the state's classrooms; voters overwhelmingly passed the lottery in November 2004.

Other highlights of his first term in office include augmenting early childhood education, medical malpractice tort reform, crafting a strategy to raise the pay of Oklahoma teachers, obtaining voluntary relocation assistance for the troubled Tar Creek region, expanding

> preschool programs, upgrading college campuses across the state, and advancing a landmark anti-methamphetamine measure which has resulted in a dramatic decline of meth lab seizures and has become a model for the rest of the nation.
>
> On November 7, 2006, Governor Henry was re-elected overwhelmingly, becoming only the third governor in the state's history to earn two consecutive terms. He won 66.5% of the vote, one of the largest margins ever for an Oklahoma gubernatorial election.
>
> Despite the demands of office, Brad Henry remains a committed family man. The Henrys have long been active members of the Shawnee community, participating in a number of civic organizations and local causes. They are also members of the First Baptist Church of Shawnee where both have served as Sunday school teachers. The Governor has also served as an ordained deacon at that church.
>
> Governor Henry is working to build a better Oklahoma by strengthening the state public education system and making healthcare more accessible and affordable to the citizenry. In his inaugural address, he urged citizens to celebrate Oklahoma's many accomplishments, put aside their differences and rally together for the good of their beloved state. As he often likes to say, "We are all Oklahomans first."

Governments, 2003). All of these requirements and resources are designed to ensure that the governor is able to fulfill the primary roles required by the office.

Table 5-1
Compensation for the Oklahoma Governor

Annual Salary	Number of Staff	Transportation Provided	Travel Allowance	Official Residence
$140,000	40	Automobile Airplane	Included in Office of the Governor budget and Department of Public Safety budget	Mansion (including guest quarters)

III. ROLES OF THE GOVERNOR

Vested with many responsibilities, governors must use their power to enhance the governmental process of Oklahoma. Governors are often described in terms of the policy and procedural roles that they play. These roles include serving as the chief executive, chief legislator, chief bureaucrat, chief economic leader, and various other roles that are often dictated by circumstances.

Chief Executive

As the chief executive, the governor provides leadership for the executive branch from the top down. The governor is responsible for protecting the public in general, enforcing laws of the state, and conducting state business with the national government and other states. However, with the exception of the power to appoint some officials within the executive branch, the Oklahoma governor is bestowed with little formal power. In the absence of real power, the governor uses influence to fulfill these responsibilities. As a result, a governor's power to impact state government can be limited in that it is indirect.

The governor as the **chief executive** can be analogized as the "head coach." While a head coach of a football team is the leader, a head coach is not the individual that throws the blocks, scores the touchdowns, or kicks a winning field goal in the final seconds of a game, but, like the governor, they are the leaders at the top of the triangle-shape organization setting goals, making plans, and developing strategies (see Figure 5–1).

The circumstances in which the governor operates are remarkably similar. When the system is not meeting the objectives set, the governor (or coach) is the one who is held responsible. When things are going well, it is usually the governor who claims credit. Just as a head coach is the administrator over the assistant coaches that help the players to do the things necessary to win, the governor administers the appointed officials

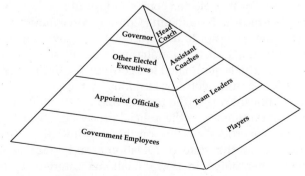

FIGURE 5–1 Administrative Structure

as they implement the policies necessary to enforce the laws of the state. Oklahoma governors do have several formal powers, including the power to issue executive orders, grant pardons and parole, participate in the selection of some judges, and extraditing accused and/or convicted criminals.

An **executive order** represents the governor's policymaking power. It is best described as a policy or regulation issued by the governor that has the effect of law. Executive orders are designed to allow implementation of policies and give administrative authority to enforce legislative statutes and the state constitution and/or to establish or modify practices of state administrative agencies (Oklahoma Almanac, 1998). In 2007, for example, Governor Henry imposed a state agency hiring freeze by way of an executive order. Combined with the role of chief bureaucrat, this power allows the governor to effectively govern within the executive branch and impact almost all of the other areas in Oklahoma state government.

As chief executive, the governor has the power to pardon and parole. **Pardons** are defined as legal release from punishment, while **parole** is defined as the conditional early release of a prisoner who has served a portion of the assigned sentence. From statehood to the adoption of a state constitutional amendment in 1944, governors had exclusive power to pardon or parole any individuals they deemed fit to be released. However, in 1944, the State Pardon and Parole Board was established to advise the governor on these issues. The board is composed of five members, three appointed by the governor, one appointed by the presiding Judge of the Court of Criminal Appeals and one appointed by Chief Justice of the State Supreme Court. As a result, in order to pardon or parole an individual today, the governor must receive a favorable recommendation from the board. However, the governor can grant a **reprieve,** which is a delay in carrying out a sentence, or a leave of absence to convicted criminals (for a maximum of sixty days) without recommendation from the board (Strain et al., 1997).

Governors also play a role in the selection of some judges. As discussed in Chapter 7, Oklahoma utilizes both elections and a non-partisan judicial selection process. For non-elected courts and for filling many vacancies, a thirteen-member Judicial Nominating Commission submits no more than three names to the governor to fill a vacancy. The governor then makes a nomination from the Judicial Nominating Commission's recommendations. While individuals nominated to a court under this process are eventually subject to retention votes or elections by the people, the governor does play a significant role in the process and is often able, over time, to have a significant influence on the judicial process in Oklahoma.

In addition, governors are responsible for initiating the return of alleged criminals to the state of Oklahoma and granting extradition requests from other states. In 1998, Oklahoma entertained ninety-three formal extradition requests from other states and made 136 formal requests for accused criminals to be returned to Oklahoma.

Chief Legislator

Historically, Oklahoma's executive branch has been weak in comparison to the legislative branch. The governor's role as chief legislator is strictly limited by the state constitution to four basic functions. These "legislative powers" include delivering messages to the state legislature, preparing and introducing a state budget, calling the legislature into special session, and vetoing acts of the legislature (Strain et al., 1997).

At the beginning of each legislative session, the governor delivers a message known as the **State of the State address.** In this address to a joint meeting of the legislature, the governor outlines the objectives of the administration and a plan to achieve those objectives. It is important to recognize that the legislature is not required to consider or accept the governor's plan and objectives. The fact that the governor has no real power to direct the legislature usually reduces the State of the State address to an opportunity for the governor to gain exposure and to posture against Oklahoma legislators. This posturing can create a tenuous relationship between the two branches particularly when the governor is of a different political party than the leadership in the legislature.

Perhaps the most important function of state government is the development of the state budget. It is from this budget that government initiatives, programs, and jobs are sustained. It is the governor's responsibility to prepare and submit a state budget to the legislature, but the legislature is not required to accept the governor's budget. Indeed, the legislature controls all individual funding decisions. In times of divided government, when legislative and executive branches are controlled by different political parties, the threat of a budget stalemate becomes a real danger. As a result, the two branches must work towards a compromise that keeps the state functioning.

If a governor is not satisfied with the work of the legislature over a particular issue or as a whole, the power to call the legislature into **special session** to deal with specific issues can be exercised. In 2006, for example, Governor Henry called a special session to give the House and Senate more time to strike an agreement on the 2007 budget. However, once the legislature has convened, the governor cannot force action on the particular legislation or concern that led the governor to call the special session. Indeed, the governor's power is limited to calling them into session. The legislature has the power to adjourn the special session at any time.

The power to **veto** legislation is the only significant power the governor has over the legislature. Any legislation that passes the House and Senate must be presented to the governor for final approval. If the governor signs the legislation, it becomes Oklahoma law. However, if the governor does not agree with the legislation, the governor's veto can be used. A vetoed piece of legislation is returned to the legislature to be changed, dropped or have the veto overridden by two-thirds vote in both houses.

There are two other types of veto power that are available to the Oklahoma governor. These other types of vetoes are the **line item veto** and the pocket veto. The line item veto was granted to the governor by the state legislature in 1994 (Council of State Governments, 2003). This type of veto power allows the governor to veto individual lines or items of proposed legislation without vetoing the entire bill. This power gives the governor the ability to make significant changes to legislation before it is signed into law. The **pocket veto** is exercised when the legislature passes a bill, adjourns, and the governor does not sign the bill. If the legislature adjourns, any bill not signed by the governor within fifteen days is rendered invalid. By putting such legislation in a "pocket" and not signing it into law, a governor effectively causes the legislation to die. If the state legislature wishes to reconsider the bill, it must be reintroduced, and then the bill is subject to the entire legislative process all over again.

In addition to the power of "final say" on what does or does not become Oklahoma law, governors can shape legislation by threatening the author of a bill with a veto. By telling the legislature what will or will not be accepted, governors can influence legislation before it reaches their desk for approval (Strain et al., 1997). While a legislature has the power to override a veto with two-thirds vote of both houses, an override majority is generally difficult to secure. As a result, the legislative authors are often willing to compromise with the governor.

As chief legislator, Oklahoma governors are limited to an advisory role. Governors advise and persuade the legislature with the State of the State address, the budget process (by introducing the first draft), the prerogative to call the legislature into special session, and by the threat of a veto. The governor's ability to influence the legislative process without significant formal power is what determines their effectiveness in this role. The ability to establish a strong track record of accomplishment in shaping the legislative process is often how the public measures the success of the governor.

Chief Bureaucrat

The governor as the **chief bureaucrat** refers to the power to appoint over 2,500 positions to over 300 offices, boards, and/or commissions. These appointees act as the assistant coaches and players under the head coach. The governor can use this appointive power to initiate, implement, and enforce policies and promote the objectives of the administration. While the majority of these appointments do not add to the institutional power of the governor, it is safe to say that the role of chief bureaucrat does add to the governor's prestige in a political sense.

Because each appointment is an extension and reflection of the governor, the process of choosing appointees must be carefully executed. It is generally not expected that the appointee share all specific views of the governor. It is important, however, to ensure basic agreement on political and philosophical principles. In addition to agreeing on these basic principles, there are usually stipulated requirements associated with appointed positions. Examples of such stipulations include, but are not limited to: professional qualifications; residence requirements; business experience; and, party affiliation in cases where appointments are to be made in the spirit of bi-partisanship. Because the responsibility of appointments is so intensive, governors must commit a number of staff members to handle nothing but the research and recommendation of appointments.

Chief Economic Leader

Governors also serve as an **economic leader** and developer. In today's international economy, the governor accepts the responsibility of representing the state to businesses and industries interested in building infrastructure in Oklahoma. With an increasing importance being placed on international trade and national economic development, the governor, now more than ever, must make such issues top priority. The key to success in this role is finding a competitive edge over other states that are similar to Oklahoma in terms of geography, social, economic, and demographic areas. Governors strive to establish Oklahoma as an attractive place for business and industry. They work with the legislature to make Oklahoma competitive in the world economy by providing an educated workforce, tax incentives, and a high-quality standard of living for employees.

Other Roles

In addition to the procedural and policy roles of the government, there are also two other roles governors have: Chief of State and Party Chief. As the **Chief of State,** the governor is the ceremonial leader of the state. In this role, governors become the premier representative of the state during the times of tragedy and triumph. The role played by Governor Frank Keating in the aftermath of the Murrah Building bombing in 1995, as well as the devastating tornadoes that affected five Oklahoma counties in 1999, are excellent examples of the governor acting as chief of state. In both situations it was the responsibility of the governor to represent all of the citizens of Oklahoma, comforting those who suffered tragic losses, and facilitating a return to normality in the lives of everyone affected.

In the role of **Party Chief** the governor is the recognized leader of his or her political party. As the leader of the party, the governor can exert political power through **patronage**—appointing faithful members of the same political party—or by trying to discipline other elected officials of the same party to support the policies of the administration. Another way that the governor exerts political pressure is by agreeing to use the high-profile position to campaign for a particular program or for a particular candidate. Finally, governors can reward loyal supporters in the legislature by supporting funding for local projects, or tax incentives to industries in their legislative district.

Chapter Five

IV. IMPEACHMENT

No account of the Oklahoma executive branch would be complete without an explanation of impeachment. The act of impeachment is authorized by Article I of the Oklahoma State Constitution. The process outlines the steps to be taken by the Oklahoma State House of Representatives and State Senate if they wish to remove the governor, or other state elective officers, for willful neglect of duty, corruption in office, habitual drunkenness, incompetence, or any offense involving moral turpitude committed while in office. The process itself consists of the House impeaching, or accusing the governor or other state elective officers, in one or more of the above mentioned infractions, followed by the state Senate decision on whether or not the governor, or other state elective officer, should be convicted and allowed to remain in office (Fischer, 1981). The Senate impeachment trial is prosecuted by "trial managers" appointed by the House of Representatives, and the impeached official is responsible for mounting his or her own legal defense. A simplified analogy of the impeachment process would be to consider the state House impeachment proceedings as an accusation or indictment of the elective officer, and the state Senate trial proceedings as to a determination of guilt (which would result in removal) or innocence (which would result in preservation of the particular officials standing in office). Impeachment does not necessarily mean removal from office; it is possible for a state elective official to be impeached, but not removed.

The threat of impeachment is sure to gain attention and create dramatic pretence, but in practice, the act of impeachment is not all that common. Only two Oklahoma governors have actually been impeached and removed from office. In 1922, Governor Jack C. Walton was elected governor, impeached, and removed from office in the same year under seventeen articles of impeachment. The charges ranged from calling out the militia without cause on three separate occasions (incompetence), corruption, and improper campaign expenditures. After a Senate impeachment trial, Walton was removed from office on eleven of the seventeen articles of impeachment. The summary of the Senate's judgments stated that Walton was found to be incompetent and corrupt.

Governor Henry S. Johnston was elected in 1927 and impeached two years later on eleven specific charges of impeachment. All of the charges accused Johnston of being incompetent, since he willingly admitted doing things that the House claimed to be illegal. The specific articles ranged from granting irregular pardons and restitution, to diverting funds for the purpose of hiring special agents for his office. The Senate trial lasted for almost two months and eventually concluded with the removal of Governor Johnston for incompetence. The Senate held that, while his actions were not criminally motivated, his actions proved him to be incompetent (Fischer, 1981).

V. The Cabinet

A **cabinet** is a group of formal advisors to the governor. By Oklahoma statute, a gubernational cabinet is created by the governor and all members of the cabinet serve at the pleasure of the governor. A governor's cabinet is generally composed of elected and appointed officials. Their primary function is to advise the governor on policy issues that arise while they fulfill their responsibilities as leaders of the state. In addition to their advisory role, cabinet members generally head state government agencies or departments within agencies. The governor's current cabinet has fifteen members in addition to the Lieutenant Governor and meets at the chief executive's discretion. Appointed members of the cabinet are typically close political allies of the governor and are in general agreement with the governor's agenda. The governor relies on the cabinet to initiate, implement, and enforce the policies that agree with the goals of the administration.

VI. A Partisan Affair

When Frank Keating became governor in 1994, he became only the third Republican to hold the highest office in the executive branch since statehood in 1907. The other two Republican governors were: Henry Bellmon, serving as chief executive from 1963–1967 and again in 1987–1991; and, Dewy Bartlett serving as chief executive from 1967–1971. Out of twenty-six Oklahoma chief executives, only three have not been Democrats (Oklahoma Almanac, 2004). It is safe to assume that to this point, occupying the governor's chair has been a partisan affair.

VII. Back to Back

George Nigh, Frank Keating, and Brad Henry are the only Oklahoma governors to serve consecutive four-year terms. In 1983, Governor Nigh was re-elected to the office of governor and secured his place in Oklahoma history as the first governor to complete two full terms in office. A career politician, Nigh served as the governor for eight years, and as Lieutenant Governor for sixteen years (Oklahoma Almanac, 2004). On his retirement, Governor Nigh realized he was not governor or Lieutenant Governor for the first time in his twenty-four-year career saying, "It didn't hit me until I left the house and jumped in the back seat of the car and we didn't go anywhere." (Both the governor and Lieutenant Governor are provided a car and a driver).

In 1998, Frank Keating achieved a truly remarkable distinction when he became only the second governor in nearly ninety years to be re-elected. Eight years later, Brad Henry joined the same exclusive club by winning re-election with 66% of the vote.

Henry's vote percentage was the state's highest since 1958, when Democrat J. Howard Edmondson swept into office with 74% of the vote.

VIII. Lieutenant Governor

The **Lieutenant Governor** is elected at the same time as the governor and serves the same four-year term as the governor. Like the governor, the Lieutenant Governor must be a citizen of the United States, be at least thirty-one years-of-age, and a qualified voter in the state for ten years prior to taking office (Council of State Governments, 2003). Although they are not elected together, the Lieutenant Governor is required to be a member of the governor's cabinet and is held accountable to the governor for duties that the chief executive assigns.

The two primary roles of the Lieutenant Governor are to replace the governor when necessary and to preside over the state Senate. In the instance that the governor is absent from the state, is removed from office, resigns, becomes permanently disabled, or dies while serving the elected term, the Lieutenant Governor is responsible for assuming the duties of the governor until the next scheduled general election. In presiding over the Senate, it is presumed that the Lieutenant Governor serves as a link between the executive branch and the legislative branch. The actual function of presiding over the Senate is an important one. When voting on any piece of legislation, the possibility of a tie exists. In such instances, the Lieutenant Governor breaks the tie. This is the only instance in which the Lieutenant Governor is allowed to vote as president of the Senate.

It was a breakthrough in Oklahoma history in 1994 as Lieutenant Governor Mary Fallin assumed the highest office held by a woman in Oklahoma state politics. Although the powers of Lieutenant Governor are limited, her accomplishment is an extraordinary step for Oklahoma women. In addition to being the first woman, she is also the only Republican Lieutenant Governor in Oklahoma history. Her successor in that office, Jari Askins, continues the trend of female Lieutenant Governors, while returning the office to the Democratic Party.

IX. Other Elected Executive Officials

Oklahoma ranks fourth in the nation in the number of elected executive officials other than the Governor and Lieutenant Governor, within the executive branch (see Table 5–2). These officials include the Attorney General, The Superintendent of Public Instruction, the State Auditor and Inspector, the State Treasurer, three Corporation Commissioners, the Commissioner of Insurance, and the Commissioner of Labor.

The **Attorney General** serves a four-year term and is the chief legal counsel to the state. This office is generally regarded by the people as the primary authority for interpretation of the law. In addition to the roles

LEADERSHIP PROFILE

LIEUTENANT GOVERNOR

JARI ASKINS, born and reared in Duncan, Oklahoma, was sworn in as Oklahoma's fifteenth Lieutenant Governor in 2007, giving her the rare distinction of being involved in public service in all three branches of government. Askins served as Special District Judge for the District Court of Stephens County for eight years, from 1982–1990. During that time, she became the first woman officer in the Oklahoma Judicial Conference. In 1991, the Governor appointed her to the Pardon and Parole Board, which elected her as its first woman Chairman. She later served as Executive Director of the Pardon and Parole Board and as Deputy General Counsel to the Governor. These experiences helped develop criminal and juvenile justice issues as her special expertise.

Elected to the Oklahoma House of Representatives in 1994, she was named Vice-Chairman of the Criminal Justice Committee. Following re-election in 1996, she served as Chairman of the newly-created Government Operations and Agency Oversight Committee and became the first woman Assistant Majority Floor Leader. In 1998, after re-election without opposition to a third term, Askins was appointed Chairman of the Subcommittee for Judiciary and Law Enforcement Appropriations and served on the Speaker's leadership team. She was elected to a fourth term in 2000 and was named Deputy Floor Leader, while continuing to serve on the House Speaker's leadership team.

Askins served in the House for twelve years, earning the position of Democratic House Leader in 2005, and becoming the first woman to lead a caucus in the Oklahoma Legislature. She won statewide election as Lieutenant Governor in 2006, becoming the first Democratic woman to attain that position. She was sworn in as Lieutenant Governor on January 2, 2007 to fill the unexpired term of Mary Fallin, who resigned as Lieutenant Governor to serve in the U.S. House of Representatives.

As Lieutenant Governor, Askins is President of the State Senate. She also serves on numerous boards and commissions and chairs

> the Oklahoma Tourism and Recreation Commission and the Oklahoma Film and Music Advisory Commission. The Lieutenant Governor is an advocate for children and for greater efficiency in government. She participates in and promotes various economic development projects and supports legislation and innovative means of providing greater hope and opportunity for Oklahoma's citizens.

played by the Attorney General, the office itself serves as a vital link between the executive branch and the judicial branch.

The **Superintendent of Public Instruction** serves a four-year term and is the head administrator for all formal forms of public education in the state. In conjunction with the State Board of Education, the Superintendent supervises Oklahoma's public school system. The public generally regards this office as the primary authority for Oklahoma education.

The **State Auditor and Inspector** serves a four-year term and is regarded by the public as the "watch dog" of the state government. On the first of November of every year, the State Auditor and Inspector reports the findings concerning financial records of the state and county treasurers, as well as the records of all state offices, to the governor.

The **State Treasurer** serves a four-year term and is the state's chief financial officer. The office is a depository for all state agencies and maintains accounts of all monies received and dispersed by the state. The public generally regards this office as responsible for the state's financial stability.

The **Corporation Commission** is composed of three elected officials that serve staggered, six-year terms. Corporation Commissioners super-

Table 5–2
Elected Executives and Their Agencies

Elected Executive	Agency
Attorney General	Office of the Attorney General
Superintendent of Public Instruction	Oklahoma State Department of Education
State Auditor and Inspector	Office of the State Auditor and Inspector
State Treasurer	State Treasurer
Corporation Commissioners (3)	Corporation Commission
Commission of Insurance	Insurance Commission
Commissioner of Labor	Oklahoma Department of Labor

vise and regulate the rates of all utility, transportation, and transmission companies charging for their services. The public generally regards this office as the regulator of public services.

The **Commissioner of Insurance** serves a four-year term and is the administrator for laws relating to the insurance industry in the state. This office enjoys the reputation as protector of the people from insurance fraud. In doing so, the office certifies all insurance companies as well as collects and disperses taxes from those companies doing business in Oklahoma.

Finally, the **Commissioner of Labor** serves a four-year term and is the administrator of all laws that relate to labor in manufacturing, mechanical, and transportation industries in the state. The Commissioner of Labor enforces all provisions and regulations that affect the health and well being of the labor force in Oklahoma (Strain et al., 1997).

While they do not receive the same amount of attention as the governor and Lieutenant Governor, the other elected executives perform valuable and necessary duties by administering agencies that fall under the executive branch. It is interesting that out of all to the elected officials in Oklahoma, the only executive limited to two consecutive terms of service is the governor. All other elected executives are allowed to serve an unlimited number of consecutive terms (Council of State Governments, 2003). In an era when a majority of Oklahomans has supported term limits for the governor and legislators, it is important to note that the other elected officials are not held to the same standard.

X. Conclusion

As the most visible and popular branch of government, the executive branch sets the tone for the state. The elected and appointed executives are responsible for leading those who run the state government. As both the administrative leader and the figurehead of Oklahoma, the governor must find a way to function within a pluralistic executive branch. Oklahoma's Constitution weakens the executive branch by splintering it into several separate power bases. Numerous officials, ranging from Insurance Commissioner to Superintendent of Public Instruction to Corporation Commissioners, are elected in statewide races. Add to this the fact that independent Boards and Commissions control many of the basic functions of state government, and it becomes clear how challenging it is for governors to effectively coordinate and manage state government.

In this type of governing situation, all elected executives must realize that the entire executive branch is evaluated on its ability to initiate, implement, and enforce effective policies. Such policy must be timely and must be in accordance with the needs of the people. Within the executive branch, effectiveness is measured by the use of political influence as a means to an end. The ability to be effective is vital because the roles and responsibilities of all of the executives directly impact the public and set the direction for Oklahoma.

Because of issues like pluralism and limited power, one might ask why anyone would want to be governor. The answer lies in the head coach analogy. If a team enjoys success, the coach is generally credited for promoting and creating ways to maximize achievement. Just as coaches are confident in their ability, anyone endeavoring to be governor must possess the full conviction that they will succeed. As fate has it, some are more successful than others. This success depends upon each governor's ability to transcend the pluralism and limited power issues, and establish strong administrative leadership. By being successful as the leader of a state government, Oklahoma governors can ensure success of their goals and that their name appears in history as one to be remembered.

CHAPTER SIX

PUBLIC ADMINISTRATION IN OKLAHOMA

Brett S. Sharp

Become part of something bigger than you, but better because of you.

Lane Graves Perry III, higher education executive

Business and public administration are alike only in all unimportant respects.

Wallace Sayre, public administration scholar

I. INTRODUCTION

On April 19, 1995, a terrorist bomb exploded near the Alfred P. Murrah federal building in Oklahoma City. At that time, it was the worst terrorist incident to have ever occurred on American soil. Ultimately, 168 people were known to be killed. The capacity of the federal level of government was severely crippled. Public servants from all across Oklahoma's state and local jurisdictions as well as numerous nonprofit agencies immediately responded. Fire, police, and emergency rescue personnel were on site and communicating with the incident command within the first half hour. The world's attention turned to Oklahoma City.

How well did Oklahoma's bureaucratic organizations respond to this unprecedented crisis? By almost all accounts, they handled the operation superbly. In fact, Oklahoma's public administrators earned tremendous praise for their interagency cooperation, hospitality extended toward rescue workers, and skillful work in keeping the public informed. Their work came to be known within the wider, national emergency response community and later to the general public as "the Oklahoma standard." For a time, the public servants in Oklahoma's state and local bureaucracies became heroes to the world. Afterwards, they shared their expertise with numerous other jurisdictions.

The dreadful experience of Oklahoma City's bombing even proved invaluable for recovering from the terrorist attacks on September 11, 2001. In addition to the periodic acts of courage and self-sacrifice by state and city employees in the case of the Murrah bombing or more typically in the aftermath of destructive tornadoes, they also serve Oklahoma citizens in

LEADERSHIP PROFILE

WILLIAM CITTY
Chief of Police, City of Oklahoma City

BILL CITTY, born and bred an Oklahoman, was born in Oklahoma City in 1953. He attended North West Classen High School and graduated in 1971. After graduation, he attended the University of Central Oklahoma for a short time, with an emphasis on business and marketing. Citty soon transferred to Oklahoma State University where he changed his major to sociology. At the time, he had an interest in psychology and had served internships at several nonprofit and juvenile facilities. Although he very much enjoyed helping young adults, he was disenchanted with the success rate of many juvenile programs.

He finished his degree in Sociology, but had turned his interest back to business and marketing. In 1977, he hired on at the Oklahoma Police Department as "just a job." At this time, he had no special interest in police work, but thought it might be interesting, and was attracted to their willingness to pay for his graduate degree.

After working for about three years on the street, he transferred to narcotics where he worked undercover. Although he had come to enjoy working for the police department, the undercover work began to wear him out. Visiting strip clubs and bars while being required to stay on good terms with shady people was not something he wanted to do for very long. Citty was soon promoted to Detective after about two years working undercover, where he mainly worked on prostitution and gambling cases. While working with Criminal Intelligence, he again went undercover to help work a major gambling operation.

After about eight years on the force, Citty was promoted to Captain and attended the FBI Academy. He considered leaving the department and going federal, but after extensive research and consideration, decided he would rather continue working in Oklahoma instead of relocating. Over the next few years, Citty held several different positions within the department. He headed up the Animal Welfare Division for a short period of time. He was also a hostage negotiator

> and even commander of the tactical team. He was appointed Chief in October of 2003. Citty says that being Chief was never his conscious goal. He was just there to do his job to the best of his ability. Even so, Chief Citty is proud to head such a fine department.
>
> *Michelle Strickin*

numerous ways often unrecognized and little appreciated. This chapter explores the nature of Oklahoma's state and local bureaucracies and the unique challenges faced by public employees within this state's often cynical and sometimes downright hostile environment.

II. UNSUNG HEROES FOR A SKEPTICAL PUBLIC

Despite the unchallenged heroism of many of Oklahoma's public employees during disasters, the majority of Oklahomans tend to be skeptical about the size of their state government. They keep a sharp eye on the taxes that they pay and how those taxes are spent. Following a long populist tradition of holding the line on government spending, Oklahoma voters have tightly restricted the possibility for tax increases. Through an amendment to the state constitution approved by the Oklahoma voters (State Question, 640), a super-majority of legislators is now necessary to increase taxes without going to a direct vote of the people. Consequently, the state is left with a rigidly conservative tax structure. On one hand, state government is not likely to experience out-of-control growth. On the other, the current tax system may not be sufficiently flexible to respond to future budget shortfalls or to adequately anticipate demographic shifts and economic trends (Oklahoma 2000, 1996, pp. 5, 191).

Already, state employees in Oklahoma are relatively underpaid when compared to their counterparts in the relevant labor market. The latest official compensation analysis indicates that state employee pay continues to lag behind the market by nearly 12% (Oklahoma Office of Personnel Management, 2006, p. 1). Over half of state employees make less than $34,000 per year. Less than 3% of state employees make more than $50,000 per year (Oklahoma Office of Personnel Management, 2003b, p. 90). State employees are awarded cost-of-living increases only sporadically, and proposed raises are always contingent upon availability of funds.

Oklahoma citizens are generally resistant to fully funding public programs and service delivery. The activities of Oklahoma's public agencies are viewed with a degree of distrust. Well-funded policy think tanks such as the Oklahoma Center for Public Affairs regularly issue critical reviews of government performance in Oklahoma. Stories presented in newspaper articles and local television news shows are much more likely to show the dark side of state and local governments than to portray their successes. In spite of this critical eye, political leaders have been successful in promoting major initiatives requiring new tax support—at least at the local level.

These initiatives include Tulsa's Vision 2025, the Oklahoma City Metropolitan Area Projects (MAPS), Oklahoma City Metropolitan Area Public Schools Trust (Maps for Kids), and there's even been talk of a MAPS III (Brus, 2007). Democrats and Republicans alike have been extremely interested in overhauling the state's current tax structure but have yet to agree on the particular features of a new system.

Generally, Oklahoma citizens get what they pay for. In metaphorical terms, Oklahomans seem only willing to pay for a used pickup truck and yet they expect the delivery of a shiny new sports utility vehicle with all the bells and whistles. According to research conducted by David Osborne and Peter Hutchinson, Oklahomans are only willing to pay about fifteen cents on every earned dollar for taxes to support state and local governments (2004, p. 56). If much above that amount, Oklahomans start actively resisting taxes by electing anti-tax candidates and passing anti-tax initiatives. Go much below that amount and critical services begin to be cut to unacceptable levels.

III. Holding Oklahoma's Bureaucracy Accountable

While politicians are voted into office by the people, they ultimately must depend upon an unelected part of government known as the *bureaucracy* to accomplish the work that needs to be done. The term *bureaucracy* has been associated—both fairly and unfairly—with red tape, inefficiency, waste, and corruption. In actuality, it simply refers to a large organization composed of specialized professionals. They operate according to rules established within a defined command and control structure. Bureaucracies are not institutions unique to government. Large and successful corporations such as Wal-Mart and General Electric are also examples of bureaucracies.

Even governmental bureaucracies can be quite successful in their endeavors. Bureaucracies have sometimes been compared to elephants. Like elephants, bureaucracies are thought of as large and cumbersome. But elephants "can run very fast" and some bureaucracies can "perform very well" (Rainey and Steinbaurer, 1999, p. 1). Many of the greatest feats of mankind—from the building of the ancient pyramids to the landing of man on the moon—have directly resulted from bureaucratic effort. On a daily basis, Oklahoma bureaucracies serve the public in countless ways. These organizations provide necessary institutional support for all three branches of government: executive, legislative, and judicial.

The difficulty remains as to the legitimacy of this large and powerful bureaucracy which has evolved for all practical purposes into an unelected branch of government. Fortunately, the demographic categories that make up the state government workforce roughly mirrors the state workforce overall. This diversity means that Oklahoma citizens are served by a **representative bureaucracy**. In other words, Oklahoma's bureaucracy looks like the public it serves.

LEADERSHIP PROFILE

JAMES D. COUCH
City Manager, City of Oklahoma City

JAMES D. COUCH was appointed City Manager of the City of Oklahoma City on November 9, 2000. He serves as the Chief Administrative Officer of the City responsible for the management and day-to-day operation of City government. Oklahoma City is a full-service City with nearly 4,300 employees and a total budget of $700 million.

Couch serves on a variety of city-related boards and agencies: Oklahoma City Airport Trust, Oklahoma City Water Utilities Trust, Oklahoma City Zoological Trust, and the Central Oklahoma Transportation and Parking Authority. Also, Couch serves as General Manager of the Oklahoma City Metropolitan Area Public Schools (OCMAPS) Trust, which oversees a half-billion-dollar construction program.

Before being appointed as City Manager, Couch already had a distinguished career with the City of Oklahoma City. He served as Assistant City Manager and MAPS Director as well as Water/Wastewater Utilities Director. In those capacities, he served as the General Manager of both the Oklahoma City Water Utilities Trust and the McGee Creek Authority and was responsible for the Water/Wastewater Utilities budget of $100 million annually, as well as the $390 million Metropolitan Area Projects capital construction program.

Prior to his career with the City of Oklahoma City, Couch held positions as the Assistant City Manager for the City of Edmond, Oklahoma; Public Works Director for the City of Casper, Wyoming; and Office Director for Buell, Winter, Mousel and Associates, Consulting Engineers. He received a Bachelor of Science in Civil Engineering from the South Dakota School of Mines and Technology, and is a Licensed Professional Engineer in the States of Oklahoma and Colorado.

Outside of his professional career, Couch serves on the YMCA of Greater Oklahoma City Board of Directors and the United Way of Metro Oklahoma City Board of Directors. Additionally, he is active in various church activities at Peace Lutheran Church.

TABLE 6-1
State Government Workforce Representation 2007
(Excluding Higher Education)

Race	Male	Female	Total
White	35.5	43.3	78.8
Black	3.1	6.8	9.9
Hispanic	.9	1.4	2.3
American Indian/ Alaskan Native	3.4	3.9	7.3
Asian/Pacific Islander	.7	1.0	1.7
Totals	43.6	56.4	100

SOURCE: Oklahoma Office of Personnel Management 2007.

Running state and local government is a labor-intensive process. According to the Bureau of Labor Statistics, one out of every seven workers in the United States works for a state, county, municipality, school system or special district—nearly twenty million state and local government employees altogether. Excluding those who work in education, state and local governments employ nearly eight million workers making this sector "one of the largest in the American economy" (Bureau of Labor Statistics, 2006, p. 279). In the state of Oklahoma, state government is the largest single employer with over 35,000 employees—and that figure does not even include higher education (Hamilton, 2003, p. 968). The key personnel that keep these public operations running are called public administrators. A *public administrator* is someone who is compensated by a government or not-for-profit agency for managing a program or supervising people.

Public administrators who run state and local agencies in Oklahoma are important because this state has traditionally denied strong formal powers to its governor and mayors. Career administrators fill in this power vacuum by default. Often, these public administrators use their *administrative discretion* when working under the color of vague or conflicting legislation. Administration discretion implies a certain amount of flexibility when applying the law. The classic example is when stopped by a police officer for a traffic violation, we hope that he or she uses administrative discretion in our favor. In other words, we hope to receive a warning rather than a ticket. While citizens must trust their elected representatives to make laws in their stead, legislators must trust public administrators to interpret and implement laws in the face of new and unforeseen circumstances. As much justice is probably done at the administrative level than in all the courts of law in the land.

Citizens tend not to think very much about bureaucracy when it works well. In a classic study reviewing numerous surveys over time, organizational theorist Charles T. Goodsell concluded, "Most citizens are satisfied with their personal experiences with bureaucracy most of the time" (1994, p. 29). The few bad experiences that citizens have with government probably become more salient due to the fact that alternative services are rarely available. Moreover, citizens rightly believe that they are the "owners" of the public enterprise since they support it with their tax monies. Bureaucratic features take on added significance in the public sector since government agencies are not directly constrained by the bottom line of profit. The public understandably desires to hold these institutions accountable. The quest is to find accurate and relevant strategies for measuring and improving the performance of government.

IV. Improving Bureaucratic Productivity

State leaders attempt to reform Oklahoma's bureaucracy on a fairly regular basis. Usually these efforts are spearheaded by new gubernatorial administrations. Reform efforts may take the form of re-organizations or the application of new managerial techniques. While the goals are often similar, the labels attached to these efforts are not. A major barrier to improving productivity in the public sector is the short tenure of elected officials. Governors have expended very little effort in preserving a sense of continuity to productivity improvement efforts. While these productivity improvement activities are often short-lived, some programs do become institutionalized within the bureaucracy. For example, Governor Henry Bellmon encouraged a "State of Excellence." His program was certainly influenced by the fashionable management strategy promoted in the book by Peters and Waterman, *In Search of Excellence* (1982). In addition, Bellmon's administration became one of the early champions of the **Certified Public Manager** (CPM) program which still provides comprehensive management training for public administrators statewide. Many politicians routinely employ the business model to run state and local governments. While sometimes helpful, the business model demonstrates little appreciation for the stark differences between the private and public sectors. Bellmon proved to be more sophisticated in his actual approach by implementing a successful human resources development program.

Subsequently, Governor David Walters adopted a **Total Quality Management** or "TQM" approach. The aim of TQM as applied in the public sector is to continuously improve customer services. Special trainers guide state employees in applying quality improvement processes and techniques within a systems perspective. This original TQM initiative was built upon a cooperative relationship between the Xerox Corporation, a recipient of the prestigious Malcolm Baldrige National Quality Award, and the state of Oklahoma. Remnants of this total quality management initiative have persisted well beyond the Walters administration due more to bureaucratic momentum than support by later administrations. For example, the network of quality teams that began under Walters continued to meet even though not recognized for months by Governor Frank Keating.

Keating put his own imprint on Oklahoma bureaucracy by creating the Governor's Performance Commission modeled after Vice President Al Gore's National Performance Review. Both the national and state performance reviews rode the wave of **reinventing government** as inspired by a book of the same name authored by Osborne and Gaebler (1992). Reinventing government promoted the use of market mechanisms, decentralization, outcomes measurement, and managerial empowerment. It emphasized revamping and even eliminating existing rules and regulations in order to increase the flexibility and capacity of public administrators to do their jobs. The assumption was that public administrators were overly fearful of taking risks. Reinventing government promoted a philosophy of tolerating reasonable mistakes when bureaucrats invested in more entrepreneurial approaches. The Governor's Performance Commission assembled numerous teams that interviewed a variety of stakeholders throughout the state. The Commission ultimately made recommendations on such wide-ranging areas as education, finance, health, human resources, management systems, social services, and transportation. Many of these recommendations were incorporated into law and policy.

Before he was first elected to public office, Brad Henry described state government as wasteful and said that Oklahoma has "too many boards and agencies. Some should be consolidated or terminated altogether" (Legislative Candidates, 1992). Since becoming Governor, Henry has not initiated a comprehensive reform of state bureaucracy. However, he has tinkered with reform at the edges. He issued an executive order placing the Oklahoma Employment Security Commission, the Oklahoma Workforce Investment Board, and other related agencies under the supervision of the Department of Commerce (Monies, 2003). He has also advocated innovative financial management techniques such as **zero base budgeting.** This technique discourages the typical assumption that agencies should receive roughly the same amount of funding as the previous fiscal year. Under zero base budgeting, agencies must defend their current roster of programs as if they did not already exist.

The state legislature has also advanced its version of improving the performance of the state bureaucracy. It recently considered recommendations by its Quality Improvement Task Force passing legislative requirements for agencies to adopt five-year strategic plans. **Strategic plans** are systematic efforts to prepare an organization to meet future demands and challenges. The new majority of Republicans in the state House of Representatives will likely approach its responsibilities for **bureaucratic oversight** by emphasizing the business model to ensure accountability.

V. The Structure of Oklahoma's Bureaucracy

The state of Oklahoma has almost 200 separate state agencies. This patchwork of agencies, boards, and commissions represents nearly a century of attempts by Oklahoma government to respond to a wide variety of emerging policy problems. With its progressive heritage, the state began with a fragmented executive branch. While there have been sporadic attempts to consolidate Oklahoma bureaucracies and executive leadership, the overall trend has been in the direction of growing complexity. Currently, state bureaucracy can be subdivided into agencies under the direction of the governor's cabinet, agencies under the direction of other elected officials, and numerous independent agencies, boards, and commissions.

Governors David Boren and George Nigh experimented with a **cabinet system** in order to strengthen and centralize their leadership. A cabinet is composed of top administrative officials, usually heads of major state departments, who work together to advise the governor on important policy matters. The legislature implemented a formal cabinet system in

Table 6–2
The Governor's Cabinet as of May 2007

Adjutant General	Major General Harry M. Wyatt III
Agriculture	Terry Peach
Central Services	Pamela W. Warren
Commerce and Tourism	Kathryn L. Taylor
Energy	David Fleischaker
Environment	Miles Tolbert
Health	Terry Cline
Human Resources & Administration	Oscar B. Jackson Jr.
Human Services	Howard Hendrick
Revenue and Finance	Scott Meacham
Safety and Security	Kevin Ward
Science and Technology	Dr. Joseph W. Alexander
State	Susan Savage
Transportation	Phil Tomlinson
Veterans Affairs	Norman Lamb

1987 under Governor Henry Bellmon. State law stipulates that the cabinet system shall consist of no fewer than ten and no more than fifteen functional areas. Within these legislatively established limits, successive Oklahoma governors in turn have tailored their cabinets to meet their particular needs. Currently, there are fifteen separate cabinet appointments over agriculture, central services, commerce and tourism, energy, environment, finance, health, human resources and administration, human services, military, public safety, science and technology, state, transportation, and veterans affairs.

Most of these cabinet officials have direct administrative authority over one or more state agencies. Sometimes the status of cabinet level officials is more honorific than substantive. "If a cabinet member lacks operational responsibility for an agency, that person becomes little more than a staff adviser to the governor" (Morgan, England, and Humphreys, 1991, p. 114). For example, Governor Frank Keating appointed Dr. Floyd Coppedge in 1996 to serve as Education Cabinet Secretary. Such an appointment provided little more than symbolic leadership given the fact that oversight of common education at the state level was provided by another elected official, Sandy Garrett, State Superintendent of Public Instruction. Higher education is of course managed by the State Regents.

The Number of Oklahoma State Government Employees

The number of state employees in Oklahoma remains a matter of continuing controversy. Several interest groups have become involved in the public discussion. The Oklahoma Center for Public Affairs, the Research Institute for Economic Development, and Citizens Against Government Waste are examples of groups that have issued reports pointing to an excess of state employees. As expected, the Oklahoma Public Employees Association voices a much different perspective. Numbers used come from different sources including the U.S. Census Bureau, the Oklahoma Office of Personnel Management, the Office of State Finance, and the State Regents for Higher Education. The exact definition of who is or is not a state employee is key to the debate. Do you count "bodies" or "hours worked." The number of people actually receiving state payroll checks would obviously yield a different employee count than calculating the amount of paid hours. According to the *Tulsa World*, "the so-called **full-time equivalents** (FTE)—the number of employees divided by a standard 173-hour-work month—is down to around 64,000 and inching toward the lowest level in six years. In other words, more people are working fewer paid hours" (Krehbiel, 2003). Other considerations include seasonal variations or whether to include employees within the legislative or judicial branches. Teachers often are identified mistakenly as state employees, but actually they are paid by the school districts. In fact, the only parts of the state workforce showing growth over the past twenty years have been in higher education and public safety including

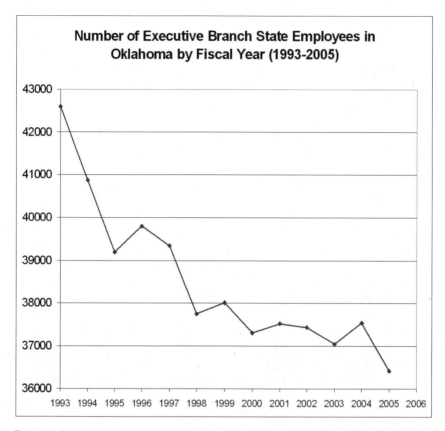

FIGURE 6-1

corrections. The sharp rise in higher education employment is due mostly to "increased research grants that generated additional jobs" (Greiner, 2003). Contrary to popular perception, the total number of state employees working in the executive branch has actually declined over the past several years (see Figure 6-1).

According to the its latest annual report, the Oklahoma Office of Personnel Management reports that the total number of **classified** employees—those covered under the merit system—is about 26,461. Including those unclassified, the number rises to 34,050. When you add in higher education, the total number of state employees is well over 60,000. Please note that these are not FTE counts, but rather body counts based on the number of employees who receive a check. For example, the higher education number includes adjunct professors. A person who teaches one class at four different institutions will be counted four times. Student work-study employees are counted also. With the complete implementation of the state's new **human resources information system** (HRIS), more accurate and detailed information will be available soon.

Direct comparison with other states is not always useful since relevant variables are difficult to take into account. "Because Oklahoma is a large state geographically, services must be provided even in sparsely populated, more remote areas" (Delcour, 2004). States with greater populations covering less area can often take advantage of economies of scale not available to a state like Oklahoma.

VI. Development of Oklahoma's Merit System

The U.S. Congress encouraged adoption of **merit systems** when it incorporated a provision into the federal Social Security Act that required governments to use rational personnel practices when staffing federally supported programs. Oklahoma voters adopted the Social Security Amendment in 1936 which led to the creation of the state's first true merit system. The purpose of the merit system is to promote a professionalized public service free from undue political interference.

In 1959, the state legislature allowed the extension of the Merit System to other agencies besides those directly receiving federal funding through executive orders. In 1982, the state of Oklahoma once again adopted the federal model by passing the Oklahoma Personnel Act. This law created the Office of Personnel Management as the administrative arm of the governor on human resource management issues. A separate board now called the Oklahoma Merit Protection Commission was also set up as an independent watchdog to ensure continued implementation of proper merit system standards.

Several other reforms were initiated throughout the past several years to allow state agencies to handle human resource matters with greater flexibility. The goal has been to change the role of the Office of Personnel Management from its perceived heavy-handedness and rigidity in enforcing personnel rules to provide a more consultative style of support to state agencies. As a result, the Oklahoma human resources system has become a model throughout the United States for its balancing of merit system principles with the needs of modern public agencies to quickly respond and adapt to changing conditions. The overall structure of the state's personnel system is well established. Recent managerial reforms such as creating more flexible job classifications (called **broadbanding**), opening salary ranges to reward performance (see Figure 6–2), strategic management, and developing a true employee performance management system have only been possible because of the previous existence of a well defined human resources system. Oklahoma's current personnel system has taken great advantage of modern management practices. In many areas, it has been on the cutting edge. The next challenge is to move this personnel system forward to the next level by making it competitive with the market. The potential is for Oklahoma to have a world-class public service.

LEADERSHIP PROFILE

Oscar B. Jackson, Jr.
Cabinet Secretary of Human Resources and Administration

OSCAR B. JACKSON, JR. is the rare public administrator to be appointed to a cabinet-level position by multiple governors of opposing parties. In 1991, Governor David Walters named Oscar B. Jackson, Jr. as the new Administrator of the Office of Personnel Management and Cabinet Secretary of Human Resources. In January 1995, Governor Frank Keating re-appointed him to both positions, and in January 2003, Governor Brad Henry also re-appointed Jackson to both positions. The Office of Personnel Management is a strategic agency for the governor administering a comprehensive and multi-functional human resources system for state government.

Jackson has a Bachelor's degree in Business Education from the University of Oklahoma, and has completed graduate work in Public Administration, with an emphasis in Public Personnel Administration.

He is extremely active in a wide variety of organizations that serve the state of Oklahoma. Jackson is a member of the Board of Trustees for the Oklahoma Public Employees Retirement System, the Employees Benefits Council, the Committee for Incentive Awards for State Employees (Vice-Chair), the State Agency Review Committee for the Oklahoma State Employees' Charitable Contribution Campaign (Vice-Chair), the Human Resources Management Advisory Committee (Chair), and the Mentor Selection Advisory Committee (Chair). He serves on the Board of Directors of The Oklahoma Academy, a non-partisan organization that identifies critical issues facing Oklahoma's future, and promotes public consideration of the issues, builds consensus, develops recommendations, and supports their implementation; and the Board of Directors for Leadership Oklahoma, a statewide leadership development program designed to identify, teach and challenge the present and future leaders of Oklahoma. He is also a member of the Central Oklahoma Workforce Investment Board

Chapter Six

(serving Canadian, Logan, and Oklahoma Counties, and the City of Oklahoma City).

Jackson is a past-President of the National Association of State Personnel Executives. He currently serves on the Executive Council of the International Public Management Association for Human Resources (IPMA-HR), the IPMA-HR Public Human Resource Certification Council, and the National Public Service Award Executive Committee for the American Society for Public Administration and the National Academy for Public Administration.

He is a 1995–1996 graduate of Leadership Oklahoma. Jackson received the 1995 "Administrator of the Year" Award from the Oklahoma Chapter of the American Society for Public Administration; the "1997 National Public Service Award" from the National Academy for Public Administration and the American Society for Public Administration; the "1997 Eugene H. Rooney, Jr. Award for Leadership in State Human Resources Management" from the National Association of State Personnel Executives; the "1999 University of Oklahoma African American Outstanding Alumni Award"; the "1999 University of Oklahoma Regents Award"; and the "1999 Outstanding Board Member of the Year Award" from the Urban League of Greater Oklahoma City, Inc. In 2005, he was selected as an inaugural member of the University Of Oklahoma College Of Hall of Fame.

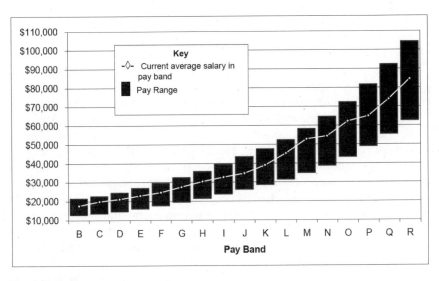

FIGURE 6–2

VII. CONCLUSION

In the wake of the events of September 11, 2001, state and local governments have been forced to respond. The reduction of vulnerabilities to terrorism and the prevention of future attacks very much depends upon the professionalism and dedication of this nation's public administrators at all levels of government. As usual when confronting a new policy problem, our political leaders search for a bureaucratic response. One of the most recent developments in Oklahoma bureaucracy is the creation of the Oklahoma Office of Homeland Security charged with the mission to coordinate responses to potential and actual terrorist attacks in this state. The creation of this new agency exemplifies the fact that bureaucracies are not created in a vacuum. They are in fact established to help solve real human problems. Their successes are rarely trumpeted and their failures are obvious. As responsible citizens, we should be careful to engage in constructive criticism of the public servants who help make our lives better rather than engaging in reflexive acts of bureaucrat bashing.

CHAPTER SEVEN

THE OKLAHOMA JUDICIARY
Keith R. Eakins

Scarcely any political question arises in the United States that is not resolved, sooner or later, into a judicial question.
Alexis de Tocqueville, *Democracy in America*

I. INTRODUCTION

Like the courts in most states, the Oklahoma judiciary jumps in and out of the public's consciousness in episodic fashion. We tend to focus on the courts during times of scandal, such as when revelations of bribery rocked the Oklahoma Supreme Court in 1965, or in the midst of high profile cases, such as the state trial of Terry Nichols, the co-conspirator in the bombing of the Murrah Building in Oklahoma City. After the general interest in these incidents wane, the courts retreat to their usual position of low prominence (see Baum & Kemper, 1994).

Astute students of politics realize that the courts deserve more consistent attention than is given them by the public. Oklahoma courts make important decisions each year which impact the lives of citizens in consequential ways. The rights, duties, and liability of those involved in criminal code violations, personal injury occurrences, real estate transactions, business contracts, divorce litigation, and numerous other matters are determined by decisions from Oklahoma appellate and trial courts. For example, if a college student suffers a broken nose in a barroom brawl in Norman, Oklahoma and she sues the bar owner, Oklahoma tort doctrines—products of the Oklahoma Supreme Court's jurisprudence—are used to determine whether the bar owner is liable in an Oklahoma trial court. It is an Oklahoma trial court judge who will decide the admissibility of evidence, guide the jury's decision making in a jury trial, or determine liability herself in a bench trial. In fact, most of the legal questions and conflicts encountered by Oklahomans are governed by the decisions and policy making of Oklahoma trial and appellate courts. Oklahoma courts are important, not only due to the impact they have on individual cases, but also because the sum total of their case decisions shape the contours of the legal landscape that affects how we live our lives.

This chapter examines several different aspects of the Oklahoma courts. First, we look at the structure of the Oklahoma judiciary starting with the trial courts and ending with the high courts of appeals. Next, we examine

Chapter Seven

how criminal and civil cases proceed through the courts, and pay particular attention to the role of plea bargaining in criminal cases. Then, we look at the various judges and justices in Oklahoma and how they are chosen, and discuss the advantages and disadvantages of the different selection systems. Finally, we consider the types of cases heard by the Oklahoma courts and examine some of the impact of the high courts on policy within the state, nationally and internationally.

II. THE STRUCTURE OF THE OKLAHOMA JUDICIARY

The judiciary of Oklahoma is unique in its design and operation (see Figure 7–1). Most notably, it features two "courts of last resort" which hear final appeals of issues of state civil and criminal law. With the exception of Texas, every other state features only one high court. The structure of the Oklahoma judiciary reflects both the traditions of the state's Populist past as well as more modern efforts at reform. In this section, we will explain how the various Oklahoma courts operate at both the trial and appellate level, and discuss the different types of jurisdiction, or authority to hear cases, they possess.

FIGURE 7–1 THE OKLAHOMA COURT SYSTEM

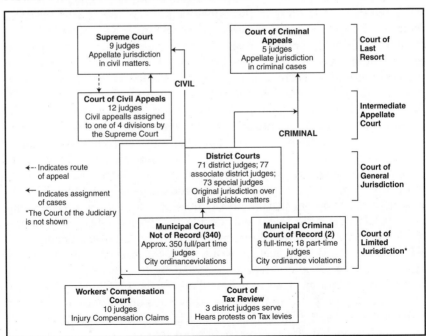

SOURCE: State of Oklahoma. The Judiciary. Annual Report, FY-94, Administratrive Office of the Courts, 1994.

An Introduction to the Trial Courts of Oklahoma

Trial courts are the courts that consider cases as they first enter the legal system. At this level in the court system, one judge presides over a case involving one or more plaintiff and defendant (both of whom can be referred to generically as "parties"). The **plaintiff** is the party who files a civil or criminal action, and the **defendant** is the party who defends himself in a criminal case or denies a claim brought in a civil case. A **criminal case** is one in which the government attempts to punish someone for conduct that has been deemed a crime by a legislative body. For example, a woman was charged for violating the Oklahoma statute 21 O.S. 1971 § 22 forbidding "willfully and wrongfully committing an act injurious to public morals and openly outraging public decency" when she danced naked in close proximity to a male patron's face in the "Satan's Lounge" in Tulsa, Oklahoma (see *State v. Walker* 568 P.2d 286 (1977)). A civil case, on the other hand, can involve any other issue that is not criminal in nature. Specifically, a **civil case** is one that is brought to enforce, redress, or protect the rights and duties individuals and organizations might legally owe each other.

For example, if an Oklahoma man abandons his family and takes off to Alaska to work with his girlfriend on a fishing scow, his wife might file a divorce action seeking to end the marriage. Or suppose an Oklahoma concert promoter enters into a contract with the rock band "The White Stripes" to put on a show in Muskogee, Oklahoma, and the group fails to show up because the lead singer was jailed for assaulting a fan during the last concert. The concert promoter might sue the band to recover the revenue lost from the cancelled show.

Trial courts are often featured in dramatic, legal thriller movies as well as television reality shows such as "Judge Judy" and "The People's Court." At the trial court level, attorneys introduce evidence related to the case. This may include examining one or more of the parties on the witness stand, presenting alibis for their clients, cross-examining witnesses against their clients, introducing physical evidence such as a gun found at a murder scene, or presenting expert witnesses such as a plastic surgeon who testifies about a botched "extreme makeover." The judge sits as a trial gatekeeper deciding which evidence to allow the jury to consider, and which to exclude based on a lack of credibility, relevance, prejudicial impact, or other reasons. Cases are decided in either **jury trials** where, depending on the type of case, six to 12 members of the community determine the fate of the litigants, or **bench trials** where the judge assumes the role of the jury.

The Types of Oklahoma Trial Courts

The trial courts of Oklahoma are broken down into two basic types: courts of limited jurisdiction and courts of general jurisdiction. Jurisdiction is defined as the authority of a court to decide a case. **Courts of limited**

jurisdiction are those that only have authority to hear specific types of cases. There are four Oklahoma courts of limited jurisdiction: (1) the **workers' compensation courts** which consider claims of employee-related injuries; (2) the **court of tax review** which determines tax-related complaints; (3) the **court on the judiciary** which hears complaints against judges and has the authority to remove them for bad behavior; and (4) the **municipal criminal courts** which only hear cases involving minor criminal violations of municipal laws (League of Women Voters of Oklahoma, 1994). The municipal criminal courts are the most common of the courts of limited jurisdiction and also hear the lion's share of cases. A typical example of a municipal court case could involve a student who is speeding down Main Street in Edmond, Oklahoma 20 miles per hour over the speed limit and is pulled over and ticketed by an Edmond police officer. The speeding ticket is a formal accusation of violating an Edmond ordinance, so if the student contests the ticket, the case would be heard in the Edmond Municipal Court.

Courts of general jurisdiction have the authority to consider cases involving a broad range of legal issues. The **district courts** are the only courts of general jurisdiction in Oklahoma. They decide all civil cases originating under state law and all cases involving violations of state criminal statutes. Oklahoma is divided into 26 judicial districts and all but four encompass more than one county (Lawler and Spurrier 1991). However, each courthouse in Oklahoma's 77 counties has an operating district court. So if an Oklahoma City woman, Crystal Method, is arrested and charged with operating a methamphetamine (meth) lab in her basement, she would appear in the Oklahoma County District Court to face the state criminal charges. Or if a Tulsa man, Cliff Clumsy, sues Wal-Mart for negligence after he slips and falls on a box of super-sized McDonalds french fries left on the discount store's floor, his civil action would be filed in the Tulsa County District Court.

An Introduction to the Appellate Courts of Oklahoma

Appellate courts have appellate jurisdiction: the authority to review cases that have been decided previously in a trial court. Typically, appellate courts receive cases when one or more parties is dissatisfied with the outcome in a trial court and files an **appeal**—a formal request to review the decision of the trial court. In Oklahoma, like every other state in the country, everyone is entitled to one "appeal of right." In other words, every person involved in a formal legal proceeding is guaranteed the right to have the decision reviewed by a higher court to ensure it was fair. So if the case of the alleged Oklahoma City meth lab operator goes to a jury trial and the defendant is found guilty, she has the right to appeal the case to an appellate court and present arguments that her conviction should be reversed. For example, if her attorney was incompetent, showed up intoxicated in court, and slept through the trial, the defendant may be able to get the appellate court to overturn her conviction on the grounds she was denied her Sixth Amendment right to have effective legal representation. Or if Wal-Mart loses its "slip and fall" case in a jury trial, it could file an appeal asking for a reversal alleging that the trial court jury erred in finding the superstore negligent since the store had put up orange cones next to the french fry mess and the plaintiff had been born with six toes on each foot which made him uniquely susceptible to falling.

Thus, appellate courts are decidedly different from trial courts because of their appellate jurisdiction. Yet they are also very distinct in how they operate. Unlike trial courts which have one judge on a case, these courts have between three and nine judges who participate in reviewing and deciding cases. Appellate courts also typically do not consider any additional evidence when they review the decisions of the trial courts. For example, in the hypothetical above, Wal-Mart would not be allowed to have its employees testify for the appellate court reviewing the case. Only the attorneys representing the parties are permitted to communicate with the appellate court. The exception to this rule is if a party forgoes legal counsel and chooses to represent himself.

In deciding cases, appellate court judges peruse the **record** (transcribed recording) from the lower court case, and consider the **briefs** (written legal arguments) of the plaintiffs' and defendants' attorneys. In some cases, the court holds **oral arguments** where attorneys present legal and policy arguments to the judges and respond to their questions. The judges later meet in a **conference** where they discuss the case and vote on its outcome. For a party to win, he or she must get a majority of the judges' votes. One of the judges in the majority group is assigned to write the **opinion of the court.** Often with the assistance of one or more law clerks, the judge researches the case issues in more depth and writes an opinion giving legal and policy justifications for the case outcome. If the other judges in the majority group agree with the reasoning in the opinion, they sign it and it becomes the official opinion of the court majority. Any judges not part of the majority vote may also write a **dissenting opinion** where they express disagreement with the majority opinion. However, it is the opinion of the majority of the court that is authoritative and determines the outcome of the case.

The Types of Oklahoma Appellate Courts

There are two classifications of Oklahoma appellate courts: intermediate courts of appeals and courts of last resort. An **intermediate court of appeals** is called so because its decisions can be appealed to a higher court or court of last resort. A **court of last resort,** on the other hand, is the final court of appeal in the state system.

The **Oklahoma Court of Civil Appeals** is an intermediate court of appeals which hears appeals of civil cases from the Oklahoma trial courts. There are four divisions in the Court of Civil Appeals, each having three judges. Two of the divisions are located in Oklahoma City and two in

Tulsa. In most states, an initial appeal is filed directly with the intermediate court of appeals. However, in Oklahoma an appeal is filed first with the Oklahoma Supreme Court which then usually assigns the case to one of the four divisions of the Court of Civil Appeals. After receiving the case, the division's three-judge panel reviews the trial court record, the briefs of the attorneys, and—in rare occasions—holds oral arguments (Simpson, 2000). One of the three judges on the panel is assigned the task of writing the opinion, and it must be supported by at least one of the other panel judges to be adopted as the opinion of the court. If a party is dissatisfied with the decision, he or she may seek further review with the Oklahoma Supreme Court.

The **Oklahoma Supreme Court** is the court of last resort for all civil cases involving issues of Oklahoma law. As mentioned above, all civil appeals are filed with the Oklahoma Supreme Court, but most are assigned to one of four three-judge panels of the Court of Civil Appeals (Simpson, 2000). A party can appeal a decision of the Court of Civil Appeals by filing a **petition for a writ of certiorari** with the Oklahoma Supreme Court. Yet, unfortunately for the appellants, the court declines to hear the majority of these "cert" petitions since it has the authority to pick and choose only those cases it deems worthy.

What types of cases does the court consider "cert worthy"? There is no precise answer to this question, but the court has set forth some considerations. Cases concerning issues of law over which there is disagreement among the lower courts, cases conflicting with Oklahoma Supreme Court or U.S. Supreme Court decisions, or cases involving important and novel issues may be more likely to be heard or granted cert (Administrative Office of the Courts, 1995b).

The Oklahoma Supreme Court also has the authority to hear initial appeals, and thus may choose to not assign some cases to the Court of Civil Appeals, if it determines that the case involves "new, first-impression issues, or important issues of great public concern . . ." (Administrative Office of the Courts, 1995b, 14). However, as mentioned above, the vast majority of initial appeals are assigned to the Court of Civil Appeals.

Finally, the Oklahoma Supreme Court has powers beyond hearing civil appeals. The court has general superintending control over all lower courts, and all agencies, boards, and commissions created by law. And it has original jurisdiction over (i.e., it is the first court to decide) initiative and referendum petitions, as well as cases involving the executive and legislative departments of state government (League of Women Voters, 1994).

The Oklahoma Supreme Court has nine members, and decides cases **en banc** (with all of the members). In order for a party to win a case being considered by the court, he or she must attract a majority vote (at least five of nine) of the justices. If a party loses in the Oklahoma Supreme Court, he or she can file a petition for a writ of certiorari with the Supreme Court of the United States if the case involves a question concerning the U.S.

LEADERSHIP PROFILE

MARIAN P. OPALA
Vice-Chief Justice, Oklahoma Supreme Court

MARIAN P. OPALA was born in 1921 in Lodz, Poland. After living an idyllic childhood, Opala was forced to flee as the Nazis invaded his home country. He eventually made his way to England where he joined the British army. Toward the end of the war, he was airdropped back into Poland but was captured by German forces. American forces subsequently liberated him from a prisoner-of-war camp in Germany. An army captain from Oklahoma sponsored Opala to come to the states. He became an American citizen in 1953. He graduated from the Oklahoma City University School of Law the same year. In 1957, he earned a BSB degree in Economics from Oklahoma City University and in 1968 his master-of-law degree from New York University School of Law.

Opala began his legal career as assistant county attorney in Oklahoma County and held this position until 1956 when he entered private practice. He first served the Supreme Court of Oklahoma as a referee from 1960 to 1965. Later he was staff lawyer for Justice Rooney McInerney.

For nine years (from 1969 to 1977) Opala directed the state's court system as its first administrative director. He served as judge on the State Industrial Court when it was renamed (in 1977–1978) the Workers' Compensation Court. On November 21, 1978, the then Governor, now OU President David Boren appointed him to the Supreme Court of Oklahoma. Voters retained him in 1980 for the unexpired term of his predecessor. In 1982, 1988, and 1994 he was retained for six-year terms. He served as the court's Chief Justice from January 1, 1991 to December 31, 1992.

The author of numerous legal papers, Opala is an adjunct professor in three law schools—at the University of Oklahoma, Oklahoma City University, and the University of Tulsa—and a frequent lecturer at various national judicial and legal education programs. Since 1982 he has been an Oklahoma commissioner in the National Conference of Commissioners on Uniform State Laws. A member of the Order of the Coif and the American Law Institute, he was appointed in December 1993 as a public member of the Administrative Conference of the United States.

Constitution. But fewer than 2% of those appeals are granted (Epstein et al., 2003).

The **Oklahoma Court of Criminal Appeals** is the court of last resort for criminal cases originating in the Oklahoma district and municipal courts. Appeals of all criminal cases, ranging from traffic violations to murder, are decided by this court. There are five members of the court who, like the justices of the Oklahoma Supreme Court, hear cases en banc. In order to win a case in the Court of Criminal Appeals, litigants must get at least three votes from the five justices.

III. THE OKLAHOMA CRIMINAL COURT PROCESS

The Formal Stages of the Oklahoma Criminal Court Process

Criminal cases begin with a district attorney filing one or more charges against a defendant. A **charge** is a formal accusation that one has violated an Oklahoma statute forbidding a criminal activity such as bigamy, murder, driving under the influence of alcohol, etc. The next step is the **arraignment,** in which a judge reads the charges alleged against the defendant and the defendant enters a plea of guilty or not guilty. If the accused faces a possible sentence of incarceration, he or she has a constitutional right to have an attorney represent her. Typically, those who can afford it hire private counsel, and those who cannot afford private counsel get an attorney appointed to them by the trial court free of charge. Defendants usually plead not guilty at this stage, and many are freed with the understanding they must later return to court for subsequent court proceedings. Some of those freed pending trial may be required to post a **bond,** a sum of money that is forfeited if they fail to return. In considering the amount of the bond that must be posted, a judge will consider the severity of the crime, the defendant's criminal record, ties to the community, and the danger he or she may pose to the community.

After arraignment, the vast majority of the criminal cases are resolved without ever going to trial. At least 90% of all criminal cases in state and federal courts are resolved through plea bargaining (Carp & Stidham, 2004, 218). **Plea bargaining** is an agreement reached between the prosecutor and the defense counsel whereby the defendant agrees to plead guilty in exchange for some leniency promised by the district attorney. If a plea bargain cannot be reached, then most cases go to a preliminary hearing. At the **preliminary hearing** the judge decides whether there is enough evidence against a defendant to force her to stand trial. Specifically, the prosecutor must present evidence and testimony to prove there is sufficient "probable cause" that the defendant committed a crime. Sometimes, the defendant's attorney will cross examine the prosecution's witnesses and cast doubt upon the evidence in an attempt to make the prosecution's case look weak and get the charges dismissed. If the judge decides that probable cause has been met, the case will be set for trial and pre-trial motions.

Before the trial, the district attorney and defense attorney usually appear before the trial court judge and make **pre-trial motions.** At this stage, the attorneys argue that some evidence should be kept out of the trial, that some witnesses must or cannot testify, or that the case should be thrown out. For example, in drug trafficking cases it is common for the defense attorney to move to suppress, or keep out of the trial, drugs that were found by police. The Fourth Amendment requires that police conduct searches properly, and if a police search was done illegally, such as a home search without a warrant, the trial judge may rule that the 25 pounds of marijuana discovered are inadmissible in court. Or in a rape case, the district attorney may argue that an alibi witness for the defendant, who claims the defendant was not at the rape scene, is mentally ill and incompetent to testify. After the pre-trial motions are decided, the case is ready to go to trial.

During the **trial,** the prosecution presents its evidence against the defendant and asks for a "guilty" verdict and conviction. Defendants also have the opportunity to discredit the physical evidence and testimony introduced by the prosecution, and may choose to offer their own evidence. After both sides have presented their case, the jury (and sometimes a judge if the defendant has requested a "bench trial" instead of a jury trial) meets to determine the guilt or innocence of the defendant. The jury will find the defendant guilty if they believe the prosecution has proven **"beyond a reasonable doubt"** that the defendant committed the crime. Under Oklahoma law, if the case involves a "petty" crime that is punishable by incarceration of six months or less, then the "guilty" verdict of the jury need not be unanimous. However, if it is a serious crime punishable by more than six months in prison, then a jury finding of "guilty" must be unanimous.

If a defendant has been found guilty by a jury or judge, he or she must be sentenced by the trial court. In a jury trial, juries may recommend a punishment. Typically, **sentencing** occurs right after convictions for minor offenses, or when a defendant has pled guilty. In more serious cases, such as those involving felonies, formal sentencing will occur at a later hearing after the judge receives a pre-sentence report. **Pre-sentence reports** are sentence recommendations prepared by the probation department reflecting assessments from the prosecutor, the defense attorney, and the probation officer. The judge also must consider the legal range of punishments for the crime. For example, if a defendant is convicted of participating in a riot and encouraging other riot participants to engage in acts of violence, he or she faces imprisonment for two to ten years under Oklahoma statutes. In determining the length of the sentence, the judge, in addition to considering the pre-sentence report, would also take into account any criminal record of the defendant, prospects for rehabilitation, remorse, the societal harm stemming from the criminal act, and any other relevant factors.

Finally, a defendant who has been found guilty has the right to appeal his or her conviction to the Oklahoma Court of Criminal Appeals. In an appeal, the individual convicted asks the Court of Criminal Appeals to overturn the conviction or sentence imposed. Typically the convicted individual, now known as the "appellant," has an attorney who files an **appellate brief** with the Court of Criminal Appeals arguing that the conviction and/or sentence was unfair or based upon legal mistakes. The district attorney, now known as the "appellee," also files a brief with the Court of Criminal Appeals arguing that the conviction and sentence should be upheld. The court also may schedule oral arguments in important cases. During the **oral arguments,** the defense attorney and District Attorney present their legal arguments to the judges who probe them with legal questions. This procedure involves only the court and the attorneys from each side arguing the legality of the original trial. In other words, no new evidence of any kind is submitted—neither the defendant nor any other witnesses testify. After reviewing the briefs from the appellant and appellee, and the transcript (a record of every word and piece of evidence), and hearing the oral argument (if one was scheduled), the Court of Criminal Appeals meets in a conference to make a decision. The court's **decision** need not be unanimous—a majority vote of the five judges is all that is required to reverse or affirm the trial court (see *The Appellate Courts* section above). This decision is final unless the case is appealed to and accepted by the Supreme Court of the United States, an occurrence which is highly unlikely since the Court rejects more than 98% of the cases filed with them.

Plea Bargaining: The Norm of the Oklahoma Criminal Court Process

While it is important to understand the formal steps of the Oklahoma Criminal Court process discussed above, it is equally important to understand the process of plea bargaining since the vast majority of cases never make it to trial. Generally, prosecutors and defense attorneys strike a plea bargain that allows both sides to resolve the case with some certainty as to what charge, if any, the defendant will be convicted of and what type of penalty will be received. These "deals" may be scrutinized by the trial judge who examines them for appropriateness. The trial judge typically approves the agreements. Plea bargaining involves either **charge bargaining, sentence bargaining,** or a combination of both.

Charge bargaining involves either **charge reduction,** where a prosecutor agrees to reduce a charge to one less serious; **charge deletion,** where a district attorney drops one or more charges against a defendant formally accused of multiple crimes; or a combination of both (Carp & Stidham, 2004). For example, in 1992, while serving a sentence in an Oklahoma state prison, Gary Ray Preston and three co-defendants murdered another inmate. Preston was charged with first-degree murder but pled guilty to a reduced charge of second-degree murder. If he had been convicted of first degree murder, he would have been eligible to be punished by death, but since the charge was reduced to second-degree murder, the worst possible sentence was imprisonment for life. (Preston received an 80 year sentence.) Here, the prosecutor and Preston entered into a charge reduction plea bargain.

Sometimes district attorneys will agree to drop a criminal charge in order to get a conviction on other charges. In 1999, Mississippian James Harold Smith pled guilty to felony counts of kidnapping and assault in exchange for the Woodward County, Oklahoma Assistant District Attorney dropping a maiming charge. Smith had locked up his common-law wife in the sleeper cab of his truck, denied her food and water, and periodically beat and tortured her with a modified cattle prod. Smith received a suspended sentence, a fine, and was ordered to receive mental health treatment (Associated Press, 1999a).

Sentence bargaining occurs when the district attorney promises to request that the judge impose a lighter sentence if the defendant agrees to plead guilty. Usually, a defendant and his or her attorney can count on the fact that a district attorney's sentence recommendation will be followed by the judge. If such sentencing recommendations held no sway, then the plea bargaining system upon which all parties, including judges, rely would break down. In the case of James Harold Smith, it appeared that a sentence bargain was entered into along with a charge deletion bargain. The victim had fled back to Mississippi, was in hiding, and refused to testify against Smith. Facing a very shaky case without the victim's testimony, the prosecution stated "Under [the] circumstances we felt that obtaining the two major felony convictions with the treatment provisions was as good as could reasonably be expected" (Associated Press, 1999a). In other words, faced with the very real possibility of acquittal, the prosecution most likely recommended a suspended sentence as an inducement to obtaining guilty pleas, which amount to convictions, on two of the three felony charges.

The realities of the criminal justice system are that all of the players—district attorneys, defense attorneys, and judges—depend upon a system of plea bargaining. Plea bargaining offers distinct benefits to everyone involved in a criminal case. First of all, going to trial is risky for both sides. As one Oklahoma County District Court judge recounted, "You never know what will happen. Sometimes I preside over cases where I would have bet my house that the jury would have convicted the defendant and did not. And then other cases where I thought the D.A. had a weak case, the jury finds the defendant guilty." So plea bargaining guarantees the prosecution a conviction in the case, while at the same time guaranteeing defendants they will not get the most severe punishment possible. The judge and the district attorney benefit because plea bargaining saves time and allows faster resolution of the case docket. A jury trial can be very lengthy, and judges constantly feel the pressure of an overwhelming caseload, so the more plea bargains that are reached the more efficiently judges can do their jobs. Finally, the victims of crime may prefer to resolve a case through plea bargaining to save them the agony of reliving the experience through a prolonged trial. A victim of rape, for example, may need to testify against the accused and face a humiliating and emotionally painful cross-examination by a defense attorney. Defense attorneys in rape cases often take the "nuts and sluts" tactic of defending their client by portraying the victim as promiscuous and consenting to the sex act, claiming the accuser is mentally unstable, fabricating her story, or both. In summary, since all of the parties often have much to gain from the certainty and expediency of resolving a case through plea bargaining, it is not surprising that the norm of "let's make a deal" predominates the legal culture of the criminal justice system of Oklahoma and the rest of the United States as well.

Despite its prevalence, the practice of plea bargaining has some strong opponents. Some proponents of "victims' rights" decry the practice as one that lets criminals "off the hook" and receive less punishment than is fair. And some concerned with the rights of the accused attack the system as one that pressures those in a vulnerable position to give up their constitutional rights to confront their accusers and be judged by a jury of their peers. Yet some scholars who study plea bargaining view it as a rational and efficient way of resolving cases. They suggest that the outcome is generally fair since the final "deal" reflects the reasoned judgment of professional lawyers who consider the strength of the evidence against the defendant, the defendant's prior criminal record, the likelihood of conviction, and the preferences of the victim (Padgett 1985).

IV. THE OKLAHOMA CIVIL COURT PROCESS

The majority of cases filed in the Oklahoma courts are civil matters. This is typical in other state courts as well, because civil cases encompass a wide spectrum of issues from abandonment to zoning. Yet, civil cases tend not to attract the same attention as criminal cases, probably because the issues involved are often not as dramatic and salacious as those in criminal cases. On the other hand, civil cases sometimes spring from the very same incident that gives rise to a criminal case because the criminal action also violates civil laws designed to protect personal rights. For example, after O.J. Simpson was acquitted for the murders of Nicole Brown Simpson and Ronald Goldman, he was found liable in a civil action against him for "wrongful death." In losing the civil case, Simpson did not face incarceration, a penalty in criminal cases, but was ordered to pay the victims' families millions of dollars to compensate them for the loss of their loved ones.

The following section explains the formal stages of how civil cases move through the Oklahoma courts. While reading, keep in mind that the legal system in our society has a way of filtering out cases early on. In fact, approximately 90% of the civil cases in Oklahoma and the country never make it to a formal trial.

The Formal Stages of the Oklahoma Civil Court Process

In Oklahoma, most civil cases begin when one or more parties involved in a dispute file a petition in a district court. A **petition** is a formal legal statement that briefly sets forth the grounds for the lawsuit and asks for some kind of relief in the form of money, specific performance, etc. The party who files the petition is designated as the plaintiff and must **serve** the petition to the defendant either personally or by certified mail so the defendant has notice of the lawsuit. The defendant files an **answer** to the petition which either: 1) denies the allegations in the petition; 2) offers defenses to the petition; 3) makes counter-claims against the plaintiff; or 4) alleges any combination of the three. At this point the defendant could also file a motion to dismiss the petition alleging the plaintiff failed to state a claim recognized by law. These formal allegations by the parties of their claims and defenses are referred to as **pleadings.**

Imagine that Brittany Notsobright, a student at the University of Oklahoma who wanted to get a base tan for Spring Break, went to a tanning business, "Leatherfaces Unlimited," fell asleep in the tanning bed, and woke up two hours later with first degree burns. Her lawyer, Petty Fogger, files a petition in the district court making these allegations against the company and seeks $3 million in damages for pain and suffering, medical expenses, and compensation for the physical disfigurement Brittany must now endure due to the company's negligence. After being served the petition, Leatherfaces Unlimited files an answer denying some of Brittany's allegations and claiming that Brittany was already burned when she came in to tan, was intoxicated, and set the timer herself so Leatherfaces Unlimited was not responsible for Brittany's misfortune.

If the petition is not dismissed, then the case goes to the discovery phase. During **discovery,** parties try to get useful evidence from each other to use at trial. The purpose of discovery is to allow both sides to get evidence related to the case so the trial can be fair, and one side won't be surprised with evidence at the time of trial. It is also designed to facilitate settlement of the case without a trial. Mechanisms of discovery used by attorneys typically include depositions, interrogatories, requests for production of documents, requests for permission to enter upon property to conduct inspections, requests to admit facts or authenticate documents, requests for an examination of a party by a physician, and subpoenas for witnesses to appear with documents. Some of these discovery tools are self-explanatory, but others require brief explanation.

Depositions involve lawyers from one side questioning the party or witnesses from the other side under oath. The depositions are recorded and transcribed, and copies are given to both sides. In addition to the useful information provided by depositions, attorneys may use them to contradict a witness if he makes contradictory statements during the trial.

Interrogatories are questions given to the opposing side asking for written responses. This is also useful for finding information and discovering documents relevant to the case. And requests for an examination of a party by a physician may be ordered by a court if the physical or mental health of a litigant is at issue (Carp et al., 2004).

In our hypothetical case, there are a number of potential discovery requests. Brittany's lawyer, Petty Fogger, would want a copy of her tanning contract to see if she agreed to assume any risk in tanning or to see whether Leatherfaces Unlimited followed the contract's stated tanning procedures. And Petty Fogger may want to have a tanning bed expert to visit the tanning business to examine the tanning bed in question for defects. Leatherfaces Unlimited may want to depose Brittany to ask her questions such as how much alcohol she consumed before tanning, how much tanning she had done before the incident, whether she really fell asleep or just purposely reset the timer for an extra 90 minutes, etc. And the tanning company may also want their own physician to examine Brittany to see if she really suffered injuries as severe as she claimed. If there are any disagreements between the parties on providing evidence during discovery, it is the responsibility of the district court judge to resolve them.

Because the process of discovery often eliminates the uncertainty over what evidence each side has, most cases are "settled" and some are resolved through "summary judgment." A **settlement** occurs when both parties agree to resolve the dispute in lieu of proceeding to a trial. A **summary judgment** occurs when a judge grants a party's motion to decide the case in his or her favor because no legitimate issues exist which necessitate a trial.

If the parties are unable to reach a settlement and the matter is not resolved through a summary judgment, the case gets scheduled for a pre-trial conference. **A pre-trial conference** is set by the trial court judge to discuss the case with the lawyers and to allow the lawyers to share a list of witnesses and evidence they wish to present at trial. The conference is also used to get both sides to stipulate or agree to certain uncontested facts in order to narrow the focus of the trial to only those issues in dispute. For example, the lawyers for Brittany and Leatherfaces Unlimited may stipulate that Brittany entered the tanning establishment at 2:00 p.m., signed in, and then left at 4:15 p.m., so these facts will not have to be established at the trial. These conferences are also used by many judges to try to persuade the parties to resolve the case before trial. Many district court judges face heavy caseloads and desire to resolve their case dockets efficiently, and the easiest way to do this is to avoid a time-consuming trial.

Sometimes parties in a dispute are unable to negotiate a settlement and opt to take the case to **trial,** which is conducted in a manner similar to the criminal trial mentioned above, yet is guided by different rules of procedure. In a typical civil trial, the judge or jury will decide in favor of a party's claim if it is supported by the "preponderance of the evidence." It is important to note that this standard of proof is much lower than the criminal standard of "beyond a reasonable doubt." To prove a case by a **preponderance of the evidence** one must establish only that it is "more likely than not" that a claim is valid. Criminal cases require a higher standard of proof because conviction often carries with it a unique stigma and severe punishment, such as incarceration. Thus, it is not surprising that in some cases (such as that involving O.J. Simpson discussed above), one is acquitted of criminal charges yet found liable in a civil case stemming from the same incident.

In a civil case decided by a jury, Oklahoma law requires that only three-fourths of the jurors agree in order to render a verdict. If the defendant is found liable by a judge or jury, then a **judgment** is issued. In other words, a remedy must be determined or damages must be assessed in the case. For example, let us assume that Petty Fogger was able to convince a jury that Leatherfaces Unlimited was negligent in allowing Brittany Notsobright to be burned by a defective tanning bed. The jury would then decide the **damages**—the amount of money that must be awarded to Brittany.

Since it lost the case at trial, Leatherfaces Unlimited may now file an appeal which will likely be assigned to the Oklahoma Court of Civil Appeals. Both parties will file briefs arguing their side of the case, and the litigant receiving the majority of the votes from the three-judge panel will win the case. If the Oklahoma Court of Civil Appeals affirms the trial court decision and decides in favor of Brittany Notsobright, Leatherfaces Unlimited can file another appeal with the Supreme Court of Oklahoma through a petition for a writ of certiorari. However, unlike the first appeal which the court must consider, the second appeal is up to the discretion of the nine-member court and is typically not granted. If the Oklahoma high court chooses to "grant cert," they will review the briefs of the parties, the decisions of the lower courts, the trial court transcript, and may hold oral arguments where the attorneys for both parties present their sides of the case. The court then issues an opinion either reversing or affirming the decision of the Court of Civil Appeals (see *The Appellate Courts* section above).

Pre-Trial and Out-of-Court Settlements: The Norm of the Oklahoma Civil Court Process

Typically, only about 3% of all civil cases are "actually disposed of by jury or bench trial verdict" (U.S. Department of Justice, 2004, 2). Civil cases tend to be resolved through **pre-trial** and **out-of-court settlements** for reasons similar to those explaining the prevalence of plea bargains in criminal cases. Namely, parties may feel pressure to settle a case for fear of "losing it all" if they go to trial (Smith, 1999). Resolving cases before trial reduces uncertainty and allows the parties to control the outcome since the matter is removed from consideration by a judge and jury. Furthermore, trial judges in civil cases face the same pressures to process their crowded case dockets. The typical civil case is assigned to an Oklahoma district court judge with a sizable criminal caseload in addition to his or her civil case docket. Thus, trial court judges may take an active role in facilitating settlement of the cases pending before them. In fact, attorneys often complain of judges being "overbearing" during pre-trial negotiations, and may feel "coerced" into accepting settlement offers (Melone & Karnes, 2003, 187). Finally, civil litigation can be very time-consuming and expensive. The average civil suit takes nearly two years from start to finish (U.S. Department of Justice, 2004). And those involved in lawsuits may often pay exorbitant legal fees and endure other costs in the form of psychological stress, lost productivity, and general disruption of their daily lives. Thus, there are several important incentives for litigants to resolve their disputes before taking the costly and uncertain step of going to trial.

Recall the previous example of Cliff Clumsy who sues Wal-Mart for negligence after he slips and falls on a box of super-sized McDonalds french fries, both Cliff Clumsy and Wal-Mart may be better off to settle their case. If Wal-Mart offers to pay Cliff's medical expenses and a reasonable sum for his pain and suffering, they avoid an expensive trial and a potentially large damage award if they lose. And if Cliff accepts the settlement, he will avoid the risk of losing the case, be able to pay his outstanding bills, and maintain his household until he can get back to work. However, saying that both parties may be better off does not imply that the outcome is necessarily fair.

It is often the "big guys" like Wal-Mart who come out ahead in litigation, because being able to withstand the inevitable delays in civil litigation, they are in a superior bargaining position compared to the "little guys" like Cliff Clumsy who cannot afford a lengthy legal battle (see Galanter, 1974). Cliff may feel forced to settle for an amount less than he considers fair because the fall made him unable to work and pay his bills, and he will lose his house and car if he doesn't get money soon. On the other hand, Wal-Mart, a large corporation with "deep pockets," has the ability to keep operating its business without disruption and will not be bothered by any case delays that operate to the detriment of Cliff Clumsy.

V. Judges and Judicial Selection in Oklahoma

Introduction: The Scandal and Resulting Reform

In Oklahoma, a variety of methods are used for selecting judges. Depending on the type of court on which they serve, judges may be chosen through non-partisan elections or by appointment. However, the current multiplicity of selection systems did not always exist. It is the result of a compromise produced from a political cauldron bubbling over from a judicial modernization movement, a major scandal in the highest echelon of the Oklahoma judiciary, and a clash over reform between state lawmakers (Simpson, 2000).

Prior to 1969, most state judges were elected on partisan ballots much in the way that a state representative or governor is chosen. From the office of supreme court justice down to the now defunct office of justice of the peace, Oklahoma judges were elected to terms of two to six years, depending on the type of court on which they served. Elections made judges somewhat accountable to the people, but their inherent partisan and political nature made some question whether the system produced judges who could maintain fairness and impartiality in deciding cases. In the early 1960s a national judicial reform movement took hold in Oklahoma. Prominent public organizations, such as the Oklahoma Bar Association and Oklahoma law schools began to endorse changes such as the "Missouri Plan" of judicial selection, which placed nominations of judges in the hands of a commission (Simpson, 2000).

Ironically, while reformers were pushing for an end to judicial partisan elections in Oklahoma, a shocking scandal erupted in the Supreme Court of Oklahoma. Three justices on the Supreme Court were accused of taking bribes which influenced their decisions in key cases. N.S. Corn, a former justice convicted of income tax evasion, admitted to taking bribes while on the court. Corn also testified that two of his brethren on the court, Justices Earl Welch and Napoleon Bonaparte Johnson, had similarly accepted bribes. Corn's revelations ended the careers of Welch and Johnson. Welch resigned his position to avoid imminent impeachment, while Johnson was impeached and removed from office by the Oklahoma legislature (Lawler & Spurrier, 1991).

This scandal was almost perfectly timed for those seeking changes in the Oklahoma courts, as it fueled the fires of reform into a raging inferno. In 1966, Earl Sneed, a former law school dean from the University of Oklahoma, spearheaded a court reform initiative which was well-received by the press and would appear on a ballot for voter approval in 1968. Leaders in the Oklahoma Legislature were now under enormous pressure to develop their own reform proposal, although many state lawmakers remained adamantly opposed to changing the status quo. In general, rural lawmakers wanted to keep the ability to elect their own local judges, whereas urban lawmakers favored the Missouri Plan which would take away selection decisions from the voters. Eventually, a compromise proposal was reached where the Missouri Plan would be implemented for appellate court selection, and non-partisan elections would operate to choose district court judges. This proposal was presented to voters as an amendment to the state constitution, and passed in the summer of 1967. Beaten to the punch by the Legislature's compromise reform, Sneed's initiative went down in defeat in 1968 (Simpson, 2000).

Selection in the District Courts: Nonpartisan Elections

The judges serving in the district courts of Oklahoma hear all cases arising under state law. There are 71 district judges and 77 associate district judges, and each is chosen through nonpartisan elections for four-year terms. In **nonpartisan elections,** voters choose district judges and associate district judges without the benefit of viewing party labels on the ballot. If a district court judge draws no challenger for his or her office after serving a term, that judge is, in effect, retained for an additional term, and the office is not listed on the ballot. When a district judge or associate district judge position becomes vacant then it is filled by the judicial nominating commission and governor in the same way an appellate judgeship is selected (League of Women Voters of Oklahoma, 1994).

Judicial elections tend to be staid, uneventful, and lacking in substance. Judges are restricted from discussing actual cases and how they would rule on specific issues, so the campaign rhetoric is typically limited to vague claims of candidates possessing "solid experience" or being "a law and order" judge. Voters typically know very little about the candidates, and, since Oklahoma judicial races are nonpartisan, they do not have party cues to guide their voting decisions. Consequently, voters may base their decisions on considerations such as which candidate has a last name that sounds familiar or bespeaks a favorable ethnic background (Baum & Kemper, 1994).

Occasionally, though, judicial races involve feuds and campaign shenanigans just as colorful and "down and dirty" as the scrappiest of nonjudicial races. A case in point is the 1998 Pottawotomie County, Oklahoma race for associate district judge between Paula Sage and John D. Gardner. Campaign fliers were distributed showing Ms. Sage baring her breasts at a Halloween party. The flier claimed Sage would be "a disaster and embarrassment" if elected and listed "10 reasons ranging from allegations of unprofessional behavior to having a temper and a foul mouth." Ms. Sage claimed the woman who took the photo worked for her opponent. "It was just kind of a lark deal. You grab the bottom of your shirt and flash a little bit. Someone grabs a camera and . . . I'm evidently the most unlucky woman in the world." Sage explained further, "I think people are going to see this for what it is, which is extremely, extremely dirty politics." Sage ended up losing the race by 355 votes (Associated Press, 1998).

Judicial candidates may not always follow the letter of the law that limits what they can say on the campaign trail. Oklahoma County District Judge Susan Caswell, a former prosecutor, waged an aggressive and ultimately successful campaign in 1998 by chiding her opponent, touting her experience prosecuting cases involving crimes against children, and vowing to continue to fight for victims if elected. Her campaign literature stated that she believed "justice requires a fair system for all, especially little children who may be too small or unable to speak for themselves." Because of this campaign, Caswell received a great deal of unwanted attention after she took office. Judge Caswell was investigated for ethics violations related to her campaign statements, and in a separate proceeding was ordered by the Oklahoma Court of Criminal Appeals to disqualify herself from a child abuse trial. The court justified its decision stating, "[i]n this case . . . the facts demonstrate Judge Caswell's impartiality might reasonably be questioned." The court elaborated: "Because of the close proximity of the election and the filing of charges in this case and the campaign rhetoric exuded in this election, we understand appellant's concerns about getting a fair trial before this judge" (Associated Press, 2000a).

Selection in the Courts of Limited Jurisdiction

Municipal judges are selected for two-year terms according to the provisions of the charter of a particular city. A common practice is appointment by the mayor subject to approval by the city council or city commission. Workers' compensation court judges are appointed in a fashion similar to the selection of appellate court judges. Three nominees are chosen by the judicial nominating commission, and the governor selects one for a six-year term. However, no retention elections are held. When a term expires, the judicial nominating commission comes up with new nominees, but the governor may also select the incumbent for an additional term.

The court of tax review and the court on the judiciary do not employ their own judges. Judges serving on these courts come from the district courts, the Court of Criminal Appeals, and the Supreme Court of Oklahoma, and are provided "necessary expenses" for their duties. The court of tax review is comprised of district court judges chosen by the Oklahoma Supreme Court. The court on the judiciary is divided into a trial division and an appellate division. The trial division is comprised of eight district judges chosen by the secretary of state, and one attorney chosen by the Oklahoma Bar Association Board of Governors. The appellate division is comprised of five district judges picked by the Secretary of State, two Supreme Court justices chosen by their fellow justices, one Court of Criminal Appeals judge tapped by that court, and one attorney selected by the Oklahoma Bar Association Board of Governors (League of Women Voters of Oklahoma, 1994).

Selecting Judges in the Appellate Courts of Oklahoma

Today, judges in the appellate courts of Oklahoma—the Court of Civil Appeals, the Criminal Court of Appeals, and the Supreme Court—are chosen through an appointive process. Named after the state where it was first adopted, the **Missouri Plan** features a judicial nominating commission, an appointment by the governor, and a retention election for the appointee.

The **Judicial Nominating Commission** is made up of 13 members who serve staggered, six-year terms. Six are attorneys chosen by the Oklahoma Bar Association, six are non-lawyers chosen by the governor, and the thirteenth member is chosen by a vote of the other 12. When a vacancy occurs in one of the appellate courts, the nominating commission interviews applicants and prepares a "short list" of their top three candidates for the open slot. Eligible candidates must be at least 30 years of age and a licensed practicing attorney or judge for at least five years. The list is then forwarded to the governor who chooses one of the three for appointment to the position.

If the successful appointee is in office for at least one year before the next general election, he or she must face a retention election. The **retention election** is nonpartisan in that there is no party label on the ballot, and noncompetitive in that the sitting judge is not running against any other candidates. Voters must decide whether the judge or justice should be retained in office—they mark the ballot either "yes" or "no." If a majority of votes is received, he or she can serve the remainder of the six-year term. Thereafter, judges and justices sit for retention elections every six years if they wish to serve additional terms. There are no term limits for judicial offices in Oklahoma (Lawler & Spurrier, 1991).

If job security is a central concern in one's career choice, one could do much worse than serving as an appellate court judge or justice. To date, no judges or justices in Oklahoma have lost a retention election. Such electoral safety is not an anomaly unique to Oklahoma. A study found that out of 4,588 such elections only 52 judges were unseated—in other words, judges lose retention contests only about 1% of the time (Aspin, 1999). Yet, as the statistics show, justices occasionally do lose retention elections. And often these losses are the result of interest groups and others taking aim at individual judges for political reasons. For example, Tennessee high court justice Penny White lost her first retention contest after the Tennessee Conservative Union, the Republican Party, and Republican Governor Don Sundquist all actively campaigned against her (Carp et al., 2004). Despite the relative safety of Missouri Plan judicial seats, the system still allows for the unseating of judges who would have kept their seat but for being a target of organized political opposition.

The Effects of Selecting Judges through Elective and Missouri Plan Systems

The elective and Missouri Plan systems used to select judges in the Oklahoma district and appellate courts, respectively, each place different emphases on two features: judicial independence and judicial accountability. Both are qualities that are valued by Oklahoma citizens. **Judicial independence** means that judges are insulated from political pressures and have the freedom to apply the law as they see it. **Judicial accountability**, on the other hand, is the principle that judges in a democratic society are responsible to the people through mechanisms that allow popular control. In reality, there is a distinct tension between independence and accountability. One way to view it is as a continuum or "trade off"—the more independence judges are given, the less accountable to the people they become and vice versa. Figure 7–2 shows where the elective and Missouri Plan systems fit on this continuum.

FIGURE 7–2 THE METHODS OF JUDICIAL SELECTION ON THE CONTINUUM OF JUDICIAL INDEPENDENCE AND ACCOUNTABILITY

Independence ←—X————————X————————X—→ Accountability
Lifetime Appointment   Missouri Plan   Partisan Elections

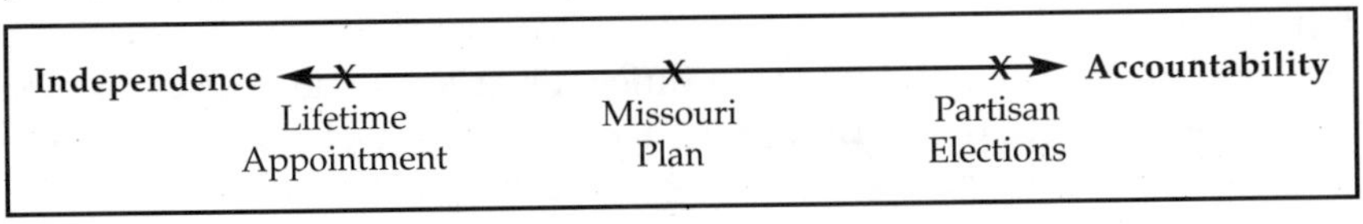

The clearest example of a high independence and low accountability system can be seen in the lifetime appointment of federal judges (and a small number of state judges). These judges can act freely with little fear of political repercussions or losing their jobs since they are rarely removed from office. In fact, in the history of the United States only seven have been impeached and removed from office. The "down side," for example, is that a federal judge can be verbally abusive to litigants and lawyers, have a drinking problem, and ignore clear case precedent in making a decision, all with impunity. Yet, this freedom also allows a federal judge to make decisions he or she strongly believes are morally right without regard to political consequences.

Conversely, the more accountable judges are to the people, the less leeway they have to act according to their own beliefs and the more they have to consider their political environment. This is the case for elected judges. For example, an elected judge might feel pressure to make decisions against his or her conscience, and sense of justice and may favor the prosecution in high profile criminal cases fearing challengers or political groups will attack him or her as "soft on crime" in the next election. But the electoral check on judges also allows for easier removal of those who abuse their power or engage in dubious conduct on the bench. Since judges are important policy makers, many argue that the elective system makes them more representative of and responsive to the values of the community in which they serve.

In between the extremes of the continuum of judicial accountability and independence lie the Missouri Plan judges. Their accountability is relatively low since they routinely win retention elections, yet it is greater than that of federal judges since some Missouri Plan judges, albeit in states other than Oklahoma, have been removed after being targeted by political groups seeking to further their policy goals. These judges enjoy considerable independence since their decision making is not constrained by the prospect of a contested election, yet it is less than that possessed by federal judges who need not fear the political ramifications of their policies.

Which System Is the "Best"—Elective or Missouri Plan?

Academics and politicians alike disagree on the question of which method of selection leads to the most fair and just legal system. As noted before, this debate played out in the Oklahoma legislature decades ago, and the resulting political compromise produced a variety of selection processes in the state. Recently this debate resurfaced when Brad Henry, the current governor who was then a state senator and chairman of the judiciary committee, sponsored bills in 1999 and 2000 to change the selection method of district judges from nonpartisan elections to the Missouri Plan. Henry's bill was precipitated by some nasty election incidents in 1998, such as the improper, bare-fisted campaign rhetoric splashed about in Judge Caswell's successful bid, and the indecent, bare-chested fliers flashed about in Paula Sage's unsuccessful race. While the bill looked promising and enjoyed some support, it faced great opposition and ultimately died after failing in two legislative sessions, because many legislators preferred the local control of elections which the Missouri Plan lacked (Associated Press, 1999b, 2000b).

The current multiplicity of selection systems in Oklahoma bespeaks the difficulty in determining which method is "the best." Like most important questions, there is no simple answer. What is "fair" and "just" is not agreed upon by all. So a worthwhile approach may be to examine the *impact* of the elective and Missouri Plan systems—in other words, what differences result from the two selection methods. Interestingly, when one analyzes both systems, what becomes most evident are their similarities (Baum, 2004).

One striking commonality is the influence of the governor. Even the elective system for the district courts is impacted by the governor because a judicial vacancy is filled in accordance with the Missouri Plan—the governor selects one of the nominating commission's three candidates. After the governor appoints a replacement, that judge is typically successful in winning re-election for as many terms as he or she desires. Considering that a large number of district judge slots are filled in this way, the governor's imprint on the composition of the court can be considerable. Another notable similarity is the characteristics of the judges selected. Proponents of the Missouri Plan often suggest that it produces judges with stronger qualifications than those elected. However, studies refute this and find no significant differences attributable to selection systems in judicial traits such as experience and education (Baum, 2004; Glick & Emmert, 1987; Smith, 1999). This has led scholars to conclude that there is no single system that is clearly superior in recruiting to the bench the best legal talent in the state (Porto, 2001).

So what of decision making? Are there any significant differences between the behavior of elected versus Missouri Plan judges? On this question, there is not a great deal of evidence, but it seems likely that both systems make judges somewhat conscious of public opinion when they decide high profile cases. For example, because voters care greatly about criminal justice issues, and death penalty cases tend to be the most prominent in voters' minds, judges facing retention or competitive elections are probably more likely to approve death sentences than those who do not face election (Baum, 2004).

Although judges facing retention elections have a lower probability of defeat than those running against challengers, they are aware that their seats are not completely safe. They know of the potential for bad publicity and the prospect of organized political opposition if they make unpopular decisions on hot button issues. Nevertheless, it is possible that elected judges, who face greater political pressures, will consider their constituents and political supporters in their decision making to a greater extent than their Missouri Plan counterparts.

Does the Missouri Plan Remove "Politics" from the Selection Process?

The Missouri Plan is often touted as a process that modernizes judicial selection and cleanses it of political considerations. However, judicial scholars who have studied the operation of the Missouri Plan note that such an assertion is naiive (see Watson & Downing, 1969). In theory, the task of the plan's nominating commission is to choose nominees solely on the basis of merit—this is why the Missouri Plan is often referred to as a "merit selection" system. The reality is that the work of the nominating commission tends to be influenced by other considerations such as personal and family ties, partisanship, and political loyalties—especially to the governor. Because the governor typically appoints the non-lawyer commission members, they may often be sympathetic to the governor's selection goals (Baum, 2004). One study found that a number of commissioners surveyed believed their commissions to be "controlled by gubernatorial appointees whose commission membership is a political 'thank-you' and who select whomever the governor wants" (Henschen et al., 1990, 334).

Other studies cite bar association politics at work in the selection of the attorney members to the nominating commission. Researchers found that "[w]hile some attorneys are interested in judgeships personally, and work to get their commission member selected whom they think will favor their candidacies, most are concerned with "policy payoffs," not patronage—that is, they want to get persons on the bench who will be sympathetic, or at least not hostile to their clients' interests" (Watson et al., 1967, 67). The stakes of the policy payoffs tend to pit the corporate attorneys, who favor judicial decisions and policies benefiting businesses, against the plaintiff attorneys, who desire court policies and outcomes favoring individuals (Watson et al., 1967). Interestingly, these same factions tend to clash over the same "policy payoffs" in elective judicial systems.

The politics involved in the Missouri Plan system was also evident to some Oklahoma legislators who opposed Henry's plan to change district judge elections to Missouri Plan selection. Said Representative Opio Toure from Oklahoma City, "the [Missouri Plan] system is essentially a political process and it's closed door." "We need to open it up so we can have a wider pool to select from" (Associated Press, 1999b).

VI. CASES AND POLICY MAKING IN THE OKLAHOMA COURTS

Cases in the Oklahoma Courts

The trial and appellate courts of Oklahoma decide cases spanning a wide range of issue areas from abandonment to zoning. Each year approximately 500,000 new cases are filed in Oklahoma, most of them flowing into the district courts. Criminal cases account for roughly 60% of the filings, however, most of these do not involve events that tend to come to mind when one thinks of a "criminal case." Gruesome murders, brutal beatings, savage rapes, daring bank robberies, and even small-time burglaries make up a small percentage of criminal case filings. The boring reality is that the majority of criminal case filings are simple traffic cases. In fact, traffic cases usually account for more than 1/3 of all the cases filed in Oklahoma (Administrative Office of the Courts, 1994, 1995a, 1999).

This prevalence of traffic cases is not unique to Oklahoma. It is characteristic of the composition of state court dockets throughout the country. Civil matters comprise about 40% of the cases filed in Oklahoma. The greatest number of civil case filings arise from **small claims**—cases that involve claims of less than $4,500. Small claims comprise approximately 40% of the civil case docket and 16% of the entire caseload of Oklahoma courts. **General civil cases**—involving matters such as breach of contract, property rights, personal injury, or civil and privacy rights—typically represent approximately 30% of the civil case docket and 12% of the total caseload of Oklahoma courts (Administrative Office of the Courts, 1994, 1995a, 1999). Table 7–1 presents some summary statistics of cases filed in the Oklahoma Courts.

TABLE 7–1
Summary of District Court Cases Filed July 1, 1993–June 30, 1994

Civil Cases:	
General Civil:	58,030
Domestic Relations:	45,394
Adoptions:	2,196
Probates/Estates	
Distributions/Trusts:	9,277
Mental Health:	6,816
Guardianships/	
Conservatorships:	2,597
Small Claims:	76,450
Criminal Cases:	
Felony (Total):	36,432
Murder I:	182
D.U.I.:	3,566
Other:	32,684
Misdemeanor (Total):	50,134
D.U.I.:	9,444
Other:	40,690
Traffic:	168,811
Juvenile Cases:	11,348
Total Cases:	467,485

SOURCE: State of Oklahoma. The Judiciary. Annual Report, FY-94, Administrative Office of the Courts, 1994.

Policy Making in the Oklahoma Courts of Last Resort

The number of cases decided by the Oklahoma Supreme Court and Court of Criminal Appeals is miniscule compared to that heard by the lower courts, but the policy making power of these high courts is considerable. Through their case decisions these courts create precedents, which the lower courts are legally obligated to follow, in numerous important areas of law. In other words, the Oklahoma courts of last resort have the final word in interpreting and deciding all issues of Oklahoma law. For example, on March 30, 2004, in a unanimous opinion, the Oklahoma Supreme Court upheld the constitutionality of a ban on cockfighting approved by Oklahoma voters several months earlier. Nevertheless, James Tally, president of the Oklahoma Gamefowl Breeders Association, vowed to continue the fight. "This is going all the way to the U.S. Supreme Court," he exclaimed in an interview with the *The Oklahoman* newspaper (The Oklahoman, 2004).

Oklahoma high court decisions which raise federal constitutional issues can be reviewed by the Supreme Court of the United States, but this occurs infrequently. Only about 2% of all state high court decisions are appealed to the Supreme Court of the United States (Glick, 1991, 87), and only a very small fraction of these cases are heard by the Court on the merits (Kagan et al., 1977, 121). Moreover, it seems unlikely the Supreme Court of the United States would consider a state ban on cockfighting to be a legitimate federal constitutional issue, so the prospect of the case receiving cert approval appears dim.

The policy making influence of the Oklahoma courts of last resort is considerable outside of the state as well. Although precedents made by Oklahoma high courts are legally binding only within the state, they can have *persuasive* value outside of Oklahoma. It is common for judges on state supreme courts to borrow or reject the reasoning from decisions of other state high courts when grappling with making and justifying a difficult decision of their own. Especially when addressing legal issues uncharted in his or her state, an appellate judge may seek out solutions provided by the courts of respected sister states. In a study of the reputation of state supreme courts, the Supreme Court of Oklahoma faired relatively well. It ranked 16th among the 50 states in its tendency to have its decisions cited by other high courts (Caldeira, 1983).

Oklahoma high courts have also distinguished themselves nationally and internationally through their progressive and innovative jurisprudence. For example, a study of state judicial innovativeness showed that Oklahoma ranked fifth among the 50 states in adopting new tort law doctrines in the post-war period (Canon & Baum, 1981). And recently, the Oklahoma Court of Criminal Appeals received worldwide attention for a ground-breaking decision in which the high court acknowledged that international treaties and their interpretation by the International Court of Justice (ICJ), the highest court of the United Nations, were binding upon state courts. On May 13th 2004, the Oklahoma high court halted the execution of Osbaldo Torres—a Mexican national who was not informed of his right of access to the Mexican consulate. In reaching their decision the court relied upon a decision of the ICJ which had held that pursuant to the Vienna Convention on Consular Relations (VCCR), a treaty ratified by the United States, German nationals sentenced to death in the United States must be informed of the right of access to their consulate. The Oklahoma high court extended this ruling to the case of Torres, holding that his failure to be notified of the right to access to the Mexican consulate constituted a violation of the VCCR. This case is significant in that the court makes a strong statement, which may be echoed in the future by other state high courts, that international law is enforced in the United States, and it signals to the world community that the United States respects the rights of non-citizens (Leavitt, 2004).

VII. Conclusion

The purpose of this chapter was to provide students of politics an overview of the Oklahoma judiciary by examining its structure, methods of judicial selection, processing of cases, and impact on public policy. Although some of the discussions focused solely on the courts without reference to other political players and institutions, keep in mind that this was a heuristic choice made for the sake of clarity. The courts of Oklahoma do not operate in a political vacuum—they are very much a part of, and affected by, the greater political arena.

This was proven in dramatic fashion when the Oklahoma legislature supported structural reform of the courts in 1967. And it was demonstrated to a lesser extent in 2004 when, amid a storm of controversy, the Oklahoma legislature passed a tort reform bill limiting the amount of monetary damages that can be awarded in product liability, medical malpractice, and other personal injury cases. Yet, the influence of politics on the Oklahoma courts is not limited simply to the ability of outside political forces to impose *institutional* change. The *decisions* of judges and courts are *also* affected by external political considerations as well as internal beliefs and attitudes. The common perception that courts are bastions of objective, rational, and formalistic decision making and unaffected by political factors may be a comforting notion to some, but it is clearly inaccurate. Judges are political actors with distinct policy preferences who pursue self-interested goals. Their decisions are made within a complex and politically charged environment where they are often called upon to interpret broadly written laws and apply them to novel and unforeseen situations. Armed with case precedents proffering various and conflicting policy interpretations (which may be only tangentially related to the specific issue at hand), judges, particularly at the appellate level, enjoy great flexibility in employing these cases as rhetorical tools to justify decisions which are distinctly political. Stumpf (1998) describes the nature of judicial decision making aptly:

> Each and every judicial decision rewards some interest or viewpoint and deprives another. Decisions are thus allocative of society's scarce resources, making them, by definition, political. This is the great paradox of the judicial role (p. 50).

Yet, despite the inevitable wading into political waters to make legal policy, the courts enjoy a high degree of public support. Polls show that the public holds favorable views of American courts (Stumpf, 1998). Oklahoma and other state judges are routinely retained by large margins and receive scant criticism unless they become embroiled in a public scandal or are targeted by outside interest groups. Their popularity and ability to weather controversial decisions are partly due to the "mythology of the court": the persistent notion that judges are different from other politicians and "above politics." The courts are steeped in a culture that is quite adept at perpetuating this myth. Judges are presented as a select group of sages who alone are capable of divining and interpreting the law. They wear majestic black robes, sit in elevated benches, and use a special language unknown to the public. And the "engrained need of the people for assurance, security, stability—a need to know all is well—sustains the myth" (Stumpf, 1998:49).

Not everyone, however, has a sanguine view of the judiciary as objective interpreters of the law. One's views of the courts may be less favorable if they have a stake in a matter and end up on the wrong side of a court's policy decision. As a case in point, after being informed of the unanimous vote of the Supreme Court of Oklahoma to uphold the state's ban on cockfighting, state Senator Frank Shurden exclaimed "I didn't have any doubt. I think they've been prejudiced all along" (The Oklahoman, 2004).

The fact that courts are inherently political institutions, and much like the other branches of government despite their unique culture, should not be a cause for alarm. History has shown that the American judiciary is quite adaptable and responsive to the needs of society. The courts are generally in step with the values and policy preferences of the public, yet on occasion they act courageously against the "tyranny of the majority" and make decisions protecting the rights of disfavored groups.

CHAPTER EIGHT

OKLAHOMA AND THE U.S. SUPREME COURT

Danny M. Adkison

The federal Constitution is perhaps the greatest of human experiments.

Louis D. Brandeis, Associate Justice, U.S. Supreme Court

I. INTRODUCTION

At one time or another, all states, in different capacities, find themselves before the highest court in the United States. Article VI of the nation's Constitution makes that document (along with constitutional federal laws and treaties) the "supreme law of the land." Article III describes the jurisdiction of the Supreme Court and lower federal courts the Congress may create. Some states may find themselves or citizens of their state in federal court due to the presence of a "federal question." States are one of the parties cited in Article III that can be in federal courts even if the issue they raise does not involve a federal question. Furthermore, long ago it was decided that decisions by a state's highest court (civil or criminal) could be appealed to the Supreme Court (if the case raised a federal question or if the state were a party to the dispute).

The state of Oklahoma has been involved in some important, even landmark, decisions issued by the U.S. Supreme Court. In some the state is an actual party in the dispute. In others, residents of Oklahoma have been parties to cases that have had far reaching consequences.

Below are the facts surrounding some of these cases (room does not permit discussing every case). Those cases discussed deal with the Fourteenth Amendment's stipulation that states not deprive citizens of "equal protection of the law," issues pertaining to criminal justice, the notion of fundamental rights, and the constitutional right to "keep and bear arms." As is sometimes the case, some of the cases deal with more than one constitutional issue.

II. EQUAL JUSTICE UNDER LAW

There are four words etched in stone on the front of the U.S. Supreme Court building: Equal Justice Under Law. The Supreme Court did not get

Chapter Eight

its own building until the 1930s, making it one of the newest. Likewise, guaranteeing equality came late to the U.S. Constitution. There was no specific reference to constitutional guarantees of equality until ratification of the Fourteenth Amendment in 1868.

Although Oklahoma would not become a state until 1907, it would play an important role in the development of the legal protection of equality on two different occasions.

In the 1940s it was illegal in Oklahoma for a public university to enroll students of different races. State law also provided for fining any professor in a public university who taught a class containing different races. Finally, any student attending such a class could also be fined.

Like many other states, Oklahoma did provide public education for African-Americans. Langston University, centrally located near the center of the State, was just such a school. In doing this, Oklahoma, like many other states, was merely following the doctrine of **"separate but equal"** which had been the law of the land since 1896.

In 1946 Miss Louise Sipuel, having graduated from Langston University, applied for admission to the University of Oklahoma School of Law. President Cross informed Miss Sipuel that although she was academically qualified, state law prevented the University from admitting her. There was no separate law school for African-Americans, and therefore, Miss Sipuel would have to go elsewhere to earn a law degree.

The NAACP approached Miss Sipuel about initiating a suit against the University of Oklahoma Law School. The NAACP often used the tactic of "test cases" to challenge the constitutionality of state laws. Miss Sipuel agreed to allow the NAACP lawyers to initiate the case. They supplied her with a lawyer—Thurgood Marshall—to assist her in her lawsuit.

Marshall argued before the Oklahoma courts that Miss Sipuel's rights to equal protection of the law, as guaranteed by the Fourteenth Amendment, had been violated. The Oklahoma courts ruled against Miss Sipuel. Marshall appealed her case to the U.S. Supreme Court. The U.S Supreme Court disagreed with the Oklahoma court, ruling that Oklahoma was required to provide Miss Sipuel (and by implication all African-Americans who were qualified) with a legal education as soon as it would provide one for Whites. The Court probably assumed that Oklahoma would respond by admitting Miss Sipuel to the O.U. law School. The Oklahoma Regents, however, came up with a different response.

In the few weeks prior to the beginning of the Spring term, the Regents created the Langston University School of Law to be located at the State Capitol building in Oklahoma City. The school had two Professors and one Dean. Thurgood Marshall.

Viewing Oklahoma's actions as a sham, several other African-Americans enrolled in several different graduate programs at the University of Oklahoma leaving the Regents with the option of either admitting them or denying them admission (time and expense prevented the State from creating many new graduate schools). One of these students was George McLaurin.

Oklahoma University did admit Mr. McLaurin, but it seated him in a janitor's closet (with a view of the blackboard) and assigned him his own table to use in the library and the cafeteria. Neither McLaurin nor Sipuel thought these responses satisfied the requirements of the Fourteenth Amendment, which stipulated that no state was to deny and individual the equal protection of the law. In the end, the U.S. Supreme Court agreed.

It is important to note that both of these cases reinforced the "separate but equal" doctrine. That doctrine would not be successfully challenged until the *Brown v. Board of Education* decision in 1954. Yet, these two Oklahoma cases were very important. They put states on notice that although the doctrine of "separate but equal" endorsed by the Court in *Plessy v. Ferguson* (1896) was still the law of the land, the Court was going to place greater emphasis on the "equal" component of that doctrine. Looked at in this way, these two Oklahoma cases, along with similar cases in other states, indicated that the Court was becoming increasingly dissatisfied with "separate but equal."

* * * * *

In 1971 the U.S. Supreme Court, for the first time in its history, struck down a state law because it treated men and women differently (*Reed v. Reed*). In striking down laws mandating racially segregated public schools the Supreme Court relied on a very tough standard. For a law treating races differently to be upheld the government had to convince the Court that the State was, due to the circumstances involved in the case, compelled to pass such laws. As decades of cases would demonstrate, this standard would result in nearly all laws treating races differently as unconstitutional.

Would the Court use the same standard when judging the constitutionality of laws treating men and women differently? The Court did not give a definitive answer to this question until a 1976 case originating in Oklahoma.

In the mid-1970s, Craig, an Oklahoma State University student, left a party to purchase more beer. When he went to purchase the beer he was told that he had to be 21 years old to purchase the beer; he also learned that state law treated males and females differently concerning purchasing intoxicating 3.2% beer. The minimum age for females to purchase 3.2% beer was 18; males had to be 21. Craig was enrolled in an introductory American government course at the time, and he complained to his instructor about the different ages established in Oklahoma law. His instructor explained the law to him, and sensing that he was very upset, nonchalantly suggested he could always sue if he was that passionate about the issue.

Craig did sue. How could Oklahoma justify treating males and females differently when it came to purchasing 3.2% beer? The lawyers arguing on behalf of Oklahoma's law argued that statistics proved that more males than females were arrested for driving under the influence of alcohol, and that more males than females were injured or killed in automobile accidents. Oklahoma's law was predicated on the assumption that when couples are together, it is more likely the male will be driving; hence the greater age (and by assumption more maturity) desired in males. The lower court agreed with this logic and upheld Oklahoma's law.

Five members of the Supreme Court, however, voted to overturn this decision. They noted that the arrest differences between males and females were slight (2% to 1.8% respectively) and had other shortcomings.

When *Craig v. Boren* was decided in 1976, the Supreme Court had two tests it used when judging the constitutionality of laws treating people differently. It used the rigorous **"strict scrutiny"** test in cases where the law treated ethnic races differently or where a law treating people differently deprived someone of a constitutional right in the process. The "strict scrutiny" test was a very difficult test for any law to pass, since the Court required the government to demonstrate a compelling need for the different treatment. The other test used to judge laws treating people differently was the **"rational basis"** test. Under this test the Court tended to defer to the lawmaker (state legislatures or Congress) as long as there was a rational basis for the law. Most laws would be able to pass such a test.

With *Craig v. Boren* the Court articulated a test that it had begun to form in its 1971 *Reed v. Reed* decision. Some had hoped the Court would use the same test for gender discrimination cases as it was using in race discrimination cases. The Court refused to do so, but neither did the Court leave laws that discriminated on the basis of gender to be judged in the same way that all other laws treating categories of people differently ("rational basis"). Rather, the Court articulated its new test for gender discrimination cases: **"heightened scrutiny."** Under this test, for a law treating males and females differently, the government would have to show that the law furthered important governmental objectives and must be substantially related to the achievement of those objectives.

III. Keep and Bear Arms

The Second Amendment to the U.S. Constitution is one of the briefer amendments. It consists of a single sentence: "A well regulated Militia, being necessary to the security of a free State, the right of the people to keep and bear Arms shall not be infringed."

In spite of its brevity, the Amendment has been subject to a great deal of controversy. Why did the First Congress include this in the 12 amendments it proposed in 1789, 10 of which when ratified would be called the Bill of Rights? What does the amendment actually protect? It is common for pro-gun forces to rely on this Amendment as proof that Americans have a right to purchase guns, and to attack any attempt by the government to regulate the purchase or use of guns.

While the amendment has been passionately debated in recent decades, very few cases dealing with the meaning of the amendment have reached the U.S. Supreme Court. One of the most important cases on this issue started with two individuals in Oklahoma.

In 1934 Congress passed a National Firearms Act. This Act made it illegal for certain types of guns to be transported across state lines except under certain specific conditions. Congress' authority for passing the law was based on the clause in Article I, Section 8 stipulating that Congress can regulate commerce among the states. A few years after this law was passed, Jack Miller and Frank Layton were stopped by Oklahoma authorities as they left Claremore, Oklahoma on their way to Siloam Springs, Arkansas. They had in their possession a double barrel 12-guage Stevens shotgun with a barrel less than 18 inches in length.

Miller and Layton were charged with violating the federal law. Their lawyers made two arguments to the District Court. First, they argued the National Firearms Act was a violation of the Constitution by allowing Congress to regulate matters that should have been regulated by the states. In other words, the federal law violated the police powers of the states. Second, the lawyers argued that the federal law violated the Second Amendment by depriving their clients of their right to "keep and bear arms." The federal District Court was sympathetic to the Second Amendment argument. On direct appeal, the U.S. Supreme Court issued its decision in 1939.

There are two major interpretations as to what the First Congress meant when it proposed the Second Amendment. One is called the **individual right interpretation.** According to this view, the Amendment clearly allows states to have militias, but it also recognizes an individual's constitutional right to own a gun. Another interpretation of the Amendment, the **collective right interpretation,** asserts that it was inserted in the Bill of Rights because states feared the newly created national government would first use its extensive powers to disarm a state's militia and then use its newly authorized standing army to march on the states.

If the individual right interpretation is correct, then the 1934 national firearms act probably would violate the Second Amendment. If, however, the collective right interpretation is the accepted meaning of the Second Amendment, individuals would have to base their argument that they have a right to own a gun on something other than the Amendment.

The Supreme Court, in what has come to be regarded as the definitive interpretation of the Second Amendment, surveyed the history of the writing of the Amendment and concluded that it was designed not to protect each individual's right to own a gun but as a guarantee to states that Congress could not disarm their militias (now referred to as the National Guard).

Neither Mill nor Layton was a member of the National Guard of Arkansas or Oklahoma. Furthermore, a double-barrel sawed-off shotgun would not ordinarily be the type of weapon issued by a state's militia. Therefore, Miller and Layton could not rely on the Second Amendment to challenge the constitutionality of the 1934 National Firearms Act.

Interpreted this way, the Second Amendment recognizes a collective right: the right of the people of a state to establish and arm a militia. It should also be pointed out that by taking this interpretation of the Second Amendment as the correct one, the Supreme Court was not denying that people have an individual right to own a gun. It merely meant that an assertion that individuals do have a right to a gun must rely on some authority other than the Second Amendment. Nor did the decision mean that all guns (except those issued by the state) are illegal. States can, as Oklahoma has, make possession of guns legal. But, if the government were to decide it wanted to strictly regulate possession of guns, the Second Amendment would not, as currently interpreted, stand in the way.

IV. Privacy Rights Issues

Few are surprised today to hear a reference to the right to privacy. Yet, just a few decades ago the U.S. Supreme Court had not specifically recognized the constitutional right to privacy. It did so in a 1965 decision dealing with an individual's right to procreate (*Griswold v. Connecticut*). But the stage was set for this decision by *Skinner v. Oklahoma*, a 1942 case that also raised questions about the state's control over an individual's right to procreate.

In 1935 the Oklahoma Legislature passed into law the Habitual Criminal Sterilization Act. The law sought to address the problem of repeat criminal offenders. Its solution for such "habitual criminals" was to sterilize the repeat offender, preventing him or her from producing offspring. What might have made the state legislature think such a law would be judged constitutional by the U.S. Supreme Court?

The answer to that question can be traced to the Court's 1927 decision of *Buck v. Bell*. In that case the Court relied on eugenics and upheld a Virginia law allowing the sterilization of individuals held in state institutions for the mentally insane (or, in this particular case, the feeble-minded). In upholding the law, Justice Holmes asserted, "Three generations of imbeciles are enough."

Not only was the Court relying on what it thought was the best science of the time, but clearly the Court was also influenced by Social Darwinism, which was the dominant way of thinking in America in the late nineteenth century.

The Supreme Court was given the chance to judge the constitutionality of Oklahoma's Habitual Criminal Sterilization Act when Oklahoma sought to sterilize a man named Skinner following his conviction of three felonies. Skinner was convicted of three crimes: (1) stealing chickens; (2) robbery with a firearm; and, again (3) robbery with a firearm. He was serving time in the penitentiary when Oklahoma initiated proceedings, under the Habitual Criminal Sterilization Act, to force him to undergo a vasectomy. Under that law, all the government had to prove to a jury in order to mandate the surgery was that the operation would not be detrimental to his general health. Having convinced the jury of this, the State ordered the surgery and Skinner appealed to the Supreme Court.

Skinner argued the Habitual Criminal Sterilization Act was unconstitutional for two reasons. First, the law was founded on the faulty notion that criminal behavior could be transmitted genetically (and thus was a violation of the Fourteenth Amendment's due process clause), and second, the law was a violation of the Eighth Amendment's prohibition against cruel and unusual punishment.

Perhaps as an indication of the difficulty the Court was having struggling with the decision in this case, the Court, after noting the arguments made by Skinner, stated, "We pass those points without intimating an opinion on them." The Court had found another reason for ruling that the law was unconstitutional. The Court ruled that since some crimes were included in determining which criminals were "habitual offenders" while others (like embezzlement) weren't, the law was a violation of the Fourteenth Amendment's equal protection clause.

The Court in the Skinner case seemed tempted to rule that procreation was too fundamental a right for the government to be allowed to regulate it. The opening sentence in the decision began, "This case touches a sensitive and important area of human rights." The decision ends by asserting, "We are dealing here with legislation which involves one of the basic civil rights of man."

It would be over 20 years later, however, before a majority of the Court, ruling in *Griswold v. Connecticut* (1965) (striking down a Connecticut law making it illegal to use birth control devices) would explicitly recognize privacy as an unenumerated right protected by the Constitution. The *Skinner* decision was a precursor to that decision and the many privacy rights cases that followed.

V. CRIMINAL JUSTICE

The Fourth Amendment to the Constitution prohibits the government from conducting unreasonable searches and seizures. What makes a search or seizure reasonable?

The Amendment itself provides the answer to this question. First, a search or seizure must be based on **"probable cause."** The Amendment does not define "probable cause," but we know from Court cases that it is greater than a "high suspicion" but less than an "absolute certainty." Second, there must be a warrant issued by a magistrate. Finally, the warrant must provide specificity concerning the place to be searched and the persons or things to be seized.

This much concerning the Fourth Amendment is fairly straightforward. Complexity enters in the execution of this Amendment in particular circumstances. The case law dealing with the subject of this Amendment is vast, due to the fact that there are so many unique situations calling for unique solutions. Because of this, it is very difficult to state a general prin-

Chapter Eight

LEADERSHIP PROFILE

MICHAEL C. TURPEN
Attorney and Counselor at Law

MIKE TURPEN is a partner at Riggs, Abney, Neal, Turpen, Orbison, and Lewis, a prestigious law firm with several offices throughout Oklahoma and one in Denver, Colorado. He graduated with a Bachelor of Science in History and went on to graduate from the University's College of Law in 1974. Among Turpen's many accomplishments, he received the "Oklahoma Bar Association Outstanding Young Lawyers Award." He began teaching law at the Oral Roberts University College of Law and proceeded to teach at the National College of District Attorneys. He served as Police Legal Advisor for Muskogee County, and later became the District Attorney for the same county. Turpen served as the President of the Oklahoma District Attorney Association for a year. Afterwards, he was elected Oklahoma Attorney General where he served from 1982 to 1986. In that capacity, he argued before the U.S. Supreme Court on a death penalty case.

He grew up in north Tulsa where he was mentored by his parents, "Aunt Mildred," and his gym teacher, Mr. Hales. Turpen was a down-to-earth guy who worked as a waiter at Steak-n-Ale. This work experience taught him the significance of service and humility. He was even Santa Claus one year at the local Sears, which helped him to learn about humor and kindness. E.M. Guillory, an older African–American man from Muskogee, is the person Turpen credits for teaching him the most about leadership. Guillory was very creative and told Turpen a story:

"A young child goes to an older man and says, 'Oh wise man, I wrote my name in the sand on the beach, but when the tide came in, my name was washed away. I carved my name in the bark of a tree, but when the tree grew, my name was gone. I chiseled my name in stone on the side of a mountain, but when the wind blew it eroded my name away. Oh wise man, what really matters in this life? Give me a reason for living and dying.' The old wise man replied,

'Inscribe your name in the hearts of your fellow man and you shall live and endure forever and ever and ever.'"

Turpen says, "We leave our name in the hearts of others by how we treat each other, how we help each other, how we respect each other" (2007). The most important leadership trait is to lead by example—with passion and purpose. It is far more important to live it than to just talk about it. Turpen says, "If you catch on fire with enthusiasm and spirit, people will come from miles around just to watch you burn." People do come from miles away to see Turpen's ability to lead others as an authentic charismatic leader. Thousands of other Oklahomans just stay in their living rooms and on Sunday mornings watch Turpen verbally duke it out with his conservative counterpart, Burns Hargis. Both have leveraged their unsuccessful gubernatorial campaigns into perhaps the most successful political commentary show on state politics in the nation, the award-winning *Flashpoint*.

Turpen has become very well known for his time in public office, his political campaigns (who could forget his "It's Turpen Time!" campaign slogan?), his legal accomplishments, and his late blooming career as a colorful television personality.

Tiffany Palmer

---

ciple that summarizes the Court's application of the conditions specified in the Amendment. The Court has created numerous "exceptions" to these conditions. For example, the Court does not require a warrant if the police are engaged in "hot pursuit." Another noted exception is the **"automobile search"** (which would include not just automobiles but any easily moved vehicle). Police may search a vehicle if they have, in their opinion, probable cause to do so, but without having to get a warrant from a neutral magistrate. Police may also search a person subject to valid arrest and seize any evidence in the suspect's immediate surroundings that is in plain view. This can be done without a warrant, and any evidence that might establish the guilt of a suspect can be used in court. Another exception the Court has recognized is the so-called **"stop and frisk"** rule. Under this rule a police officer could, without a warrant and with only a "high suspicion" stop an individual and pat down the outer garment (without reaching inside a pocket) in order to detect any illegal behavior.

While the Court has recognized other exceptions to the conditions specified in the Fourth Amendment, one that played an important role in a case from Oklahoma is the public school environment. Probably the most noted case dealing with the public school exception is the 1985 case of *New Jersey v. T.L.O.* The case determined that the public school environment was unique and thus school officials could conduct warrantless searches as long as the search, under the circumstances, was reasonable.

This exception was extended in *Veronica School District v. Acton* (1995). In *Veronica* the Court upheld suspicionless random searches of students participating in competitive athletics. This too was extended in a 2002 case from Oklahoma.

In 1998 Pottawatomie County in Oklahoma adopted a Student Activities Drug Testing Policy. This policy required all students who participate in competitive extracurricular activities to submit to drug testing. Students participating in such activities as choir, marching band, and the academic team were required to take a drug test and be subject to random testing while participating. Two students at the Tecumseh school (located in Pottawatomie County) sued, challenging the constitutionality of the policy. Lindsay Earls was a member of the choir, marching band, academic team, and honor society. Daniel James participated in academic team. One argument they used against the policy was that there was no drug problem at the Tecumseh school.

Relying on earlier rulings like Veronica, the U.S. District Court upheld the policy, but the Tenth Circuit Court in Denver, Colorado reversed it, indicating that suspicionless searches should not be allowed where there was no evidence of a drug problem. The Supreme Court took the case and ruled in favor of the school policy.

Writing for the Court, Justice Thomas noted that it was already established in law that public schools need not be bound by the Fourth Amendment's requirement for a warrant based on "probable cause." To require this "would interfere with the maintenance of the swift and informal disciplinary procedures that are needed" at public schools. What of the privacy rights of students? The Court noted that when students participate in competitive extracurricular activities they waive some privacy rights. In summary, Thomas explained, "Finally, we find that testing students who participate in extracurricular activities is a reasonably effective means of addressing the School District's legitimate concerns in preventing, deterring, and detecting drug use."

Four of the Court's Justices disagreed with this gradual erosion of student privacy rights. Their view was expressed in a dissent by Justice Ginsburg: "Although special needs inhere in the public school context, those needs are not so expansive or malleable as to render reasonable any program of student drug testing a school district elects to install."

These Justices might agree that the Court had moved a long way from the position it took in *Tinker v. Des Moines Iowa School District* in 1968 when, in upholding the right of students to symbolically protest the Vietnam War by wearing black armbands to school, the Court asserted that students do not shed their constitutional rights at the schoolhouse gate.

CASES CITED

Board of Education of Independent School District No. 92 of Pottawatomie County v. Earls, 536 U.S. ____ (2002).
Brown v. Board of Education, 347 U.S. 483 (1954).
Buck v. Bell, 274 U.S. 200 (1927).
Craig v. Boren, 429 U.S. 190 (1976).
Griswold v. Connecticut, 381 U.S. 479 (1965).
McLaurin v. Oklahoma State Regents, 339 U.S. 637 (1950).
New Jersey v. T.L.O., 469 U.S. 325 (1985).
Plessy v. Ferguson, 163 U.S. 537 (1896).
Reed v. Reed, 404 U.S. 71 (1971).
Skinner v. Oklahoma, 316 U.S. 535 (1942).
Sipuel v. Board of Regents of the University of Oklahoma, 332 U.S. 631 (1948).
Tinker v. Des Moines School District, 393 U.S. 503 (1969).
U.S. v. Miller, 307 U.S. 174 (1939).
Veronica School District v. Acton, 515 U.S. 646 (1995).

RECOMMENDED READINGS

1. Adkison, D.M. & McNair Palmer, L. (2001). *The Oklahoma State Constitution.* Westport, CT: Greenwood Press.
2. Alderman, E. & Kennedy, C. (1991). *In our defense: The Bill of Rights in action.* New York: William Morrow and Company, Inc.
3. Aldrich, G. (1973). *Black heritage of Oklahoma.* Edmond, OK: Thompson Book and Supply Co.
4. Killian, J.H., ed. (1987). *The Constitution of the United States of America: Analysis and Interpretation.* Washington, D.C., U.S. Government Printing Office.
5. Gibson, A.M. (1981). *Oklahoma: A history of five centuries.* Norman, OK: University of Oklahoma Press.

CHAPTER NINE

PARTIES, ELECTIONS, AND POLITICAL PARTICIPATION IN OKLAHOMA

Jan C. Hardt

I'm not a member of any organized political party. I'm a Democrat.

Will Rogers

I. INTRODUCTION

Oklahoma is a hard state to categorize when it comes to politics. At first glance, Oklahoma looks like a Democratic state. The state legislature has been majority Democrat since 1921, most state offices have been held by Democrats, and Democrats have held the edge in voter registration over any other party, including the Republicans. Oklahoma has also had mostly Democratic governors throughout its history. Yet, since 1960 Oklahoma has voted only once at the presidential level for a Democratic candidate—Lyndon Baines Johnson in 1964. Moreover, many of its congressional seats have been held by Republicans. And, if you asked most Oklahomans, except in the Southeast corner of the state, they would probably tell you that there are more Republicans than Democrats in Oklahoma. They would also tell you about some of the more well-known Republicans that have held state office in Oklahoma, including Frank Keating who was governor from 1994 to 2002.

Yet, despite this lack of categorization, Oklahoma has lots of rules that govern both its political parties and its elections. Sometimes, these rules have given Oklahoma national attention. For example, after the chaos of the 2000 presidential election, Oklahoma was one of the few states applauded for its election process; Oklahoma's sophisticated voting system would have eliminated almost all of the problems that happened in Florida. In 2004, Oklahoma again captured national attention during the presidential election. The Oklahoma legislature moved the date of Oklahoma's primary up to the third week of the presidential nomination season, instead of in the middle. Relatively, small Oklahoma became a major player in helping to determine the presidential nominee. Suddenly, all of the major party candidates wanted to visit and spend money in Oklahoma.

At times, though, some of the national attention has not been desired. In that same 2004 presidential election, some national pundits poked fun at Oklahoma because the endorsement of John Edwards (NC) by Barry Switzer, a former college football coach, seemed to be a deciding factor in voting for Edwards. In 1998, Oklahoma attracted national attention, again for the wrong reasons, because there was concern that Oklahomans would vote for a dead candidate whose name appeared on a ballot and could not be removed by state law, and because old nude pictures of a judge candidate showed up during a campaign.

One of the cardinal rules of politics is that political rules are never neutral. Someone always wins when a new rule is established, and of course someone always loses. New rules change how the game is played. That is certainly the case in Oklahoma. This chapter will seek to examine some of these rules and many others that have consequences for how Oklahomans participate in politics.

First, this chapter will examine political parties in Oklahoma and the rules that govern them. Not surprisingly, the rules have kept certain candidates from getting on the ballot, and might have determined the outcome of some races. This is particularly true in state legislative races in Oklahoma after 2004, as one of Oklahoma's new rules, the term limit for state legislators, has now taken effect. This has already brought change to the state legislature in 2004 and 2006, in the form of open seats, very competitive races, and the subsequent turnover in both houses of the legislature. Second, this chapter will examine redistricting. Redistricting after the 2000 census changed many of the rules that govern Oklahoma elections. Oklahoma not only lost one congressional seat, but also saw the shapes and thus the constituencies of its congressional districts, its state House districts, and its state Senate districts, change. This was a process that saw the redistricting map decided in the courts, rather than the state legislature, where it is supposed to be decided. Third, this chapter will examine some of Oklahoma's election rules. Oklahoma is a bit of a puzzle when it comes to election rules. As a state, on certain aspects, it leads the country, such as in voting technology, but in other aspects, it has older rules that many other states have long abandoned. Fourth, no chapter on parties and elections could be complete without looking at voter turnout. No candidate or party can win unless the voters go to the polls. In Oklahoma, voter turnout varies considerably depending upon the geographic region. Finally, this chapter will examine the outcomes. Who has won elections in Oklahoma? Who has lost? Which party seems to be getting more candidates elected to office?

II. Political Parties in Oklahoma

Political parties are regulated by both the federal and state governments. Without party regulation, voters could face hundreds of candidates on any given ballot. In order to regulate political parties, it is necessary to define them. In Oklahoma, a recognized **political party** is a political organization whose candidates' names appeared on the general election ballot in 1974 "and those parties which shall be formed according to law" (Strain, Reherman, and Crozier, 1990). New parties can be formed in Oklahoma after filing a statement of intent, and then filing a petition containing the signatures of registered voters equal to at least 5% of the total vote cast in the last general election for governor or for presidential and vice-presidential elections.

Party Structure and Organization

In the United States, the political parties are organized on three levels: national, state, and local. Although most people believe that the **national party organizations**, such as the Democratic National Committee or the Republican National Committee, have all the power, this is far from the actual case. The national party organizations do hold presidential conventions every four years to select the presidential nominees. The national parties also provide their parties' candidates with services best done at the national level. The national organizations might provide polling information on current issues to their candidates or produce national campaign ads to be run in most districts. The national organizations also create party platforms at their conventions to guide their candidates. Moreover, in a very competitive race the national parties might help their candidates with campaign funds.

Yet, despite these responsibilities, national party organizations in the United States do not have that much power. Most of the major rules and decisions are made by the **state party organizations**. This has led some political scientists to call the national party organizations "loose confederations of state organizations" (Morgan, England, and Humphreys, 1991). Although the national party organizations create policy platforms, no major party has required its members or its candidates to support the platform. Each state party may create its own **platform**, which can be different and sometimes in opposition to that of the national party. Moreover, the states decide who can get on the ballot. For major party candidates this is usually not an issue, but concerns third party and independent candidates who must petition their way onto each ballot.

State parties also determine the type of **party nomination elections**. These elections are used in the United States to determine who will be the nominee for each political party. There are currently two types of party nomination elections. The first is the **direct primary**, where voters go on a specific day and vote for a presidential nominee in a voting booth. About 75% of states used some sort of primary system. Direct primaries can be either open or closed. An **open primary** allows both Democrats and Republicans to vote for either party, and sometimes independents are included. A **closed primary** means that only Democratic registrants can vote for the Democratic nominees, and only Republicans registrants can vote for the Republican nominees. Independents cannot usually vote in a closed primary. Oklahoma has a closed primary. The remaining 25% of the states, including Iowa, typically one of the most important early presidential contests, hold the second type of party nomination election, a **caucus**. Caucus elections usually occur over several states, and usually involve series of meetings amongst the voters supporting each of the candidates. These meetings are designed to create coalitions of voters that winnow the field, and rally support behind just a few candidates. There is typically one final vote at the end of a caucus weekend which reveals the winner.

There sometimes remains an uneasy tension between the national and state party organizations. On the one hand, state parties are not disciplined from deviating from the national platforms. In fact, the state parties contain diverse groups and individuals, making it difficult to write one national platform for the state parties. Each state party has thus developed its own identity. Yet, on the other hand, the state parties are also supposed to be united by one common national party organization. For the most part, the two major parties are separated by their past histories and their different views on certain political issues.

In Oklahoma, each of the two major parties has its own structure and organization as shown in Table 9–1. The Oklahoma Democratic Party

TABLE 9-1
The Democratic and Republican Parties in Oklahoma

	OKLAHOMA DEMOCRATIC PARTY	OKLAHOMA REPUBLICAN PARTY
LEADERS	Chair: Ivan Holmes Vice-Chair: Kitti Asberry	Chair: Gary Jones Vice-Chair: Cheryl Williams
CONVENTION	Elects its officers every two years. Holds a convention every year.	Elects its officers every two years. Holds regular state conventions every year except the gubernatorial election year, or every three out of four years.
MISSION STATEMENT	"To get Democrats elected in Oklahoma."	"To continue moving the state toward a Republican legislature."
STAFF	Two full-time staff members and one part-time staff member. Normally, two interns are hired per semester.	Three full-time staff members and one part-time staff member. Three or four interns during busy periods.
STRUCTURE OF THE PARTY	Democratic National Committee State Executive Board State Party Organization 5 Congressional District Organizations 77 County Organizations 2115 Precinct Organizations	Republican National Committee State Executive Committee Republican State Committee 5 Congressional District Committees 77 County Central Committees 2115 Precinct Organizations

began in the 1880s and as of May 2007 is chaired by Ivan Holmes and its vice-chair is Kitti Asberry. The Democratic Party elects its officers every two years, and holds a convention every year.

The Oklahoma Democratic Party has a simple, but effective, mission statement: "to elect Democrats in Oklahoma." According to its mission statement adopted in April 2003, the party has several beliefs which include: 1) government helping to encourage success to all its citizens; 2) public education as the oldest method to improve the quality of life for all Oklahomans; 3) providing incentives for business and freeing it from needless regulation; 4) supporting the rights of working men and women; and 5) protecting the environment. To help achieve these goals, the Democratic party has two permanent full-time staff, and two part-time staff members. Lisa Pryor serves as the Executive Director. The party also usually hires about two interns per semester.

The Democratic Party has a hierarchical structure. It has an executive board consisting of the state party officers and the leadership of the five congressional district party organizations (chair, co-chair, and secretary). The Democratic Party has seventy-seven county organizations and 2115 precinct organizations each with its own separate chair, co-chair, and secretary. The party includes in its leadership all Democratic state House and Senate members as well as all Democratic officials elected statewide (Oklahoma Democratic Party, 1999).

The Republican Party tended to dominate pre-statehood politics, officially forming as a party on June 12, 1892, in McAlester, Oklahoma. Today, the goal of Oklahoma Republicans is to "continue moving the state toward a Republican legislature" (Oklahoma Republican Party, 1999). To meet this goal, Oklahoma Republicans hold state conventions every year except the gubernatorial election year, or every three out of four years. The convention elects a chair and vice-chair for two-year terms.

As of May 2007, the Chair of Oklahoma Republican Party is Gary Jones and the Vice-chair is Cheryl Williams. Other members of the leadership include a man and woman from each county, county chairs and vice chairs, and several other chairs. As part of its organization, Oklahoma Republicans also include all Republican statewide officials, Republican members of the legislature, Republican members of Congress, and their past party chairs. The Oklahoma Republican Party in 2004 had three full-time members, and one part-time member. It is also not uncommon for the party to have three or four interns at any one time.

Third Parties in Oklahoma

Third parties do exist in Oklahoma. Third parties face several substantial challenges when competing against the two major parties, the Democrats and the Republicans. The first challenge is to get their candidates on the ballot. Unlike the major party candidates who receive an automatic place on the ballot, third parties must collect petition signatures to get on the ballot in Oklahoma. In 1996, the Reform Party could officially be recognized as a

Chapter Nine

LEADERSHIP PROFILE

GARY JONES
Chairman and Executive Director, Oklahoma Republican Party

GARY JONES, born at Fort Sill, Oklahoma, and raised in Lawton, graduated from Lawton Eisenhower High School in 1972 and earned a Bachelor of Business Administration from Cameron University in 1978. Jones is a Certified Public Accountant, farmer and rancher, and he is also involved in commercial real estate.

Jones and his wife of twenty-nine years, Mary Jane, reside on their farm southwest of Cache, Oklahoma. They have two grown children, Kelly and Chris. Kelly is a student, and is married to Brandon Dollarhite, a minister at the First United Methodist Church in Comanche, Oklahoma. Chris manages the family farm. Jones and his wife also have a two and a half-year-old grandson, Blake, whom Grandpa calls "Buck" and a newborn granddaughter, Lauren.

Jones and Mary Jane have attended the First United Methodist Church in Cache for the last twenty-seven years where Jones has been a Sunday School teacher and served on the board of trustees.

Jones has been involved in grassroots Republican politics for years, having served as precinct chairman, Comanche County Vice-Chairman, and Fourth District Republican Chairman. Jones also serves as the Executive Director of the Oklahoma Republican Party in addition to State Chairman. In 1994, Jones was elected Comanche County Commissioner. In 2002, he ran a very competitive race for State Auditor and Inspector but lost by only a couple of percentage points.

---

third party in Oklahoma by getting more than the 49,751 required signatures on a petition seeking ballot recognition. The Reform Party actually collected 49,853 signatures. The U.S. Taxpayers Party also sought ballot recognition in 1996, but their petition was declared insufficient. But in 2002, both the Reform and Libertarian parties were no longer recognized by the state to field their party candidates on the Oklahoma election ballot.

As a consequence, neither party fielded candidates in 2004 and 2006 elections. Thus, it is not surprising that in the 2004 US presidential elections, Oklahoma was the only state in the nation whose voters were limited to just two choices, Democrat and Republican, for president in 2004. Half of the states had at least six names on the ballot, and Colorado had twelve names (see www.oklp.org/obar/issues.html). Thus, voters in forty-nine states had the opportunity to vote for Libertarian nominee Michael Badnarik, and voters in thirty-six states had the opportunity to vote for independent/Reform candidate Ralph Nader on the ballot. Oklahoma voters, however, were not given these choices, despite attempts by Libertarians in Oklahoma to get on the ballot in 2004. The problem for third-party voters came with the ballot access laws. Oklahoma has some of the toughest ballot access laws of any state, which require that party officials file petitions with voter signatures equal to 5% of those voting for governor or president in the last general election. To remain on the ballot, a new party's candidate for governor or president must draw at least 10% of the vote in the next election. Thus, it took a petitioning requirement of 51,781 signatures for a third party to secure full party ballot access, and 37,027 signatures to place a presidential candidate in the 2004 elections.

Despite several failed attempts to pass Oklahoma Ballot Access Reform (OBAR) laws in the state in 2004 and 2005, not much has changed, and in fact it has gotten worse. Because of the daunting odds facing a third party and the belief that the rule is unfair, the Libertarian Party took Oklahoma's ballot-access law to court in March 2007. Unfortunately for the party, the Oklahoma Court of Civil Appeals turned down the party's claim that the state's requirements for gaining recognition for a party are constitutionally restrictive. The Libertarian Party next planned to take its battle to the Oklahoma Supreme Court in late 2007. As of May 2007, the Libertarian Party was unsure whether it would field a candidate in the 2008 presidential election, because of the need to get 48,500 signatures in order to get a presidential candidate on the 2008 election ballot.

Once on the ballot, third parties face a second challenge—getting their voters to the polls. Many voters view a third party vote as a wasted vote, and as a result third parties have to work hard to overcome these impressions. The Reform Party was so worried about its outcome in the 1996 elections that it filed suit in October 1996, alleging that the Election Board and the state of Oklahoma had made some serious errors. The party alleged that the state failed to notify voter registrars of the existence of the Reform Party. Reform party state chairwoman, Dale Welch Barrow of Tulsa, also noted that the Election Board failed to list the Reform Party on voter application forms and failed to post notices at registration sites recognizing the party.

Finally, the third challenge faced by third parties comes on election day—getting enough votes. In Oklahoma, third parties experienced one of their best years ever in 1992, when Ross Perot as an independent was on the presidential ticket. He received 319,878 votes that year, while the

Libertarian party received 4,486 votes. In 1996, however, Ross Perot in conjunction with the Reform Party was only able to get 130,788 votes, while the Libertarian party received 5,505 votes (Oklahoma Department of Libraries, 1997).

Party Competition

Having party competition in a state is important. First, without at least two competitive parties, voters often find themselves without a choice of candidates. In such a state, the minority party may not even field candidates, forcing those voters in the minority party to either not vote, or switch to the other party. Second, competition is the fundamental basis for a democracy. Without competition, voters can effectively lose their right to vote. Third, competitive parties serve a crucial function for the state government as well. Without an opposition party, the majority party can often run unchecked, making policies that perhaps may be unwise. The opposition party, therefore, can often serve as a watchdog for the interests of the people.

At the national level, there definitely has been true party competition at the state legislative level. In 2004, there was only a sixty-two-seat difference between the two parties, out of 7,382 total seats, or less than a 1% margin. Republicans controlled this seat edge so it is not surprising that they also had an advantage in terms of the number of states controlled, with twenty-one states controlled by Republicans, and only seventeen by Democrats. But the parity among the parties can be seen if one does some math. Only thirty-eight states are controlled by the Republicans or the Democrats, and if Nebraska is eliminated because of its non-partisan elections, leaving eleven states where party control is divided. One of those states was Oklahoma in 2004. After the 2006 elections, the trend seemed to shift towards the Democrats. The Democrats seized control in all of the chambers that changed hands outright in 2006; thus, the Democrats now control twenty-three states, while the Republicans only controlled fifteen, and eleven are still split (National Conference of State Legislatures, 2007).

In Oklahoma, both parties do field candidates, yet in the past, the Democratic Party has seemed to dominate. Oklahoma was thus classified as a **Democratic majority** state. Majority party rule is defined as one party winning the governorship at least 40% of the time and both houses of the legislature over 50% of the time. The other seven Democratic majority states include many southeastern states, including Kentucky. Five states in the South, however, are as classified as **Democratic dominant**, meaning that the Democratic Party holds most of the offices and most party registration in the state. Only two states, South Dakota and Utah, are classified as **Republican dominant**; the rest are either classified as **competitive two-party** or **Republican majority** (Morgan, England, and Humphreys, 1991).

Oklahoma's classification does need some explanation. After all, some people could look at the Oklahoma legislature and notice that since statehood, the legislature has been majority Democrat all years except 1920,

1921, 2004, and 2006 making it a state traditionally dominated by Democrats. The question of party competition, however, depends heavily on how party competition is measured. One needs to look at not only the party composition of the state legislature, but also whether a party won the vote for President, the congressional seats, and most state offices.

In looking at the vote for president, the picture is very clear in Oklahoma. Since 1960 Oklahomans have voted Republican for President in every election except 1964, when Oklahomans voted for Lyndon Baines Johnson from Texas. The average presidential vote in Oklahoma from 1960 to 1996 was 55.3% Republican, considerably above the national average of 48.1%. The 2000 and 2004 presidential elections were nationally vigorously contested elections, but not in Oklahoma. In 2000, Republican George W. Bush got 60.3% of the vote in Oklahoma, while Democrat Al Gore received only 38.4% of the vote. In 2004, Bush did even better, winning with 65.6% of the vote in Oklahoma, compared to John Kerry's 34.4%.

With Congressional seats, the picture is a bit more mixed. Traditionally, Oklahoma has had a split delegation with some Democrats and some Republicans. But in 1996, Oklahoma elected its first entirely Republican delegation to the U.S. Congress (Oklahoma Department of Libraries 1997; Wayne, 1997). These results were repeated in 1998 as again Oklahomans elected the same delegation to the U.S. Congress. Yet, in 2000, Democrat Brad Carson won the open seat held by Steve Largent (R) when he decided to run for governor, and he won again in 2002. In the 2004 elections, Brad Carson's Second Congressional district seat became open when he vacated that seat in an unsuccessful bid to capture the US Senate seat. Several candidates competed to take his place, and Dan Boren, a Democrat, emerged as the victor with 65.9% of the vote. In the 2006 elections, four of the five incumbents including Dan Boren decided to run for re-election, so there was only one truly competitive race. That was for the Fifth Congressional district, since Republican Ernest Istook vacated that seat in a failed bid for Governor in 2006. But alas, the Republicans had nothing to worry about; David Hunter, the Democrat, really never had a chance against Mary Fallin, the former Republican Lieutenant Governor, who won with 60.4% of the vote in the solidly Republican district. So as of May 2007, four of the five congressional seats are held by Republicans, and the fifth is held by a Democrat.

With state offices, however, another picture appears. Not only has the state legislature been mostly majority Democrat, but Republicans until just recently have captured few statewide offices. Oklahomans did elect some Republicans, including Tom Daxon as Auditor/Inspector in 1978, Henry Bellmon as Governor in 1986, Robert Anthony and J.C. Watts as Corporation Commissioners in 1988 and 1990, and then Claudette Henry as State Treasurer in 1990. The real change, however, came with the 1994 general elections when Oklahomans not only elected Republicans Frank Keating and Mary Fallin as Governor and Lieutenant Governor, respec-

LEADERSHIP PROFILE

MARY FALLIN
Member of Congress, Fifth District—Oklahoma

MARY FALLIN represents the Fifth District of Oklahoma, which includes most of Oklahoma County and all of Pottawatomie and Seminole Counties. Overwhelmingly elected in November 2006, she is the first woman to represent Oklahoma in Congress since 1920. Fallin currently serves on the Committee on Transportation and Infrastructure and the Committee on Small Business. She also serves on the Executive Committee of the National Republican Congressional Committee, Small Business Chair on the Republican Policy Committee, and Vice Chairman of the Women's Caucus.

Fallin is no newcomer to public service; she first took office in 1990 as a state legislator. During her two terms as a State Representative she was recognized by the American Legislative Exchange Council as Legislator of the Year and named "Guardian of Small Business" by the National Federation of Independent Business.

Fallin became Oklahoma's first woman and first Republican Lieutenant Governor in 1995. As Lieutenant Governor, Fallin served as President of the Senate and on ten boards and commissions that impact the quality of life and business in Oklahoma, including the Tourism and Recreation Commission, State Board of Equalization, Oklahoma Land Commission, and Film Advisory Commission. She pursued an aggressive agenda focusing on economic development, education, healthcare and government reform during her twelve years in office.

Fallin worked to promote economic growth and increase economic opportunities for Oklahomans throughout her three terms as Lieutenant Governor. In the Cabinet-level position of small business advocate during the Keating administration, Fallin championed the cause of small business in Oklahoma by fighting the rising cost of health insurance and excessive government regulation. Fallin was also instrumental in initiating several economic development events including the first-ever Oklahoma Aerospace Summit & Expo, Small Business Day at the Capitol, and Telecommunications

Day at the Capitol. She also hosted the Lieutenant Governor's Invitational Turkey Hunt.

Fallin has also worked hard to keep Oklahoma's children safe and ensure them a bright future. In the wake of the tragic Oklahoma City bombing, she formed a task force to rebuild the childcare center lost in the disaster. Fallin also initiated Project Homesafe, a gun safety program that has distributed more than 80,000 free cable gun locks to Oklahomans.

Many organizations and civic groups have recognized Fallin for her service over the years. She has been honored with numerous awards including "Women in Communication's Woman in the News Award," induction into the "Oklahoma Women's Hall of Fame," "Clarence E. Page Award," induction into the "Oklahoma Aviation Hall of Fame," "1998 Woman of the Year in Government," and "1993 Legislator of the Year."

Fallin comes from a family with strong ties to public service. Her mother and father both served terms as mayor of Tecumseh, where she was raised. A native of Tecumseh and a current resident of Oklahoma City, Fallin is a long-time resident of the Fifth District. She is a graduate of Tecumseh High School and attended Oklahoma Baptist University in Shawnee. Fallin also holds a degree from Oklahoma State University. She and her two children, Christina and Price, make their home in Oklahoma City, where they are active members of Crossings Community Church.

---

tively, but also elected Republicans to be Commissioner of Labor, Insurance Commissioner, Corporation Commissioner, and to the U.S. Senate. For the first time, a majority of statewide offices were now held by Republicans. Yet as of 2004, most of the state offices again are held by Democrats. Democrats not only captured the governor's office in 2002 with the upset of Brad Henry over Republican Steve Largent, but also control every other major state office except Lieutenant Governor and Corporation Commissioner. In 2006, the Republicans also lost the Lieutenant Governor seat when Jari Askins, a Democrat, beat Todd Hiett, a Republican, in a bid to replace Mary Fallin, who ran successfully for the Fifth Congressional district seat. Thus, the Democrats now control all but the Corporation Commissioner seats. The biggest pickup in 2006 was undoubtedly the Lieutenant Governor's seat, because the Oklahoma Senate that year went twenty-four to twenty-four, giving the Lieutenant Governor the deciding vote on all ties.

Despite all of these facts, Oklahoma is still not a true two-party system. [not true] Most measures of party competition focus not only on statewide offices, but also on those for the legislature. Over the years, this is where Oklahoma is truly not competitive, until recently. Prior to the 2004 elections, Oklahomans had a Republican legislature in only two years, 1920 and 1921. In 1996, Oklahoma Republicans held out hope that they might capture the state legislature, but it did not happen. Republicans failed to gain a seat in the state House and only managed to gain two seats in the Senate. In the 1998 elections, the Republicans gained four seats in the House, and the party ratio stayed the same in the Senate. In 2000, Republicans gained eight seats total, winning three open seats held by Democrats, and defeating five incumbent Democrats. In 2002, the Democrats lost two seats, but picked up three for a gain of one seat and then had a fifty-three to forty-eight majority. In the Senate, the Republicans lost one seat and gained three open seats held by Democrats, giving Democrats a twenty-eight to twenty advantage. Yet as of 2004, the combined number of seats for Republicans stood at sixty-eight, their highest number ever, which would seem to bode well for the 2004 elections.

Indeed, it did. Oklahoma Republicans had one of their most victorious moments in Oklahoma history in 2004, capturing the Oklahoma House with fifty-seven seats, with the Democrats having only forty-three seats. Thus, the Republicans now controlled the House for the first time in Oklahoma in over eighty years as the Republicans last held control in 1921–1922. The Republicans, while hopeful, that they could win the Oklahoma Senate, alas only gained two seats, but with twenty-two seats in the Senate, the Republicans now controlled a combined total of seventy-seven seats. In 2006, the Republicans almost reached the ultimate victory, control of both the Oklahoma House and the Senate. But the Republicans were only able to pick up four seats in the Senate, instead of five, creating a twenty-four to twenty-four tie in the Oklahoma Senate. With a Republican in the Lieutenant Governor's seat, the Republicans would have held the advantage in any tie vote, but that office went to Jari Askins, a Democrat, instead of Todd Hiett, the Republican. With these recent gains, perhaps Republicans could improve their ranking in one of the most commonly used measures of party competition, political scientist Austin Ranney's party index. This index looks at four factors: the vote by Democrats for governor, the seats held in the state House, the seats held in the state Senate, and all terms in which Democrats controlled the governorship, Senate, and the House. Using this measure, Oklahoma was classified as a modified, one-party Democratic state, not a competitive two-party state.

III. Redistricting in Oklahoma

One of the major events affecting politics in Oklahoma for the 2002 elections was redistricting. **Redistricting** is the redrawing of both congressional and state legislative district lines to reflect the shifts in populations between states. Because of *Baker v. Carr* and several other Supreme

Court decisions decided in the 1960s, one person equals one vote, and thus, districts must be roughly equal in population. Every ten years the U.S. census measures those changes in population and determines whether a state has gained or lost population relative to other states. According to the 2000 Census, Oklahoma actually gained in population, but lost in population relative to other states. Thus, Oklahoma was destined to lose a seat in Congress in 2002. This meant that all the congressional districts needed to be redrawn to move from six seats to five. Simultaneously, state legislative districts were also being checked for population changes, and some of those districts needed to be redrawn as well. According to the U.S. Constitution, it is the state legislature that is responsible for redrawing these district lines.

Thus, the Oklahoma legislature had two major goals to accomplish after the 2000 Census and before the 2002 elections: drawing the district lines for the congressional districts and drawing the state district lines as well. This was not going to be an easy process because there were numerous players that had a stake in the system and wanted their political interests protected. Besides the 101 incumbent state legislators and six incumbent members of Congress, then Governor Frank Keating, a Republican, the state Democratic and Republican parties, and potential challengers to those incumbents, all wanted to control the outcome. Numerous redistricting plans, several court decisions, and several lawsuits later, Oklahoma did get two redistricting plans, but only after the Oklahoma legislature agreed to turn over the decision to the courts. Oklahoma did avoid some of the embarrassing situations that befell other states in their attempts at redistricting. Just south of the Red River in Texas, Democratic state legislators actually left the state en masse on several occasions so that they could protest the Republican plans, and thus giving Ardmore, Oklahoma, a temporary tourist boost. Yet at the same time, it is probably safe to say that few people are happy with the final Oklahoma redistricting plan. But that is politics!

Even in 2003, several efforts were underway to revisit Oklahoma's congressional district plan. Why all the controversy? Because in redrawing the districts, the Oklahoma legislature had to consider numerous factors: protecting incumbents, dealing with Democratic versus Republican interests, retaining Oklahoma's seniority in Congress, individual election decisions, and rural versus urban power. The old and new congressional districts in Oklahoma look vastly different. The new district map (see Figure 9–1) gives the major metropolitan areas, Tulsa and Oklahoma, basically districts by themselves. Thus, in the Fifth District, where Oklahoma City was represented by Ernest Istook, it used to take him five hours to travel the district from one end to the other, but now it takes his successor, Mary Fallin, ninety minutes. But of the 690,000 people in the redrawn Fifth District, 300,000 are new constituents. The end result of creating two metropolitan districts, though, is that the remaining three districts are now very spread out geographically. For example, the new Second District stretches from Kansas

FIGURE 9-1 2002 OKLAHOMA CONGRESSIONAL DISTRICTS

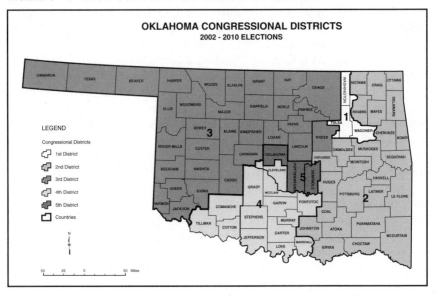

to Texas. Even more spread out is the new Third District which starts with the Panhandle, and then cuts a diagonal swath across most of the northwestern half of the state. That district now encompasses nearly 34,000 square miles and about 48% of Oklahoma's territory.

Moreover, redistricting means that not only did the congressional districts need to change, but the state House and Senate districts changed as well. This meant that many state legislators now faced fairly new districts with new voters, new concerns, and new issues to face. State legislators had to campaign harder than ever to meet their new constituents, while making sure that they did not isolate their old ones. This was not easy for some legislators, and as a result, nine seats, five in the House and four in the Senate, changed parties in 2002.

IV. OKLAHOMA ELECTION RULES

Rules on Election Day

Oklahoma has a number of rules that govern the election process. **Electioneering** is prohibited within 300 feet of a polling place, while intoxicating liquor is prohibited within a half mile. To prevent further undue influence, voters cannot disclose how they vote to any other person within a precinct polling place and ballots cannot be removed or brought into a polling place. In 2006, Oklahoma voters passed State Question 733 which lifted the ban on package stores selling alcoholic beverages on election days while the polls were open.

Oklahoma Ballots

There is one election rule in Oklahoma, however, that is different from other states. While many other states have adopted an **office-column** ballot where a voter votes separately for each office, Oklahoma has a **party-column** ballot. With this type of ballot, it is much easier to vote for a single political party for all candidates because the ballot is organized that way. Oklahoma is the only state in the nation, however, where a voter must mark the party for each office in order to vote a straight-party ticket. For example, in 2004 an Oklahoman voter wanting to vote for all candidates of the same party needed to vote four times—for President, Congress, state offices, and the state legislature. This can make it much more confusing for voters because they have to remember how many times they need to vote for their party. The Oklahoma Election Board has made a special effort to remind voters of this process, through news reports and at the polling booth. Although Oklahoma has a party-column ballot, this ballot rule may influence the outcome of elections, by actually discouraging a straight-party vote. Oklahoma Democrats were convinced that this happened in the 2006 elections in the House District 25 race when initially Democrat Darrell Nemecek beat Todd Thompsen of Ada by two votes. But a recount was conducted shortly after the election, because four votes were thrown out because an incorrect ballot was mistakenly given to four voters for in-person absentee voting. The loser in that recount, Darrell Nemecek, blamed the straight-party voting system, saying that it was confusing to some voters who may have marked straight-party voting for statewide offices, but not for local offices which included the legislative races. Thus, both Senator Kenneth Corn, D-Poteau, and Representative Neil Brannon, D-Arkhoma, said that they would file a bill in the 2007 legislature to eliminate straight-party voting in Oklahoma. A similar measure was passed in the 2003 legislature, but was vetoed by then Governor Frank Keating. The move to eliminate straight-party voting has occurred in other states as well, with only seventeen states having such an option in the 2000 general election.

At the top of an Oklahoma ballot, the traditional symbols for the major parties are also missing. Rather than use a donkey for the Democrats and an elephant for the Republicans, an Oklahoma ballot features a rooster for Democrats, an eagle for Republicans, a statue of liberty for the Libertarians, and for the Reform party, a five-pointed star in 1996. The rooster and eagle symbols were chosen by the first state legislature so they remain today. The legislature believed ballot symbols were necessary because at that time many voters were illiterate. Thus, symbols would make it easier to understand the ballot. In filing their candidacies in Oklahoma, candidates can neither adopt nor assume famous names, or can they take the names of persons in office or publicly declared candidates for office, under election law. Candidates are also not allowed to place titles or prefixes before or after their names on the ballot. Such titles as Mr., Mrs.,

Miss, Dr., Rev., Prof., Judge, Sen., Col., or Sgt., are not allowed on the ballot (Strain, Reherman, and Crozier, 1990).

Voter Registration

In order to vote in Oklahoma, one must register with a political party or as an independent. According to registration figures available from the Oklahoma Election Board, the percentage of Democrat registrants has decreased, while the percentages of Republican and independent registrants have increased. As of January 15, 2007, 1,045,490 (50.4%) of voters were registered as Democrats, compared to 1,022,442 (59.0%) in 2004. The Republicans, meanwhile, increased from 720,121 (34.9%) voters in 2004 to 805,607 (38.8%) in 2006 (Oklahoma Election Board, 2004 and 2006). In looking at the independents, however, it is much harder to calculate the numbers of independents. This is because several third parties, most notably the Reform and Libertarian parties, lost their officially recognized status with the state in 2004, and thus by state law, any voter that registers with an unrecognized party by the state is automatically recorded as an independent. But the 2004 registration figures (as of January 15) showed twenty-five voters registered with the Reform Party, 455 voters as Libertarians, and 195,334 as independents (Oklahoma State Election Board, 2004).ABt Oklahoma had 224,464 (10.8%) independents as of January 15, 2007.

In looking at Oklahoman registration, since 1960 every year more Oklahomans have registered as Democrats than as Republicans. Given the higher percentage of Democrats, it is not surprising that a large percentage of counties are majority Democrat as well. But here there has been a major change since January 2004. In January 2004, only eight of Oklahoma's seventy-seven counties were majority Republican. These eight Republican counties were mostly in the Northwestern part of the state, with the exception of Tulsa and Washington counties in the Northeast. Counties in the Southeast were particularly Democratic, with Choctaw, McCurtain, and Pushmataha having less than 6% Republican registered voters. But as of January 15, 2007, there has been a remarkable change. Following the percentage increase in Republican registration, there are now twenty-one counties, or 27.3% which are majority Republican, including more counties such as Logan, Noble, Oklahoma, Canadian, Kingfisher, Cleveland, etc. which are located in the center of the state.

The 38.8% total for Republicans in January 2007 represented the largest percentage ever for the Republican Party in Oklahoma. The Republican Party has also has experienced the most increase in new registrants, receiving 45% of all new registrants from January to June 1996, with the Democrats signing up only 30% (Money, 1996). Thus, in the surge of registration that occurred in the eight days prior to the 2004 elections, it is not surprising that many of those new voters were Republican. During that time period, 77,859 Oklahomans registered to vote or 41% more than during that time period in 2000. Of those new voters, 39,393 were Republicans or 50.6%, while only 25,506 were Democrats, or 32.8% (Greiner,

2004). The largest change in Oklahoman voter registration since 1960 came in 1981. From 1960 to 1980, only 20.2% of voters were registered Republicans, but from 1981 to 1997 there were 30.9% registered Republicans (Oklahoma Department of Libraries, 1997). Most suggest that this increase is due to the influence of former President Ronald Reagan (Morgan, England, and Humphreys, 1991). Thus, while most of Oklahoma is generally registered Democrat, Republicans are experiencing increases, particularly in some Northern and even central counties.

Voter registration can be done at tag agencies or in local government offices. Oklahoma also allows registration by mail for all voters. The closing date for registration before an election in 2004 was twenty-four days. One must be a resident of the county where one is registered to vote for at least thirty days. Moreover, Oklahoma is one of just thirteen states to allow **unrestricted absentee voting**. Oklahoma registered voters can vote by absentee ballot for any reason and without notarization. Oklahoma is also one of seven states to offer **walk-in early voting**. First used by Texas in the 1988 presidential election, early voting allows voters the chance to vote in person at their county clerk's office or a satellite office usually twenty to forty days before Election Day. Oklahoma is only one of six states to offer both of these forms of voting, which together tend to encourage voter turnout.[1]

The National Voter Registration Act was implemented in Oklahoma in 1995. More commonly known as **motor voter**, this law allows voters to register by mail at any tag office, welfare office or disability office, with the burden placed on the voter to give the correct information. During its first eighteen months, the law resulted in a record registration of twenty million people, or nearly a million per month (Wayne, 1997). A news station in Tulsa, Oklahoma, sought to show in 1996 that motor voter's failure to request identification when registering to vote could lead to voter fraud. The news station successfully registered several animals to vote, including those with such names as Rover and Muffy. Unfortunately for the station, it faced some legal problems as a result of this investigation for a short period of time. It is illegal to misrepresent a voter when registering to vote. To guard against voter fraud, several US Attorneys in Oklahoma created special election boards in 1996 to monitor election fraud in both the Tulsa and Muskogee areas.[2]

Like most states, Oklahoma does **purge** its voter registration records to remove voters who have either died or moved away from their county. Purging records can also substantially reduce voting fraud (Wayne, 1997). Traditionally, the Oklahoma Election Board, which governs elections in Oklahoma, has removed nonvoting voters after a four-year time period, but in 1994, the Board purged the rolls of voters after purging in 1992. These two purges sharply reduced the number of registered voters in Oklahoma from 2.3 million in 1992 to about 1.98 million in 1996.

In its January 2004 presidential primary, Oklahoma also implemented a federal law, **the Help America Vote Act**, for the first time. This law requires that voters show identification the first time they vote in a federal election. Without an acceptable form of identification, voters have to sign an affidavit, and their votes are considered provisional, meaning that their votes are not counted until election officials can verify the information on the affidavit.

Party Nominations

The political parties each election year select candidates to represent that party for each office. These are called **nomination elections**. The type of election is determined by the political parties in the fifty states. Prior to the 1890s, most nomination decisions were made by party elites. Political parties typically used conventions open only to elites to select candidates for the major offices, with almost all recommendations for the nominations coming from the elites as well. The 1890s, however, saw the rise of the **Progressive Movement**. Many believed that politics had become too corrupt. Not only did the political process seem to ignore the masses of people who were not party elites, but there was massive political corruption as well. Dead people voted, ballot boxes were stuffed, and alcohol from nearby pubs was often used as a bribery tool for votes. Much of the power in this system rested with urban political party machines that doled out jobs and other services in exchange for party loyalty, otherwise known as **patronage**.

The Progressive Movement sought to give power to the masses by taking the power away from the political party machines. First, the movement encouraged the adoption of the Australian ballot. The **Australian ballot** is a secret ballot that is not color coded or otherwise marked to reveal candidate preferences. Second, the movement strongly recommended that many government employees be hired on the basis of merit and not party loyalty. The end result was that many states, including Oklahoma, began to add a **merit-based system** for selecting government employees. Finally, the Progressive Movement urged the adoption of a **primary election** in all states. A primary election allows the voters to select the candidates for the party nominations directly through a ballot. From 1902 to 1955, the existing forty-eight states all adopted some sort of primary election.

There are four types of primaries today. Thirty-nine states including Oklahoma have a **closed primary**. A closed primary specifies that only those who registered to vote in the party can vote in that party's primary election. With this type of primary, a candidate is more likely to be acceptable to the party, because only those registered with the party can vote for that candidate. In five of these states, the political parties can call a convention instead of holding a primary. The second type of primary is an **open primary**. Eight states have an open primary where voters can vote for candidates of either party, regardless of how they are registered. In these states, voters typically do not register with a particular party. Those supporting an open primary suggest that the eventual winners of these primaries are more likely to appeal to all the people, whether Democrat,

Republican, or independent, because voters can vote for all candidates. Two states, Alabama and Washington, have a **blanket primary**. With this type of primary, voters can choose office by office the party in which they will cast their vote. The only restriction is that they can only cast one ballot per office. Only the state of Louisiana has a **single primary** system. Louisiana voters can vote for candidates of both parties on the same ballot during the primary. Instead of holding general elections, Louisiana then holds a runoff between the top two candidates for an office.

How Oklahoma Conducts Its Primary Elections

Oklahoma's primary elections are relatively late compared to most states. Rather than in April or June of each election year, the Oklahoma Republican and Democratic parties hold their primaries on the fourth Tuesday in August in each even numbered year, including presidential election years. Primary runoff elections also exist in Oklahoma. If either candidate fails to receive a majority of the votes, a runoff election will take place. The runoff election is held between the top two candidates in the primary election. Primary runoff elections usually occur in states in which the voters are predominantly of one party (Strain, Reherman, and Crozier, 1990). These two rules often make it difficult for challengers to compete against incumbents. With a late primary and a potential runoff, as well as a general election, this usually means that candidates have to compete in either two or three elections in the short time span between August and the first week in November. This makes it easier for candidates who have substantial campaign funds and built-in name recognition to win their races, because there is not a lot of time to campaign. Thus, incumbents typically have the advantage.

A recent change in Oklahoma statutes authorizes the two parties to allow independents to vote in primary elections, but neither party has done so. Hence, most people register with one of the two major parties. In 2007, Oklahoma's polling hours were from 7:00 a.m. to 7:00 p.m. All citizens of Oklahoma, who are citizens of the United States, aged eighteen or over are eligible to vote, with only a few exceptions. The Oklahoma Constitution declares ineligible citizens who have been judged guilty of felonies (until their sentences are expired), persons in prisons, and persons committed to mental institutions or who are patients in institutions for the mentally retarded. Persons in the military services do not satisfy residence requirements merely because they are stationed in Oklahoma. Nor do they lose their residency in this state because they are located elsewhere in the line of duty (Strain, Reherman, and Crozier, 1990).

Oklahoma Presidential Elections

Presidential elections essentially consist of three stages: 1) the presidential nomination season, which runs typically from February to June of a presidential election year, although the candidates usually start campaigning in states much earlier, 2) the national party conventions typically held during the summer, and 3) the general election season, which usually starts after the conventions are over and runs until the election in November.

The first stage is the presidential nomination season in which each state holds an election from February to June of a presidential election year so that its parties can select their nominees. Oklahoma adopted a **presidential preference primary** as its preferred form of election in 1986 and such a primary was held for the first time in March of 1988. Each vote for a candidate on the primary ballot actually represents a slate of delegates committed to vote for that candidate at the presidential convention. The political parties in each state can decide whether their presidential primary contests will use winner-take-all or proportional representation. Most Republican state party organizations, including Oklahoma, have chosen **winner-take-all**, meaning that the winner of each presidential primary receives all of the delegates to the convention for that state. Most Democratic party organizations have chosen **proportional representation**, meaning that candidates who do not win the primaries can still receive some representation at the convention depending on how well they do in that primary. In Oklahoma, Democratic presidential candidates who receive 15% or more of the vote are entitled to receive delegates, thus using a proportional representation system.

As stated previously, Oklahoma's 2004 presidential primaries were earlier than usual, conducted on February 3, 2004, rather than in March. This meant that the primary was held during the third week of primaries and caucuses, making Oklahoma one of the very first states. As a result, the presidential candidates paid more attention to Oklahoma visiting the state numerous times, running numerous campaign ads on television, sending direct mail to Oklahoma voters, and holding several political rallies and debates the week before Oklahoma's primary. General Wesley Clark won the Democratic primary in Oklahoma with Senator John Edwards, and Senator John Kerry coming in second and third, respectively. President George W. Bush easily won the Republican primary in Oklahoma.

The second stage of a presidential election is the convention season. The Oklahoma Democratic Party sent forty-seven delegates, including seven unpledged delegates, to its July 2004 **national convention** in Boston, Massachusetts, who voted for John Kerry as their chosen Democratic nominee. The Oklahoma Republican Party, on the other hand, sent forty-one delegates to its August 2004 national convention in New York, and used winner-take-all as its method. Of the forty-one delegates, fifteen were "allocated on a winner-take-all basis to the candidate who receives the most votes district-wide in the primary." The twenty-six at-large delegates were "awarded on a winner-take-all basis to the candidate who receives the most votes statewide in the primary" (www.rnc.org—"delegate selection rules by state," February 10, 2004). In Oklahoma, since George W. Bush was easily the winner in all congressional districts as well as statewide, he received all forty-one of the delegates to the Republican National Convention in 2004.

The third stage, the **general election**, is much less straightforward. In the United States, voters essentially cast two votes in November—a popular vote for president and the selection of **electors** to represent Oklahoma at the **electoral college**. The framers of the U.S. Constitution did not trust the masses in voting for President and Vice-President of the United States. They thus created the Electoral College as an institution where party elites, or electors, could choose the president and vice-president based mainly on the wishes of the masses. The winner of the popular vote of the state receives all the electors for that state, with those electors committed to vote for that candidate at the Electoral College. The electors are selected by the state delegate conventions of the political parties in Oklahoma. It is a misdemeanor in Oklahoma for a presidential elector to vote for someone other than the candidate he/she nominally represents. All electors in Oklahoma must sign an oath at least ninety days before the presidential election. The state of Oklahoma has seven electors after redistricting with the 2000 census. The number of electors is equal to the number of Senators and members of the House of Representatives who represent Oklahoma in the U.S. Congress. Oklahoma electors meet in the State Capitol in Oklahoma City, on the first Monday after the second Wednesday in December following the general presidential election (Strain, Reherman, and Crozier, 1990). In 2004, Oklahoma voters cast their ballots for their favored presidential candidate. With no surprise, George W. Bush won easily with 65.6% of the votes in Oklahoma, while John Kerry only won 34.4% of the votes.

V. Political Participation in Oklahoma

Because of populist attitudes in Oklahoma, political participation for Oklahomans goes far beyond just turning out to vote. The strong populist tradition in Oklahoma suggests that citizens should have more control over the political affairs in Oklahoma. In Oklahoma, this can be seen through turnout rates higher than the national average.

Voting Turnout in Oklahoma

One of the measures of political participation is **voting turnout**. It is measured by the percentage of voters that are age-eligible to vote that actually turnout at the polls. Voting turnout in Oklahoma has been just slightly higher than the national average with 57.5% for the ten presidential elections between 1960 and 1996. The national average for that same time period was 55.3%. In 1996, Oklahoma had a very high turnout rate, 63%. The highest presidential year turnout in Oklahoma was in 1960 with 89% when a highly competitive presidential race between John Kennedy and Richard Nixon encouraged voters to vote. In 2000, despite the closeness of presidential election between George W. Bush and Al Gore, Oklahoma's turnout rate was only 55.3%, although this was still higher than the national turnout rate of 51.2%. In 2004, Oklahomans set a voting record when 1,463,875 voters cast ballots, the most voters ever. Turnout in nonpresidential election years, however, tends to be substantially lower than in presidential election years. Oklahoma had a turnout rate of only 38.7% in 1990, 41.8% in 1994, and 46% in 1998. (Council of State Governments, 1996, for the 1990 and 1994 elections; Oklahoma State Election Board for the 1998 election). In 2002, voter turnout was 38.4%. (www.fairvote.org). In 2004, Oklahoma had a turnout rate of 45%, which was higher than the national average of 39% and also meant that about 110,000 more Oklahomans voted than in 2002, the last gubernatorial election (Greiner, 2006).

Voting turnout varies substantially by geographic region in Oklahoma. The northeastern part of the state (North of Interstate 40 and east of Interstate 35) tends to have the highest voter turnout, while Southern Oklahoma tends to have the lowest voter turnout. This is particularly true in the southeastern section of Oklahoma known as "Little Dixie." This geographic area closely resembles the South in terms of its voting patterns, with less voter participation and more support for Democratic candidates. This area also tends to be the poorest and least educated part of the state. Most studies of voter turnout, whether at the national or state level, show that the most important determinant of voter turnout is education (Jewell and Olson, 1982). Those voters with a high school education are much more likely to turnout to vote. Education and income usually are strongly correlated, and as a result, the southeastern part of the state has the lowest voter turnout. There is also a strong tradition of paternalism and elite domination in the Southeast, which also explains the voter turnout (Morgan, England, and Humphreys, 1991). On the other hand, the northeastern part of the state has some of the highest levels of education, with wealthier voters and more Republicans. All of these factors encourage the higher voter turnout found in that region.

One of the issues that may affect voter turnout in Oklahoma is the number of uncontested seats. During the 2004 elections, nearly 80% of the nation's 7,382 seats were up for re-election, but about a third of them went uncontested. Oklahoma was one of those states that had a high number of uncontested seats with 53 (52.4%) seats of the 101 House seats unopposed in 2004, which compares with 37.6% of state legislative seats nationally (www.okies.info/reasons.html). But in 2006, there were fewer uncontested seats, with five Senate races and forty House seats uncontested. Still, with the eventual election result of twenty-four to twenty-four in the Senate, perhaps if some those seats had been contested there might have been a change in one of those seats. Uncontested seats should be viewed with mixed emotions. They could be seen as a sign of voter satisfaction with the current crop of candidates, but they could also be the result of voter apathy or the lack of party competition. Either way, uncontested seats can depress voter turnout because there are fewer candidates on the ballot, and thus fewer reasons for voters to vote.

VI. Recent Election in Oklahoma

Presidential Elections in Oklahoma

Unlike 1996 and 2000, when candidates barely visited the state, Oklahoma in 2004 became one of the presidential candidates' prime destinations because of the early February primary. Senator Edwards, for example, made fourteen separate visits to Oklahoma. A major debate was held in October in Stillwater, Oklahoma, and several candidates debated healthcare just a few days before the Oklahoma primary in Edmond, Oklahoma. The weekend before the primary saw a flurry of campaign ads, including one thirty-minute spot by General Wesley Clark, and numerous campaign rallies daily by the candidates. The eventual winner was Clark (AR) who ended up spending the most of any the candidates on campaign ads and mail circulars. Senator John Edwards (NC) who received an endorsement from former University of Oklahoma football coach Barry Switzer came in second, while Senator John Kerry (MA), the winner of the Iowa and New Hampshire elections came in third. Democratic voter turnout for the race, the only one on the ballot, was 29%, while Republicans had only 9% with George W. Bush easily defeating a Los Angeles T-shirt maker to win Oklahoma's Republican delegates. In the 2000 General Election, George W. Bush easily defeated John Kerry, the eventual Democratic nominee in Oklahoma, taking 65.6% of the vote.

With several states moving up their presidential primary dates in 2008, most notably California, the 2008 presidential election race started fast, with about twenty candidates declaring early, roughly split between the two parties. Notable early candidates included Hillary Clinton, Rudolph Giuliani, Barack Obama, John McCain, Fred Thompson, Mitt Romney, and John Edwards. Several candidates visited the state in early 2007, including Rudy Giuliani, John Edwards, Barack Obama, and Bill Richardson, all before May 2007. Thus, Oklahoma seems to be having not only more presidential candidates visit the state, but they also seem to be visiting earlier than usual. This is not a surprise given the early primary dates of California, Oklahoma, and many other states for the 2008 presidential elections.

Congressional and State Elections

The last twelve years (1994–2006) has not been a good one for the Democrats, but has been good for Republicans as shown in Table 9–2. Although Oklahoma has voted for Republican presidential candidates since 1960, it usually was considered a Democratic state because most of its state offices, including a majority of the legislature, were held by Democrats. Yet in 1994, Oklahoma experienced the electoral equivalent of a tornado. For the first time, Oklahomans voted in Republicans for a majority of the state offices, including Governor Frank Keating and Lieutenant Governor Mary Fallin. The 1996 and 1998 elections brought more changes. After the 1996 elections, for the first time in Oklahoma history its congressional

Chapter Nine

TABLE 9-2
Changes in Oklahoma Congressional and State Seats

	1998 ELECTIONS	2000 ELECTIONS	2002 ELECTIONS	2004 ELECTIONS	2006 ELECTIONS
1ST SEAT IN CONGRESS	Steve Largent (R)	Steve Largent (R)	John Sullivan (R)	John Sullivan (R)	John Sullivan (R)
2ND SEAT IN CONGRESS	Tom Coburn (R)	Brad Carson (D)	Brad Carson (D)	Dan Boren (D)	Dan Boren (D)
3RD SEAT IN CONGRESS	Wes Watkins (R)	Wes Watkins (R)	Frank D. Lucas (R)	Frank D. Lucas (R)	Frank D. Lucas (R)
4TH SEAT IN CONGRESS	J. C. Watts (R)	J. C. Watts (R)	Tom Cole (R)	Tom Cole (R)	Tom Cole (R)
5TH SEAT IN CONGRESS	Ernest Istook (R)	Ernest Istook (R)	Ernest Istook (R)	Ernest Istook (R)	Mary Fallin (R)
6TH SEAT IN CONGRESS	Frank Lucas (R)	Frank Lucas (R)	Lost to redistricting	Lost to redistricting	Lost to redistricting
OKLAHOMA SENATOR	Don Nickles (R)			Tom Coburn (R)	
OKLAHOMA SENATOR			James Inhofe (R)		
GOVERNOR	Frank Keating (R)		Brad Henry (D)		Brad Henry (D)
LIEUTENANT GOVERNOR	Mary Fallin (R)		Mary Fallin (R)		Jari Askins (D)
CORPORATION COMMISSION CHAIR			Jeff Cloud (R)		
CORPORATION COMMISSION COMMISSIONER		Bob Anthony (R)			Bob Anthony (R)
CORPORATION COMMISSION VICE-CHAIR	Denise Bose (R)			Denise Bose (R)	
STATE TREASURER	Robert Butkin (D)		Robert Butkin (D)		Scott Meacham (D)
SUPT. OF PUBLIC INSTRUCTION	Sandy Garrett (D)		Sandy Garrett (D)		Sandy Garrett (D)
COMMISSIONER OF LABOR	Brenda Reneau (R)		Lloyd L. Fields (D)		Lloyd L. Fields (D)
ATTORNEY GENERAL	Drew Edmondson (D)		Drew Edmondson (D)		Drew Edmondson (D)
INSURANCE COMMISSIONER	Carroll Fisher (D)		Carroll Fisher (D)		Kim Holland (D)
STATE AUDITOR AND INSPECTOR	Clifton H. Scott (D)		Jeff A. McMahan (D)		Jeff A. McMahan (D)
TOTAL SEATS HELD BY EACH POLITICAL PARTY	5 seats Democrat 14 seats Republican	6 seats Democrat 13 seats Republican	8 seats Democrat 10 seats Republican	8 seats Democrat 10 seats Republican	9 seats Democrat 9 seats Republican

NOTE: A blank space indicates the seat was not up for re-election that year. The officeholder thus remains the same as the previous year.

delegation was represented entirely by Republicans. In 1998, the Democrats lost four seats in the State House, raising the hopes of Republicans that they could capture the House in 2000. Alas, that did not happen. In fact, while Republicans celebrated as George W. Bush won the most competitive race in presidential election history, Democrats cheered because they picked up another prize—the Second district seat in the U.S. Congress won by Brad Carson. Yet Republicans did console themselves with their gains in the state legislature. They won three open seats formerly held by Democrats and defeated five incumbent Democrats, making Republicans just five seats short of the Democrats' fifty-three-seat majority in the legislature.

The 2002 elections brought some political turmoil to Oklahoma in more ways than one. First, Oklahoma's gubernatorial election was a surprise to most political experts. Former Representative Steve Largent had resigned his House seat to campaign for governor and spent $3.18 million, more than any of his competitors, and was viewed as the clear frontrunner for most of the race. But then came independent Gary Richardson who ended up spending $2.63 million on the race, mostly from his own funds. That money bought campaign ads which Richardson aired on television at least one year before the race, and before most of his competitors. On the Democratic side, there appeared to be more disarray at first than a strong challenger. Brad Henry, although a state legislator was relatively unknown throughout the state and faced well-financed businessman Vince Orza in the primary that was close enough to need a runoff election. But Henry won the runoff election, and was able to use that momentum to carry him to the governor's office. Henry ended up spending the least of the three major competitors, only $2.28 million, but probably benefited greatly from a ballot proposition on cockfighting which increased voter turnout particularly in the Democratic counties, and Gary Richardson's being in the race who mostly attacked Largent since he was the frontrunner. What was the end result? Oklahoma had its closest gubernatorial election in thirty-two years, with Henry getting 43.3% of the vote, Largent with 42.6% of the vote, and Richardson with 14.2% of the vote.

In 2004, there were very few statewide races in Oklahoma, only those for corporation commissioner and US Senator. The former was very uneventful; Denise Bode, the Republican, won as predicted with 63.6% of the vote. The exciting race instead was the race for US Senator between Democrat Brad Carson, Republican Tom Coburn, and independent Sheila Bilyeu. With Don Nickles (R) retiring, this became an open seat, and thus it featured high-quality candidates. Both Carson and Coburn had represented the state of Oklahoma before as US House members. Thus, this was widely predicted to be a competitive race. One of the more interesting features of this race was the involvement of the national parties. By the time the race was finished, both the Democratic National Committee and the Republican National Committee had given about $600,000 each to their respective candidates because it was feared by both parties that this race could decide the US Senate. With some well-placed campaign advertising including one featuring Brad

Carson as a puppet of the Democratic Party and one that called Brad Carson too liberal for Oklahoma, Tom Coburn was able to overcome some mistakes during the campaign to defeat Brad Carson, 52.8% to 41.2%. Perhaps because of all the negative campaigning during this race, Sheila Bilyeu did surprisingly well for an independent candidate, getting 6% of the vote.

In 2006, Oklahoma statewide races were also generally uneventful. This even included the Governor's race which at one point featured five to six Republican candidates vying to spar against the incumbent Brad Henry (D) for his seat. But in the end, Henry easily defeated Ernest Istook (R), the former member of Congress, 66.5% to 33.5%. Other races such as that for attorney general, state treasurer, superintendent of public instruction and all five US congressional seats followed a similar pattern, with one candidate typically getting at least 60% of the vote. The exceptions to this during the 2006 came with the previously noted Lieutenant Governor's race, where Jari Askins (D) won with only 50.1% over Todd Hiett (R) who had 47.5% and the Insurance Commissioner and State Auditor and Inspector races where both Democratic candidates, Kim Holland and Jeff McMahan, won their races with about 52% of the vote. The closest statewide race came with the Commissioner of Labor seat where Lloyd Fields (D) competed against the incumbent Brenda Reneau (R). This was a rematch of the 2002 election when Fields only lost to Reneau by 44,000 votes. Alas, this time Fields was victorious, but winning by just over 2,700 votes.

Term Limits in Oklahoma

In 1990, Oklahoma became the first state in the nation to adopt **term limits** for its state legislators. These term limits require that state legislators can only serve twelve consecutive years in the either the Oklahoma House and/or Senate. As adopted, term limits apply only to state legislators, but did not completely take effect on Oklahoma's state legislators until 2004. Fifteen states including Oklahoma circulated petitions in the states to examine term limits at the congressional level. In U.S. *Term Limits v. Thornton*, the U.S. Supreme Court held that the states cannot impose term limits on Congress. To maneuver around this ruling, fourteen of the fifteen states, including Oklahoma, have adopted **instruct and inform laws**. Candidates for state legislative and congressional races, under these laws, would be required to sign a pledge that they will do everything in their power once elected to adopt a constitutional amendment to limit congressional terms. Failure to adhere to the pledge exacts a price: the words "disregarded voters' instruction on term limits" will appear next to their names on the ballot when they run for re-election (Rafool and Warnock, 1996). The impact of term limits on the 2004 elections was substantial. In the Oklahoma House alone, there were twenty-eight seats that were left open because of term limits, and when combined with the nine members who left office or who lost in other primary races, this meant the Oklahoma legislature experienced thirty-seven new House members after the 2004 elections. In 2006, there were twenty open seats. In other states where terms limits have already been enacted like California, there is typically not an influx of new, inexperienced candidates coming into office, but rather, many of the experienced candidates just rotate offices. This has already happened in Oklahoma. Examples of this include the following term-limited legislators who ran for higher office: Representative and former Speaker of the House Todd Hiett (R) and Representative Jari Askins (D) who competed against each other for the Lieutenant Governor position in 2006, as well as Senator Cal Hobson and Representative Fred Morgan who both ran for the U.S. Congress position now held by former Lieutenant Governor Mary Fallin.

Some Conclusions

Oklahoma is a strong state politically. In recent years elections have become more competitive, providing genuine competition for most statewide offices in Oklahoma. The two major parties themselves have also been strengthened considerably, with more resources, more organization, and more staff. Recent elections in Oklahoma have seen major changes, with Democrats dominating at the state legislative level, but with Republicans capturing many other state offices and congressional seats. Oklahomans have also voted mostly Republican at the presidential level.

WWW RESOURCES

Oklahoma Election Board:	www.ok.gov/~elections
Oklahoma Democratic Party:	www.okdemocrats.org
Oklahoma Republican Party:	www.okgop.com
Democratic National Committee:	www.democrats.org
Republican National Committee:	www.rnc.org
Libertarian Party:	www.lp.org
New Party:	www.newparty.org
Patriot Party:	www.patriotparty.us/
Socialist Party:	www.sp-usa.org
Tulsa World:	www.tulsaworld.com
Lawton Constitution:	www.lawton-constitution.com
Daily Oklahoman:	www.oklahoman.com
Political Sites:	www.hillaryclinton.com
	www.joinrudy2008.com
	www.barackobama.com
	www.mittromney.com
	www.okies.info/reasons.html

NOTES

1. The five other states to offer both early walk-in and unrestricted absentee voting are Arizona, Colorado, Iowa, Nevada, and Texas. Alaska, California, Idaho, New Mexico, Oregon, Washington, and Wyoming offer unrestricted absentee voting only. Tennessee offers walk-in early voting only (Busch, 1996).
2. See "Unit to Target Voting Rights Infractions," Tulsa World Online, November 2, 1996, at http://www.tulsaworld.com.

CHAPTER TEN

INTEREST GROUPS AND CAMPAIGN FINANCE IN OKLAHOMA

Jan C. Hardt

So much money is being spent on the campaign that I doubt if either man, as good as they are, are worth what it will cost to elect him.

Will Rogers

I. INTRODUCTION

Oklahomans are very active in politics. As part of the populist movement in Oklahoma, Oklahomans believe that they should have a major stake in how political decisions are made. As a result, Oklahoma has a number of very active interest groups. Interest groups help Oklahomans to participate in politics by organizing the citizens around groups of particular interests. As these groups have become more active in Oklahoma politics, concerns have been raised about their power and influence. Fortunately, the Oklahoma Ethics Commission has placed more effective restrictions on these interest groups and how they can lobby the legislature, as well as other aspects of the government. The Ethics Commission, for example, has tightened its definition of who is a lobbyist, meaning that more lobbyists are now regulated by the Ethics Commission. It has also enacted very specific laws about how these interest groups can be involved in campaigns, and how much they can donate to politicians.

The populist movement in Oklahoma is also very evident in Oklahoma's active initiative and referendum process. These measures allow Oklahomans the right to change the state constitution and statutes directly. Unlike citizens of some other states, Oklahomans can use both the initiative and the referendum, and in the past have used them often. There are usually eight to ten such measures on the ballot each year, dealing with everything from property taxes to wine making.

Finally, Oklahomans also participate in politics by donating money. It is often said that the more money a candidate receives, the more likely that candidate is going to win the race. This turns out to be true in Oklahoma, although the money spent varies tremendously with the type of seat being sought, whether there is an incumbent in the race, the type of challenger, and the amount of competition in the race.

This chapter will examine the populism in Oklahoma by looking at the growth of interest groups and their lobbying, particularly the lobbying efforts behind the effort to get cockfighting banned in Oklahoma. Then, this chapter will explore how Oklahomans actively participate in politics, both through the initiative and referendum process as well as through donating money to candidates.

II. Lobbying in Oklahoma

What Is Lobbying and Who Does It?

Lobbying is most often done by interest groups seeking to influence decisions made by the executive, legislative, or judicial branches of government. **Lobbying** can be defined as the communication of data or opinion by someone other than a citizen to a governmental decision-maker in an effort to influence a specific decision. **Interest groups** are individuals with common needs who seek changes in public policy. Oklahoma tends to be an active state in terms of both the numbers of lobbyists and the numbers of interest groups participating.

Lobbyists and Interest Groups in Oklahoma

In 1948, American journalist John Gunther identified some of the earliest interest groups in Oklahoma politics. He found that the most active interest groups were the Baptist Church, oil interests, the elderly, the education lobby, and county rings. In 1960, the five same groups were still influential, but Stephen Jones, an Enid lawyer, added labor unions and newspaper organizations to the list as well.

In order to represent their interests, most groups rely on **lobbyists**. Lobbyists are individuals who are usually paid by interest groups to represent their interests to the legislature or other government entities. Lobbyists tend to be highly educated with 46.5% having a Bachelors degree, and another 46.5% having a Masters degree (31.4%), Doctorate (5.0%), or law degree (10.1%) according to a 2006 survey. In the same survey it was found that 72% of the lobbyists surveyed in Oklahoma were male, that their average age was a little more than fifty-one years of age, and that they averaged over eleven years in lobbying (Davis, Metla, and Herlan, 2006). The annual income from lobbying in Oklahoma is $86,525, which is low compared to most states since Oklahoma ranks forty-fourth among the fifty states in the average yearly income for lobbyists (Coleman, 2006).

The number of registered lobbyists in Oklahoma has grown steadily, with eighty-three lobbyists in 1976, 343 lobbyists in 1986, 410 lobbyists in 1997, and 417 lobbyists in 2004, but only 374 in 2007. Of the 374 lobbyists in 2007, 83% came from Oklahoma, while 17% were out-of state, or the same percentages as 2004. Lobbyists can represent single interests such as Jenifer Zeigler, a lobbyist who works for Institute for Justice based in Arlington, VA, who lobbies the Oklahoma legislature, or a lobbyist can work for multiple interests, such as Sandra Ruble who works in Norman, OK, for forty-eight different interests. Many of the lobbyists, including Sandra Ruble work for consulting firms, who not only lobby for multiple interests, but these interests can also be very diverse, and not necessarily in the same field of expertise. Ruble, for example, lobbies not only for Remington Park, but also for Enterprise Rent-a-Car, 3M, Chesapeake Energy Corporation, and Oklahoma state government among others. Of the 374 lobbyists, 112, or 30% work for multiple interests, with an average of 10.1 interests per lobbyists among those with multiple interests. Most of the lobbyists registered with the state in 2007, 82.9% or 310, were based in Oklahoma, while only sixty-four lobbyists were based outside of Oklahoma.

In contrast to the early years of studying lobbyists (1976 and 1986) when oil and gas companies had the most lobbyists, today business interests have the most lobbyists, as shown in Table 10–1. The percentage of business lobbyists in 2007 (50.9%) represents an increase from 2004, when they represented 29.2% of all lobbyists.[2] Over the years, there has been some variation in terms of which group has the most lobbyists after business. In 1986, the second and third largest lobbying groups were realty organizations and the banking community, with 13.4% and 11.7%, respectively. Surprisingly, given the fact that Oklahoma has the reputation of

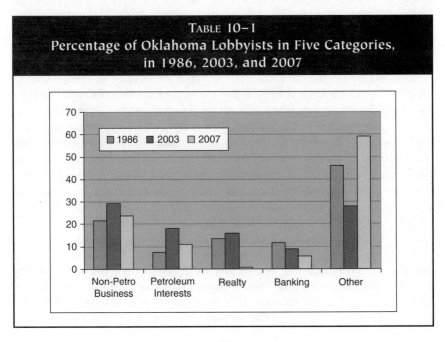

TABLE 10–1
Percentage of Oklahoma Lobbyists in Five Categories, in 1986, 2003, and 2007

being an oil and gas state, the petroleum community in 1986 had only the fourth largest group of lobbyists, representing 7.3% of all lobbyists registered in Oklahoma. In 2007, however, oil and gas still remained in fourth place, as health lobbyists and consultant lobbyists represented the second and third largest groups of lobbyists. What has really dropped is the number of lobbyists representing only realty organizations, with only two in Oklahoma in 2007 (Oklahoma Ethics Commission, 1997; Morgan, England, and Humphreys, 1991).

Over time, some have asked whether there are too many lobbyists per legislator in Oklahoma. Davis, Metla, and Herlan (2006) found in their sample in 2006 that were 2.6 lobbyists to each legislator. In 2007, that number had dropped to 2.5 lobbyists per legislator, with 374 lobbyists and 149 legislators. According to a study conducted by Rawls (2005), only seven states had fewer lobbyists per legislators, with four being in the Northeast (New Hampshire, Pennsylvania, Vermont, and Maine), and only one of these, Pennsylvania, considered to be a large state. The three states with the most lobbyists per legislator were all large, including New York (18:1), Florida (13:1), and Illinois (12:1), but being a large state does not necessarily guarantee a large number of lobbyists per legislator as indicated by the example of Pennsylvania (Rawls, 2005). Thus, Oklahoma with its 2.5:1 ratio is actually on the small side in terms of the number of lobbyists per legislator, ranking it about thirty-ninth in the nation, and under the national average of 5:1 lobbyists per legislator (Rawls, 2005).

Having more lobbyists, however, does not always mean that an organization has more influence. In 1986, legislators were asked their perceptions of the most influential lobbyists. The three most influential groups have not even been mentioned yet—education, labor and professional groups. Banking and finance, public employees, oil, and business lobbyists round out the list of lobbyists legislators think are most influential (Morgan, England, and Humphreys, 1991).

This list by no means exhausts the types of interest groups active in Oklahoma. By looking at only the most numerous or influential groups listed in a broad survey, one can miss single-issue interest groups that can be very powerful when activated. For example, in a frontier state like Oklahoma, the strength of the gun lobby, including the National Rifle Association, cannot be overlooked. The gun lobby has been very influential in Oklahoma, placing pressure on public officials to oppose gun control policies. This lobby has not only waged several independent expenditure campaigns against pro-gun-control candidates, but also fought successfully in 1995 for legislation permitting Oklahomans to carry a concealed weapon if certain restrictions were met. Another powerful interest group lobby includes Native Americans. In 2004, a gaming issue came up before the legislature. In order to save the horse racing industry in Oklahoma, proponents argued that more gaming would have to be present at the racetracks. This issue featured an unusual combination of lobbyists arguing for the measure: education interests who would get some of the profits, the horse racing industry, and Native-American gaming interests. More recently, Native Americans, business interests, and others were active in bringing a state lottery to Oklahoma. The state lottery became a state question on the 2004 election ballot which passed, and thus Oklahoma had its first state lottery starting in 2005.

On occasion, there can be a heated battle between lobbyists on different sides of an issue. That is certainly the case between Oklahoma grape growers and vintners who are trying to get the legal ability to sell their wine directly to retail outlets who are competing against a few, but well-funded liquor wholesalers. Currently, under Oklahoma law, any wine produced in Oklahoma must go through a wholesaler who can then sell the wine directly to the retail outlets. In 2000, the voters of Oklahoma approved overwhelmingly the right for in-state wine to be sold directly to retail outlets, bypassing the wholesaler. But in November 2006, the U.S. District Court ruled that the state question was unconstitutional, stating that by extending a privilege to in-state wine growers to sell directly to retail outlets, and not out-of-state growers, the Oklahoma question violated the interstate commerce law. The 2007 Oklahoma legislature considered more than a dozen bills regulating wine sales, with eight measures directly addressing the subject of wine shipment. Some of the bills were designed to give Oklahomans the ability to have wine shipped directly to their doors, as is available in 38 other states. But all of these measures except one died in committee. The lone remaining bill, HR 1753, reaffirmed the existing system of alcohol distribution, but also allowed Oklahoma wineries to ship their products to customers in other states, but not to customers within the state of Oklahoma. According to Danny Morgan (D-Prague), the minority leader in the Oklahoma House, this created another inequity between Oklahoma wine growers and those of other states, and just seemed to make the problem worse. In grappling with this issue in the future, state legislators will need to consider many interests: the needs of forty-eight state bonded wineries who produced more than 200,000 liters of bottled wine in 2006 alone, the fact that the current system allows for the efficient collection of $13 million in taxes on wine purchases, the large wholesale industry in Oklahoma with its extensive payroll, including one company, Central Wholesalers, who has an Oklahoma payroll of $25 million, and the state's need to control excessive alcohol purchases, including those by minors. Thus, it does not look like this issue will be decided anytime soon.

How active are Oklahoma's interest groups compared to those of other states? Two political scientists, Thomas and Hrebrenar (1990), sought to measure the impact of interest groups in each of the fifty states by looking at how interest groups are able to work with other political actors in the state. They came up with five categories of effectiveness: dominant, dominant/complementary, complementary, complementary/subordinate, and subordinate. In a dominant interest group state, interest groups play a large role in setting the policy agenda. There are many active interest groups and they make their presence known in all three branches of government. New Mexico is an example of a dominant state, where there are many active interest groups. Dominant interest groups typically come closest to being true **pluralism**, with multiple, competitive actors all fighting for and winning the attention of policy makers. In a complementary state, interest groups and lawmakers need to work together. Neither is stronger than the other, and the interest group's impact on policy making is moderate. Finally, in subordinate states, interest groups are fairly weak. They neither have much of a presence nor have much of an impact on making public policy. Oklahoma is classified as a **dominant/complementary state**. Interest groups in Oklahoma are strong as indicated above, but face some limitations because of the strengths of the legislature and the governor. Oklahoma is usually listed among the strong interest group states because of the power of economic interests (particularly oil and gas) as well as the lack of strong two-party system (Thomas and Hrebrenar, 1990).

III. What Do Interest Groups Do?

The Functions of Interest Groups

The wide variety of interest groups in Oklahoma serves several important functions. First, interest groups make it easier for people to participate in the political process, and may often give voters their first introduction to active politics. People will often need to join interest groups because of their jobs. Many occupations, including education, labor, and the healthcare profession, have established interest groups so that those employees can be aware of legislation affecting their interests. Individuals may also join interest groups because of their hobbies, activities, or interests. Perhaps a person who recycles gets upset with the lack of recycling facilities in his/her community and decides to join the Sierra Club. Perhaps a gun owner may decide to protect the right to have a gun by joining the National Rifle Association. On the opposite side of the fence, a gun control advocate might also decide to join Handgun Control Incorporated. Interest groups, however, can be distinguished from certain recreational groups by looking at the amount of political activity involved. Most boating groups, for example, are not considered purely political, unless they decide to fight for a change in boating laws such as placing limits on those boaters who drive their boats drunk.

Second, interest groups also provide key information about a specific policy area. This information may be provided to the public, to legislators when crafting legislation, or to other government officials. In June 1997, for example, the Southern Baptist Church decided to call for a boycott against the Disney Corporation because of the benefits that it gives to gay employees and its sponsorship of activities for the gay community. The public who heard about this boycott found out not only that Disney provides these benefits, but also that it is a major media conglomerate. The Disney Corporation includes the theme parks and films as well as several sports franchises, ABC television and radio networks, and 80% of ESPN.[3] Thus, a potential boycott of Disney meant not only the theme parks but the other companies like ESPN that it owns as well. On the other side, several gay rights organizations informed the public about what gay benefits mean to the gay community. Finally, interest groups can advocate the needs of a certain group of individuals. Whether it is education policy, boating policy, or crime policy, interest groups help to meet the needs of members and to articulate those needs to both policy makers and public.

What Do Interest Groups Do?

Most political interest groups are involved in some sort of lobbying. There are two types of lobbying: direct and indirect. **Direct lobbying** refers to efforts made by interest groups to convince policy makers through personal contact. This personal contact can include talking to policy makers directly, giving them information, sending information through the mail, or testifying before legislative or executive hearings. A 1986 survey of professional lobbyists in Oklahoma found that 98% of them use personal contacts; another 84.5% help in drafting legislation, appear before committees, and present research results. Of the lobbyists, 85.1% also engage in contacts with executive branch personnel (Morgan, England, and Humphreys, 1991).

Another common form of lobbying is for interest groups to give money to candidates or other election campaigns. Most interest groups will form a political action committee, or a PAC, for this purpose. PACs are the segregated campaign funds of a group of persons seeking to influence the political process. The PAC must be a segregated campaign fund, meaning that it is legally separate from the other funds of the organization. PACs according to Oklahoma law can only give $5,000 per candidate per calendar year.

Lobbyists may also give gifts directly to legislatures, under Oklahoma law. In the past lobbyists could spend up to $300 per year on each state employee or non-elected state official, but now that amount has dropped to merely $100. The amount for elected state officials, thus including state legislators, however, has remained unchanged at $300 per year. Lobbyists are required to report gifts that total more than $50 in a six-month period, according to Oklahoma Ethics Commission rules. Thus, lobbyists can still entertain elected state officials by giving them items such as tickets to concerts, professional sporting events, college bowl games, speech honorariums, and sometimes wine tours, provided at out-of-state conferences. In 2006, two Republican lawmakers from Tulsa, Dennis Adkins and Ron Peterson, received the most from lobbyists with $4,200 in gifts for Adkins and nearly $3,300 for Peterson. With these amounts, both legislators far outpaced their counterparts in both the Senate and the House. In terms of the contributors, the University of Oklahoma and Oklahoma

State University top the list of lobbyist principals, with OU giving $31,800 in season football tickets, and OSU $22,000 in tickets in 2006. Among companies and organizations, AT&T ranked highest on the list with nearly $9,000, Global Health Inc. was second with about $8,375, the Oklahoma State School Board Association was third with about $6,000, and Chesapeake Energy Corp. was fourth with nearly $5,000. The largest single giver among lobbyists was Lisette Barnes, a lobbyist for Global Health, Capital West Securities, and the Oklahoma Association of Youth Services who gave more than $10,000 in 2006, and second was Gary Huddleston who spent nearly $5,000.[4]

Interest groups in Oklahoma are also asked to testify before the legislature about the potential impact of a bill on the community, whether it be farming interests or those representing the horse racing industry in Oklahoma. For example, the testimonies of several different interest groups were heard by legislature in 1997 during the discussion of SB 715, a bill that established a procedure for those who do not wish to be resuscitated in cases of heart or lung failure. The Oklahoma legislature not only heard from the medical community and the state Council on Aging, but also Oklahomans for Life. Lawmakers also heard from several families that had made the decision not to resuscitate. The bill passed only because the legislators were able to get these groups to compromise on the various provisions of the bill.

Indirect lobbying, on the other hand, refers to the activities of interest groups designed to influence policy makers indirectly, usually by using an intermediary. The most common form of indirect lobbying involves using the public. Some interest groups hope that by influencing the public through campaign advertising, news reports, or mailings, that the public will be so moved that they will immediately call their public officials to get them to change some public policy. A 2006 survey of professional lobbyists seemed to suggest that both inside and outside lobbying strategies have been used in Oklahoma. When asked which lobbying techniques are used most often, the professional lobbyists stated that political fundraising (60%), directly trying to persuade officials (59%), getting influential constituents to contact officials (52%), engaging in informal contacts with officials (49%), and mounting grassroots lobbying efforts (48%) were the most common. Getting influential constituents to contact officials directly (an inside technique) and mounting grassroots lobbying efforts (an outside technique) were used very often 52% and 48% of the time, respectively (Davis, Metla, and Herlan, 2007). Yet, several prominent interest group campaigns in 1996 and 1997 used campaign advertising to make their interests heard. Voters watched television and radio ads about hogs, the elderly, telephones, education initiatives, and the Oklahoma oil and gas industry. The latter campaign was particularly expensive. Not only has this industry run ads both in and out of the legislative session, but many of the ads aired during the prime viewing (and therefore more expensive) hours such as during the Summer 1996 Olympics.

IV. Lobbyists and Lobbying Regulation

Who Are the Lobbyists?

There are many different types of lobbyists. The type of lobbyist depends heavily on how that lobbyist was acquired. First, some lobbyists are **in-house** lobbyists. These lobbyists are usually members of interest groups or employees of a corporation and are hired to lobby for a particular interest. In-house lobbyists represent 15–25% of all lobbyists in state capitols. Many lobbyists are **contract** lobbyists. These lobbyists are professionals, hired by an interest group or corporation solely for the purpose of lobbying. Often, contract lobbyists may work for several different lobbying organizations at one time, particularly if they are part of a lobbying firm. Much different are **volunteer** lobbyists. While they are usually members of an interest group, they are usually not paid and have agreed to lobby because they were asked to by their interest group. Volunteer lobbyists may not have the professional experience of some paid lobbyists, but often volunteer lobbyists are more devoted to their issue, and use emotion to effectively persuade policy makers. Finally, there are **government** lobbyists, or lobbyists who are hired by a government to represent its interests before policy makers. The governors of all fifty states and even mayors have organizations that represent their interests in Washington, D.C. Similarly, local communities in Oklahoma may send representatives to the Capitol to lobby for policy changes.

Lobbying Regulation

Why is lobbying regulation necessary? Without it, members of special interest groups could spend money and seek to influence officials in the state without any regulation. Lobbying or **ethics laws** make it possible for the public to know how much is being spent, which organizations have lobbyists, and which candidates have received the money or other services from lobbying. According to the Council of State Governments, Oklahoma's ethics laws fall into the moderate category, along with fourteen other states. There are twelve states who have tougher ethics laws than Oklahoma. One example of such a state is Kentucky. After a federal investigation in Kentucky called BOPTROT, several lawmakers and lobbyists were sent to prison. One of them was the House Speaker Don Blandford, convicted of both extortion and racketeering. Because of these scandals, Kentucky changed its ethics laws so that they are now the toughest in the country. Lobbyists in Kentucky cannot contribute to legislative campaigns, hold fundraisers for candidates, or serve as campaign treasurers. Legislators also face a two-year **revolving door** restriction on lobbying the legislature after they leave it. One last law allows lobbyists to spend up to $100 per legislative year for meals and drinks. However, this same law also requires *complete* disclosure. The result is that during the first month after the law took effect, legislators in Kentucky received a grand total of $26 in lobbyist spending for food and drink for the month.

Oklahoma ethics laws are not this stringent, but since 1990 when the Oklahoma legislature revamped its commission on ethics, the lobbying laws in Oklahoma have clearly changed. Formerly the Oklahoma Council on Campaign Compliance and Ethical Standards, the Ethics Commission in 1990 not only shortened its name but also strengthened the state's ethics laws. There are specific statutes to regulate the activities of those that lobby members of the Oklahoma legislature. Under state statutes, any person who spends in excess of $250 in a calendar quarter for lobbying activities, who receives compensation in excess of $250 in a calendar quarter for lobbying services rendered, and/or whose employment duties in whole or part require lobbying is considered to be a **lobbyist**. Every quarter lobbyists also must file expenditure reports with the commission when an expenditure on any one member of the legislative, executive, or judicial branch exceeds $50. These lobbying rules satisfy the requirements for **disclosure**. Disclosure is important because it can give the citizens of Oklahoma and other candidates the chance to see how lobbying money is being spent.

Unfortunately, despite these reporting requirements, there were few readily available published records of PAC or lobbyist contributions in Oklahoma. Prior to the 2006 elections, Oklahomans seeking information on lobbying and PAC contributions, needed to either visit the Ethics Commission in the State Capitol and copy each report by hand or rely on newspapers which provided only ad hoc information at best on PAC contributions and lobbying disclosure. This, despite the fact, that many other states such as California, had made their lobbying/PAC information available online allowing it to be easily searched. The Oklahoma Ethics Commission started in the summer of 1997 to allow access to ethics information on the Internet, thus making this valuable information more available to all citizens. But unfortunately, after an initial trial period, the state legislature recalled its earlier mandate that campaign finance information must be disclosed, and made that information voluntary for candidates instead. As a result, only about 15–18% of the candidates made their campaign finance information available on the Internet from 1997 to 2006 and any full study of Oklahoma campaign finance required a trip in person to the State Capitol and extensive digging through paper documents to get the material desired. Fortunately, this has now changed starting with the 2006 elections where the Oklahoma Ethics Commission began to require mandatory online filing from all candidates.

In the 2004 legislature, Oklahoma legislators also considered legislation that would have limited the revolving door for lobbyists. House Bill 1888 introduced by Representative John Trebilcock would outlaw lawmakers from getting "anything of value" for two years following their last day in office. Thus, lawmakers would have to wait two years before becoming a registered lobbyist. Trebilcock also introduced another bill in December 2003 that would prevent the distribution of campaign contributions in the State Capitol or other state government buildings.

V. A Profile of One Lobbying Effort in Oklahoma

Since 1999, a battle has been going on in Oklahoma. The battle is over cockfighting. The Oklahoma Coalition Against Cockfighting, the Humane Society, and several other opponents of cockfighting started gathering initiative petition signatures to get a ban against cockfighting on the Oklahoma ballot. They argued that cockfighting causes animal cruelty and can lead to human violence as well. They also point out that illegal drug users and dealers make numerous deals at cockfights. As a result of some of these issues, most states have banned the practice of cockfighting. Leading the fight against cockfighting opponents were the Oklahoma Gamefowl Breeders Association and others. Proponents of cockfighting argued that cockfighting was essential to the economy of many rural communities in Oklahoma; they pointed out that gamefowl breeding has been more than a $100 million industry in Oklahoma. Cockfighting opponents were also worried that other animal-related activities, such as rodeos and hunting, might be banned as well.

Sufficient signatures were gathered and SQ687 appeared on the November 2002 ballot. The specific wording of SQ 687 stated that it would be a felony for anyone to pit birds in a fight, participate in running a fight, or maintain a site for cockfighting. Spectators at a cockfight could be charged with a misdemeanor. Felony convictions would be punishable up to ten years in prison or a fine up to $25,000, while misdemeanor offenders could receive up to one year in prison or a fine up to $500. Leading up to its appearance on the ballot, both sides used a variety of lobbying techniques to advocate their positions on this issue. They ran extensive television and newspaper ads shortly before the November 2002 vote. The supporters of the ban featured graphic ads with animals, while the opponents ran advertisements talking about their civil liberties, such as the "Freedom Alert Special" inserts that appeared in the Tulsa World and other papers in the state. Both sides also raised substantial funds to wage their campaigns, with cockfighting opponents raising more than $600,000 and cockfighters spending about $140,000 (Killman, Hinton, and Hoberock, 2007). Opponents also received outside assistance from several groups, particularly the animal cruelty opponents. There were also rumors of more nefarious activities, including private investigators hired to monitor the cockfighting opponents' movements, threatening phone calls, and infiltrators secretly monitoring Internet chat rooms.

In November 2002, after a hard-fought campaign, the people of Oklahoma finally got to vote. Oklahomans voted 56% to 44%, or a 125,000-vote margin, to make cockfighting a felony. The cockfighting vote was largely a geographic one, with voters in urban and suburban areas voting for the cockfighting ban, and rural areas voting against it. Once the vote took place, the ban on cockfighting took effect immediately that weekend after the vote was certified.

The November 2002 vote did have an economic impact on the gamebreeders and the more than three dozen game clubs in the state. Because of the ban, many out-of-state cockfighting supporters were still coming to Oklahoma, but they were coming as spectators and not as cockfighters. Moreover, some gamefowl breeders have faced other charges. Thirty Oklahoma gamecock owners were cited in November 2003, ironically about one year after the ban's passage, for violating the Migratory Bird Treaty Act for allegedly setting traps to snare hawks and owls preying on their gamebirds.

However, the battle over cockfighting did not end there, by any means. Within days of the vote, cockfighting supporters went to court to block the law's enforcement, winning injunctions in thirty-six of the state's seventy-seven counties. The injunctions allowed the cockfighting to continue, from Guymon to Quapaw to Thackerville, but mainly in eastern Oklahoma. Yet even this was in some doubt. Attorney General Drew Edmondson stated that the law was still in effect while the challenges were pending, but enforcement of the law has been enjoined in some counties.

Perhaps to encourage a quicker resolution of this issue, around 500 cockfighters rallied at the Capitol in February 2004 to push for legislation to permit cockfighting on a county-option basis. While the cockfighting continued because of the injunctions, the Oklahoma Supreme Court considered a challenge of the law's constitutionality which was filed quickly after the election. As soon as it was filed, the two groups immediately fought over whether the issue should even go to the Oklahoma Supreme Court or to the District Courts in Oklahoma who were holding the injunctions. Cockfighting supporters argued that the Oklahoma Supreme Court justices were biased against cockfighters. However, a high court referee ruled that ban opponents offered no evidence of this bias. Then, in March 30, 2004, the Oklahoma Supreme Court upheld the constitutionality of the cockfighting ban, effectively voiding the injunctions and making cockfighting illegal in the state of Oklahoma. Later on May 27, 2004, Senate Bill 835 authored by Senator Frank Shurden, D-Henryetta and Representative Randall Erwin, D-Nashoba, was defeated. This bill proposed reducing the charge for cockfighting from a felony to a misdemeanor.

In more recent times, the issue has changed on two fronts. First, cockfighting has become a greater federal issue. Under prior U.S. federal law, anyone who was involved in the interstate or foreign transportation of animals for fighting purposes could be charged only with a federal misdemeanor. In the largest Oklahoma cockfighting case to date, seventy people in Oklahoma pleaded guilty to misdemeanors for a cockfight that took place on July 22, 2006. In early 2007, an anti-cockfighting bill sought to changes these penalties by now making it a federal felony to be involved with such transportation of animals for fighting purposes. This bill passed the U.S. House and Senate in early 2007 and was awaiting President Bush's signature. Oklahoma's U.S. Senator, Tom Coburn (R) believed that the legislation was not needed and worked hard to kill it, although he was unsuccessful. As of 2007, Louisiana is the only state where cockfighting remains legal.

Second, it has become an issue that now concerns tribal sovereignty. On June 14, 2004, Lawton's Mike Turner, founder of the Kiowa Association for Cultural and Rural Lifestyles, was arrested along with five others at a cockfighting pit near Randlett. Turner then became the first person to challenge the state law under the banner of tribal sovereignty. Although Turner had been warned prior to the event not to engage in cockfighting, Turner chose to do so anyway, arguing that he was operating on American Indian land and under the legal protection of the tribal-recognized Kiowa Association for Cultural and Rural Lifestyles. However, the tribe's attorney has said that the Kiowa Tribe does not recognize Turner's organization and the land in question is also on the Cotton County tax rolls. This case is currently being decided in the courts, and has not been resolved yet. Thus, this issue, although decided by the voters in November 2002, continues to this day.

VI. THE COSTS OF OKLAHOMA ELECTIONS

As with elections at the federal level, the costs of state elections just continue to increase. In 1994 for the first time, the cost of all state and local elections reached $1 billion. The costs are highest in the most populous states and in states where there is heavy use of electronic media. Oklahoma as a smaller state has seen remarkably consistent spending in its state level elections. Candidates for the state House and Senate, for example, spent $8.9 million in total in 1998, $8.94 million in 2000, $8.96 million in 2002, and $15.04 million in 2006. The spending for all state-level races in 2002 was $29.3 million and was $41.1 million in 2006. Campaign spending by candidates in Oklahoma is regulated by two distinct sets of laws. Candidates for the U.S. Congress seats in Oklahoma are federal election candidates so they are governed by the Federal Election Campaign Act of 1971 and 1974. This law was largely amended by the Bipartisan Campaign Reform Act, which increased the $1,000 individual donation to $2,000 and banned soft money contributions, among other things. Since these laws only deal with federal election candidates (President, U.S. House, and U.S. Senate) all other candidates in the various states, including Oklahoma, are covered by separate state laws created by each state. All fifty states now have some regulation over campaign finance for state and local elections. All states, for example, require that election campaigns disclose their sources of funds. State campaign finance laws vary considerably, however, on how much must be disclosed, what the candidates can spend, the sources of campaign funds, and when they must disclose that information.

Campaign Finance Laws

An important Supreme Court decision, *Buckley v. Valeo* in 1976, set specific restrictions on the federal government and states in terms of how campaign finance can be regulated. This decision said that candidates can spend as much of their own personal money as they need to run their campaigns. Therefore, governments are only allowed to limit the personal spending of a candidate if the candidate agrees to accept public funding. Thus, for the few states that have public financing, they can place an overall limit on how much a candidate may spend on the campaign. Otherwise, all overall limits on campaign spending were eliminated by the Buckley decision. This decision also stated that governments could put limits on other sources of funds, such as those from a family member, from labor organizations, and other groups. Governments can also limit the use of leftover campaign funds; a state can specify, for example, that money raised for campaign purposes may not be used later by a candidate to defray personal expenses.

The Buckley decision, FECA, and BCRA have guided the campaign finance laws of Oklahoma and the forty-nine other states. Only eight states equal or better the existing federal limits established by FECA. The toughest state law is in Florida and places $500 limits on both individual and group contributions to candidates. Eight states place no limits on individual or group contributions, including three of Oklahoma's neighbors—Missouri, New Mexico, and Colorado.[4] Oklahoma's campaign finance laws are classified as moderate by the Council of State Governments. Oklahoma's laws for state and local elections are slightly weaker than those established for federal elections. Unlike the federal government, Oklahoma provides no public funding for its campaigns. Thus, there are no limits on the overall amount of money that candidates can spend for their races for governor, state legislature, and other seats. Few states, however, have opted for public funding. The truest comparison between Oklahoma's laws and that of the federal government comes in the area of contributions. The contribution limits on individuals in Oklahoma are certainly weaker than the federal limits. While individuals can only contribute $2,000 per candidate per election in federal races under the new BCRA law, Oklahomans can donate up to $5,000 to a candidate in a calendar year.

Oklahoma's campaign finance laws, however, are tougher than federal election laws in several aspects. First, there are more restrictions on the donations that can be made by Oklahoman interest groups and corporations. Corporate donations, for example, are expressly prohibited under Oklahoma law, although many corporations can form PACS that can donate to candidates. Corporate employees in Oklahoma also can give separately to election campaigns. Labor organizations in Oklahoma can spend only $5,000 to a candidate committee in a calendar year, while the federal law allows for $5,000 per candidate per election. Since most candidates will have a primary, a general, and maybe even a runoff election, this can more than double the amount that labor organizations can spend on federal elections. Most interest groups getting involved in elections will form a **political action committee**, also called a PAC. PACS at the federal level are allowed to donate $5,000 per candidate per election, usually meaning that they can spend $10,000 on a candidate. PACs in Oklahoma can only spend $5,000 per calendar year per candidate. Second, there are also stricter laws on who can donate. State highway patrol officers and supernumerary tax consultants are prohibited from making contributions, while state officials, state employees, judges, and classified employees *should* not make contributions (Council of State Government, 1996). Third, Oklahoma also prohibits the use of leftover campaign funds for personal use. The federal government has been relatively slow in applying this law to presidential and congressional candidates.

In January 2004, the Oklahoma State Ethics Commission changed the amount that a contributor can give to a state political party under certain circumstances. The state limit on contributions to a state political party is still $5,000 per family per year. But with the enactment of BCRA at the federal level, a new category of contributions was created called Levin Funds. These contributions must be earmarked to help a party with registering voters or getting them to the polls, otherwise known as get-out-the-vote activities. A contributor may now give up to $10,000 to a state political party if that amount is earmarked for Levin Funds. This new change in the law took effect from July 1, 2004.

Independent Expenditures

One of the most difficult types of campaign activity to regulate is the **independent expenditure**. This occurs when a person or group campaigns either positively or negatively on behalf of a campaign, without that campaign's knowledge or cooperation. These independent expenditures commonly take the form of campaign advertising, but can often result in flyers, mailings, and newsletters. Independent expenditures are difficult to regulate because it is often hard to tell whether a given activity truly occurred independent of a campaign. Independent expenditures can often pose problems for candidates as well. Interest groups can run a negative campaign against a candidate, thereby forcing that candidate to spend large amounts of money responding to the attack. This money could have been spent on other activities, including positive ads run by that candidate. Only six states currently have laws requiring public disclosure. Of those, only Florida has a law specifying that the creators of independent expenditures notify all candidates within twenty-four hours of obligating the funds. This specific disclosure law allows the receiving campaign the chance to respond without infringing upon the original group's right to freedom of speech. Oklahoma's ethics laws allow independent expenditures, but those independent expenditures cannot be made by candidates on behalf of another candidate.

Campaign Spending in Oklahoma Races

Oklahoma's campaign spending is fairly predictable. In looking at this campaign spending, this report will tend to focus on the 2002 and 2006 statewide races because it makes for an easier comparison as these are both non-presidential election years. Even at the state level, fundraising in presidential election years tends to be significantly higher than those in non-presidential election years. Those in statewide races (Governor, Corporation Commissioner, etc,) tend to spend more than those in non-statewide races. This can be seen in Table 10–2.

Table 10-2
Average Money Spent by Type of Seat Sought for the 1998, 2002, and 2006 Elections

	1998	2002	2006
Attorney General			$385,493.86
Corporation Commissioner			$412,301.03
District Attorney	$32,340.20	$30,163.50	$412,301.03
Governor	$577,095.90		$1,220,915.88
House	$25,969.55	$24,062.36	$33,571.75
Senate	$57,082.29	$71,954.59	$86,397.48
Insurance Commissioner	$168,056.80	$185,327.28	$258,487.77
Justice, OK Sup Ct.	$67,220.59	$30,673.63	
Associate District Judge	$4,424.78	$5,101.84	$8,788.54
District Judge	$19,467.66	$11,798.68	$17,031.29
Labor Commissioner	$102,746.50	$63,085.15	$146,035.12
Lieutenant Governor	$843,953.50	$236,734.50	$700,250.33
State Auditor and Inspector	$224,756.10	$79,467.85	$367,010.95
Sup. of Public Instruction	$2,724.92	$71,954.60	$168,773.57
Treasurer			$1,002,452.34

As can be seen in Table 10–2, the only races where candidates spent more than $100,000 on average were those for statewide seats (Governor, State Auditor and Inspector, etc.). Even with the same type of seat, though, there is still considerable variation in campaign spending. Redistricting after the 2002 elections meant that several Senate candidates spent more for their seats, but this did not seem to affect the House, as shown above. The quality of the challenger and the number of years the incumbent has been in office also have an impact on campaign spending. In 1998, when she was first elected, Lieutenant Governor Mary Fallin faced a tough challenger, and as a result the Lieutenant Governor's race was an expensive one, with $843,953.50 spent on average, but in 2002, with Fallin having more experience in that seat, only $236,734.50 was spent on average. In the 2006 elections, Governor Brad Henry faced substantial competition, particularly among the Republicans for his seat, and thus $1,220,915.88 was spent on average by the candidates in that race alone. Another competitive race in 2006 was the race for State Treasurer, with Scott Meacham, the Democrat, facing two Republicans, Howard Barnett and Daniel Keating. In this race alone, over $3 million was spent, with Barnett spending almost $1.7 million and Meacham spending almost $1.2 million.

What can also be seen in Table 10–2 is that state Senate candidates spent considerably more than state House candidates during every election. Senate candidates not only have more constituents because they have larger districts, but they are elected every four years instead of every two. Because of the greater prestige, Senate seats also tend to attract better candidates (those with State House experience, those with name recognition, etc.) than the House seats. For the 2006 elections, the average amount raised by House candidates was $38,900, while the average amount raised by Senate candidates was $172,253, for a significant difference of $133,353. In 2002, the amounts raised by House and Senate candidates were $20,046 and $71,954, respectively, for a difference of only $51,908. Thus, the gap between these types of seats has gotten much larger over time.

Even more interesting is when the amounts raised and spent are divided even further by looking at who won or lost the race. The losers simply could not compete with the winners, both at the ballot box and in raising money. In the 2002 elections, House winners raised $35,633 on average, while House losers only raised $14,766. In the Senate, the story was similar, although the gap this time was even wider: $99,309 for the winners, and $48,373 for the losers. This pattern continues for the 2006 elections with House winners raising $58,062.91, while the losers raised only $26,923.68. The Senate winners raised $207,668.68 on average, while the losers raised only $74,872.42 on average. Thus, there is a consistent gap of at least 2:1 between the winning and losing candidates in the Oklahoma legislature, no matter which house or which year. This gap in money raised can buy advertisements, circulars to deliver door-to-door, and other campaign essentials that make it much harder for the loser to be competitive.

One significant change has been in fundraising by the party candidates. Typically, the party in control is able to raise more money. In the past, that has always been the Democrats. Thus, in 2002 the Democratic House candidates were able to raise $27,509 on average, while House Republicans raised only $24,036. The Democratic Senate candidates similarly raised $71,055 on average, while Republican Senators managed only $50,262. Yet after Republicans captured the House in 2002, there has been a change. This can be seen in the average amounts raised by the Democratic and Republican House candidates for 2006. The House Democrats were only able to raise $30,573.21 on average, while the Republicans managed a whopping $51,201.13 on average. The Republicans, however, were not so lucky in the Senate where that body currently is tied at twenty-four Republicans and twenty-four Democrats after the 2006 elections. Here the remnants of Democratic power can still be seen with the Senate Democrats raising $125,764.13 on average and the Republicans getting only $86,470.08.

Given these results, it should be no surprise that most of the top recipients of campaign contributions for both the 2002 and 2006 elections are Senators, not Representatives, since the Senate usually raises more money on average than the House. In 2002, sixteen of the top seventeen recipients of campaign contributions were Senators, and in 2006, fourteen of the top seventeen recipients were Senators. The top recipients with their expenses as well for the 2002 and 2006 elections are listed below in Table 10–3.

What it is also noteworthy about these two charts is that the impact of term limits can be seen. In looking at the 2002 and 2006 charts in Table 10–3, there are only two names duplicated, Cliff Branan and Johnnie Crutchfield. Most of the other candidates on the 2002 list do not appear because they were term-limited during this time period and thus are no longer in office. This includes such candidates as Stratton Taylor, Cal Hobson, and Kevin Easley, the top three recipients on the list.

Obviously, it takes a lot of money to win some state legislative seats in Oklahoma. Comparatively speaking, for example, it currently takes about $1.2 million to be competitive on average to win a U.S. House seat, but many seats are won with only $400,000–450,000 or even less and so some of the Oklahoma state legislators would probably be competitive, running for the U.S. Congress, at least in terms of money.

It is probably not a surprise, but many of the same state legislators who are on the top recipient list for 2006 also received the most PAC contributions for 2006 as well, as shown in Table 10–4. The most was Mike Schulz who raised $183,450 from PACs alone for the 2006 election. He's #8 on the above list, but others on the PAC recipient list include Brian Bingman (#2 in PAC donations), Ami Shaffer (#3), Lance Cargill (#4), Mark Wofford (#5), Mary Easley (#6), and Thad Balkman (#7). Moreover, the top PAC recipient in 2002, Jonathan Nichols, only raised

TABLE 10–3
2002 and 2006 Top Recipients/Spenders in Oklahoma State Legislative Races

2002					2006			
CANDIDATE	OFFICE	CONTRIBUTIONS	EXPENSES		CANDIDATE	OFFICE	CONTRIBUTIONS	EXPENSES
Stratton Taylor	S	$413,945.91	$488,855.17		Michael Burrage	S	$651,754.78	$639,492.68
Cal Hobson	S	$383,976.84	$200,338.67		Lance Cargill	H	$445,675.00	$423,357.41
Kevin Easley	S	$362,365.55	$259,638.46		Robbie C. Kerr	S	$419,042.70	$406,109.20
Jim Walker	S	$242,555.10	$222,189.34		Brian Bingman	S	$399,913.46	$398,977.51
Cliff Branan	S	$236,245.74	$163,386.39		Thomas Ivester	S	$384,692.72	$369,678.29
Johnnie Crutchfield	S	$220,961.30	$158,711.41		John Hunt Sparks	S	$374,359.34	$336,504.65
Steve Harry	S	$173,758.50	$165,024.66		Mike Schulz	S	$369,024.67	$361,149.46
David Boren	H	$169,561.37	$161,464.59		Cliff Branan	S	$325,136.58	$329,353.49
David Herbert	S	$162,819.80	$139,269.22		Patricia Potts	S	$293,646.50	$293,533.18
Harry Coates	S	$161,652.45	$152,817.68		Mary Easley	S	$273,105.52	$254,476.77
Joe Smith	S	$153,205.83	$131,754.61		Andrew Rice	S	$268,918.69	$204,933.08
Jay Paul Gumm	S	$142,715.61	$122,942.56		Johnnie Crutchfield	S	$256,025.00	$46,668.34
Tom Leonard	S	$131,812.74	$39,380.05		Ami Shaffer	S	$251,725.46	$246,544.51
Ted Fisher	S	$129,275.50	$119,073.77		Todd Russ	S	$248,187.88	$236,368.77
David F. Myers	S	$121,929.01	$51,311.09		Thad Balkman	H	$246,023.92	$232,696.24
Jim R. Maddox	S	$113,853.99	$107,374.30		John Mark Young	S	$232,620.74	$169,323.13
Randall Brogdon	S	$111,614.24	$106,492.68		Glen Coffee	S	$230,807.00	$174,330.93

TABLE 10-4
Top 10 PAC Contributors in Oklahoma State Legislative Races, 2002 and 2006

2002 TOP 10 PACS—By Average Donation (Min 20)

1. OK State Republican Senate Committee	$3,050.00
2. Republican Majority Fund	$2,537.00
3. OK State AFL-CIO	$2,278.00
4. Transportation Workers Union	$2,065.00
5. Republican State House Committee	$2,008.00
6. OK Republican Party	$1,438.96
7. Chesapeake Energy Corporation PAC	$1,414.89
8. Center for Legislative Excellence	$1,107.88
9. Lawyers Encouraging Government and Law (LEGAL)	$1,105.62
10. Working Oklahomans Alliance PAC	$1,061.36

2006 TOP 10 PACS—By Average Donation (Min 20)

1. OK State Republican Senatorial Comm	$4,166.67
2. Repub State House Comm	$3,576.09
3. Central Oklahoma Business Alliance	$2,981.48
4. Republican PAC to the Future	$2,785.71
5. Lawyers Encouraging Govt & Law (LEGAL)	$2,724.14
6. Fund for a Conservative Future	$2,479.17
7. Energy for Oklahomans	$2,017.24
8. Working Oklahomans Alliance PAC	$1,964.29
9. Sooner Fund PAC	$1,934.03
10. Center for Legislative Excellence	$1,786.99

$100,050 in PAC contributions, which is not only 54.5% of what Mike Schulz received in 2006, but if Jonathan Nichols had raised that amount in 2006, he would only rank eleventh in total PAC contributions received. Clearly, candidates are raising more PAC money than ever before.

PACs in Oklahoma tend to follow certain trends. Of all the PAC money contributed in the 2006 elections, 89.7% of those came from in-state PACs, while only 10.3% came from out-of-state PACs. In-state PACs also gave a lot more money on average ($956.45) than out-of-state PACs ($542.12). Yet certain candidates count on the out-of-state PAC contributions because they come from particular interests, especially oil and gas as well as health interests. Examples of these include Duke Energy Corporation, BP North America, and Marathon Oil as well as Merck, Wyeth, Pfizer, and Johnson and Johnson.

Very few PACs tend to give the maximum amount possible,$5,000, to candidates under Oklahoma election law. The exceptions to this rule tend to be PACs representing the political parties or ideological organizations. Examples of this include three of the top four PAC donors who gave over twenty donations by average donation in the 2006 elections: The Oklahoma State Republican Senatorial Committee which gave $4,167 on average to candidates in the 2006 elections, the Republican State House Committee ($3,576), and the Republican PAC to the Future ($2,786). Seven of the top ten PACs by average donation in 2006 were either PACs representing the Oklahoma Republican Party or PACs that typically give to only one party or another. The Central Oklahoma Business Alliance (Third on PAC list with $2,981) and the Fund for the Conservative Future (Sixth with $2,479) gave all their money to Republicans, except for one Democrat, Senator Connie Johnston. Legal (Lawyers Encouraging Government and Law—fifth at $2,724) and the Working Oklahomans Alliance (Eighth at $1,964) only gave to four Republicans total. This top ten PAC donor list is also bad news for Democrats. Five of the top six PACs on the list gave almost entirely to Republican candidates, while only LEGAL (#5) gave consistently to Democrats.

In looking at the list of PACs that give the most contributions in terms of the number of contributions donated, however, a completely different set of PACs emerges as shown in Table 10–5. PACs that give a lot of contributions tend to give smaller amounts, typically either $250 or 500, but will distribute their money to many more candidates. These include PACs that encourage employee contributions as well as PACs from professional associations.

The Oklahoma Optometric Association, SURE (Speak Up for Rural Electrification), the OK Ag Fund, the Oklahoma Osteopathic PAC, and the Oklahoma Dental PAC were ranked high on this list, with the Oklahoma Optometric PAC giving the most at 167 contributions in the 2006 elections. This is fairly significant considering that there are only 149 candidates in the Oklahoma legislature. These top five PACs, however, gave an average contribution of only $481.33, which is considerably less than the $2,000 or $3,000 contributions given by the party PACs. The largest PACs by the total amount donated to state legislative candidates in 2006 were the Chesapeake Energy Corporation ($139,250) and the Center for Legislative Excellence ($130,450), which was also second on the list in 2002. The top PAC on the list for 2002 was the Oklahoma Independent Energy PAC (OKIE PAC) which came in third for 2006; thus, the top PACs seem to fairly consistent over the years, even if the amounts have increased.

TABLE 10-5
Top 10 PAC Contributors in Oklahoma State Legislative Races, 2002 and 2006

2002 TOP 10 PACS—By Total Amount Donated

1. OK Independent Energy PAC	$164,700
2. Center for Legislative Excellence	$161,750
3. Chesapeake Energy Corp PAC	$133,000
4. Republican Majority Fund	$104,000
5. Lawyers Encouraging Govt and Law (LEGAL)	$98,400
6. Republican State House Committee	$82,350
7. OK State AFL-CIO COPE/PAF	$77,450
8. OK Republican Party	$74,826
9. Southwestern Bell Communications Employee PAC	$71,250
10. Transportation Workers Union of America	$64,000

2006 TOP 10 PACS—By Total Amount Donated

1. Chesapeake Energy Corp PAC	$139,250
2. Center for Legislative Excellence	$130,450
3. Okla Independent Energy PAC (OKIEPAC)	$128,100
4. OK Ag Fund	$100,200
5. Okla State Republican Senatorial Committee	$100,000
6. Working Oklahomans Alliance PAC	$96,250
7. Realtors PAC of Oklahoma	$86,600
8. Repub State House Committee	$82,250
9. Central Oklahoma Business Alliance	$80,500
10. Lawyers Encouraging Govt & Law (LEGAL)	$79,000
11. Republican Media Fund	$79,000

The amount that PACs give varies considerably depending on the political party, the type of office contested, and whether the candidate was a winner or a loser. With the political parties, PAC money in 2006 constituted a higher percentage of the money raised by Democratic candidates (32.2% PAC) compared to Republicans (23.3%), by House candidates (29.3% PAC) more than Senate candidates (26.3%), and by winners (32.1% PAC), more than losers (20.1%).

LEADERSHIP PROFILE

Saundra Naifeh
Executive Director, Oklahoma Association of Optometric Physicians

SAUNDRA NAIFEH is the Executive Director of the Oklahoma Association of Optometric Physicians (OAOP). In this capacity, she represents the interests of over 500 optometrists in Oklahoma's political and regulatory arenas. Through her leadership, Naifeh helps OAOP maintain public awareness of issues pertinent to the optometric profession. Oklahoma is the only state where optometrists are legally allowed to perform incisional eye surgery. OAOP has been at the forefront of several successful efforts to maximize the types of eye care that optometrists can provide to their patients. As one might expect, the ophthalmologists in the state have banded together to argue that only fully credentialed medical doctors should be allowed to provide these types of eye surgery. So far, their efforts have been effectively resisted by the skillful lobbying efforts of OAOP.

Previously, Naifeh served as the Mayor of the City of Edmond. She was elected to her first term as Mayor of Edmond in May 2001 and served until 2007. Community beautification, increasing citizen participation, cultivating next generation leadership, and expanding Edmond's influence in our state and nation were Naifeh's priorities. Her accomplishments included approving an agreement with the Trust for Public Land in which Edmond was named the state's first Green City, and establishing a weeklong youth council program. Under her leadership, an ordinance was passed to allow the appointment of young people as full voting members to the city's various board and commissions.

Consistent with Naifeh's goal of community beautification, a Visual Arts Commission was established, and numerous sculptures for the downtown area have been acquired. In addition, a simple process has been established for residents who support public art in the community to make a donation to the city for future purchases. Under her direction, the City First Building, the new administrative

> center, has a permanent "wall of history" with historical photographs and paintings. Naifeh also initiated a campaign to acquire artifacts for public display from previous mayors and their families. The new office building features rotating displays of the works of various artists.
>
> Naifeh was a founder and first president of both the Edmond Women's Club and Keep Edmond Beautiful. She is a past president of the Edmond Chamber of Commerce, Edmond Community Theatre, Central Business Development District, Retired Senior Volunteer Program, and the Oklahoma Institute for Child Advocacy. Naifeh has served on the Edmond Medical Center Board, the Edmond Board of Appeals and Adjustments, and the steering committee for "Tomorrow's Edmond." She has served on the Board of the Oklahoma Academy and Oklahoma Higher Education Council, as well as working with the Oklahoma Literacy Council. Naifeh is a graduate and Alumnus of Leadership Oklahoma. In 1996, Naifeh was inducted into the "Edmond Hall of Fame." She was named "Edmond Citizen of the Year" in 1982, and was chosen as one of the Journal Record's Top 50 Oklahoma Women. Naifeh has a Bachelor's degree in Government and Education from the University of Central Oklahoma, where she has been honored as a "Distinguished Former Student."
>
> A longtime resident of Edmond, Naifeh is active in the First Presbyterian Church of Edmond where she is a Stephens Minister. She is married to Frank Naifeh and has two stepchildren.

What was really surprising, though, was the average PAC contribution. As will be shown, this depends entirely on whether one looks at only those state legislative candidates who received PAC contributions versus all state legislative candidates. As seen in Table 10–6 below which shows only those candidates who received any PAC contributions, Republicans got more on average from PACs in 2006, particularly in the Senate where Republicans received $1,796.77 while the Democrats only received $913.62 on average. But the real surprises came with the winners and losers and the incumbents versus the challengers. Although PAC donations constitute a smaller proportion of the money raised by losers as shown above, losers do manage to receive a larger contribution on average than do winners, and this is true in both houses. Again, the difference seems to be magnified in the Senate, where Senate winners received only $965.06 in PAC contributions on average, while the losers received a whopping $2,653.03 on average. These differences can probably be explained by looking at the type of PAC money received. The win-

Table 10-6
2006 AVG PAC Contributions—by House & Senate Looking at Only Those State Legislative Candidates Who Received PAC Contributions

	House	Senate
Winners	$624.81	$965.06
Losers	$928.26	$2,653.03
Democrats	$535.27	$913.62
Republicans	$779.35	$1,796.77
Incumbents	$582.98	$863.15
Challengers	$955.37	$4,492.18
Open Seats	$894.06	$1,177.48

ners are getting contributions from almost every PAC, including those that give large donations like the parties, but also the employee and professional PACs which typically give the smaller donations. The losers who received PAC money, however, got most of their money from the parties and ideological PACs, who typically give $3,000 or $4,000 donations. Why? These two groups know that these candidates represent the potential to pick up a seat from the other party, and so they will donate heavily to these candidates hoping to provide the seed money to make that happen. Thus, these results are less surprising than they first appear. The same results happen when incumbents versus challengers are examined, with the largest difference in the Senate. House incumbents received $582.98 on average from PACs, while House challengers received $955.37, with House open seat candidates being in between at $894.06. But in the Senate, the incumbents received only $863.15, which is more than the House incumbents, but certainly less than the Senate challengers at $4,492.18. The Senate open seat candidates received again in between at $1,177.48.

Yet when one looks at all the state legislative candidates in 2006, including those who received no PAC contributions at all, the picture reverses. Yes, the Republicans still get more than the Democrats in both houses, but the difference narrows considerably, particularly in the Senate with Senate Republicans only getting $788.93 on average compared to the Senate Democrats who got $701.24 on average from PACs. But the real change comes with the comparison between winners and losers and incumbents versus challengers. The House losers got only $342.83 in PAC money on average, while the House winners got $590.87. The Senate losers fared poorly as well, receiving only $673.12, compared to the

Senate winners who received $867.12. Again, with incumbents versus challengers, the same change appears with the incumbents receiving more PAC money on average than the challengers.

Another huge difference between the winners and losers and the incumbents versus challengers appears when the total number of PAC donations to all state legislative candidates in the 2006 elections are examined, as shown in Table 10–7. Basically put, the House losers and challengers were able to garner very few donations. The losers got only five donations per candidate, while the winners got 32.1. The incumbents got 33.4 donations per candidate, while the challengers got 2.9 donations and the open seat candidates got 10.4 donations. These differences are even more magnified in the Senate, where the winner received 60.5 donations and the loser only received 10.3. A similar picture emerges for the incumbents and the challengers as the Senate incumbents received only 36.5 donations and the Senate challengers received 9.2. The open seat candidates fared better as expected with 23.0 donations on average.

Finally, once PAC information is collected by candidate, it is now possible to examine the PACs by categories. For the first time, we can truly see how much money is donated by various interests in Oklahoma. Table 10–8 shows PAC contributions for the 2006 elections divided by category. Within each category, the total amount donated, the number of donations, the percentage of that total amount, and the average donations are given because each column truly yields different information. In looking at the categories alone for example, it is clearly evident that some interests are more powerful than others. Although the top three interests remained the same from the 2002 elections to the 2006 elections, the order has switched. In 2002, Oil/Gas PACs gave the largest amount of donations, with political party PACs second, and Health PACs third. For 2006, political party PACs gave the largest amount, with Health PACs in second, and oil/gas PACs in third. This change is significant for several reasons. First, political party PACs give a lot more money on average than these other types of PACs. The candidates depend on these large donations to get elected. It also makes it easier while fundraising, when a contributor gives a large amount because it means that fewer donors have to be sought. Second, this has significant partisan implications because as can be seen in the chart, almost all of the increase in the political party donations has come from the Republicans, not the Democrats. Thus, while the Democrats were able to give 27.2% of the party money in the 2002 elections, they were only able to give 7.5% of the party money in 2006.

In looking at average donations in 2006, some of the same interests still top the list, but compared with the 2002, there are more of them. In 2002, the only interests that were able to raise an average donation greater than $1,000 were the political parties. Yet, in 2006, the Democratic Party was clearly unable to do this, but the Ideology, Health PACs, and Other PACs were able to give over $1,000 on average as well as the Republicans. Again, this is more bad news for the Democrats. Not only did they have a significantly smaller

Table 10-7
Average PAC $, Average Number of PAC Donations, Average PAC Donation Amount, Average Receipts and Average Expenditures to All State Legislative Candidates in the 2006 Elections

HOUSE	Average PAC$	Average # of PAC Donations	Average PAC Donation Amt	Average Receipts	Average Expenditures
Democrats	$8,159.04	15.21	$328.13	$30,573.21	$22,415.66
Republicans	$15,458.75	19.33	$581.13	$51,201.13	$45,672.72
Independents	$0.00	0	$0.00	$1,543.23	$996.42
Winners	$20,529.34	32.14	$590.87	$58,062.91	$51,592.44
Losers	$4,931.23	5.04	$342.83	$26,923.68	$22,054.79
Incumbents	$19,786.92	33.35	$482.22	$50,399.09	$44,994.65
Challengers	$2,807.04	2.94	$295.19	$16,427.16	$15,361.68
Open Seats	$9,440.62	10.42	$501.77	$45,038.21	$37,139.98

SENATE	Average PAC$	Average # of PAC Donations	Average PAC Donation Amt	Average Receipts	Average Expenditures
Democrats	$25,047.63	26.52	$701.24	$125,764.13	$105,724.60
Republicans	$28,775.00	22.27	$788.93	$86,470.08	$75,516.98
Independents					
Winners	$57,969.79	60.54	$867.12	$207,668.68	$171,244.02
Losers	$16,618.66	10.29	$673.12	$74,872.42	$69,477.88
Incumbents	$31,236.38	36.53	$792.99	$111,002.51	$81,717.90
Challengers	$19,857.89	9.16	$675.92	$59,818.39	$53,974.22
Open Seats	$27,664.97	23.03	$758.97	$138,111.76	$127,776.91

average donation than the Republicans ($765.24 to $3,521.55), but the Health (69.4%) and Ideology PACs (75.9%) gave most of their money to Republicans as well. Other significant PACs in terms of average donations in the 2006 elections were Business PACs, Oil/Gas PACs, and Labor PACs, and PACs in the "Other" category. Most surprising here was the low average donations given by guns, tobacco, and even agriculture interests. Oklahoma is

Table 10-8
2002 vs. 2006 Elections—Type of PAC—Which Ones Give the Most and Least?

Type of PAC	2006 Elections				2002 Elections			
	Sum	%	#	Avg	Sum	%	#	Avg
AGRICULTURE	$201,735.00	3.33	327	$616.93	$32,450.00	0.77	135	$240.00
BANKING	$234,250.00	3.87	458	$511.46	$189,535.00	4.52	598	$316.95
BUSINESS	$387,918.44	6.41	455	$852.57	$192,697.00	4.59	565	$341.06
CONSTRUCTION	$76,750.00	1.27	140	$548.21	$126,364.82	3.01	413	$305.97
EDUCATION	$97,930.00	1.62	279	$351.00	$127,266.92	3.03	505	$252.01
ENVIRONMENT	$4,200.00	0.07	11	$381.82	$4,300.00	0.10	11	$390.91
GUNS	$17,210.00	0.28	69	$249.42	$24,250.00	0.58	172	$140.99
HEALTH	$747,434.00	12.35	1,187	$629.68	$377,518.00	8.99	1211	$311.74
IDEOLOGY	$390,518.20	6.45	209	$1,868.51	$103,500.00	2.47	117	$884.62
INSURANCE	$86,650.00	1.43	145	$597.59	$81,400.00	1.94	354	$229.94
LABOR	$222,625.00	3.68	315	$706.75	$251,850.00	6.00	285	$883.69
OIL AND GAS	$587,275.00	9.71	706	$831.83	$540,011.00	12.86	970	$557.00
OTHER	$519,433.34	8.58	297	$1,748.93	$349,328.00	8.32	433	$806.76
PARTY—ALL	$974,980.64	16.11	352	$2,769.83	$468,446.38	11.16	328	$1,483.62
PARTY—REPUBS	$901,518.00	14.90	256	$3,521.55	$341,074.00	8.13	157	$2,172.45
PARTY—DEMS	$73,462.64	1.21	96	$765.24	$127,362.00	3.03	80	$1,592.02
PROFESSIONAL	$303,550.00	5.02	438	$693.04	$263,050.00	6.27	628	$419.79
PUB EMPLOYEE	$9,550.00	0.16	16	$596.88	$80,486.00	1.92	115	$699.88
SENIOR	$11,650.00	0.19	33	$353.03	$2,950.00	0.07	8	$368.75
TELECOMM	$79,450.00	1.31	167	$475.75	$211,950.00	5.05	453	$500.00
TOBACCO	$2,500.00	0.04	11	$227.27	$20,100.00	0.48	109	$182.72
TRANSPORTATION	$67,800.00	1.12	131	$517.56	$124,450.00	2.96	278	$447.66
UTILITIES	$52,150.00	0.86	222	$234.91	$157,441.00	3.75	600	$262.40

typically known nationally as a "gun and pickup" state, with lots of cowboys riding the plains, but these numbers show that these groups are not big contributors in Oklahoma. That is probably because they know that Oklahoman legislators would already be supportive of those interests.

In comparing the House versus the Senate on Table 10–9, other trends emerge. Because of the smaller size of the state Senate, its prestige, and the four-year terms, it was expected that PACs would give more to Senate candidates. With only a few exceptions, Banking PACs, Gun PACs, and Youth PACs to name a few, most PACs gave more to Senate candidates. There were several interests, though, where the difference in the size of the average donation was substantial. State Employees ($1,293.75 vs. $52.00), the Democratic Party ($1,731.55 vs. $477.95), Other PACs ($2,025.44 vs. $1,150.30), and Business PACs ($1,373.35 vs. $505.38) gave much more on average to Senate candidates than they gave to House candidates.

Table 10–10 also shows the different categories of PACs broken down by political party. For many interests, the Democrats and Republicans received roughly the same amount in terms of the average donation. This was true for Banking PACs, Construction PACs, Labor PACs, and Utility PACs. Probably among these, the labor PAC similarity is the most surprising. This, however, is when total donations given should be looked at. Although Democrats ($725.00) and Republicans ($706.02) received about the same average donation, the Republicans received only twelve donations for a total of $8,700, while the Democrats got 303 donations for a total of $213,925. Yet there were some key differences. The Republican candidates did much better than the Democrats in receiving PAC money on average from the political parties ($1,959.45 vs. $765.23) and ideological PACs ($2,056.27 vs. $1,552.14). But this was counteracted or the Democrats by donations from some of their traditional interests, including the greater money from Labor already mentioned as well as the Youth ($3,192.86 vs. $750.00 on average), and Professional PACs ($993.33 vs. $627.78). One surprise with the difference came with Transportation PACs who have traditionally given to the Democrats; however, in 2006, they gave more to the Republicans ($1,046.58 vs. $368.97).

Table 10–11 compares the PAC donations received by the winners and the losers in the 2006 elections. In looking at this table, two items need to be viewed simultaneously, the total amount given by an interest and the average donation. The reason for this is that if one just looks at the average donation, there will be some surprising results. For most of the interests, the loser received an average higher donation than the winner. This was especially the case for Business PACs, Democratic Ideology PACs, Other PACs, Professional PACs, Senior PACs, and Transportation PACs. Yet with all of these, the total amount given to the winners was much greater than that for the losers. For a few interests, the average donation was higher for the winners, including the Fire PACs, the State Employee PACs, and the Utility PACs.

As with the differences between the winners and losers, a similar pattern emerges with the PAC donations to incumbents and challengers as shown in Table 10–12: the incumbents like the winners generally received

TABLE 10–9
2006 Elections PAC Contributions by Type of PAC, Divided by House and Senate

TYPE	HOUSE			SENATE		
	NUMBER	AMOUNT	AVERAGE	NUMBER	AMOUNT	AVERAGE
Agriculture	216	$106,885.00	$494.84	111	$94,850.00	$854.50
Banking	444	$227,900.00	$513.29	14	$6,350.00	$453.57
Business	273	$137,968.44	$505.38	182	$249,950.00	$1,373.35
Construction	90	$35,200.00	$391.11	50	$41,550.00	$831.00
Education	178	$43,955.00	$246.94	101	$53,975.00	$534.41
Environment	7	$2,600.00	$371.43	4	$1,600.00	$400.00
Guns	41	$15,550.00	$379.27	28	$1,660.00	$59.29
Health	858	$492,634.00	$574.17	329	$254,800.00	$774.47
Ideology	106	$174,968.24	$1,650.64	103	$21,500.00	$2,092.72
Insurance	100	$46,200.00	$462.00	45	$40,450.00	$898.89
Labor	225	$129,500.00	$575.56	90	$93,125.00	$1,034.72
Oil & Gas	477	$368,975.00	$773.53	229	$218,300.00	$953.28
Other	111	$127,683.34	$1,150.30	171	$346,350.00	$2,025.44
Party All	246	$337,661.54	$1,372.61	106	$237,419.10	$2,239.80
Party (Democrats)	74	$35,368.54	$477.95	22	$38,094.10	$1,731.55
Party (Republicans)	172	$302,293.00	$1,757.52	84	$199,325.00	$2,372.92
Professional	194	$122,050.00	$629.12	94	$108,100.00	$1,150.00
Senior	14	$8,550.00	$610.71	2	$1,000.00	$500.00
State Employees	25	$1,300.00	$52.00	8	$10,350.00	$1,293.75
Telecommunication	123	$56,050.00	$455.69	44	$23,400.00	$531.82
Tobacco	4	$1,000.00	$250.00	7	$1,500.00	$214.29
Transportation	89	$28,750.00	$323.03	42	$39,050.00	$929.76
Utilities	158	$27,750.00	$175.63	64	$24,400.00	$381.25
Youth	10	$33,900.00	$3,390.00	5	$11,500.00	$2,300.00

Table 10-10
2006 Election PAC Contributions by Type of PAC, Divided by Democrats and Republicans

Type	Repub			Dem		
	Number	Amount	Average	Number	Amount	Average
Agriculture	164	$118,410.00	$722.01	163	$83,325.00	$511.20
Banking	293	$152,800.00	$521.50	165	$81,450.00	$493.64
Business	287	$284,748.44	$992.15	168	$103,170.00	$614.11
Construction	56	$30,050.00	$536.61	84	$46,700.00	$555.95
Education	75	$21,570.00	$287.60	204	$76,360.00	$374.31
Environment				11	$4,200.00	$381.82
Fire	14	$5,550.00	$396.43	136	$67,850.00	$498.90
Guns	5	$1,200.00	$240.00	64	$30,950.00	$483.59
Health	724	$518,250.00	$715.81	462	$228,934.00	$495.53
Ideological	142	$291,990.14	$2,056.27	60	$93,128.10	$1,552.14
Insurance	106	$70,100.00	$661.32	39	$16,550.00	$424.36
Labor	12	$8,700.00	$725.00	303	$213,925.00	$706.02
Oil & Gas	433	$379,550.00	$876.56	273	$207,725.00	$760.90
Other	131	$226,450.00	$1,728.63	151	$247,583.34	$1,639.62
Party	256	$501,618.00	$1,959.45	96	$73,462.64	$765.24
Professional	153	$96,050.00	$627.78	135	$134,100.00	$993.33
Senior	11	$7,750.00	$704.55	5	$1,800.00	$360.00
State Employees	12	$7,100.00	$591.67	21	$16,250.00	$773.81
Telecommunication	113	$56,800.00	$502.65	54	$22,650.00	$419.44
Tobacco	5	$10,250.00	$2,050.00	4	$10,250.00	$2,562.50
Transportation	73	$76,400.00	$1,046.58	58	$21,400.00	$368.97
Utilities	111	$37,600.00	$338.74	111	$34,550.00	$311.26
Youth	1	$750.00	$750.00	14	$44,700.00	$3,192.86

TABLE 10–11
2006 Election PAC Contributions by Type of PAC, Divided by Winners and Losers

TYPE	WINNERS			LOSERS		
	NUMBER	AMOUNT	AVERAGE	NUMBER	AMOUNT	AVERAGE
Agriculture	266	$155,535.00	$584.72	52	$43,450.00	$835.58
Bank	406	$207,050.00	$509.98	45	$24,650.00	$547.78
Business	380	$267,450.00	$703.82	64	$116,668.14	$1,822.94
Construction	114	$59,450.00	$521.49	26	$17,300.00	$665.38
Education	221	$69,730.00	$315.52	51	$26,450.00	$518.63
Environment	6	$2,350.00	$391.67	5	$1,850.00	$370.00
Fire	108	$53,900.00	$499.07	42	$19,500.00	$464.29
Guns	53	$17,100.00	$322.64	14	$14,450.00	$1,032.14
Health	1003	$598,894.00	$597.10	145	$134,350.00	$926.55
Ideological Republicans	90	$183,340.00	$2,037.11	53	$111,400.00	$2,101.89
Ideological Democrats	41	$53,828.10	$1,312.88	19	$39,300.00	$2,068.42
Insurance	126	$72,800.00	$577.78	14	$11,600.00	$828.57
Labor	207	$134,475.00	$649.64	107	$87,650.00	$819.16
Oil & Gas	611	$493,975.00	$808.47	55	$53,650.00	$975.45
Other	207	$299,983.36	$1,449.19	73	$173,600.00	$2,378.08
Party Democrats	43	$34,143.85	$794.04	53	$39,318.79	$741.86
Party Republicans	159	$324,373.00	$2,040.08	97	$177,245.00	$1,827.27
Professional	255	$181,500.00	$711.76	30	$47,450.00	$1,581.67
Senior	14	$6,800.00	$485.71	2	$2,750.00	$1,375.00
State Employee	18	$13,650.00	$758.33	15	$9,700.00	$646.67
Telecommunications	151	$72,500.00	$480.13	10	$4,450.00	$445.00
Tobacco	9	$2,500.00	$277.78			
Transportation	118	$48,950.00	$414.83	12	$18,350.00	$1,529.17
Utilities	198	$63,150.00	$318.94	16	$4,850.00	$303.13
Youth	7	$9,950.00	$1,421.43	8	$35,500.00	$4,437.50

TABLE 10–12
2006 Election PAC Contributions by Type of PAC, Divided by Incumbent, Challenger, and Open Seat

Type	Challenger			Incumbent			Open Seat		
	#	Amount	Average	#	Amount	Average	#	Amount	Average
Agriculture	8	$15,000.00	$1,875.00	212	$115,135.00	$543.09	107	$71,600.00	$669.16
Bank	6	$2,950.00	$491.67	359	$183,700.00	$511.70	92	$47,300.00	$514.13
Business	31	$62,690.00	$2,022.26	325	$195,288.44	$600.89	99	$130,000.00	$1,313.13
Construction	9	$2,750.00	$305.56	89	$48,050.00	$539.89	42	$25,950.00	$617.86
Education	5	$1,400.00	$280.00	184	$54,280.00	$295.00	90	$42,250.00	$469.44
Environment	3	$1,100.00	$366.67	3	$1,300.00	$433.33	5	$1,800.00	$360.00
Fire	10	$4,400.00	$440.00	87	$44,250.00	$508.62	53	$24,750.00	$466.98
Guns	4	$3,000.00	$750.00	47	$14,200.00	$302.13	18	$14,950.00	$830.56
Health	29	$49,350.00	$1,701.72	852	$481,834.00	$565.53	305	$218,550.00	$716.56
Ideological R	39	$91,998.89	$2,358.95	37	$77,391.25	$2,091.65	2	$300.00	$150.00
Ideological D	2	$1,100.00	$550.00	1	$1,000.00	$1,000.00	68	$125,600.00	$1,847.06
Insurance	8	$14,650.00	$1,831.25	110	$57,450.00	$522.27	27	$14,850.00	$550.00
Labor	38	$23,850.00	$627.63	133	$91,275.00	$686.28	144	$107,500.00	$746.53
Oil & Gas	14	$21,450.00	$1,532.14	562	$415,825.00	$739.90	130	$150,000.00	$1,153.85
Other	23	$59,900.00	$2,604.35	146	$179,200.00	$1,227.40	113	$264,933.34	$2,344.54
Party D	20	$7,668.85	$383.44	22	$20,539.83	$933.63	54	$45,253.96	$838.04
Party R	62	$121,215.00	$1,955.08	83	$198,013.00	$2,385.70	111	$183,390.00	$1,652.16
Professional	7	$22,500.00	$3,214.29	216	$139,900.00	$647.69	65	$67,750.00	$1,042.31
Senior				14	$8,550.00	$610.71	2	$1,000.00	$500.00
State Employee				14	$7,900.00	$564.29	19	$15,450.00	$813.16
Telecomm	2	$600.00	$300.00	126	$60,400.00	$479.37	39	$18,450.00	$473.08
Tobacco				8	$2,250.00	$281.25	1	$250.00	$250.00
Transportation	4	$15,500.00	$3,875.00	101	$32,900.00	$325.74	26	$19,400.00	$746.15
Utilities	1	$200.00	$200.00	176	$57,400.00	$326.14	44	$14,250.00	$323.86
Youth	2	$5,500.00	$2,750.00	4	$6,450.00	$1,612.50	9	$33,500.00	$3,722.22

smaller average donations from most interests, but the incumbents and the winners did receive more overall contributions, both in the quantity and the amount than their competitors. A few examples of this include Business PACs, Health PACs, Insurance PACs, and Oil/Gas PACs. The Business PACs, as an example gave only $600.89 on average to incumbents, but a whopping $2,022.26 to challengers on average. But when the totals are revealed, the Business PACs gave only thirty-one contributions or $62,690 to challengers, while they gave 325 contributions or $195,288.40 to incumbents. There are some exceptions to this pattern most notably the Republican Party, which gave $2,385.70 on average to incumbents, but only $1,212.15 to challengers. The Democrats did the same, but on a smaller scale, giving only $383.44 to challengers, but $933.63 to incumbents. There are also some types of PACs that did not give any money to challengers at all, including Senior PACs, State Employee PACs, and Tobacco PACs. The only good news for challengers with this is that these three types of PACs each gave very few donations overall. With the open seat candidates, their PAC averages generally fell between the challengers and the incumbents for the most part.

VII. Initiatives, Referenda, and Recalls

Besides turning out to vote, Oklahomans can participate in Oklahoma's initiative, referendum, and recall process. An **initiative** gives voters the right to take direct action by placing questions directly on an election ballot. With an initiative, Oklahomans can change both the Oklahoma Constitution and state statutes. While twenty-one states give their voters the right to change state statutes, only sixteen states including Oklahoma allow voters to change the state constitution through the initiative process. In order to create such an initiative, voters would need to circulate a petition among other voters gathering the required number of signatures. Oklahoma requires 15% VH to change the Constitution and 8% VH to change state statutes. VH is a designation which stands for the total votes cast for the office receiving the highest number of votes in the last election. These signatures can be gathered for ninety days, and a completed petition should then be delivered to the Oklahoma Secretary of State. Once placed on the petition, signatures cannot be removed, but they do not have to be verified before submission. There is however, a $1,000 penalty for falsifying petition signatures in Oklahoma (Council of State Governments, 1996).

With a **referendum,** the legislature is reluctant to vote on a question and instead places it directly on the ballot, allowing the voters to decide. The Oklahoma Constitution provides for two kinds of referenda. The first type of referendum allows for a change to the Constitution to be made. All fifty states but Alabama have this type of referendum. The second type of referendum deals with the state statutes. Oklahoma voters have two ways to change the state statutes. First, the Oklahoma legislature may place a proposition on the ballot that they are reluctant to vote on. Second, a dissatisfied group can gather enough signatures on a petition to force a public vote on some legislative act. This type of referendum, called a citizen petition referendum, is rarely used. Nevertheless, twenty-two states allow for both types of statute referenda. The dissatisfied group will need to gather signatures equivalent to 5% VG, or 5% of the total votes cast for governor in the last election. All types of referenda can occur within ninety days of the legislative session and are not restricted to subject matter (Council of State Governments, 1996). In Oklahoma, a large percentage of legislation in the Oklahoma legislature carries an **emergency clause,** meaning that legislation requires a two-thirds vote to pass and goes into effect immediately upon the signature of the governor. If no emergency clause is attached, legislation in Oklahoma then has ninety days after the legislature adjourns before becoming effective. During that ninety-day period, the citizen petition referendum can take place. With enough signatures, the people can vote on that issue.

Oklahoma's initiative and referendum process is very active. From 1970 to 1988, Oklahomans voted on 102 state questions (initiatives or referenda). Oklahoma faces an average of eight to ten such measures every year. In the 2000 elections, Oklahomans voted on six state questions, which included a measure on streamlining millage elections, a wider selection of local wines, and a trust fund for tobacco settlement money. One measure also gave state college presidents longer contracts. In that election, however, Oklahomans rejected two proposals: "one that would allow voters in Oklahoma and Tulsa counties to increase property taxes to fund county health departments, and another to allow schools to spend a portion of School Land Commission funds" (Zizzo, 2007, p. 6). During the 2002 elections, there were eight measures on the ballot and half of them failed. Most of the media attention was devoted to the cockfighting question which passed. But Oklahoman voters also approved a local government using bonds for economic/community development, a storm shelter question, and an issue on the abatement of taxes. During the 2004 elections, there were nine measures on the ballot, several of which attracted some national attention. Oklahoma was one of many states in 2004 to include an initiative to define marriage as between a man and a woman; that measure passed easily with 1,075,216 votes for and only 347,303 votes against. Oklahoma also included several lottery measures on the ballot, all of which passed as well. Thus, in 2005, Oklahoma now had a state lottery, joining many other states. The 2006 elections only included four initiatives on the ballot, two of which attracted the most attention. With the passage of State Question #724, state legislators can no longer receive pay while in jail or prison, and with the passage of State Question #733, package stores can now sell alcoholic beverages on election days.

Like other election campaigns, efforts to get initiatives and referenda are monitored by the Oklahoma Election Board. In many initiative or referendum campaigns, special interest groups, like the elderly or educators, will contribute money to influence passage of the measure. Although the Oklahoma Constitution prohibits corporate contributions to elections, the U.S. Supreme Court has held that corporations have a first amendment right to contribute to initiative and referendum campaigns. According to Oklahoma's ethics laws, groups campaigning on state questions must report contributions in excess of $200 annually. These disclosures have revealed corporate contributions in excess of $20,000 to certain state question campaigns. In 1990, the Oklahoma legislature passed legislation that would require more stringent reporting of such campaigns so that contributors could be known. This legislation, supported by both Oklahoma Common Cause and the Oklahoma League of Women Voters, was vetoed by Governor Henry Bellmon. The Governor thought that it would hinder the public's use of the initiative and the referendum.

Oklahoma's recall process is limited compared to some other states. A **recall election** allows voters the chance to reject an elected official through a direct vote of the people after that person has already served in office. In some states, voters can recall governors, legislators, and Supreme Court judges. The state of Oklahoma does not have a recall system at the state level. Therefore, no recall elections are held for governor, state legislators, school board officials, county officials, or other state positions. This lack of a voter recall caused problems for some Oklahoma voters when Governor David Walters was governor from 1991 to 1994. Voters sought his removal in 1991 because he had illegally solicited campaign contributions. While in office, Governor Walters pleaded guilty to a misdemeanor election violation. Oklahoma voters found, however, that he could not be removed from office because the state had no recall process for governors. Given that Governor Walters would be facing a Democratic legislature, impeachment was considered as an option, but only briefly, by those unhappy with his term in office. There is, however, a recall option for voters in some municipalities. Of the fifty to fifty-five municipal governments organized under a home rule charter, about fifteen to twenty have recall elections at the municipal level (Myers, 1996). The larger cities in Oklahoma have a home rule charter. One example of such a recall election took place in Del City, Oklahoma, where a city council member faced a recall election in 1997, allegedly because of that member's effort to seek a grand jury investigation into the actions of fellow council members.

VIII. CONCLUSIONS

The populist tradition continues in Oklahoma with the numbers of interest groups and the numbers of lobbyists increasing. These interest groups have been very active on numerous measures appearing before the legislature, including those dealing with cockfighting, gambling, and others. At the same time, however, Oklahoma strengthened its ethics laws for lobbyists, interest groups, and candidates, placing much deeper restrictions on how money can be raised and spent in Oklahoma. By examining the candidate's contributions and receipts, every Oklahoman can find out whether winning or losing candidates raise more money, whether Democrats or Republican have been more successful in the money game, and how various interests give their PAC money in Oklahoma.

WORLD WEBSITES

General interest group information:	http://web.syr.edu/~jpcammar/intgroup.htm
Initiatives and referendums in the states:	http://www.pirg.org/aapc/platform/init.htm
The Tulsa World:	http://www.tulsaworld.com
Lawton Constitution:	http://www.lawton-constitution.com
The Daily Oklahoman:	http://www.oklahoman.net
Political Sites:	http://campaign.96.com/links.htm http://www.vote-smart.org

END NOTES

1. All lobbying statistics from 1997 were calculated by the author from the "Oklahoma Registered Lobbyists 1997–1998" report published by the Oklahoma Ethics Commission. Statistics from earlier years came from Morgan, England, and Humphreys (1991). 2004 and 2007 figures came from the Oklahoma Registered Lobbyists report as listed at www.state.ok.us/~ethics.

2. In trying to measure the number of lobbyists by categories of interest, some methodological issues arose. Since several lobbyists reported working for multiple associations or corporations that were not in the same issue area, the number was more difficult to measure. Percentages of time figures are not available, nor are the amounts paid by these groups to hire these lobbyists. Thus, the only way to measure the number of lobbyists by category was to count the number of associations or corporations listed and to categorize them, instead of doing it by the number of lobbyists. Also, the time for each individual lobbyist was divided based on the number of groups represented and then looked to see how many persons represented each association, as done by many human resource firms. The results were almost identical, particularly for the major categories represented.

3. Some of the other holdings of the Disney Corporation include 37.5% of A&E, 50% of Lifetime, four film studios in addition to Walt Disney (Touchstone, Hollywood, Caravan, and Miramax), several newspapers, several magazines including Los Angeles and Discover, a cruise line, and some vacation clubs.

4. These states require disclosure, but do not place any limits on the amounts that non-candidate individuals and groups may donate to campaigns: Oregon, Utah, Virginia, Idaho, and Illinois (Council of State Governments, 1996).

CHAPTER ELEVEN

THE OKLAHOMA TAX SYSTEM

Loren C. Gatch

The income tax has made more liars out of the American people than golf has.

Will Rogers

I. INTRODUCTION

Taxes provide the means by which governments turn political rhetoric into reality. In this chapter we examine briefly the patterns of taxing and their meaning as they occur in Oklahoma. After some general remarks about the different forms of taxation and their relation to American federalism, this chapter describes the various taxes that Oklahoma imposes upon its citizens, and how Oklahoma's tax system differs from those of other states. Fiscal conditions in Oklahoma are particularly influenced by the constraints imposed by the passage, in 1992, of State Question 640, which severely limits the ability of state government to raise taxes. In the longer run, Oklahoma's tax system as well as those of other states face challenges posed by the continuing shift towards a service economy, and the rise of Internet commerce. We will look at these developments and their implications for Oklahoma government.

As Justice Oliver Wendell Holmes, Jr. famously remarked, "Taxes are the price we pay for a civilized society." All the same, it is a price we are compelled to pay, and the average citizen's contact with the tax system represents our single most common experience of government coercion. Taxes transfer wealth from the private sector to the government in exchange for public services. Whatever their reasons for collecting taxes, governments do so in three basic ways. First, they may tax the *possession* of existing stocks of wealth, in the form of property or other financial assets. The most common form of the property tax is that upon homes. Second, they may tax the *creation* of new wealth, particularly in the form of income flows. Third, they may tax the *exchange* of wealth, as it occurs through domestic trade (sales and excise taxes), international trade (tariffs) or through intergenerational inheritance (estate tax).

In addition, governments may treat the services they provide citizens just as businesses would: as products provided to consumers for which various licenses or "user fees" must be paid. Although we do not commonly think of it this way, the price of a postage stamp is the tax we pay for government-provided mail delivery. This fourth way of looking at government finance has become increasingly important as popular resistance to taxation in the first three senses has grown.

II. Taxation and American Federalism

Within American federalism, some taxes are excluded either from state or national control by the United States Constitution. Other methods are shared by both levels of government. National control over tariffs excludes states from one source of transfer tax revenue. By the same token, national commerce powers also prevent states from taxing the transfer of each others' products across state lines. Conversely, the Constitution originally prohibited the national government from laying **capitation**, or "direct" taxes that focused directly upon individual wealth and income (Article I, Section 9). Although modified by the Sixteenth Amendment establishing a national income tax, the national government does not otherwise tax property directly; instead, the property tax remains a mainstay of state and especially local government. Otherwise, the power to tax income is shared by the national and state governments and, in a few cases, cities.

In a similar way, sales tax authority is divided between the national, state and local levels, with the national level limiting itself to selective (or "excise") taxes upon selective items—e.g. gasoline, cigarettes, liquor—the sorts of things that people are either addicted to or cannot do without. Despite the occasional proposal to establish a national sales tax, broad-based levies on an *ad valorem* basis are traditionally reserved for the states. In addition, states like Oklahoma which possess significant natural resources like minerals or fossil fuels will tax their extraction. Finally, as a matter of tradition, the states' police powers enable them to sell *permission* to engage in certain activities, such as practicing a profession, driving a car, and owning a dog, or to charge for **access** to certain benefits, such as state parks, public higher education, turnpikes, or museums. State sponsored lotteries, a growing revenue source for state governments are available in Oklahoma since a vote of the people in 2004, charge their customers for access to dreams of instant wealth! Taken together, licenses and other miscellaneous user fees constitute a significant revenue source for many states.

As a practical matter, then, within the American federal system, state governments enjoy three main sources of tax revenue: **property taxes, sales taxes, income taxes,** with non-tax **licenses** and **fees** representing a fourth source. Finally, a fifth important source of revenue is "intergovernmental transfers," or money given by a higher level of government to a lower level for specific purposes. Of course, money coming from the national government had to be raised somehow. But that issue is beyond the scope of this chapter.

The ability of any government to raise taxes depends upon economic conditions, and these may vary from state to state even within a broader context of expansion or recession in the national economy. Beyond this variation, however, the broad historical trend in American federalism has affected all states in a similar direction. With the expansion of the national government since the 1930s, its own revenues have come overwhelmingly from personal and corporate income taxes, as well as social security "contributions." From the point of view of the national authorities, income taxes are the ideal source of revenue in that the government's share of this income grows automatically with an expanding economy. In contrast, the main sources of nineteenth century revenue, the tariff and excise taxes, have dwindled to relative insignificance. The success of a national income tax has also depended upon a complete monetization of the economy, and the shift of income into the manufacturing and service sectors, where income flows can be regularly tracked and subject to withholding by the tax authorities.

For their part, between the 1930s and the 1970s, states have left property taxes to the localities. Since immobile property like a house is easier to tax yet requires local knowledge and manpower to assess its value, local governments most easily manage this revenue source. This shift in tax authority was accelerated by the severe decline in property values during the Great Depression, which forced states to seek more stable sources of revenue. At the same time, states began introducing their own general sales and income taxes. Indeed, Oklahoma was one of the first states to introduce a general sales tax. Miscellaneous taxes and fees, as well as expanding intergovernmental transfers (grants in aid, revenue sharing) rounded off the main revenue sources for states up until the 1970s (Winters, 1996). Since then, tighter national finances and the return of financial responsibilities to the states have had major impacts upon state budgets. Intergovernmental transfers from the national level have declined as a percentage of state funding, as have sales and corporate income taxes, while states have relied more on income taxes, "miscellaneous" revenues and higher user fees to make up the difference (Raimondo, 1996). Moreover, popular resistance to local property taxes has led to restrictions on their use in most states, forcing local governments into a greater reliance upon financial support from state governments for such critical functions as public education. In the last ten years, the growing pressure of healthcare and education costs are squeezing state finances, at the same time the states' traditional sources of revenue have failed to keep pace with new fiscal demands (Boyd, 2006).

III. THE OKLAHOMA TAX SYSTEM

In the fiscal year ending June 30, 2006, the government of Oklahoma collected the precise amount of $8,435,214,024.57, not including those sales tax revenues gathered on behalf of cities and counties but before deducting tax refunds. This amount includes $80 actually paid for "Controlled Dangerous Substance Tax Stamps" (while dealing in marijuana is illegal, it is also a felony to do so without paying the relevant stamp tax!). Of course, Oklahoma spends more than this annually; significant revenues also come from non-tax sources (the lottery, for example) and intergovernmental transfers from the federal level. What major categories of tax does Oklahoma impose, and how does its tax system fit within national patterns? How heavy a burden does the Oklahoma tax system impose upon citizens? We will consider these questions in turn.

Tax Administration

With few exceptions, the administration, enforcement and collection of state taxes is handled by the Oklahoma Tax Commission (OTC), a three-person body appointed by the Governor, subject to Senate confirmation, to staggered six-year terms. Motor vehicle registration taxes and fees are collected by motor license agents (tag agencies) approved and regulated by the OTC. In addition, the OTC provides considerable assistance to county and local governments, and to the State Board of Equalization, as they assess property values for *ad valorem* taxation. While about 70% of tax revenues flow into the state's General Revenue Fund for appropriation by the legislature, the rest are earmarked by statute for county, city, and other local uses such as roads or education and are disbursed through the OTC. Finally, the OTC handles under contract the collection of sales and use taxes for counties and cities. In particular, nearly 500 municipalities as well as most counties impose some sort of sales tax over and above that levied by the state. As a consequence, the effective sales tax rates in Oklahoma can range from 5 to 10%.

The Main Types of Taxes

Oklahoma has two main types of revenue source at the state level: an income tax (individual and corporate) and sales and use taxes. Together, they represent over 60% of the state's tax revenues. Also important are taxes on motor vehicles and their fuels. A fourth source that is peculiar to Oklahoma consists of severance taxes on oil and gas. Apart from the multitude of user fees, Oklahoma's other main non-tax source consists of transfers from the national government. At the local level, municipalities rely on the property tax and supplemental sales taxes, as well as intergovernmental transfers from the state level.

We will briefly review the features of Oklahoma's major taxes.

1) The *income tax* represents the state's single largest source of revenue. For individuals, it is levied annually upon the net income of Oklahoma residents, whether from earnings, dividends, or capital gains, irrespective of whether it was received in Oklahoma or elsewhere. Conversely, nonresidents are subject to Oklahoma's income tax in proportion to their property interests or business activities within the state. For individuals, this tax is mildly progressive, ranging from 0.5% to 6.25%. The corporate tax rate is a

LEADERSHIP PROFILE

SCOTT MEACHAM
Oklahoma State Treasurer

SCOTT MEACHAM is the seventeenth State Treasurer of Oklahoma. He was elected by the people to a full, four-year term on November 7, 2006 after being appointed by Governor Brad Henry on June 1, 2005. Prior to becoming treasurer, Meacham served as Governor Henry's Director of State Finance. He continues to serve on the governor's cabinet as Secretary for Revenue and Finance. According to the Oklahoma Constitution, Meacham chairs the Oklahoma College Savings Board and the Board of Investors for the Tobacco Settlement Trust Fund. He also serves as a voting member of the State Board of Equalization.

As cabinet secretary, chief negotiator and policy advisor to Governor Henry, Meacham helps write the state budget. During his first year as state treasurer, Meacham directed modernization of the state's $4 billion investment portfolio that resulted in a doubling of investment income—generating an extra $50 million for the taxpayers of the state.

Due to Meacham's renegotiation of contracts for state financial services, the state will save an estimated $6 million over five years. Meacham, a certified financial planner, formerly served as Chief Executive Officer of First National Bank & Trust of Elk City. He is a fifth generation Oklahoman and a graduate of Chickasha High School and the University of Oklahoma. He holds a Bachelor's Degree in Finance, a Master of Business Administration, and a law degree. Meacham, his wife, Susan, and their four children, Trevor, Evan, Kady, and Lucas, make their home in Edmond. They attend Crossings Community Church in Oklahoma City.

flat 6% upon that portion of a corporation's income obtained from Oklahoma operations. The corporate income tax amounts to less than one-twentieth of total income tax revenues, reflecting both the reluctance of government to dampen the competitiveness of business and the ability of corporations to shelter profits in lower-tax jurisdictions (Fox and Luna, 2006). Most income tax revenues go into the General Revenue Fund.

2) *Sales and use taxes* have risen over the years from 1% in 1933 to 4.5% in 1990. On top of the current basic statewide rate, counties and municipalities have been allowed since 1965 to add supplemental rates, the proceeds of which are collected by the OTC on the localities' behalf. Indeed, alongside the property tax this has become an important source of revenue for local governments. In FY 2006, the OTC collected and reimbursed over $1.5 billion for counties and municipalities. The use tax is merely the sales tax applied to items bought outside of, but delivered to, Oklahoma. Between 1933 and 1987, proceeds were earmarked to the State Assistance Fund to fund various public welfare programs. Since 1987 these proceeds have been redirected for general revenue purposes. The sales tax applies both to the sale of tangible goods and personal property, as well as to other specified services such as transportation, meals, hotel lodging, and entertainment admissions. Exemptions to the tax are numerous, ranging from certain agricultural sales and prescription drugs to the transfer of intermediate manufacturing goods.

Many of these exemptions reduce the incidence of taxation on productive activities by business, and in particular aim to avoid the problem of **tax pyramiding**, or the building up of excessive tax burdens when taxes levied early in production are passed on as price increases of intermediate goods, which then are taxed again in later stages of processing and distribution. Business exemptions of this sort alone amounted to over $2 billion in foregone taxes as of 2002 (Olson, 2004). In other cases, exemptions represent concessions to politically-influential or connected constituencies. Other items already subject to tax, such as motor fuel (see

TABLE 11–1
Major Exemptions to the Sales Tax

1. Items already subject to excise or other taxes (fuels, motor vehicles, petroleum production);
2. Sales by the state and federal governments, and nonprofit organizations such as churches;
3. Agricultural sales made directly on the farm to consumers, as well as farm implements and livestock feed;
4. Sales of prescription drugs;
5. Sales by residential utilities (electricity, gas);
6. Sales of items purchased for subsequent resale (wholesale inventories);
7. Sales of intermediate manufacturing goods and products (machinery and products used in the manufacture of products for final consumption);
8. Sales of corporations and other entities that reflect various forms of financial consolidation (mergers, consolidations, restructurings)

SOURCE: Emerson (2002).

below), are also exempt. The single most important exemption concerns the sale of services, most of which (as opposed to goods) remain untaxed. In a modern economy, increasingly driven by the service sector, this exemption has resulted in an increasing mismatch between the fiscal systems of all American states and the economy that sustains it.

3) ***Gross production taxes***, including severance taxes on oil, gas, uranium and other minerals, are significant sources of revenue for Oklahoma. These reflect the lingering importance of natural resource extraction in the state's economic profile, and seldom play the same important role in other states' finances. These taxes are based upon a percentage of the value of resources taken from the ground. Raised to their present level in 1971, severance taxes take 7% of the gross value of oil and gas and 5% of the value of uranium. Also included among gross production taxes are small excise taxes placed upon gas and petroleum. Gross production taxes are earmarked to the General Fund, to county spending for roads and schools and, in the case of severance taxes on gas, to the Oklahoma Teacher's Retirement System.

4) ***Excise taxes*** are placed upon gasoline and diesel fuels, meaning that their sale is taxed at a fixed rate per gallon, and not as a percentage of their price (as would an *ad valorem* tax). Since 1987, the gasoline tax has remained at sixteen cents a gallon, and thirteen cents for diesel fuel. An additional one-cent per gallon has been tacked on for environmental cleanup purposes. Other excise taxes relating to motor vehicle ownership and operation include a variety of registration, title and lien fees, an "in lieu" tax, and vehicle, boat and motor excise taxes. These taxes are collected for the state by gas stations and private tag agencies. The details of, and exemptions to, this tax category are numerous and complex. In particular, they include the exemption of motor fuel taxes on sales by Indian tribal authorities to tribal members. Most of the proceeds are earmarked to various transportation and road-building purposes.

A related set of excise taxes (sometimes called sumptuary or "sin" taxes) are those applied to alcoholic beverages and cigarettes. Taxes on liquor are levied per liter of spirits and wine, and per barrel of beer; cigarettes are taxed by the pack. In Oklahoma, some of the wages of sin are the following: If you drink hard liquor, you pay the state $1.47 per liter for the privilege; wines range from nineteen to fifty-five cents per liter, while beer over 3.2% is taxed at $12.50 per thirty-one-gallon barrel. If you smoke cigarettes, you pay $1.03 per pack. If you really must chew tobacco or use snuff, you are assessed 30% of the factory list price. Because of Native Americans' sovereign status, their tribal smoke shops sell tobacco products at a substantially lower tax rate than do retailers elsewhere in Oklahoma. The loss of revenue to the state has been a point of contention between the state and its Native American population.

5) ***Vehicle taxes and licenses*** generate revenue from a number of sources, the most important of which is the annual tax which motorists pay on the value (adjusted for age) of their vehicles.

6) **Property taxes** are collected by local governments as an assessed percentage of the "fair cash value" of the property. By law, personal property other than homes is included in this tax, although in practice the application of this tax beyond real estate has been sporadic, since its collection would require very intrusive measures. Over the years, the property tax system has been the subject of much revision and litigation. Property tax collections are continually politicized by the fact that county assessors are elected officials who enjoy considerable autonomy in how they value property and assess taxes on it. The key issues concern the consistency (or "equalization") of assessed valuation across counties and the widespread under-reporting of personal property other than real estate. A **State Board of Equalization** seeks to impose greater uniformity in the assessment of similar pieces of property across counties. Finally, as with other taxes, exemptions abound—particularly for "intangibles" such as financial assets and relatively easy treatment of agricultural land.

Table 11–2 provides a more detailed breakdown of Oklahoma's major revenue sources.

As noted in Table 11–2, slightly more than 70% of these revenues flow into the General Revenue Fund, to be allocated by the legislature according to its priorities. The remainder is divided among a number of earmarked uses. These numbers do not include revenue that Oklahoma earns from non-tax sources, such as tuition charged to college students.

TABLE 11–2
Oklahoma State Taxes and Collections, Amount and as a Percentage of All Revenues, by Major Source, FY 2006

Type of Tax	Amount Collected	Percentage of All Tax Revenues
Income Tax, less refunds	$3,785,151,545	37.9
Personal	3,378,966,312	
Corporate	406,185,233	
Gross Production Taxes	1,168,597,608	10.1
Sales and Use Taxes	1,866,591,366	25.5
Vehicle Taxes and Licenses	588,668,345	11.9
Motor Fuel Taxes	445,666,139	8.2
Beverage and Tobacco Taxes	301,143,913	2.3
Estate Tax	82,049,033	1.3
Other	197,346,075	2.9
(Franchise Tax and Fees; Rural Electric Tax and License; Miscellaneous Taxes, Fees, Licenses)		
Total Net Tax Collection	8,435,214,025	100

SOURCE: *Oklahoma Tax Commission, FY 2006 spreadsheet, courtesy of Carolyn Moore, OTC.* Percentages do not sum to 100 due to rounding.

Nor does it include grants and other financial transfers from the federal government to the state. What Table 11–2 does provide is a basic snapshot of the pattern and results of Oklahoma's tax system.

Oklahoma Taxes in Comparative Perspective

Comparisons among state tax systems seek to answer two basic questions. First, what sort of a burden does the Oklahoma tax system impose, relative to other states? Second, how do their mixes of revenue sources vary, both among themselves and relative to the national average? Various authorities have attempted to rank states in different ways. This chapter makes frequent use of one well-known source, Congressional Quarterly's annual *State Fact Finder* (Hovey and Hovey, 2006). While these numerical rankings are important exercises from a policy perspective, the relevance of these numbers for political debates means that we must take some care to specify what the rankings do and do not compare. In particular, the bases for many cross-state comparisons involve revenue figures that aggregate both state and local spending, and often include non-tax revenue sources. As a consequence, the aggregate revenues being compared are often more comprehensive than the snapshot of Oklahoma's state tax sources given above. In some cases, FYs in question are earlier than FY 2006, the date of the most recent data available from the OTC. Nonetheless, the resulting comparisons are useful for situating Oklahoma within broad national patterns.

Above all, it must be stressed that these rankings by themselves do not tell us whether Oklahoma is an over- or under-taxed state, and thus whether taxes are too high or too low. Those are political judgments that depend upon what the public decides it wants from its governments. That said, other important questions do arise that can be answered by fiscal analysis. For example, does the Oklahoma tax system encourage or discourage economic development? Are revenue sources stable, diversified, and well adapted to the nature of the economy from which they are drawn? Is the mix of taxes fair, if fairness can be defined in a generally acceptable way? While we cannot answer these questions in this chapter, we can at least understand the relationship between tax policy and these other issues.

The most basic comparative measure of the burden of state and local taxes can be expressed as a percentage of personal income or per capita.

Oklahoma's place in this ranking reflects a number of factors—the wealth of the state relative to others, its geography, population distribution and density, tax structures, legal limits on spending, degree of federal aid, and voter preferences. One important fact that affects Oklahoma's ranking in this and a number of other fiscal indicators is its relatively low per capita income: at somewhat over 80% of the national average, the state's relative poverty sets an overall limit to the amount of money the state can raise, from whatever revenue source. That said, taxes are high and low only relative to what populations are able to pay, so per capita

TABLE 11-3
State and Local Taxes as a Percentage of Personal Income and Per Capita, Oklahoma, Neighboring States, and the National Average, FY 2002
(National Rank Out of 50 States, 1 = Highest

STATE	STATE AND LOCAL TAXES AS A PERCENTAGE OF PERSONAL INCOME	STATE AND LOCAL TAXES PER CAPITA
Oklahoma	10.0% (37)	$2513 (42)
Texas	9.5 (42)	2708 (33)
Arkansas	10.4 (22)	2384 (45)
Kansas	10.4 (26)	2936 (25)
Missouri	9.6 (39)	2666 (35)
New Mexico	11.1 (9)	2629 (38)
National Average	10.4 —	3138 —

SOURCE: Hovey and Hovey (2006). Identical percentages with different rankings reflect rounding.

rankings by themselves may not adequately express the burden borne by Oklahoma's taxpayers.

A slightly more detailed picture emerges when we compare, in the same way, the relative burdens posed by the three largest tax sources: property, sales, and income taxes (see Table 11–4).

Missing from these data is any reference to gross production taxes, which, though important revenue sources to Oklahoma, have no counterpart in most other states. As for its two other significant tax revenue sources, Oklahoma ranked forty-third in the nation for its seventeen cents per gallon gasoline tax, and second in the nation for its motor vehicle registration fees, even after having reduced these substantially (Hovey and Hovey, 2006). What this broad comparison suggests is that, much like Arkansas, Oklahoma's relatively low property tax burden is made up by a heavier than average sales tax burden. Regional contrasts are accentuated by the case of Texas, which has no income tax and correspondingly relies far more heavily on the other two remaining legs of the state tax "tripod."

Yet another way of expressing these contrasts is to compare the relative contribution of each major tax category—property, sales, and income—to the sum of all three revenue streams.

As Table 11–5 illustrates, Oklahoma relies disproportionately on its sales and income taxes in order to make up for a relatively low property tax burden. Another consequence of this reliance follows from the inherently local nature of property taxes: compared to other states, Oklahoma's tax system is far more centralized at the state level, in the sense that the state government, as opposed to county and municipal governments, collects a greater proportion of overall tax revenues than is the case in other states.

TABLE 11-4
Property, Sales, and Income Taxes as Percentage of Personal Income and Per Capita, FY 2002
(National Rank Out of 50 States, 1 = Highest)

STATE	PERCENT OF PERSONAL INCOME		PER CAPITA	
PROPERTY				
Oklahoma	1.68%	(47)	$424	(47)
Texas	3.97	(10)	1126	(13)
Arkansas	1.61	(48)	370	(49)
Kansas	3.28	(20)	930	(24)
Missouri	2.46	(39)	684	(37)
New Mex.	1.73	(46)	408	(48)
U.S. Average	3.21	—	968	—
SALES				
Oklahoma	3.91%	(20)	$986	(32)
Texas	4.64	(14)	1316	(7)
Arkansas	5.38	(5)	1233	(12)
Kansas	3.99	(18)	1129	(20)
Missouri	3.84	(22)	1065	(27)
New Mex.	5.30	(6)	1250	(11)
U.S. Average	3.72	—	1124	—
INCOME (INDIVIDUAL)				
Oklahoma	2.59%	(17)	$654	(28)
Texas	0	(NA)	0	(NA)
Arkansas	2.52	(22)	578	(32)
Kansas	2.41	(26)	683	(23)
Missouri	2.58	(23)	693	(22)
New Mex.	2.25	(33)	530	(36)
U.S. Average	2.33	—	730	—

SOURCE: Hovey & Hovey (2006).

The wide range in ranking amongst Oklahoma's neighbors for this value does point to the structural consequences of a state's tax mix. As with other indicators provided in this chapter, Arkansas' ranking paints it as a somewhat more extreme version of Oklahoma. In contrast, the entire lack of an income tax in Texas has resulted in the opposite ranking: with the smallest relative share of state tax collections in the nation, Texas' tax system is both regressive (sales taxes weigh more heavily on poorer people) and is ill-equipped to provide aid to local governments without contentious disputes over the allocation of property taxes. Quite apart from whether a state's taxes are too high or too low, specialists in state finance recommend that a good tax system should attempt to do three things. First, it should seek diversity in its revenue streams, and not depend too much on any one source. Second, it should seek revenue streams that will

TABLE 11-5
Property, Sales, and Income Taxes as a Percentage of the Three-Tax Revenue Total, Oklahoma and Neighboring States FY 2002 (National Rank Out of 50 States, 1 = Highest)

STATE	PROPERTY	SALES	INCOME (INDIVIDUAL)
Oklahoma	20.5% (45)	47.8% (17)	31.7% (11)
Texas	46.1 (6)	53.9 (12)	0 (NA)
Arkansas	17.0 (49)	56.5 (9)	26.5 (22)
Kansas	33.9 (24)	41.2 (22)	24.9 (29)
Missouri	28.0 (38)	43.6 (19)	28.4 (19)
New Mexico	18.6 (46)	57.7 (7)	24.2 (32)
US Average	32.6 —	40.2 —	25.2 —

SOURCE: Hovey & Hovey (2006).

grow with the needs of the state. Finally, for the sake of fairness it should impose its burdens equally on the largest number of people, resulting in broad but low tax rates. On all three counts, while not as deficient as the Texas tax system, Oklahoma's is less than ideal.

Non-Tax Revenue Sources

In addition to the revenues states raise from their own citizens, an important source of revenue is federal ("intergovernmental") funding. Here, more recent data show that Oklahoma garners nearly the national average of federal funds per capita, and depends upon these funds somewhat more than the average state. Nearly a quarter of the Oklahoma's state and local general revenue consists of such transfers. Indeed, Table 11–7

TABLE 11-6
Share of State and Local Tax Collections by State Governments, Oklahoma and Neighboring States FY 2002 (National Rank out of 50 States, 1 = Highest)

STATE	PERCENTAGE COLLECTED BY STATE (RANK)
Oklahoma	68.9% (12)
Texas	48.6 (50)
Arkansas	80.9 (1)
Kansas	60.3 (25)
Missouri	57.7 (36)
U.S. Average	59.1

SOURCE: FFIS (2004).

TABLE 11-7
State and Local Intergovernmental Revenue Per Capita and as a Percent of State and Local General Revenue: Oklahoma and Neighboring States FY 2002
(National Rank Out of 50 States, 1 = Highest)

STATE	PER CAPITA REVENUES	PERCENT OF ALL STATE AND LOCAL GENERAL REVENUE
Oklahoma	1,279 (23)	24.4 (19)
Texas	1,099 (40)	21.1 (32)
Arkansas	1,364 (17)	27.5 (10)
Kansas	1,153 (35)	21.2 (29)
Missouri	1,310 (21)	25.2 (15)
US Average	1,281	21.4

SOURCE: FFIS (2004).

understates the importance of intergovernmental transfers to the tax burden, since the Census Bureau's definition of "General Revenue" includes various non-tax revenue sources that, as we shall see, Oklahoma relies upon to a greater degree than the national average. These numbers are driven in particular by rising levels of reimbursements for Medicare (health insurance for the elderly), the cost of which is shared between the national and state governments.

In other respects, Oklahoma does very well by its fiscal relationship with the federal government. In terms of federal spending in the state per dollar of taxes paid to the federal government, in FY 2003 the state ranked twelfth in the nation by receiving $1.48 for every tax dollar paid. This reflects the prominence of federal payrolls, particularly those on military bases. In a related sense, measures of Oklahoma's "terms of trade" with the federal government—the ratio between federal grants paid to all Oklahoma governments to taxes paid to the federal government—also places Oklahoma at a favorable seventeenth among states, with $1.35 received for every $1.00 paid (Hovey and Hovey, 2006). A less charitable interpretation of this relationship is that, as a relatively poor state with many of the social problems that accompany poverty, Oklahoma receives more federal assistance than richer states.

The other main non-tax revenue source available to Oklahoma uses consists of the many charges and fees that the state imposes on its citizens. The distinction between these charges and specialized taxes is sometimes one without a difference; nonetheless, if it is not collected by the OTC, (turnpike fees or college tuition, for example), then it falls into the non-tax category. Nationwide, such non-tax sources of revenue have become increasingly important, both because of popular opposition to tax increases and because of longer-term structural problems with states' traditional tax bases. In Oklahoma, for example, taxes are restrained by constitutional limitations on property tax millages and the supermajority requirements of Proposition 640 (a tax increase requires 75% vote by the legislature). Nationwide in FY 2002, taxes accounted for 68.3% of state and local revenues (excluding intergovernmental transfers), a percentage that has been in decline over the last decade. In that same year, Oklahoma ranked thirty-fourth for having a tax take that was four percentage points below the national average (FFIS 2004). As these percentages go down, the proportion of non-tax revenue within the state and local revenue mix increases. While nationwide slightly less than one-fifth of all revenues came from non-tax sources, Oklahoma ranked eleventh in its 23.9% share.

One final, and perhaps the most comprehensive, way of assessing Oklahoma's tax system is to compare the relative importance of its major components to those of other states (see Table 11–8). Care should be taken when contrasting this table with the percentages given in other tables. Unlike the others, this one includes state and local revenue sources (e.g. property taxes) as well as non-tax sources not collected by the OTC.

The importance of this table to our portrait of the Oklahoma tax system is that its comparisons point in the same direction as do the earlier tables.

TABLE 11–8
Major Revenue Sources as a Share of State and Local Own-Source General Revenue Oklahoma vs. Neighboring States, FY 2002

STATE	PROPERTY TAXES	GENERAL AND SELECTIVE SALES TAXES	INDIVIDUAL INCOME TAXES	CORPORATE INCOME TAXES
Oklahoma	10.9%	25.3%	16.8%	1.3%
Texas	28.4	33.2	—	—
Arkansas	10.4	34.7	16.3	1.8
Kansas	21.9	26.6	16.1	1.1
Missouri	17.9	27.8	18.1	1.4
U.S. Avg.	21.1	24.5	15.3	2.1

STATE	LICENSING AND OTHER TAXES	CHARGES	OTHER MISC. REVENUE	TOTAL
Oklahoma	10.2%	23.9%	11.7%	100.0%
Texas	6.8	18.7	12.8	100.0
Arkansas	3.9	20.4	12.4	100.0
Kansas	3.5	18.1	12.8	100.0
Missouri	4.5	17.9	12.6	100.0
U.S. Avg.	5.3	19.1	12.5	100.0

SOURCE: FFIS (2004).

Whether expressed as a percentage of personal income, taxes per capita, or as a percentage of all revenue sources, Oklahoma makes less use of the property tax than do other jurisdictions. Without the presence of gross production tax revenues to ease the percentages, Oklahoma's reliance upon sales taxes and stiff motor vehicle-related taxes would appear even more prominent. Finally, Oklahoma's resort to non-tax revenue sources, while part of a larger national trend, has been exacerbated locally by constitutional restrictions placed upon the ability of the state to raise revenues. It is to these restrictions, and the tax policy responses they have engendered, that we turn to by way of conclusion.

IV. Is This Tax System Right for Oklahoma?

As a general matter, each state's revenue sources mirror in important respects the economic condition and structure of the state. For broad comparative purposes, some data are more useful than others. For example, it is commonly pointed out that, in per capita terms, Oklahoma ranks near the bottom of the fifty states in various categories of taxing. Yet this is not surprising, given that Oklahoma's per capita income lags the national average. Obviously, a relatively poor state will take in, and spend less, per capita than will a rich one. Some anomalous rankings reflect interesting policy alternatives, such as Texas' lack of an income tax. In contrast, a neighboring state like Kansas possesses a tax system whose results come far closer to national averages. Indeed, to appreciate the Oklahoma tax system it is far more useful to compare its tax pattern with those prevalent nationwide.

Oklahoma's relatively low income means that it has historically relied to a greater extent than other states upon transfers from the national government, although Oklahoma's dependence in this regard has faded in recent years with the more general retrenchment in national government aid to the states. Gross production and other severance taxes naturally make an outsized contribution to state revenues, since most states lack Oklahoma's mineral resources. Yet these are notoriously unstable, depending as they do upon changes in the international oil market. During the oil boom ending in the early 1980s, severance taxes alone provided over 20% of the state's revenue, a number that, while fluctuating wildly, currently sits at something half of that (Olson,1984).

How Heavy a Burden Does the Oklahoma Tax System Impose?

As noted above, a low per-capita tax take does not necessarily mean that Oklahoma has a low tax *burden*. Even low taxes may be burdensome; depending upon how poor Oklahoma is relative to the rest of the country, its tax burden may actually be greater than elsewhere. Alternately, the relatively heavy reliance upon severance taxes may overstate this burden, since those taxes typically fall upon out-of-state consumers. Analysts are divided over the question whether or not Oklahoma is a low-tax state in

Table 11-9
"Tax Freedom Day"

STATE	DATE OF "TAX FREEDOM"	NATIONAL RANKING
Oklahoma	April 12	50
Texas	April 19	42
Arkansas	April 22	32
Kansas	April 24	28
Missouri	April 20	40
New Mexico	April 15	45
U.S. Average	April 30	—

SOURCE: The Tax Foundation, Special Report No. 152, March 28, 2007 (www.taxfoundation.org)

relative terms. As we have seen, comparisons by tax category yield mixed results. Even including intergovernmental transfers and non-tax revenues, in FY 2002 Oklahoma ranked fortieth in state and local general revenues per capita (FFIS, 2004).

Another approach to the question with great intuitive appeal is to ask how long Oklahomans collectively must work in a given year before they earn the sum of that year's state tax bill. This date, popularly known as "Tax Freedom Day," is regularly calculated by the national organization, The Tax Foundation, for each state, and for the nation as a whole. By this measure, Oklahoma has the lightest tax burden in the nation.

Whatever position one argues, it remains the case that Oklahoma's tax structure in part reflects political decisions about how to exploit the state's tax base. The resulting tax structure expresses first and foremost what voters will tolerate. Of all the deviations from the national average, severance taxes on oil and gas are most understandable, since they allow Oklahoma to shift the tax burden onto the (nonvoting) citizens of other states. Similarly, property taxes in Oklahoma are, as a percentage of the take, far below the national average—in large part because, since 1933, their assessment and administration have been left in the hands of local government and elected county assessors.

It seems proper that local resources fund local services. However, localities will skimp on their contributions if they can get the money from somewhere else. Voters will always want low property taxes. In Oklahoma, these incentives are sharpened by the relative autonomy that local assessors enjoy, despite the efforts of the Equalization Board. Oklahoma's experience illustrates the basic problem of property taxes. A tax that is best administered at a local level is also a tax that local property owners will most resist (Oklahoma Academy for State Goals, 1985).

Ironically, one result of this local autonomy is that Oklahoma exhibits greater **fiscal centralization**—the financial dominance of state governments over localities—than other states (Murry et Al., 1996). This condition is also suggested by Table 11–5. In this regard, Oklahoma is hardly alone; the movement of power and money from the local to the state level is a national trend that began in the 1980s. As federal aid to localities has decreased, states have taken up the slack, either by substituting their own grant systems, or by assisting localities in the collection of taxes (Hanson, 1996). Yet, by relying less upon property taxes than other communities, Oklahoma localities depend even more upon state-level revenue sources than do localities elsewhere.

It should be stressed these various rankings do not imply what Oklahoma taxes ought to be. Rather, they describe Oklahoma taxes *relative to national patterns*. Like all tax systems, Oklahoma taxes reflect the history of the state. The distinctive features of Oklahoma's system include: low property taxes; relatively high sales taxes; high fees and licenses; and heavy reliance upon unpredictable severance taxes on oil and gas production. In addition, the property, sales and income taxes contain many exemptions that tend to reduce their revenues. Overall, Oklahoma's tax system exhibits a structural tendency towards **inelasticity**. That is, revenues do not grow proportionally with increases in state income. This is increasingly a feature of state tax systems nationwide (Murry et al., 1996; Fox and Luna, 2006). Oklahoma's tax system reflects both past choices and the influence of powerful constituencies. Are these choices and influences necessarily bad? In an ideal world, taxes would be simple—broadly based, minimal, and fair. Oklahoma's taxes do not fit this ideal, but neither do the tax systems of any of the other forty-nine states (nor, God forbid, does the federal government's!). Any tax system that responds to popular pressure or is used as a tool of public policy will become complicated. For their part, policy reformers have a disconcerting tendency to prefer tax systems whose revenues grow in a steady and automatic fashion, beyond the reach of political interference. Fortunately, democracies have a high tolerance for political imperfections. Besides, inefficient and inequitable tax systems are also ones whose burdens do not grow as quickly as the rational "ideal." That said, one should not hesitate to point out the fiscal consequences of the tax choices that Oklahoma has made.

Like all other American states save one, Oklahoma ties itself down in advance by having a constitutional commitment to a balanced budget. In addition, the details of the state's budgeting are disciplined by the State Board of Equalization, which must certify the amount of money the legislature may spend in the coming year. Together, both of these mechanisms limit the overall budget to incremental growth. In March 1992, Oklahoma voters approved State Question 640, which forces the state to submit all tax increases to popular approval if they pass either house of the legislature by less than a three-fourths margin. A popular reaction to the tax increases of the 1980s makes this new requirement hard for Oklahoma to raise taxes.

What does SQ 640 mean for Oklahoma's fiscal future? As long as the economy grows, the government's increasing tax take means that the bite will not be felt. However, over the long run, the interaction of Oklahoma's tax system—particularly its reliance upon sales and excise taxes—with the limits imposed by SQ 640 point to the emergence of a chronic, structural shortfall in revenue growth. Unlike income tax receipts, sales tax receipts do not grow proportionally with increases in per capita income. Moreover, the absence of taxes upon *services*—an increasingly dominant sector of any modern economy—means that more and more of what is bought and sold in Oklahoma escapes taxation (Murry et al., 1996). The rise of Internet-based commerce only aggravates this trend. In 2004 alone, it has been estimated that Oklahoma lost over $200 million in sales taxes to cyber-transactions (Hovey and Hovey, 2004: 159). Within this long-term trend, the state will undoubtedly face pressures from changes in the business cycle. The painful results of these pressures reappeared with a vengeance during the recession of 2001–2002, and have prompted calls for modernization of the Oklahoma tax system (Olson, 2003). In particular, reform of the tax system might entail reducing the number of special-interest features of the tax code, such as the exemptions to the sales tax detailed in Table 11–1. Such features are generally termed **tax expenditures**, which the OTC defines as "the amount of state revenue that would have been collected but for the existence of each exclusion, deduction, credit, exemption, deferral or other preferential tax treatment allowed by law" (OTC, 2006). In 2006, it was estimated that nearly 500 separate tax expenditures reduced the state's tax take by $4.6 billion. In other words, had these various special interest provisions not been in the tax code, the state's tax revenues would have been that much higher (Krehbiel, 2006). Other, more radical, reform ideas include adoption of so-called Taxpayer Bill of Rights legislation, or TABOR. The idea behind TABOR is to prevent state lawmakers from raising revenues at a rate faster than the combined percentage of the state's rate of economic growth and population increase. Favored by advocates of smaller government, it is likely that some form of TABOR legislation will be put to a vote of the people within the next few years.

In the meantime, existing restrictions on the ability of Oklahoma to raise taxes have encouraged lawmakers to consider fee-for-service revenue sources such as a lottery, tuition increases, and turnpike tolls (Dauffenbach et al., 1994). More recently, the economic downturn that began after the burst of the stock market bubble in early 2000 has led, among other things, to dramatic hikes in the cost of tuition at Oklahoma's colleges and universities. With the election of Brad Henry as Governor, an Oklahoma lottery again became a possibility, and the voters in the November 2004 elections duly approved one. Non-tax revenue sources have their advantages and drawbacks. Lotteries in particular are politically popular because they are not seen as a tax, yet they are unreliable as revenue sources and their benefits can be overblown (Holmes, 2004). In its brief life so far, the Oklahoma lottery has produced lower revenues than anticipated. Lotteries are also faulted for encouraging civic irrationality and a spirit of gambling among those citizens who can least afford it (Claunch, 2002). Although with the proliferation of tribal gaming facilities, opposition to state-sponsored gambling looks increasingly quaint. Whatever its ultimate consequences, a lottery for Oklahoma is no long-term solution to its revenue problems. Indeed, thanks to the current surge in world oil prices and their effect upon gross production receipts, Oklahoma has gained some breathing room to think about what in the long term is best. One thing is certain, though: sooner or later the effects of SQ 640, and the erosion of state tax bases nationwide, will force Oklahoma to think hard about where it will get the funds to pay for the things Oklahoma wants.

CHAPTER TWELVE

MUNICIPAL AND COUNTY GOVERNMENT IN OKLAHOMA

Deborah D. Ferrell-Lynn

All politics is local.

Thomas P. "Tip" O'Neill,
Speaker of the U.S. House of Representatives 1977–1987

I. INTRODUCTION

Oklahoma's economic future looked dismal in 1986 as the "Oil Bust" of the late 1980s negatively impacted employment and sales tax collections statewide. Throughout the state, municipal business leaders and elected officials questioned whether their jurisdictions could emerge from the economic malaise that resulted from the dramatic drop in crude oil prices (from $ 37.60 to $11.15 per barrel, from 1982 to 1986) and the subsequent failure of Penn Square Bank. As the largest city in the state, both in size and population, Oklahoma City was particularly hard hit. Already generally overlooked as part of "fly-over country" (a derisive term for the middle section of the U.S.), Oklahoma City's downtown was in danger of becoming little more than a place where suburb-dwellers worked before returning to their "bedroom communities" and where lower-income residents dealt with declining infrastructure and little economic opportunity. By 1993, the city's primary convention center, the "incomparable" Myriad was hardly that—national business organizations and trades shows rejected the outdated and increasingly run-down event locale in favor of other cities' newer structures and nearby quality hotels (downtown Oklahoma City had <u>one</u>), restaurants, concerts, sports venues, and community events.

Civic and elected leaders hoped that landing a contract with a major employer would jump-start Oklahoma City's flagging economy. Instead, potential employers looked to other more economically progressive cities, despite the fact that Oklahoma City residents had approved dedicated sales tax initiatives to enhance public safety and the citys zoo; a 1989 infrastructure bond issue had also been approved by voters. These efforts were somewhat unusual, given that City voters traditionally rejected sales tax measures, but the local economy was severely impacted by the Oil Bust, and City leaders and residents realized that a major investment would have to be made in order for Oklahoma City to compete with other states for private sector and tourism dollars. This realization prompted voters in 1991 to approve several sales tax measures to entice two major air carriers—United and American—to build their new aircraft maintenance centers in Oklahoma City. Despite an aggressive campaign for the $1 billion United contract, Oklahoma City finished behind Indianapolis (which, ironically, faced the prospect of closing the facility in 2003).

The loss of the United Airlines contract turned out to be a blessing in disguise. Airline officials told Mayor Ron Norick that Oklahoma City was rejected because of its limited quality of life and a declining downtown area. Lack of public investment had contributed to the city's negative image. City leaders learned through a survey conducted by the Greater Oklahoma City Chamber of Commerce in the early 1990s that only 17% of residents held a favorable view of the City's image; 61% indicated a negative image. Chamber chairman Ray Ackerman summarized respondents' views in an article in *The Daily Oklahoman:* "If you asked people why they stayed here, they said they thought we had a good quality of life. But they also thought the grass was greener on the other side of the fence. They didn't have any pride" (Lackmeyer, 2003, p. 1A).

Norick, Ackerman, and other city elected and business leaders responded by proposing the Metropolitan Area Projects (MAPS), an aggressive plan to fund nine projects seen as critical to revitalizing the downtown area. Other cities had funded the building of sports stadiums and entertainment districts; Oklahoma City was proposing a comprehensive package that would include among other things construction of an indoor sports arena, a minor league ballpark, a new library, a recreational canal running through the city's burgeoning entertainment district, and renovation of several existing city structures vital to its arts and entertainment. Instead of serving simply as a "quick fix" or "band-aid" approach to economic malaise, MAPS was envisioned as a major revitalization effort that would permanently enhance the city's economy and its status as a major mid-sized U.S. city.

The campaign to win city voters over to the idea faced an uphill battle. Polling data indicated that only 37% of residents initially supported the plan and the attached tax. Previous similar redevelopment plans, like the ill-fated "String of Pearls" (derisively dubbed the "String of Beads" by critics), were cited by critics as proof that Oklahoma City could not successfully undertake such massive endeavors. Some argued that it was foolish of Oklahoma City to attempt to emulate San Antonio's Riverwalk through the building of a canal that "went nowhere."

Norick and his allies were not discouraged by such criticism, and their persistence and dedication to the vision paid off. In 1993, voters approved a five-year, one-cent sales tax to fund the $254 million plan to renovate existing structures and build new ones also viewed as vital to the project's success. During the next ten years, Oklahoma City witnessed the renovation of its Civic Center, State Fair Arena, and convention center. The 13,000-seat SBC Bricktown Ballpark, recognized as one of the finest minor league baseball venues in the country, opened in 1998. The Bricktown Canal, constructed in 1993, attracted restaurants, shops, and special community events, making it a major tourist attraction. The state-of-the-art $87 million Ford Center, the largest of the MAPS projects, has become a primary concert venue and was built to NHL and NBA standards.

The MAPS investment paid off in multiple ways. In addition to the renovation of existing cultural facilities like the 1937-vintage art deco Civic Center and the State Fairgrounds Arena, the infusion of public and private sector dollars into the Ballpark and Canal have led to increased economic development in the Bricktown Area, making it downtown's entertainment center. A new four-star hotel was erected north of the "Cox Convention Center" and high dollar apartments sprang up in the Deep Deuce section of Bricktown. Other communities and nations looked to MAPS as an innovative way for cities to reinvigorate their downtown economies. Residents of Tulsa, Oklahoma, adopted the MAPS approach, passing an $885 million historic economic development tax package in September 2003. As Oklahoma City observed the tenth anniversary of MAPS, there was much to be proud of.

Yet, there were also controversies and challenges. Critics pointed to a lack of government accountability despite the creation of a Citizens' Advisory Committee. Cost estimates for the Civic Center, Bricktown Canal, and convention center were higher than expected, leading the new mayor, Kirk Humphreys, to call for an extension of the sales tax to cover the $10 million shortfall. The public criticized the granting of naming rights of the Bricktown Ballpark to Southwestern Bell Telephone for an undisclosed amount. The 1995 bombing of the Alfred P. Murrah Federal building delayed MAPS projects as the City responded to the loss of 168 lives and destruction of several downtown buildings. The city failed to attract an NHL team to the Ford Center (this proved to be a blessing in disguise as the NHL canceled its 2004–2005 season over a labor dispute), and legal disputes have delayed construction of the new downtown library. The City of Oklahoma City's decision to fund the building of a MAPS spin-off, a Bass Pro Shop just south of the Ballpark, drew criticism from those concerned about taxpayer-funded incentives to attract private investment, despite a refund requirement. Civil rights groups argued that lower income groups were not benefiting from MAPS success and jobs creation.

Still, MAPS has been successful. All nine projects have been completed, the last being the $24 million Ronald J. Norick Library opened in 2004. Downtown investment is expected to reach into the billions. Already, millions of people have visited new downtown attractions such as Bass Pro and the multi-screen theater in Bricktown. The Ford Center became the temporary home of the New Orleans Hornets after Hurricane Katrina devastated the Gulf Coast in 2005. Oklahoma City sports fans responded overwhelmingly positive in terms of attendance and enthusiasm. The proven quality of the Ford Center as a sports venue virtually assures that the City will get its own NBA or other professional sports team in the near future.

MAPS exemplifies an aggressive response to competition among American cities for private sector investment capital and jobs creation. The project's success illustrates how important Oklahoma's cities are in enhancing their own and the state's economic well-being.

This chapter provides an overview of the structure and functions of Oklahoma's municipal and county governments and the means by which they acquire and spend funds needed to meet basic services while responding to new challenges. While the focus is primarily on municipal government, the chapter will also discuss the role and responsibilities of county government and changes that have occurred and not occurred in response to a massive scandal involving corrupt county officials during the 1980s. The issue of proposed consolidation of county governments and services will also be discussed.

II. Municipal Governments: Cities and Towns

Population and Jurisdictional Demographics

Discussion of a state's population and jurisdictional demographics is fact-based and traditionally uninspiring. However, these facts are important indicators of state's (and more specifically, a municipality's) attractiveness as a place where people want to work and live. Oklahoma's total population as of July 1, 2003 stood at 3,511,532. As part of the American "Heartland," Oklahoma is generally regarded as a primarily rural state. Population figures, however, show that the state has become more urbanized with 80% living in cities and surrounding communities. The U.S. Census Bureau identifies cities as any urban place with a population of 2,500 or more; a "Metropolitan Statistical Area" (MSA) consists of at least one urban area (a "central city") with 50,000 or more inhabitants and "adjacent communities" that are linked economically and socially with the central city. Oklahoma ranks forty-seventh among U.S. MSAs, and Tulsa ranks fifty-fourth (Statistical Abstract of the U.S.).

The two major cities in the state are Oklahoma City (also the state capital), and Tulsa, formerly a major oil center. Table 12–1 identifies the current ten largest cities (Stillwater replaces the previous number ten, Muskogee). It is important to note that for several cities, "population" must be considered in terms of both those citizens living in the cities themselves and those living in outlying metropolitan areas. In addition, three of the cities (Norman, Stillwater, Edmond) on the "Top 10" list are "university towns" with significant student populations.

"Legal Existence"—Constitutional and Statutory Aspects

The American federal system distributes governing power between the national and state governments. It not only prevents one level of government

Table 12-1
Ten Largest Cities in Oklahoma and Land Area

	2002 Population	MSA (2001–2002)	Area (Sq. Miles) 2000
Oklahoma City	519,034	1,121,000	607.00
Tulsa	391,908	878,000	182.6
Norman	97,831		
Lawton	91,333		
Broken Arrow	83,088		
Edmond	70,540		
Midwest City	54,503		
Enid	46,531		
Moore	43,739		
Stillwater	40,586		

SOURCE: Statistical Abstract of the U.S.

from dominating all others but also provides U.S. citizens with numerous government access points and elected officials accountable to the public for government actions. Article I, Section 3 of the U.S. Constitution gives the national government authority to admit states into the union. Section 4 states that "The United States shall guarantee every State in this Union a Republican Form of Government." Scholars generally agree that this language is designed to ensure that the citizens of each state are provided the legal means of electing their representatives to their respective state governments. While not specifically expressed in the Constitution, states hold the power to grant legal existence to cities, counties, towns, etc. States have established unitary relationships, individually determining the extent of power exercised by their respective individual jurisdictions. This relationship between states and cities is governed by the so-called **Dillon's Rule**, named after a nineteenth-century Judge from Iowa who articulated the concept that cities are creatures of the states. Over time, the unitary relationship has been modified to allow cities greater discretion in service delivery and expanded taxation authority.

In identifying the formal structures of and powers exercised by Oklahoma's municipalities, one needs to look no further than the state constitution and statutes. Oklahoma's constitution, specifically Article XVIII dealing with "Municipal Corporations," empowers the state legislature to *incorporate*, that is, to grant legal existence and powers to local jurisdictions and their governments. Specific rules regarding the incorporation of towns and cities are articulated in Title 11 of the Oklahoma State Statutes. Those jurisdictions consisting of more than twenty-five but less than 1,000 inhabitants may be incorporated by the state legislature as a *town*; an incorporated *city* has more than 1,000 inhabitants. Incorporation At present, there are 599 city or town municipalities in Oklahoma (Oklahoma Department of Commerce).

Cities containing more than 2,000 inhabitants may apply for *home rule* status, meaning that the city's inhabitants, through adoption of a *city charter*, are empowered to determine the form of municipal government that will operate in the jurisdiction. Home rule makes it possible for cities to engage in actions which can lead to successful economic development (like the MAPS and Tulsa's "Vision 2005" tax programs), enhanced public safety programs (such as neighborhood policing), and other problem solving/enhancement activities without first seeking state approval.

Municipal Government Structures

In examining the several forms of municipal government structure used in Oklahoma, it is important to note these structures differ in three important ways: 1) how power is distributed among several elected officials, 2) the degree and type of formal and informal power exercised by the governing body's chief executive and its impact on governance, and 3) the use of professional administrators to manage municipal operations. State statutes establish the forms of government that can be adopted by cities and towns and articulate details regarding elected officials, powers, terms of office, and other structural matters.

Unlike cities, towns are restricted regarding the form of government that can be adopted. Towns use the *aldermanic* form of city government with a mayor elected at large and one or two council members elected from each city ward. The mayor is not considered a council member when it comes to achieving quorum or for purposes of voting unless the council vote is equally divided. In this case, he or she is permitted to cast the tie-breaking vote for "questions under consideration of the council" (Title 11, Article IX). Other important officials in the aldermanic form include the city clerk, city treasurer, marshal, and street commissioner.

The processes by which cities in Oklahoma select the desired form of government first depends on whether the individual city chooses the charter or state statute route. Cities choosing government by state statute follow the rules stipulated in Title 11. Cities wishing to adopt one of the three available options must first adopt a charter and then select from among the forms of government provided by statute (Title 11, Articles IX, X, and XI).

The *council-manager* form of government provides for the election of one council member from each city ward and one elected at large. Council members elect a mayor and vice mayor (who acts as mayor during the regular mayor's absence, disability, or suspension), both of whom have almost no formal powers. For example, the mayor presides at meetings and is considered the city's chief representative for ceremonial purposes, but he is essentially in a "weak" position as he does not possess the veto power generally found in "strong mayor" governments. In addition, the mayor does not exercise sole appointment power over department heads, another feature of the strong mayor structure, but shares this responsibility with council members. The mayor does have voting power equal to each council member and participates in all discussions and votes before the council. The council-manager form is popular in Oklahoma and in medium-sized cities throughout the U.S.

Oklahoma City uses the council-manager form, but with some differences. The mayor is elected at-large while the vice-mayor position is held on a rotating basis by the eight members of the city council, each of whom is elected on a ward-based system (The City of Oklahoma City).

Professionalization of city services is facilitated by the use of a city manager, appointed by the council based on executive and administrative qualifications to appoint department heads and manage city operations. City managers are also selected based on actual experience in performing pertinent administrative duties and knowledge of accepted public management practices. It is not uncommon for city managers in major Oklahoma cities to possess masters degrees in public administration or finance or professional degrees. The current city manager of Oklahoma City, James D. Couch, holds several engineering degrees and previously served as the City's Director of Water/Wastewater Utilities.

The city manager directly supervises department heads and their departments' activities, but all city employees serve under the authority of the mayor and council, who are ultimately accountable to the citizens of Oklahoma City. Three exceptions to the city manager's supervision are the City Auditor, the Municipal Counselor, and the Municipal Court Judges, who as "council appointees" answer directly to the mayor and council.

The ***strong mayor-council*** form of government includes a mayor, elected at large, who serves as an ex officio council member at large, and one council member from each city ward. The strong mayor model provides the mayor with greater authority; not only does the mayor preside at council meetings, but he/she essentially has all of the rights, powers, and privileges of all council members, including the right to vote on questions before the council. The strong mayor is described in statute as the city's chief executive officer and the head of the administrative branch of city government due to the additional powers associated with appointing and removing department heads and supervising and controlling city operations and employees (comparable to the city manger position in the council-manager form). The strong mayor-council form is used in most large U.S. cities of one million or more in population, although it is also popular in many medium-sized cities in the Midwest (Bowman and Kearney).

One unique feature of the strong mayor-council form is the existence of a three-member personnel board, elected for staggered six-year terms by the council, to provide a measure of merit protection. The mayor and council are prohibited from appointing or promoting persons to city classified positions (FTE merit-based) for political or non-merit/job fitness reasons.

Tulsa originally used the once-popular commission form of government which empowered multiple commissioners with both executive

LEADERSHIP PROFILE

CINDY ROSENTHAL
Mayor, City of Norman, Oklahoma

CINDY SIMON ROSENTHAL'S first real job was as a newspaper reporter. She worked the city desk for the *Toledo Blade* in Ohio and covered county government for *The Monterey Peninsula Herald* in California. Her interest in government services began to grow. At some point she realized just reporting about government activities was not going to be enough. While working on her Master of Arts in Urban Studies, she served a yearlong public affairs internship with the Coro Foundation. That fellowship provided her an opportunity to observe civic leadership in the St. Louis, Missouri area. She became more fascinated with representative institutions such as state legislatures, county commissions, and city councils. She then became involved with Legis 50, an advocacy organization for the improvement of policymaking capacity of state legislatures. From there she moved to the National Conference of State Legislatures (NCSL) where she provided technical assistance to legislative leaders and their staffs. Rosenthal drew upon her journalistic skills once again as she became the Editor-in-chief for *State Legislatures*, a professional magazine published by NCSL. At that time, the circulation of *State Legislatures* was over 14,000.

When her husband Jim accepted an academic appointment to the School of Social Work at the University of Oklahoma, the Rosenthals moved along with their young daughter to Norman. Soon thereafter, she became a Carl Albert Congressional Fellow and began work on her Ph.D. in Political Science which she earned in 1995. Subsequently, she was hired by the University of Oklahoma to serve as an Assistant Professor of political science and public administration with a joint appointment to Women's Studies.

Rosenthal now serves as the Director and Curator of the Carl Albert Congressional Research and Studies Center at OU. She has become a noted scholar with a national reputation in the fields of legislative studies and women's leadership. Rosenthal has written the book *When Women Lead* (1998) and edited *Women Transforming Congress*

(2002). In addition, she has written dozens of journal articles and book chapters and presented at numerous professional conferences. Rosenthal directs the National Education for Women's Leadership (N.E.W.) program.

She has always been extremely involved in the Norman community and in the summer of 2004, she began her official service to the city as Council Member of Ward 4. "One of the nice things about academic life is that you have a great deal of flexibility of your own schedule—teaching in the evenings and writing on the weekends has allowed me to be able to balance my university commitments and my public service to the city," Rosenthal explains. "A lot of the city meetings are in the late afternoon and evenings . . . and the university is so close to City Hall—within five minutes."

Rosenthal was recently elected as Mayor. Her campaign platform emphasized maintaining quality of life for the citizens of Norman by carefully managing commercial and residential development in the city.

Both Cindy and Jim continue teaching at OU and have two grown children. In what little free time Rosenthal enjoys, she plays golf with her husband and continues her twenty-year participation in a local women's reading group.

Brett S. Sharp

and legislative powers. This form of government fell out of favor due to its lack of a single executive and professional administrator and problems associated with commissioners having virtual sole autonomy over their assigned departments with no charter requirements that commissioners possess competence, knowledge, or experience associated with the departments they headed. Tulsa adopted the strong mayor model in 1990 following approval by city voters the previous year (Tulsa City Council).

Services and Functions—What Cities Do

Oklahoma's constitution empowers cities and towns to provide services and perform functions associated with local governance. Basic traditional services generally include provision of police and fire services, clean water and wastewater management, solid waste management, street and traffic maintenance, zoning and code enforcement, and in some cases (Edmond, for instance), electricity purchased from publicly regulated, private companies.

Cities provide more than public safety services, utilities, and infrastructure maintenance. Many cities also fund and coordinate services and programs designed to enhance "quality of life" and promote economic growth and vitality; for example, Edmond established a public arts program to beautify its downtown area and encourage business growth (state lawmakers adopted a similar program statewide in 2004). Norman offers several youth-based recreation events including a fishing derby. Lawton's Arts and Humanities Council is part of the city's government. Oklahoma City sponsors or manages numerous entertainment and cultural events including the nationally known Festival of the Arts. These positive activities are designed to enhance community life and may translate into more dollars being spent in these jurisdictions by residents and visitors attracted to events and sights.

In sum, modern Oklahoma cities are no longer just concerned with picking up trash, making sure the water runs clean, and keeping city streets safe—they are now expected to provide events and programs which provide entertainment for residents and economic opportunities for downtown merchants.

The majority of general fund municipal expenditures are dedicated to personnel expenses—compensation, benefits, training, compliance with state and federal labor laws—which makes most departmental budgets "labor intensive." Fiscal year budgets, which run from July 1 of one year to June 30 of the following year, provide municipal officials with a complete breakdown of revenues, specific fund activity, and expenditures. Oklahoma law, specifically the Municipal Budget Act, prohibits expendi-

TABLE 12-2
City of Norman Select Departments and Functions

Department	Functions
Police	Law enforcement, criminal investigation, crime prevention
Fire	Fire suppression and prevention, emergency, management
City Clerk	Records management, issuance of licenses and permits, records minutes of council meetings
Public Works	Construction, maintenance, and operation of street and drainage networks
Finance	Monitors organization's financial activities, initiates and manages investment activity, prepares and coordinates budget activity
Parks and Recreation	Manages maintenance and operations at city parks, community centers, pools, and various sports facilities
Human Resources	Manages the recruitment, hiring, and training of city personnel, manages employee benefits and risk management activity

SOURCE: City of Norman.

tures for each fund to exceed the estimated revenues for each fund; in addition, no more than 10% of the total budget for any fund may be budgeted for miscellaneous purposes, such as the fund balance that carries over to the next fiscal year (Title 11—OSCN website). The Act and other legal controls are designed to prevent deficit spending and force municipalities to exercise fiscal discipline.

Pie charts for The City of Oklahoma City illustrate the type and amount of some of the spending activity that municipalities engage in (Figures 12–1 and 12–2). Not surprisingly, out of the $444,465,362 total operating expenditures, public safety (police, fire) receives the greatest amount of funding.

How They Pay For It—Municipal Finances

To meet service demands, municipal governments must collect and spend money. This money, commonly referred to as *revenue*, comes from multiple sources, including a variety of taxes and user fees needed to purchase equipment and materials and to meet employee payrolls and state and federal funding. Municipal governments also engage in capital projects to maintain and enhance infrastructure (streets, bridges, water/wastewater lines, for example) and to build or restore public buildings. States authorize local governments to levy taxes, incur debt, and make expenditures, and the distribution of state and federal aid supplements

FIGURE 12–1 FY 2003–2004 CITY OF OKLAHOMA CITY OPERATING EXPENDITURES BY FUNCTION

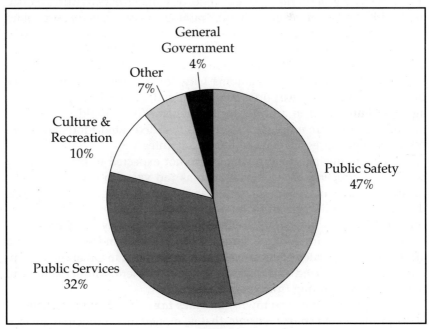

FIGURE 12-2 THE CITY OF OKLAHOMA CITY FY 2004–2005 OPERATING EXPENDITURES BY CATEGORY

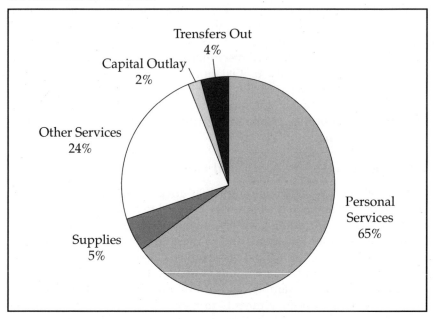

the limited resources generated directly by individual municipalities. Municipal budgets reflect the complexities associated with multiple funds. A city's *general fund*, for example, designates expenditures associated with personnel costs—payroll, training, travel, benefits, etc.—and expenditure categories. Other funds are dedicated by law to specific uses; these may include funds that are to be spent specifically on public safety, street maintenance, public recreation, and other categories (see City of Edmond in Figure 12–3). Oklahoma City, for example, has twenty-five designated funds (e.g. Airports Enterprise Fund, MAPS, Emergency Management Fund, etc.) in addition to the general fund. Rigid budget and accounting rules are employed to ensure that dedicated funds are spent for specific purposes as required by state statutes.

Initially, municipal governments were not expected to provide many services, so *property taxes*, also known as "ad valorem" taxes, were the primary source of revenue. As urban populations grew and public demands for additional and expanded services increased, governments sought to identify new sources of revenue. Modern-day cities now tax a variety of sources including income, food and merchandise, tobacco and alcohol products, sales of goods, and certain services. In Oklahoma, property taxes are collected and used by state government. Municipalities do not derive any funding from this source.

For Oklahoma cities and towns, the *sales tax* on food and merchandise is the primary *own source revenue*, that is, money that municipal govern-

FIGURE 12-3 CITY OF EDMOND GENERAL FUND REVENUE BY SOURCE FY 2000-2001 (BY PERCENT)

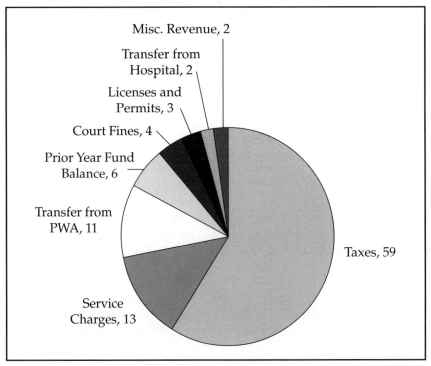

ments raise through taxation of purchases made within their respective jurisdictions.

While cities and towns can raise some of the money needed to fund services, they generally do not have the tax base ("tax capacity") to raise *all* of the funds required to meet residents' service needs and expectations or federal and state policy mandates. Because of this, cities and towns must also rely on (a) state and federal fiscal assistance, i.e., intergovernmental transfers and revenue sharing, and for some, (b) home rule status, which provides municipal government with some autonomy in how revenues are generated and spent.

In FY 2001-2002, the total generated sales/use tax (the sale or rental of tangible personal property and from the furnishings of specific services) for the State of Oklahoma was $1,520,610,183.36 with 93% (or $1,422,902,928.14) being from sales tax alone. Of the sales tax collected, $1,004,909,232.93 was city sales tax; $45,208,494.38 was city use tax (Oklahoma Tax Commission).

Municipal governments are charged with collecting the sales tax, comprised of a 4.5% state sales tax and the individual city/town sales tax. The rate of sales tax charged by Oklahoma's cities and towns varies from 1.0% in towns like Aline, Sawyer, and Texola to 4.5% in Beggs and Rush

Springs. Larger cities tax at rates similar to each other: Oklahoma City charges 3.875%, while Edmond and Tulsa charge 3.25% and 3.0%, respectively (Oklahoma Tax Commission). The importance of the sales tax cannot be overstated. Two recent policy/economic issues, elimination of the sales tax for grocery items and internet taxation, have featured prominently in municipal government discussions over how to protect and enhance this important revenue source. Oklahoma municipalities raised an estimated $98 million in grocery sales tax revenues in FY 1996–1997 increasing to an estimated $178 million for FY 2000 (Oklahoma Municipal League).

Some concern has been raised in recent years over the regressive nature of the sales tax as it places a greater burden on lower income residents who spend a higher proportion of their income on food and other "non-luxury" items (alcohol and tobacco are not included). Support for elimination of the state grocery tax has generated debate at the state and local level with many municipal leaders arguing that the loss of this revenue would force an increase in taxes on other goods and services or force reductions in municipal services; for smaller municipalities, which rely even more heavily on the sales tax than do the larger ones, the loss of this revenue source is particularly problematic. One suggested strategy for off-setting the loss of grocery sales tax is to expand the taxation of services (Oklahoma currently allows taxes of approximately thirty-two different types of services, such as utilities) to include dry cleaning, legal and medical services, barber and beauty shops, lawn maintenance, and other forms of professional and personal services. While most agree that eliminating the sales tax on groceries is justified because of its regressivity, there is disagreement regarding the impact that a sales tax on services would have on lower income residents and concerns regarding the cost of municipal compliance and state administration of compliance activities (UCO College of Business Administration).

Related to the general sales tax issue and sales vs. service debate is the issue of Internet taxation, currently the subject of legislation at the federal level. State and local governments lose an estimated $343 million annually to online purchases not subject to state and local taxation. Midwest City Mayor Eddie Reed summed up state and municipal arguments for imposing an Internet tax by stating, "When a special class is created for sales by Internet or catalog, local communities lose funds to support services. At the same time, it hurts local businesses that must compete with this protected class . . . the Simplified Sales and Use Tax Act, addresses the issue of equity . . ." (Oklahoma City Business). The Act, passed by both houses of Congress in 2003, is an attempt to simplify sales taxation and establish equal treatment between local merchants and remote (Internet) sellers.

While other cities throughout the U.S. rely on ***corporate and personal property*** and ***income taxes*** to add to their revenue, Oklahoma restricts the imposing of these taxes to state government and, in the case of the property tax, for limited purposes. This tax can only be used to retire city debt for specific capital projects but not for day-to-day operations; otherwise, it is distributed to counties and school districts.

Other forms of revenue enhancement contribute to municipal coffers. *User fees*, generally accepted as the "fairest" form of taxation, are paid by the user for services (trash pick-up) and goods (water, parking garages) received. *Franchise fees* are paid by privately owned business establishments (ex: gas stations) located on city easements. *Fines and forfeitures* are collected for violation of criminal, parking, traffic, and code ordinances. Cities and towns charge for various *licenses* and *permits* (ex: garage sales and special events). *Interest* and *investment income* on collected revenues can also be generated.

Finally, local government may call upon residents to approve the issuance of municipal *bonds* through special elections for the purpose of funding long-term capital projects that will require payment over time. Bonds, the most commonly-used form of long-term borrowing, are attractive forms of investment due to federal and state tax breaks for private investors. The attractiveness of bonds is also enhanced by a city's *bond rating*, a measure of the city's "fiscal health" as determined by the subjective/objective rating system established by the nation's top rating firms, Moody's Investor's Service and Standard and Poor's Corporation. The passing of a bond issue creates a debt obligation that municipal residents must assume until the debt is paid off.

Two types of bonds are used by local governments to finance capital projects such as street construction and resurfacing, major computer systems, construction of new public facilities, and other one-time, non-recurring expenditures. *General obligation (G.O.) bonds* are secured by the "full faith and credit" of the local jurisdiction that issues them and are paid off with regular revenues. *Revenue bonds* are also paid off over time with the fees collected from those using the service or product (ex: parking garages). The payment period for both types of bonds is usually between five and twenty years. While bond projects represent a rational approach to planning and spending (they force municipal elected and appointed leaders to plan and prioritize), there is no guarantee that the public will approve them in specially called elections

Challenges for Municipal Governments

Oklahoma's municipal governments have recently faced numerous challenges, including fiscal uncertainty. Declining revenues associated with the impact that the September 11 attacks had on the national economy impacted state budgets (Oklahoma's tax collections dropped from approximately $6 billion to $5 billion between July 2001 and July 2003) forcing municipal leaders to cut city budgets leading to reductions in force. Oklahoma City, for example, estimated that mandatory budget cuts in city departments (2% for police and fire, 11% for other departments) would be needed to offset an estimated $4 million shortfall for FY 2003–2004.

The improved national economy prompted City officials to predict moderate sales tax gains for FY 2004–2005 (The City of Oklahoma City).

Oklahoma's state and municipal governments have responded to the national effort to deter and mitigate terrorist attacks. Already cognizant of the damage and loss of life associated with terrorism, the State of Oklahoma created the Oklahoma Office of Homeland Security (OKOHS) in 2002 to "develop and coordinate implementation of a comprehensive statewide plan to secure the State of Oklahoma from the results of terrorism . . ." As part of this effort, OKOHS distributes federal grant funds to local governments An example of this is $32 million for programs associated with law enforcement, terrorism prevention, interoperable communications, security, and continued funding of citizens' corps which render assistance in community emergencies (OKOHS).

Other challenges have prompted municipal governments to engage in ambitious and non-traditional efforts to respond to community needs. Tulsa's Vision 2025 is similar to MAPS as an economic development program, but unlike Oklahoma City's plan, Tulsa's includes regional as well as city improvements. Oklahoma City partnered with the Oklahoma City Public Schools to develop and promote the MAPS for Kids plan designed to renovate dilapidated schools and provide enhanced academic programs through a $500 million tax initiative and $180 million bond issue passed by city voters in 2001. This partnership is unique in that The City of Oklahoma City has no formal role in the administration and funding of the city's public school system, but city leaders were persuaded to participate in development and passage of MAPS for Kids as the quality of the school system was seen as critical to the city's overall success (Oklahoma City Chamber of Commerce).

While these do not encompass the entire scope of municipal challenges and are not an exhaustive accounting of what is happening at the municipal level, they do illustrate the fact that Oklahoma's cities are concerned with more than ensuring that routine operations are conducted efficiently.

III. COUNTY GOVERNMENT

County Government—Purpose and Functions

Oklahoma counties, established in Art. XVII of the Oklahoma Constitution, are traditionally described as "creatures" or "agents" of state government; that is, they carry out the functions of state government at the local level. This makes it possible for state government to operate throughout the state without having to establish government offices with state employees in locations outside the capital. This decentralized system provides country officials with greater autonomy over how operations are to be managed but also provides local voters with the opportunity to elect their own county officials and hold them more accountable than they could state officials.

Nationally there are 3,066 of these "discrete subunits" of state government; Oklahoma has seventy-seven counties, the largest of which (population-wise) are Oklahoma County (660,448) and Tulsa County (563, 299). The two smallest counties are Cimarron County (3,148) and Harmon County (3,283) (U.S. Census). Many of Oklahoma's counties, including Choctaw, Comanche, Osage, Pottowatomie, and Pawnee, are named for Native American tribes. A rather detailed description of each county's jurisdictional boundaries is provided in Article XVII Section 8 of the Oklahoma Constitution.

Originally, Oklahoma counties consisted of 400 sq. miles of taxable area with at least 15,000 in population and $2.5 million in taxable wealth. Statutory changes expanded the area requirement to 500 sq. miles with the population requirement increased to 20,000; the taxable wealth requirement was also expanded to $4.0 million.

Oklahoma's counties engage in services determined via the state constitution and statutes. Traditional services have included road and bridge construction and maintenance, law enforcement and adjudication, and maintenance of county records [(Oklahoma has 86,820 miles of road and 15,000 bridges that are twenty feet or longer), births, deaths, marriages, land transactions, etc.]. County services have expanded in recent years to include provision of healthcare and medical services, economic and industrial development, social services, and informal adult and youth education programs in science and agriculture, among others, often working with educational institutions located within country borders. For example, Payne County, in cooperation with Oklahoma State University provided courses in agricultural enterprises, natural resources and environmental management, and education in nutrition, food, and health safety in 2003 through the Payne County OSU Cooperative Extension Center.

County services are supported through a variety of fiscal resources: tax levies (on personal property, real estate), aircraft registration fees, sales tax on some products and services, occupation taxes on liquor establishments outside municipal boundaries, and state-collected fees used for county roads, bridges, and highways. Title 74 of the Oklahoma State Statutes authorizes counties to engage in interlocal agreements to share the cost of some road projects with adjacent municipalities and other counties. These agreements are used to combine fiscal and manpower, equipment, and material resources and planning expertise needed for construction of county roads and bridges that cross county and city jurisdictions. County road funds come primarily from state and federal fuel taxes, motor vehicle excise taxes, and gross production taxes.

The Structure of County Government

All counties in Oklahoma employ the "plural executive" system comparable to that used at the state level. The sharing of authority among several elected officials is seen as beneficial to citizens who can now hold multiple government figures accountable for what country government

LEADERSHIP PROFILE

JOHN SMALIGO, JR.
Tulsa County Commissioner for District #1

JOHN SMALIGO, shortly after graduating from the University of Central Oklahoma, ran for a seat in the Oklahoma House of Representatives. He lost. But since he received 48% of the vote in his first race, he was encouraged enough to come back in 2000 for another try. He won with less than 300 votes. His namesake and father, John Smaligo, Sr. held the very same House seat but had lost it in a re-election bid. He took his son proudly the next morning to have breakfast in his opponent's hometown. During much of his tenure in the House, Smaligo was the youngest person serving. Recently, he shifted his political career to the local level by being elected to the Tulsa County Board of Commissioners.

Smaligo was born in Council Bluffs, Iowa but has lived most of his life in Owasso, Oklahoma. He experienced his first political campaign while working a parade for Frank Keating's successful bid for governor in 1994. He has chaired the Tulsa County and Rogers County Republican Conventions and has been a delegate to the State Republican Convention. Smaligo was elected a few years ago to be the Vice-Chairman of the Republican caucus. He served on the Rules, Transportation, Environment & Natural Resources, Tourism and Recreation, Appropriations and Budget committees.

His proudest moment on the legislative floor was when he rose to speak against a bill sponsored by the House and Senate Leadership. It would have placed a $100 fee on any family that wanted to take the deceased body of a loved one outside the state of Oklahoma for burial. During the debate he quoted a line from the movie, *The Sixth Sense*: "I see dead people. I see dead people funding the State of Oklahoma and I think that's wrong." Smaligo used the collapse of the I-40 bridge and the crash of the private plane with several Oklahoma State University basketball team members and officials as examples of why it would be tasteless to extort money from out-of-state families just to get back their loved ones. Smaligo noted that when his own mother died in 1994, his family

> buried her in her home state of Iowa. The bill failed seventy-nine to fourteen.
>
> Despite his young age, term limits quickly moved him to the top half of House seniority. With the turnover in the House of Representatives to the Republicans, Smaligo soon move into top leadership roles. He was awarded the 2004 Pathfinder Award for having a perfect score on a pro-business index. The *Daily Oklahoman* recently ranked him in the top five fewest missed votes in the last two years.
>
> He is still in school pursuing a Master's Degree in Political Science at the University of Central Oklahoma. Smaligo enjoys listening to country music, working on his house, and playing golf. But according to him, politics is still the most fun activity of all.
>
> Brett S. Sharp

does. This is consistent with Oklahoma's populist tradition. However, like its state counterpart, the "plural executive," this can also impede coordination of policymaking and related activity.

The structure of county government is essentially the same throughout the state. Each county elects (on a partisan ballot) three commissioners, a sheriff (county law enforcement and crime prevention), a county clerk (custodian of records, registrar of deeds, county's purchasing agent), an assessor (determines the true worth of real and personal property for the purpose of taxation), and a treasurer (county tax collector and banker). All persons serving in these offices must, at the time of election or appointment, be qualified residents and voters in the county they serve. By statute, regular elections can only be held on Tuesdays in November. Commissioners serve four-year staggered terms (for example, the election of a commissioner for Oklahoma County District Two will occur in 2004; the election for Districts One and Two will not be held until 2006). A county's clerk, sheriff, and court clerk serve two-year terms while the assessor and treasurer serve four-year terms. Special elections can be held to fill vacancies (Source: OSCN–Title 19, Section 131).

The state's constitution and statutes empower county commissioners to assume responsibility for a variety of administrative duties. In addition to general management and administrative efficiency responsibilities, some of the more important commissioner duties are:

- Audit the accounts of all officers handling county money
- Exercise direct control over the county highway system
- Make general financial plans for the county including the county budget
- Approve bids for major purposes or construction projects
- Develop personnel policies for the county

- Selling or purchasing public land for improving efficiency of county government

(Source: Association of County Commissioners of Oklahoma)

County commissioners, like their elected counterparts at the municipal level, must also deal with state and federal unfunded mandates, some of which include drug and alcohol testing for persons holding state-issued commercial drivers licenses, meeting environmental requirements for roads and bridges, complying with ADA employment and public facilities access requirements, and providing training for various county personnel.

Recent Challenges—Scandal, Reform, and Consolidation

County government in Oklahoma has not always been viewed in a positive light. Statewide investigation of purchasing and expenditure practices in the early 1980s led to the conviction of 220 commissioners and other county personnel from sixty of the state's seventy-seven counties in what federal prosecutors dubbed "Okscam." The scandal caused Oklahoma's citizens and lawmakers to take a hard look at the structure of county government and the system which facilitated such widespread corruption.

In their study of the scandal, Holloway and Meyers determined that Okscam was not primarily a product of a "culture of corruption" that had existed in the state throughout its history or at the time of the scandal (in fact, their research indicated that some, but not all county residents supported corrupt official behavior),[1] but the result of a structural and political environment that fostered corrupt activity. Specifically, they found that county commissioners had a significant amount of funding and discretion available to them for road construction with few checks on how county money was spent and for what purpose (Holloway, p. 18).

In response to the scandal, the State Legislature and then-Governor Nigh launched separate efforts to identify the causes of such widespread corruption and develop suggestions for reform of the county commissioner system. Examination of the system revealed that there was a "virtual lack of accountability" with commissioners acting on their own with little effort made to comply with state statutes governing revenue collections and expenditures.

Suggestions for reform concentrated on restructuring county government through professionalizing administration and depoliticizing elective offices. The creation of full time positions (comparable to a city administrator) responsible for administration of road construction/maintenance activities and county purchasing was proposed. Depoliticizing county government would occur through expansion of the number of commissioners (beyond the existing three) and consolidation or abolition of some elected positions (Holloway, p. 19).

A strong county lobby was effective in getting the state legislature to reject these proposals as interfering with the commissioner–constituent relationship. Ultimately, the state approved reforms proposed by Governor Nigh that altered procedures, but not structure:

- Create a county purchasing position (end the commissioner control of this activity)
- End commissioner authority to lease or purchase heavy equipment and machines (now done through central purchasing at the state level)
- Completely fund county District Attorneys' offices though the state and empower D.A.s to investigate allegations of corruption.

Interestingly, the proposal to professionalize county administration through the hiring of engineers and long range planning was "urged" but not mandated (Holloway, p. 21).

Although these reforms fell short of some lawmakers' expectations (commissioners still retained control over road projects and authority was still fragmented among several county officers), the limited institutional modifications did reduce commissioner discretions. A significant change was the legislature's passage of the County Budget Act in Title 19, which authorized the county clerk to ensure that county funds are legally spent and tracked (Oklahoma County Clerk). These, along with the successful prosecution of corrupt county officials, contributed to public support for reform (Holloway, p. 24).

Another recent major issue for counties is city–county consolidation, the merging of similar functions and operations engaged in by counties and area jurisdictions into single countywide government. Thirty-two of these regional forms of government exist in the U.S.; some of the more prominent ones include Indianapolis-Marion County (Indiana), Jacksonville-Duval County (Florida), and Nashville-Davidson County (Kentucky). Despite the rationality of having one administrative body manage and provide such operations—police, fire, water and sewer systems, etc—voters may reject the proposal as limiting their contact with those persons directly responsible for supplying needed services (Bowman and Kearney, p. 343).

While some municipal leaders, such as Tulsa's Mayor Bill LaFortune, have indicated support for consolidation as a way to reduce duplication of services, Oklahoma's county commissioners have been generally resistant to the idea of sharing or even giving up administrative and decision making authority. Arguments against consolidation have included the belief that county government works well under the current system (a view that is debatable given that several successful lawsuits have been filed due to questionable personnel practices) and that the at-will status of county workers reduces personnel problems. Suggestions that efficiency could be enhanced through county performance reviews are countered by arguments that the state already audits county operations. Because of these conflicting views, the possibility of city–county consolidation seems remote (Source: Association of County Commissioners of Oklahoma).

Chapter Twelve

Opportunities for Citizen Participation in Governance

The federal and unitary systems are intended to prevent one government from acquiring all power and to facilitate government accountability and public involvement. To that end, citizens enjoy "multiple points of access" to the two primary units of government, national and state, and the approximately 88,000 local governments that exist throughout the nation. Ideally, citizens would have a more prominent role in determining policy at the local level. National representatives work primarily in Washington, D.C., and, but for a few months of the year, do not spend extended periods of time in their home districts or states. State legislators may spend more time with their constituents, but their focus may be on the activities at their state capitols. Local representatives, such as mayors, county commissioners, aldermen, and councilors, work and live in the same jurisdictions they represent. The proximity of these representatives to the people who elect them promotes the belief that local government is closest to the people, and is, therefore, more likely to be responsive to it. An oft-quoted remark by former U.S. Speaker of the House, Tip O'Neill that "All politics is local" suggests that day-to-day actions and decisions by local government have a greater impact on the state's population and economic fortunes than some might think.

Yet, citizen participation at the local level is frequently marked by low voter turnout. While Oklahomans traditionally turn out in large numbers for presidential and some special elections (like MAPS and sales tax elections), their level of participation is sporadic for municipal and country elections. Voter turnout in the 2002 Tulsa Mayoral election was less than 20%. Lower turnout numbers are generally expected for school board and bond issues. This is not to suggest that municipal and town elections inspire little public interest. In fact, some elections, especially those that involve candidates running on the basis of two clearly competing issues (the 1999 mayoral contest in Oklahoma City where the issue was extended funding of MAPS is an example) can result in higher-than-average turnout. Oklahoma City's 2004 mayoral election achieved an unusually high voter turnout of 25% (some contend that this was due to the interjection of partisanship issues in a non-partisan election).

The problem of low voter turnout seems to stem from the great number of elections that city–county residents can participate in, a consequence of Oklahoma's populist heritage. Municipal and county elections for mayor, council members, county commissioners, sheriffs, school board presidents and members, education and general bond issues, tax measures, and special elections to fill vacancies occur throughout the year, making civic participation via voting a demanding responsibility.

While voting is generally regarded as the major form of public participation in governance, it is not the only means. Some Oklahoma cities provide additional opportunities for civic participation. Residents of Edmond (approx. seventeen miles north of Oklahoma City) can apply to the Citizens' Government Academy to learn about Edmond city government and the role played by citizens while Norman youth ages fourteen to twenty can apply to the city's Police Explorer's program to learn about law enforcement, possibly as a career. Oklahoma's Open Meetings Act opens regular and special government meetings (like budget deliberations) to the public. City council meetings frequently designate a time specifically for citizen commentary in their weekly agendas. Citizen groups may form to support and/or oppose local government actions; "Citizens for a Better Edmond," an example of a citizen-based group, played an important role in influencing The City of Edmond's decision regarding the building a Super Wal-Mart near a residential area while Oklahoma City's Neighborhood Alliance was a key player supporting the successful 3/4 cent sales tax for public safety . In short, municipal residents have multiple opportunities for accessing and influencing their governments, and in some cases, they are very successful in doing so.

NOTES

1. My mother, former Canadian County Commissioner Penny Duncan Ferrell, encountered the corrupt practices that her predecessor, a convicted commissioner, had engaged in when she received an angry note from a county resident who demanded to have her driveway paved after Ferrell refused. The resident had sent a check for payment and a request for service because that is how the last commissioner did business. Ferrell insisted on complying with state law and was scolded for it.

CHAPTER THIRTEEN

PUBLIC POLICY
Markus S. Smith and Dana K. Glencross

No policy that does not rest upon some philosophical public opinion can be permanently maintained.

Abraham Lincoln

Surround yourself with the best people you can find, delegate authority, and don't interfere as long as the policy you've decided upon is being carried out.

Ronald Reagan

I. INTRODUCTION

Gambling that they would not be caught, tattoo artists continued to flaunt their trade for many years in violation of a state law enacted in 1963 banning the practice. A person could get a tattoo, but the artist caught applying the tattoo was guilty of a criminal misdemeanor offense. Tattoo designs could be sold in Oklahoma but could only be applied legally by an artist in a neighboring state. Removing tattoos and getting permanent makeup applications, as well as body piercing, were all legal practices during this time. The Oklahoma Tattoo and Piercing Association sponsored a seminar where potential artists could learn the art by applying tattoos to pig skin (Nascenzi, p. 10).

Often, tensions between the public and public policy cause interesting situations to emerge as people attempt to change public policy. As the popularity of tattooing increased nationwide from an estimated 300 tattoo parlors in 1960 to more than 4,000 in 2005, Oklahoma was the sole remaining state with unregulated tattooing (*World's* Editorial Writers, p. A12). With a "little ink and a nod," the ABATE ("A Brotherhood Aiming Toward Education") motorcycle group even held a yearly tattoo contest and swap meet (Walton, p. A26). They gathered in spite of misdemeanor arrests, an unsympathetic public, and numerous defeated legislative attempts to legalize the art. An editorial by the Oklahoma Commissioner of Public Health even argued for legalization of the practice, drawing attention to the fact that the original legislative intent of the ban preventing tattooing for public safety and health concerns might actually cause increased safety and health risks from the too common practice of tattooing illegally without regulation (Crutcher, p. 25A). A 2004 case in Tulsa County rendered the antiquated state law ineffective when two arrested tattoo artists claimed that since tattoos could be removed, the state law prohibiting application of a "permanent indelible mark" on the skin did not apply (Mock, p. 1A).

The situation regarding enactment of a state lottery was similar in nature although in this instance Oklahoma was one of ten states without a lottery. Moral tensions defeated early legislative attempts and even a legislative referendum to legalize a lottery. A **legislative referendum** occurs when voters are asked to approve a legislative proposal. In contrast, voters previously had approved both liquor by the drink and an initiative legalizing horse racing. An **initiative** occurs when voters circulate a petition, gather the state-required number of signatures of eligible voters, have those signatures certified as authentic and then vote on the ballot measure proposing constitutional or legislative change. Success of initial gaming efforts may very well have aided later attempts to pass a state lottery. Voters eventually approved it by 64% even though a referendum to ban gay marriage appeared on the same ballot with 75% of voters disapproving of that measure (Ellis, p. 14A). Also helping to pass the measure was undoubtedly the fact that in a separate measure, voters were constitutionally assured lottery proceeds would contribute economically to the improvement of education. Interestingly, Native American Indian tribes also contributed more than half a million dollars towards passage of the lottery proposal, seemingly at cross-purposes with their existing casino interests (Thornton, p. 1A). Not long after approval of the measure, however, the "voluntariness" of the lottery was apparent when poll results showed 64% of those polled admitted they had yet to purchase a ticket (NewsOK.com, 2005).

"Scratchers," tattoo artists who were less than knowledgeable about their trade, and those wishing to become lotto ticket "scratch" winners eventually had opportunities to experience the outcomes of successful efforts to alter public policy. Everyone is affected every day by some type of public policy enacted by governments (e.g. polluted air, capital punishment, the Patriot Act, etc.). **Public policy** can be defined as "an intentional course of action followed by an actor or set of actors (usually government) in dealing with some problem or matter of concern that causes some type of distress" (O'Connor, 2006).

Segregation and discrimination are prime examples of national "matters of concern" that led to the landmark *Brown v. Board of Education* cases (1954, 1955), which ultimately led to passage of the Civil Rights Act of 1964 and the Voting Rights Act of 1965, effecting public policy changes in all states. Millions of African–Americans were finally able to attend schools, eat in restaurants, vote, and work in places where blacks previously were prohibited, not without violence and diligence, because of long-sought changes in public policy (Anderson, 1978). These policies are considered some of the most significant advances that the federal and state governments have taken in regards to civil liberties and civil rights. *Brown* demonstrated a necessary course of action to ameliorate problems that caused distress and dissatisfaction to many African–Americans during the 1950s and 1960s.

Political scientist Carl J. Friedrich gives us a more detailed definition of **public policy** as:

> *"a proposed* course of action *of a person, group, or government within a given environment providing obstacles and opportunities which the policy was proposed to utilize and overcome in an effort to reach a goal or realize an objective or a purpose (Friedrich, 1963)."*

This course of action (series of stages or sequential phases) is typically the model used to illustrate the policy-making process (see Figure 13–1).

FIGURE 13–1 Policy Making Process

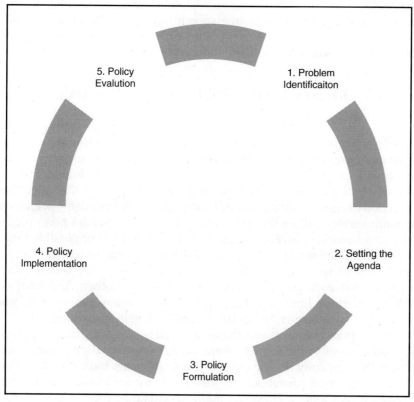

What follows below is an explanation of how such measures can and do indeed become law. Let us now look more specifically at the various stages of the policy-making process.

II. Stage One—Problem Identification

For a condition to be **identified as a problem**, *there must be some type of standard that leads people to seek some type of relief which the government can effectively remedy.* It is important to note that a condition must also be seen as appropriate and feasible for government action, and more importantly, something for which a remedy or solution is possible; because quite frankly, all distressing conditions do not automatically become problems that can be ameliorated. For example, the May 3rd tornado, which touched down in Oklahoma in 1999, was one of the deadliest tornadoes in the United States in over twenty years (Brooks, 2001). Though tornadoes have been a continuing problem in Oklahoma, they are unlikely to become a policy issue because, simply, there is little or nothing that the government can do about them directly. They are considered an act of nature or a natural disaster. Only after they occur do federal and state governments promulgate the majority of their policies to respond and cope with the aftermath. The tattoo provision in Oklahoma rose to prominence not because of a need to protect free speech but largely because of public health concerns raised by unscrupulous artist practices and the need to effectively and safely regulate the industry.

III. Stage Two—Setting the Agenda

Professors Roger Cobb and Charles Elder define **agenda setting** as a set of political controversies that will be viewed as falling within the range of legitimate concerns meriting the attention of the polity (a society or institution with an organized government); a set of items scheduled for active and serious attention by a decision-making body (Cobb, 1972). With this definition of agenda setting, it is evident that a dilemma exists—which set of controversies will be viewed? Which set of controversies takes precedence over another? In other words, out of the hundreds or possibly thousands of requests made to the government (state, local, or federal), only a small number will receive serious consideration by policy-makers. This suggests that each problem competes with one another. And because policy-makers are limited by time and resources, many controversies are put on the "back burner," so to speak, and may never be addressed.

The fact that Oklahoma was the very last state to legalize tattoo application and was one of the few remaining states to pass a lottery measure evidences this difficulty. Public polling of Oklahomans indicated that they strongly supported educational improvements for many years prior to the discussion of a lottery. However, many specific measures to achieve this outcome competed with one another and delayed action. Was the key to improving national, standardized test scores of secondary students best resolved by keeping veteran, tenured teachers or by replacing them with more recent education graduates whose training included more modern learning approaches? States such as Texas fired many veteran teachers when they failed a state-mandated professional exam only to discover that standardized test scores of students showed little if any improvement after this action was taken. Early attempts to supplement the funding sources of public education in Oklahoma, such as legalizing gambling in the form of horse racing, produced minimal increases in education funding and failed to improve educational measurements. By far, the measure HB 1017, which provided teacher salary raises through income tax increases, produced far faster results in improving Oklahoma's national ranking in teacher salaries; however, national standardized exam scores by students during this period netted only modest increases, at best. Moral dilemmas and debates concerning the best methods to improve educational quality certainly defeated the initial passage of the state's lottery; however, growing public concern over the lack of education funding sources and slow-to-improve standardized exam performance by students increased to the point that most voters were willing to take a chance on the lottery in the hope it would fund substantial educational changes and improvements in learning. Thus, controversies labeled as a "crisis" are more likely to be given attention and may specifically be given that label in an effort to secure a higher agenda status, which will help ensure that action is inevitable (Anderson, 2000).

IV. STAGE THREE—FORMULATION/ADOPTION

The third stage in the policy-making process can be defined, simply, as *the stage where the crafting of acceptable courses of action for dealing with some public issue are identified and adopted into law with requisite authority, such as Congress, the President, or a legislature.* Thus, public policies are governmental policies based on law, which means that they are authoritative and binding on people. For example, individuals, groups, and even governmental agencies can be penalized with fines, lose benefits, and are even incarcerated if they fail to comply with policies (O'Connor, 2006). Many tattoo artists in Oklahoma learned these hard lessons even as they knew that the eventual approval of legislation legalizing tattooing was imminent. One of the reasons frequently cited for eventual voter approval of the lottery was the fact many Oklahomans were crossing the state line to buy lottery tickets in neighboring states. This common practice cost the state many dollars in potential revenue.

V. STAGE FOUR—IMPLEMENTATION

The stage of the policy-making process immediately following the passage of a policy into law is **implementation**. Implementation can be

Chapter Thirteen

LEADERSHIP PROFILE

JEANETTE M. NANCE
Agency Liaison and Public Policy Specialist, Office of the Governor

JEANETTE NANCE, as one of Governor Brad Henry's designated liaisons to the rest of the executive branch, had never really thought about the hodgepodge of agencies assigned to her. Why, for example, did she have the Department of Agriculture *and* the Department of Transportation; or Public Safety, Corporation Commission, Insurance Department, Turnpike Authority, and the Secretary of the Environment? Then the necessity to coordinate these disparate state agencies became crystal clear to Nance. A series of back-to-back ice storms hit the state in January 2007. Ice and snow paralyzed large parts of Oklahoma. Nance found herself at the virtual center of a rapidly developing communications network linking these agencies to changing events on the ground. In a sense, she became eyes and ears for a host of decision makers inside and outside of the governor's office.

Nance received countless calls from citizens across the state who were facing critical needs. Thousands of homes were without power. Bitterly cold temperatures continued for days creating a host of problems. Power outages were forcing some people to lose food. Roads and highways were extremely slick and hazardous over widespread areas. The storms affected nearly every aspect of public policy in the state.

State agencies swung into action. The Corporation Commission channeled hourly updates about power outages to the governor's office. The Oklahoma Highway Patrol would then know where to keep state troopers assigned to distribute emergency water and generators. The Department of Agriculture gathered hay to deliver to assist ranchers and farmers who could not feed their cattle. A Chinook helicopter from the National Guard and a plane from the Highway Patrol dropped hay to cattle stranded due to the storms. Road crews worked day and night clearing ice and salting highways to keep open the transportation arteries of the state. The governor declared a state of emergency for all seventy-seven counties of the state allowing local governments to get reimbursed for recovery expenses.

As a junior staff member, Nance realized that she was doing something important. She had face-to-face contact with several cabinet members, the chief of staff, and even the governor himself. She fielded dozens of calls per day, worked long hours and weekends all through the month. Storms of this magnitude make it impossible to fully address the needs of each and every citizen. But as Nance says, "I had the satisfaction of knowing I at least helped some of the people some of the time." She remembers a political proverb proffered by one of her mentors, Mike Turpen, who told her, "The rule of constituent service is the people that you specifically help specifically remember, and the people you generally help generally forget."

Prior to her service in government, Nance had worked mostly in the nonprofit sector and had just recently completed her Bachelor's Degree in Political Science from the University of Central Oklahoma. As part of her educational career, Nance made a special effort to take advantage of internship opportunities. Her first internship experience was as a Carl Albert Intern for the State of Oklahoma Office of Personnel Management. Later, she served as an intern on the inaugural committee for Brad Henry. Nance also was selected to be a Carl Reherman City Management Intern for the City of Edmond. Finally, she spent a summer internship in the scheduling office for Governor Brad Henry which ultimately led to her job as Agency Liaison and Public Policy Specialist. Even more exciting, the Governor has just announced that Nance is being promoted to Director of Constituent Services.

Nance and her husband Bob, a well-respected attorney, are the proud parents of three children: Joy, Julie, and Daniel. She and her two daughters graduated at nearly the same time from the University of Central Oklahoma with degrees in political science. Both daughters are now married with children of their own. Her son is now a student at Oklahoma State University.

Brett S. Sharp

defined as *the carrying out of public policies through various actors—Congress, courts, organizations, etc.—to put the policies that have been adopted into effect in an attempt to achieve program or policy objectives.* Congress for instance, affects implementation in a variety of ways. In some cases, Congress passes legislation which may severely limit the amount of discretion administrators have available to them. Congressional concerns dealing with the particulars of the food stamp or student loan programs—who should truly be receiving the benefits and how much should be provided to each beneficiary—represent examples of congressional affects upon implementation. State funding may be detrimentally affected by a state administrator deemed to be administering program funds incorrectly although the administrator is following only vaguely-established guidelines. Disparate results in the amount of aid awarded those who qualify may occur because funding amounts vary due to particular biases placed within the policies to achieve desired end results.

The courts' relationship in implementing policies is sometimes more direct than the congressional relationship. Judicial administration encompasses a variety of issues such as the *Brown v. Board of Education* example mentioned earlier, bankruptcy, naturalization for illegal aliens, as well as criminal and divorce proceedings, to name a few. However, in many instances, the most important way in which the courts affect policy implementation results from judicial interpretation of rules or statutes. For example, in *Griswold v. Connecticut* (1965), Connecticut had a statute that made it illegal to use or provide counseling to married persons for the purposes of using contraceptives. By a vote of seven to two, the U.S. Supreme Court struck down the law on the grounds that it violated an individual's "right to privacy," as interpreted by the justices in the Constitution. Furthermore, the *Griswold* ruling also helped to declare that women have a constitutional "right to privacy" to choose to terminate a pregnancy (i.e. secure an abortion) in *Roe v. Wade* (1973). While abortions were legal at the time of the *Roe* case in some states, such as California, the plaintiff in *Roe* sued because the right was not being extended to her by her resident state of Texas, where abortions were illegal. The U.S. Supreme Court's decision in *Roe* forced all state governments to comply with the federal decision, while simultaneously giving the states some discretion in regulating abortion procedures and personal privacy rights. Thus, states were not only responsible for ensuring that doctors and medical facilities complied with the federal ruling, but they were also responsible for ensuring that this new policy was implemented within constitutional guidelines.

Implementation can also be viewed in terms of outcomes. Meaning, the outcomes of policy, hopefully, can illustrate some measurable change in the problem that was addressed by the policy or law. For example, has the quality of education improved? Or is getting a tattoo less medically risky than at the time before the adoption (or passage) of lotto and tattoo regulation/legalization policies? The questions posed illustrate the nature of policy implementation—it is neither routine nor predictable—due to the complexities of the process. And because of the complexities, uncertainties about whether a policy will actually accomplish what it was set out to do are typical. As the Oklahoma lottery continues to bring in less revenue than estimated, the potential to enhance the quality of education in Oklahoma is diminished. A medically safe tattoo is more likely but not guaranteed, with many artists still failing to comply fully with licensure requirements. Regardless of the nature of policy implementation and from a policy-making perspective, implementation is still both fascinating and meaningful due to the impact that public policies have upon the lives of people.

VI. STAGE FIVE—EVALUATION

Because the public policy process can be viewed as a series of stages or sequential phases, its final stage is policy **evaluation**. Policy evaluation can be defined as *the stage where policy-makers determine whether a course of action achieved, or is achieving, what it was set out to accomplish.* Congressional committees, qualified evaluators, social scientists, and even citizens frequently make judgments on the effectiveness and efficiency, as well as the necessity, of particular policies. Typically, studies are designed to measure or systematically examine both the short and long-term impact to determine whether these programs are achieving their specific objectives or goals (Shafritz, 2005).

The Resource Conservation and Recovery Act (RCRA) of 1976 gave the EPA the primary responsibility for the safe management (i.e. transportation, storage, treatment, and disposal) of toxic waste. Although the RCRA is a federal law, it is implemented by individual states and cities. To implement the law, a state must first: 1) provide adequate staffing; 2) establish institutional responsibility; and 3) allocate resources to carry out the intent of the law. Though the process proceeded slowly, all but six states received final authorization from 1984–1995. Some states like Delaware proceeded expeditiously, whereas other states such as Wyoming never intended to attain authorization status. This raises the question: Why the disparity in reaction times between the states?

Part of the reason was due to some of the states' inability to hire sufficient staff to implement the RCRA. Additionally, some of the states had sufficient financial resources for implementing RCRA, where others did not. Not surprisingly, research also indicated that states dominated by the petrochemical industry (e.g. Oklahoma and Texas) were "foot-draggers" in implementing RCRA. Thus, this brief illustration of RCRA implementation exemplifies the conditions that can facilitate or hinder the implementation of public policy (Lester, 2000).

Evaluation research can encourage attempts through feedback to modify and/or terminate policies and, thus, restart the policy-making process all over again. Therefore, the policy-making process can be viewed as a never-ending cycle. Oklahoma's efforts to make the tattoo industry more medically safe and towards improving education quality by providing an additional lottery funding source undoubtedly illustrate the difficulties inherent in policy success.

VII. CONCLUSION

Public policy affects each and every one of us every day—directly and indirectly—whether we realize it or not. Public policy addresses a diversity of interests. A basic understanding of the nature of public policy along with a framework for understanding the policy-making process helps to facilitate an effective means to resolve many problems that face society today.

CHAPTER FOURTEEN

OKLAHOMA ENVIRONMENTAL POLICY: CONFLICT AND COMPLEXITY IN A TRADITIONALIST STATE

John R. Wood

That's the thing about mother nature, she doesn't really care what economic bracket you're in.

Whoopi Goldberg

I. INTRODUCTION

Oklahoma is an ecologically diverse state. According to the Environmental Protection Agency (EPA), Oklahoma holds the nation's most diverse terrain for its size (Western Ecological Region, 2007). Oklahoma's environment is a mosaic of grazing land, cropland, woodland, forests, and abandoned farmland. It is one of only four states with more than ten **eco-regions**, which are areas separated by type of environmental terrain or sub-climate. The state's land varies from the cypress swamps of the Southeast to Rocky Mountain foothills in the West, tallgrass prairies in the Central and Northeast, and hardwood forests to pine-covered mountains in the South and Southeast.

Environmental policy is the implementation of governmental actions to influence natural resource use and environmental quality (Kraft, 2004). From its beginning, Oklahoma's stance toward governmental policies has been largely populist with "traditionalistic overtones" often in conflict with its physical environment (Morgan et al., 1991). From the Land Run to the Dustbowl to the controversies over Tar Creek and poultry operations, Oklahomans struggle to square their political culture with the demands placed on them by their own state's environmental regulatory complexity. Oklahoma's environmental policy is complicated by more than ten Oklahoma state agencies overlapping in their authority over environmental questions (See Table 14–1).

Oklahoma's environmental policy is made up of the state's collective decisions to pursue certain environmental goals with particular tools to

Table 14–1
Oklahoma State Environmental Agencies

Department of Environmental Quality	The state's primary environmental agency. Established in 1993. Responsible for point and some non-point source pollution; ground and surface water quality and protection, air quality, radioactive waste, solid and hazardous waste, and enforcement of Water Quality Standards. Administers Superfund, or the Comprehensive Environmental Response, Compensation and Liability Act of 1980.
Department of Labor	Regulates indoor air quality under the Oklahoma Occupational Health and Safety Act. It also regulates asbestos monitoring in workplaces.
Department of Mines	Deals with mining activities and corporations engaged in mining activities in the State. Deals with groundwater protection and the development of a Water Quality Standards Implementation Plant for these activities.
Department of Public Safety	Responsible for transportation of hazardous waste including inspection of vehicles and other carriers of hazardous waste.
Department of Wildlife Conservation	In charge of wildlife protection.
Oklahoma Corporation Commission	Authority over oil and gas conservation and exploration, drilling, development, production, processing, and underground storage tanks. It receives its jurisdiction from the Oklahoma Constitution.
Oklahoma Conservation Commission	Monitors, evaluates, and assesses waters to determine the impact of non-point source pollution. It also deals with erosion control, abandoned mines, wetlands, and environmental education.
Oklahoma Department of Agriculture	Covers both point and non-point source pollution, and runoff, from agricultural-related activities. Also enforces the Oklahoma Water Quality Standard, implementing a Water Quality Standard Implementation Plan as well as other agricultural storage facilities.
Department of Civil Emergency Management	Prepares for and deals with emergencies and disasters in the state. Also maintains an electronic emergency information system which provides access to information relating to the quantity and location of hazardous materials.
Oklahoma Scenic Rivers Commission	Establishes minimum standards for planning and other ordinances necessary to carry out the provisions of the Scenic Rivers Act. Main focus is preservation and protection of the beauty, scenic, history, archaeology, and scientific features of the Illinois River and its

	tributaries—Barren (Baron) Fork Creek, Lee Creek, Little Lee Creek, Flint Creek, and (Upper) Mountain Fork.
Oklahoma Water Resources Board	Enforces Oklahoma water quality standards. Lead agency to enforce the Clean Water Act's clean lakes program. Deals with ground and surface water rights and interstate stream compacts.
Secretary of the Environment	Charged with the protection and enhancement of Oklahoma's environment and natural resources. Administers Federal Clean Water Act funds as well as coordinates pollution control efforts to avoid duplication of state agency work.

achieve them. Not only is environmental policy a description of what the state does about the use of natural resources and protecting environmental quality, but what it *does not* do. Oklahoma's environmental history was dominated by settlers' struggles to keep food on the table, not by conserving their resources for future use. This early history is not unlike colonists' concentration on land use (Andrews, 2006). Such a policy strategy, with an emphasis on use rather than conservation, seemed to work well for the first third of the State's history. However, this policy strategy's eventual failure means that present Oklahomans ultimately inherit its consequences.

II. History From the Land Run to the Dust Bowl

A long row of excited settlers, some 50,000 on racehorses, others in wagons and on foot, toed the imaginary line of a new frontier—a new life. Little did these settlers know, but Oklahomans' policies regarding their fragile and yet often hostile environment would begin with an earsplitting trumpet call heard on April 22, 1889, at high noon. At this pivotal moment, the Oklahoma Land Run began and thousands of settlers from many states broke the line, dashing for their highly coveted prize of 160 acres of land. Overnight, Guthrie, Oklahoma swelled from nothing to 10,000 people (Oklahoma Territory Census 1890). The *Harper's Weekly* in 1889 described the new birth of a community virtually overnight:

> "Unlike Rome, the city of Guthrie was built in a day. To be strictly accurate in the matter, it might be said that it was built in an afternoon. At twelve o'clock on Monday, April 22nd, the resident population of Guthrie was nothing; before sundown it was at least ten thousand. (Howard, 1889)."

Land was plentiful at a time when Native Americans held the land in common. But this soon changed as it was opened up to homestead settlement. Poor settlers poured into the once barren territory, lured by "free land." They failed to understand that without a way to deal with this immediate and immense overpopulation, the result would be poverty and conflict (Morgan et al., 1991).

More than sixty years prior, Indian tribes were uprooted from their homes east of the Mississippi River in a series of land confiscations under the Removal Act of 1830. Over several decades they moved to what was then called Indian Territory. Today this is recognized as the eastern portion of Oklahoma. Their new home would not last for long (Heidler and Heidler, 2007). After the Native Americans settled the territory, frontiersmen eyed the area, often complaining that these Native people and only a few cattlemen were the sole occupants of these sixty million acres of treaty lands. Many government officials as well as frontiersmen felt that the Native Americans were not civilized and that they would assimilate as farmers if given individual land holdings. In his 1881 address to Congress, U.S. President Chester Arthur explains:

> ". . . there is reason to believe that the Indians in large numbers would be persuaded to sever their tribal relations and to engage at once in agricultural pursuits. Many of them realize the fact that their hunting days are over and that it is now for their best interests to conform their manner of life to the new order of things. By no greater inducement than the assurance of permanent title to the soil can they be led to engage in the occupation of tilling it" (Richardson, 2001).

As a result, the General Allotment Act of 1887, also known as the Dawes Act or Dawes Severalty Act, authorized the President of the United States to survey Native American commonly-held tribal land and break it up into allotments for individual Native Americans (Debo, 1949). During this process, the "Indian Nations" were stripped of their communally-held lands. For Native Americans, the Dawes Act was the most important method of gaining citizenship prior to 1924 (Baird and Goble, 1990). The Dawes Act tied Native American citizenship to the ultimate proof of citizenship—individual land ownership. The Dawes Act supporters not only wanted to destroy the tribal loyalties and the reservation system, but also to open up white settlement of Indian Territory. The Dawes Act opened up hundreds of thousands of acres of land after the individual 160-acre allotments had originally been made to Native Americans. These land parcels were then sold for prices to land-hungry whites though the Homestead Act, which like the Dawes Act, allowed individuals to claim up to 160 acres of publicly owned lands. Those who lived on and improved their claims over a five-year period owned this land outright.

Land ownership through the Homestead Act, however, would later come to haunt Oklahomans (Egan, 2006). The soil erosion during the Dust Bowl was a result of not only farming technique and climate, but also Oklahomans' approach to environmental policymaking. Agronomists and others advised Congress members that for Indian Territory, the division of 160 acres per settler would not work. Farmers could not make enough money to feed their families on the arid Oklahoma soils with only 160 acres of land. However, Debo (1981) argues, Congress members wanted to boost their popularity by helping as many families as possible and stuck with the 160-acre allotments.

> *"Oklahoma had a bad condition to start with: light, thin soil; large areas too rough for agriculture; and violent extremes of flood and drought. Then the method of settlement, although in the American tradition, was the worst possible method for the land. All the bad practices inaugurated at Jamestown and repeated on successive frontiers were intensified in Oklahoma" (Debo, 1981, p. 74).*

Settlers became conscious of the land's fragility soon after statehood in 1907. Farmers watched their fields become pockmarked with gullies filled with stagnant water, but did little because they were forced to squeeze every last ounce of each acre's production to feed their struggling families. By 1931, thirteen of sixteen million acres, or more than 80% of Oklahoma cropland, had been damaged with water wearing down the once fertile soil. After grasses and trees were removed to create farmlands, the resulting sandy Indian Territory soils were susceptible to erosion (Phillips and Harrison, 2004). The circumstances only grew tougher as depression hurt the economic outlook of much of the United States. The "Black Tuesday" crash of the stock market pushed people from the economic hardship in the cities to the already struggling farm lands (Carson, 2006). To make things even worse, severe drought hit the Great Plains in the mid-1930s. These problems piled up on the backs of farmers who could not plant their crops, leaving the land even more exposed to the wind. More than 300 "Black Rollers," or major dust storms, windswept what was left of the once fertile soil already worn down by standing water. Along with environmental conditions unkind to crop farming, eastern methods of farming such as straight-row farming, often plowed up and down hillsides, created gullies in the lowlands from rainfall runoff. When it did rain, it often fell at the wrong time of year to help crops. As a result of a ten-year drought, Oklahoma started to look more and more like a desert by the mid-1930s. Not surprisingly, more than 75,000 farmers abandoned their unproductive farms for other states like California in search of employment (Phillips and Harrison, 2004). As a result, U.S. environmental policy toward Oklahoma changed from **laissez faire**, or a hands-off approach, to a focus on erosion control.

Policy Reaction

Environmental policy appeared in the forefront for the first time as the government recognized soil erosion in 1929 with the Buchanan Amendment to the Agriculture Appropriation Bill enacted by Congress (Egan, 2006). In an effort to keep farmers on the farm, the federal government created the Agricultural Adjustment Act of 1933, a forerunner to today's

Farm Bill. This Act paid farmers to limit producing certain crops when prices were low and store them during times of crisis (Carson, 2006).

In response to the "Black Rollers," the federal government took a more active role by enacting the Soil Conservation Act of 1935, which created the Soil Conservation Service (SCS) within the U.S. Department of Agriculture. This is now referred to as the Natural Resources Conservation Service. Hugh Bennett, who headed the Service, took over the largest soil conservation service project called "Operation Dust Bowl." Bennett's strategy attacked the drifts of sand with contour-plowing, creating furrows or grooves in the soil to protect it from the gusting wind. In these furrows, he planted African grasses, not to grow crops, but to bring the Oklahoman desert back to life (Mundende, 2004).

By 1937, Oklahoma took a more direct role in working with landowners and acted as intermediary for federal soil conservation assistance. The resolution called for states to enact a law establishing a state soil conservation agency and procedures whereby local soil and water conservation districts could be established.

These environmental policies were a reaction to the Dust Bowl crisis and a way in which to deal with it. In debate at the time was whether the Dust Bowl was a hundred-year cycle or man made. In 1936, Bennett delivered the Great Plains Drought Area Committee to President Roosevelt concluding that it was both. The study says that only twenty inches of rainfall or less would not support dry land farming. The report noted that: "Mistaken public policies have been largely responsible for the situation." The report more specifically, made reference to "a mistaken homestead policy, the stimulation of war time demands which led to over cropping and over grazing, and encouragement of a system of agriculture which could not be both permanent and prosperous"(Egan, 2006: 267). This report shows how environmental policy can be flawed. But, the story of how the government has responded shows how such tragedy can be turned around. The Dust Bowl coupled with the Great Depression convincingly demonstrates that state efforts alone were inadequate for the responding to national economic and environmental problems. Although the New Deal itself did not adequately respond to the environmental problems, it transformed current notions of federalism by creating a presumption that national regulation was necessary for responding to national problems.

However, counter to this trend, Oklahoman's painful Dust Bowl history has contributed to a largely traditionalist political culture resistant to change, placing a premium on "business as usual"(Morgan *et al.*, 1991: 4). This might help explain why the Resource Renewal Institute's State of the State's reports finds that Oklahoma ranks forty-sixth out of fifty states in its policy innovation to improve the state's environmental programs, and in the bottom five states in pollution prevention performance in a study by the Environmental Defense Fund. Furthermore, *Governing* magazine cites U.S. Census Bureau data showing that Oklahoma ranks forty-fifth in environmental spending per capita with $661 million dollars in 2004.

Governing also finds that Oklahoma—3.8%—beats only Mississippi and South Dakota in the percentage of residents' garbage recycled.

III. RECENT POLICY CONTROVERSIES

Controversies in Oklahoma as well as elsewhere often stem from diversity and complexity. This chapter briefly discusses two cases, representing major environmental controversies. The first is the rise of Oklahoma poultry farmers, who contract with large poultry corporations in Arkansas and the second is Tar Creek, one of the nation's most polluted places. Environmental policy from the Land Run to the Dust Bowl was relatively simple because at the time little was known about the environment. But as Oklahomans and their federal counterparts have had to deal with the Dust Bowl and thereafter, policy decisions on all levels of government have become more complicated and controversial.

Poultry

The poultry house's aluminum door whirrs as it opens, revealing a dark, dank, and stale "other world." The barn's intoned vibration betrays the community of 50,000 chickens therein. The unwieldy smell of chicken waste quickly penetrates the senses without warning. "You'll get used to it, they're just chickens," the farmer says as he notices my grimace. As we enter, the chickens cluck and cluster together away from our feet as we walk across the barn. A foot thick of chicken waste has finely matted over the last six weeks as the chickens have grown to maturity. Within a week, all these chickens will ship and be slaughtered at the contractor's plant just across the state line in Arkansas. We cross to the other end of the barn to adjust the watering system. Soon, a line of chickens greedily suck on the holes neatly carved in the bottom of the long PVC pile strung alongside the length of the barn. "Man, they're a thirsty this mornin,' mighty hot out there already," the farmer says as he wipes his brow with his grimy cap in hand.[1]

In an adjacent pasture, this poultry farmer sells his chicken waste to his neighbor, a cattle rancher, in order to fertilize the land's nutrient-starved soil. The payoff is a nice stand of wheat for the neighbor's cattle. This practice has alarmed politicians, residents and scientists alike. Scientific reports have indicated that increased phosphorous from various sources, like chicken waste, has caused the Illinois River to turn abnormally green and brown from **algal blooms**.[2] These blooms take up too many nutrients, starving fish and other wildlife from precious, life-giving oxygen.

The Illinois River in Northeast Oklahoma is considered by many to be the State's most prized, scenic and pristine river. It provides numerous social benefits to the citizens of the state and region. It is a source of drinking water for Tahlequah and Watts and irrigates plant nurseries and farms in the region. It also provides a home to an abundance of wildlife, including several threatened and endangered species of plants and animals. It is additionally a popular tourist and recreation attraction and was the first river designated as a **Wild and Scenic River**[3] by the state. More than 180,000 tourists annually float the Illinois River by raft, canoe or kayak. It is estimated that nearly 350,000 swim, fish, camp, hike, bird watch and hunt, boosting $9 million into the local economy by bringing in tourists from not only Oklahoma, but also Arkansas, Missouri, Kansas, and Texas (Bality et al., 1998). In 2006, only 113,763 people floated the river, because of low stream levels and excessive heat (Kelly, 2007). However, Tahlequah Tourist Director Kate Kelly said, floaters and other tourists still contributed nearly a $12 million boost to the local economy that year.

Because of these benefits, damage to the watershed is magnified by the public. Several large corporations contract with nearly 2,000 farmers just within twenty miles of the Oklahoma–Arkansas border. Over the course of the last twenty years, many farmers in the economically-depressed northeastern section of Oklahoma have eagerly undertaken chicken and turkey farming as a lucrative alternative to traditional crop farming. Increased large-scale poultry feeding operations are on the increase, numbering forty-five million in Oklahoma and another 125 million in Arkansas (Cooper et al., 1994). Recent studies have indicated that the water quality in the Illinois River has deteriorated, particularly from chicken waste's nutrients, especially phosphorous, which seeps down into the soil and then runs off into the river (Palmer, 1994). Ed Fite, director of Oklahoma's Scenic Rivers Commission (OSRC) describes the Illinois River's headwaters as highly developed and says "my windshield impression is that the river's quality is spiraling downward" (Money, 2002). The OSRC board members are responsible for overseeing the State's river water quality. Therefore, it concerns these members when cattle ranchers buy chicken waste from poultry operators to apply to nutrient-starved pastureland. Unfortunately, the chicken waste is not applied consistently and often too liberally, creating excess nutrients that seep into the river. In 1997, legislation required soil tests on lands to which a farmer wants to apply chicken waste. This test is to be sent to a stipulated lab in order to assess phosphorous levels. Land over the designated 250 phosphorous index has enough nutrients already; therefore chicken waste cannot be applied (Stephens, 1997). Too many nutrients, such as phosphorus from chicken waste, can cause a shortage of oxygen leading to blue baby syndrome, a condition that is sometimes fatal to humans. It can also create algal blooms that take up a great deal of oxygen, subsequently hurting **biodiversity**—basically the numbers and types of different species available in the water (Palmer, 1994). More specifically, biodiversity is the representation of the variety of living organisms, their differences in genetics, and the communities and their interrelation in their associated physical environment (Oklahoma Conservation Commission, 1998).

The nutrients from chicken waste trickles into the water from multiple places, but is not seen by the naked eye. Such a phenomenon is what policy experts call **non-point source pollution**. Non-point source pollution is an undefined or diffuse source from fields to urban streets from fertilizers, pesticides, or sediment (Oklahoma Conservation Commission, 1998). Because this movement of nutrients into the water is over time and invisible, often people who live in the area play the blame game, creating conflict over what to do. For example, tourists and farmers blame each other for the decline in water quality. Riverfront property owners also blame tourists for trespassing, littering, and rowdy behavior. Many in Oklahoma blame Arkansas poultry operations and wastewater treatment run-off from Fayetteville, Arkansas. Oklahoma's fight with Arkansas eventually led to a U.S. Supreme Court decision in 1992.[4] Five years later, citizens of Tulsa worried about a perceived threat to their city water supply and pushed for a law to address poultry (Hinton, 1997). At the same time, small-scale poultry farmers face large economic pressures because when they comply with more rules and regulations, their operational costs also go up. However, passing costs off to consumers is only one problem farmers face. For example, Tyson Foods, located in Fayetteville, Arkansas, as well as other corporate poultry corporations, often threaten to pull their business and contracts with small farmers raising chicken and turkeys if costs go up (Kershen, 1997). These poultry farmers could lose their livelihood.

In 2005, Attorney Drew Edmondson brought a lawsuit against several out-of-state poultry operators declaring that they are polluting the state's rivers and in turn, its drinking water and public health. His lawsuit alleges multiple violations of federal law; for example, the Comprehensive Environmental Response Compensation and Liability Act (CERCLA), also known as **Superfund**, as well as state and federal nuisance laws, trespass and Oklahoma Environmental Quality and Agriculture Codes. "It all comes down to pollution," Edmondson says in a press release. "Too much poultry waste is being dumped on the ground and it ends up in the water. That's against the law. The companies own the birds as well as the feed, medicines and other things they put in their birds. They should be responsible for managing the hundreds of thousands of tons of waste that comes out of their birds" (Edmondson, 2005). Arkansas responded in 2006 by seeking the U.S. Supreme Court to intervene based on Constitutional grounds, but the Court rejected their claims (Demillo, 2006).

Tar Creek

"The Lawyer" and "The Sooner" are two of many heaping ten-story piles of rock, dispersed throughout Pitcher, Oklahoma, drawing dirt bikers and children (Gillham, 2006). Over the years, the townsfolk named these massive mounds of rock by ordinary and familiar names instead of by the term most everyone else outside the region uses **chat piles**. These massive piles of crushed rock like the mound locals call "Saint Joe," were left behind by miners long ago. These huge piles loom over residents and often blow contaminated dust on the populace and in schoolyards. These chat piles, some towering 200 feet in the air, are contaminated with heavy metals that pose a threat to children (CCEH & DP Research, 2007).

Chapter Fourteen

LEADERSHIP PROFILE

W. A. "DREW" EDMONDSON
Attorney General of Oklahoma

DREW EDMONDSON was elected Attorney General in 1994, and was re-elected in 1998, 2002, and 2006, winning more than 60% of the vote in his last two elections. Edmondson served as the 2002–2003 President of the National Association of Attorneys General. In 1996, Edmondson filed suit against the tobacco industry resulting in a $2 billion settlement between the industry and Oklahoma, part of the largest settlement in the history of the world. Edmondson was one of eight attorneys general asked to serve on the negotiating team for the states.

Early in his first term as Attorney General, Edmondson successfully advocated reform of the death penalty appeals process at the state and federal levels, cutting lengthy appeal times in half. He also created a victim assistance unit in the Attorney General's Office. Representing rate payers, Edmondson negotiated record-breaking rate reductions with telephone, electric and gas utilities and workers' compensation insurance.

Edmondson graduated from Northeastern State University in Tahlequah, Oklahoma with a Bachelors Degree in Speech Education. Following graduation, Edmondson enlisted in the U.S. Navy and served a tour of duty in Vietnam from 1971 to 1972. In 1974; he was elected as a Democrat to the state legislature where he served two years in the Oklahoma House of Representatives before entering the University of Tulsa Law School. After graduation, he entered private practice. In 1982, he ran for Muskogee County District Attorney where he served for three consecutive terms and was selected as "Outstanding District Attorney for the State of Oklahoma" in 1985 and the "Outstanding Death Penalty Prosecutor" in the ninth and tenth Circuits.

Edmondson's wife Linda is a noted activist—a medical social worker—for end-of-life concerns and both have worked to improve end-of-life healthcare in Oklahoma. They have two children: Mary is an attorney and Robert is pursuing a doctorate in cultural anthropology. Edmondson is a member of the Oklahoma Bar Association, the Presbyterian Church and the Democratic Party.

Although Tar Creek in Northeast Oklahoma was once a vibrant mining area where many citizens in the area patriotically produced lead and zinc for the soldiers in World War II, today the battle lines are closer to home. U.S. Senator Inhofe explains that the government must act now because abandoned mining companies were not held responsible long ago for the hazardous waste from the mines that leaked into the groundwater (Inhofe, 2003). However, he says, federal agencies have engaged in inter-agency battles over who is responsible for the clean-up. The EPA, the Army Corps of Engineers, the Department of Interior, officially admit responsibility for the clean up.

Battle lines have also been drawn between those residents who want to remain to clean up their home areas and those residents who want a "buy-out" plan. Senator Inhofe, formerly held the chairmanship of the Senate Environment and Public Works Committee, which gave him huge sway over any legislation affecting Tar Creek before he lost his seat. In 2003, the Senator asserted that instead of a buyout, he supported a $45-million plan to have the University of Oklahoma lead an effort focusing on the periphery of the Tar Creek area to remove tons of chat located in the site's epicenter (Myers, 2003). Inhofe's plan was in spite of then Governor Frank Keating's Tar Creek Superfund Task Force in 2000, which recommended a "world class wetlands". The conception of wetlands has created a backlash among residents who fear that they may be forced from their homes. In response, the EPA backed off a wetlands plan soon after (Myers, 2003).

Tar Creek, in Picther, Oklahoma, is part of the Tri-State Mining District—Northeast Oklahoma, Southwest Missouri, and Southeast Kansas. Eighty-three abandoned water supply wells along with dozens of exploratory drills mined the Boone Formation, which was particularly rich in zinc and lead. Despite the mineral riches found, the drills punctured the underlying deep Roubidoux aquifer, which serves as the drinking water supply for a large portion of Northeastern Oklahoma. The drill holes serve as pathways for abandoned toxic metals left by the mining companies as late as the 1970s when mineral deposits were exhausted. Underneath roughly 2,500 acres of this site is nearly 300 miles of tunnels and in excess of 1,300 mineshafts (CCEH & DP Research, 2007). By 1980, the contaminated water flowed down the stream, turning it bright orange, bringing media attention to the plight of Pitcher for the first time.

The Tar Creek Superfund site was added in 1983 to the EPA's **National Priority List** (NPL), which is a list of nation's dirtiest sites and eligible for funding to clean it up. Although Tar Creek was Oklahoma's first Superfund site, it is now only one of fourteen statewide. The Imperial Refining Company in Ardmore, for example, became Oklahoma's latest NPL list member in 2000. Clean-up of the refining company's **underground storage tanks** began in 2005. These tanks also leaked oil into the groundwater, often the source for drinking water. The Oklahoma Department of Environmental Quality oversees, maintains, and cleans up Superfund sites. Ignoring groundwater contamination can have its consequences.

For example, an Indian Health Services study found that 34% of the area's Native American children had lead blood levels in excess of the Centers for Disease Control (CDC) and Prevention standards. By 1996, the EPA removed and replaced contaminated soil from residents' yards with soil that is not contaminated. It took more than $40 million to clean up more than 1500 yards, with an estimated 600 left (Focht and Hull, 2004).

Resistance to a "world class wetlands" has dwindled in the area as a *Washington Times* article from February 2006 reported a collapse of a West Virginia coal mine. It reminded Oklahoma residents that the abandoned mine shafts and caverns underground could also give way. Before a jammed gymnasium at Picther-Cardin High School, the *Times* reported further, the results of an eighteen-month "subsidence" study which released two weeks prior. The in-depth study produced by six state and federal agencies—U.S. Corps of Engineers, U.S. Geological Survey, U.S. Interior Department, U.S. Bureau of Indian Affairs, the Oklahoma Department of Environmental Quality and Geological Survey—shocked locals. The study described 286 mine shafts and caverns in danger of giving way, endangering 162 occupied homes, sixteen public facilities, eighteen businesses, and thirty-three locations beneath major highways or streets (Aynesworth, 2006).

Because of this change, Senator Inhofe seemed to change his position from cleaning up the area to the "buyout" plan.

> *"With the new facts provided by the recent subsidence report we simply cannot risk the safety of Oklahomans in the Tar Creek area and that is why we are moving forward with this plan. Buying out these residents and removing them from Tar Creek will eliminate a very serious risk to these Oklahoma families"* (Inhofe, 2006).

Tar Creek residents living with the greatest risk of cave-ins are the first to receive up to $300,000 buyouts. This is out of a total of $18 million promised so far in early 2007 (Stogsdill, 2007). The residents will not be forced to leave, but if they stay, they will be responsible for their health and finances.

Gary Garrett, a longtime resident, who lives in a nearby town of Cardin, says he would take a buyout if offered. "My house is situated above one of the risk sites identified by the Corps," Garrett explains. "I have lived here 40 of my 60 years but I would move. I am afraid for my safety and for my health. It would probably scare us to death if we really knew all the risks" (Gillham, 2006).

IV. FUTURE DIRECTIONS FOR THE STATE

Many scientists, environmentalists and business leaders are focusing on **sustainable development** in the state. According to the Brundtland Commission, "Sustainable development is development that meets the needs of the present without compromising the ability of future generations to meet their own needs." This definition focuses on finding the middle ground between the present and future.

Oklahoma's Secretary of the Environment Miles Tolbert (2004) says Oklahoma is making progress as waste of all kinds released into the environment has decreased by two-thirds since 1988. However, he cites that many of Oklahoma's wildlife species are in decline, including the Prairie Chicken with a 90% drop in numbers in just a few years. Even some birds are disappearing. For example, the Arkansas River Shiner is almost extinct. Tolbert says that species decline is a result of habitats disappearing due to human development. To illustrate, 70% of the original wetlands have been drained or filled and tall grass prairies have all but disappeared. In addition, 95% of Oklahoman lands are in private owners' hand, which means that state government is limited in their ability to enforce federal regulations on those lands.

Tolbert recommends a voluntary program of riparian buffers on public and private land. **Riparian buffers** are the planting of native vegetation along stream banks to filter nutrients from getting into the stream. This simple plan has six benefits: 1) filtering pollutants from heading into the river; 2) decreasing stream bank erosion; 3) reducing the number of cattle eroding the stream bank; 4) lowering temperatures of the stream; 5) improving habitats for wildlife; and 6) making the stream look better. There are different government programs, Tolbert says. Few farmers have been aware of what the state has to offer in the past. He says he would like to enhance the visibility of these programs.

Focht (2004) finds sustainable solutions have fallen by the wayside in Oklahoma because there is a dearth of research on how to achieve sustainability and how to measure it. On top of this, people need to be a part of the process and policymakers need to know what people want and will accept to gain their buy in to achieve a movement forward toward a sustainable Oklahoma. It is also likely though as the history of Oklahoma in this chapter reveals, Oklahomans' traditionalist worldview makes for slow change, especially when it is perceived that government is the force behind that change.

Change is not only coming from state government but from business. ConocoPhillips President J.J. Mulva says that his company is planning for a sustainable Oklahoma with a focus on protecting bird habitats (Mulva, 2004). The company has also moved to **double hulls**[5] and other environmental and safety features. Additionally, ConocoPhillips supports the Nature Conservancy's work to preserve the Tall Grass Prairie in Northeast Oklahoma.

Sustainable change is also coming from non-profit citizen groups like the Oklahoma Sustainability Network (OSN), which has made sustainability a focus of their work. The OSN's mission is to connect and educate the people of Oklahoma concerning the many aspects of sustainability. OSN is a catalyst and a resource for the improvement of Oklahoma's economy, ecology, and equity (OSN, 2007). Their Sixth Annual OSN Conference, held in Oklahoma City looked toward the future with the title: "Ideas to Action: Envisioning the Next 100 Years in Oklahoma."

V. Conclusion

As the state moves through the twenty-first century, environmental conflicts and controversies may become more apparent and serious. How Oklahoma's citizens approach these environmental problems will determine the state's direction.

Oklahoma's environmental policy is complicated from the land's once fertile beginnings during early statehood to dealing with the environmental consequences of focusing on other prominent goals, such as making a living.

Deep down, environmental policy is about disagreements over values, which are basically abstract concepts evaluating what is worthwhile or right. At first blush, these conflicts might be fights about technical disagreements, for example, when a farmer is forced to test his land for phosphorous or another person is forced off their land to make way for a "world class wetland." However, environmental conflict is actually about differences in opinions on how people should interact with the environment. Often government politicians and policymakers have to step in when there are concerns over pollution and subsequently when there has to be something done about it. However, government, business, and non-profit groups can work together to facilitate change toward a more sustainable future.

NOTES

1. From the author's experience touring poultry houses in the Illinois River basin during the spring and fall of 1999.
2. An algal bloom is caused by a relatively quick increase in the population of phytoplankton algae in an aquatic system, such as a river or lake. Some algal blooms are the result of too many nutrients, i.e., phosphorus and nitrogen in a water environment. A higher concentration of these particular nutrients in the water creates an increased growth of algae and green plants. When the concentration is higher, it often causes other plants and animals to die out.
3. The Wild and Scenic Rivers Act was passed in 1968. The Act was to balance river development with river protection. In order to have this designation, Congress created the Wild and Scenic Rivers System nationwide. The Illinois River pushed in 1979 to be a candidate for Wild and Scenic designation. However, it needed a management plan. The river is considered a State Wild and Scenic River today. See Oklahoma ScenicRiver Website: http://www.oklahomascenicrivers.net/programs_next3.asp
4. An agreement was reached in 2003 between Oklahoma and Arkansas, both states agreed to reduce phosphorus output from its wastewater treatment plants by 75% over the next ten years, although it does not address poultry-farm runoff.
5. Simply, a double-hulled tanker is a ship with a hull within a hull, basically a double skin of steel separated by a distance of 2 to 3.5 meters, depending on a ship's size. A hull like this can reduce the risk of a tanker oil spill. (Valenti, 1999).

BIBLIOGRAPHY

Adkison, D. M. & McNair Palmer, L. (2001). *The Oklahoma State Constitution*. Westport, CT: Greenwood Press.

Alderman, E. & Kennedy, C. (1991). *In our defense: The Bill of Rights in action*. New York: William Morrow and Company, Inc.

Aldrich, G. (1973). *Black heritage of Oklahoma*. Edmond, OK: Thompson Book and Supply Co.

Administrative Office of the Courts (Oklahoma). (1994). *Annual report*. Oklahoma City, OK: Author.

Administrative Office of the Courts (Oklahoma). (1995a). *Annual report*. Oklahoma City, OK: Author.

Administrative Office of the Courts (Oklahoma). (1995b). *The Supreme Court of Oklahoma* (Brochure). Oklahoma City, OK: Author.

Administrative Office of the Courts (Oklahoma). (1995–1996). *The Oklahoma Court of Criminal Appeals*, Brochure.

Administrative Office of the Courts (Oklahoma). (1998). *Annual report*. Oklahoma City, OK: Author.

Anderson, J., Brady, D. & Bullock, C. (1978). *Public policy and politics in America*. CA: Wadsworth Publishing Company, Inc.

Anderson, J. E. (2000). *Public policymaking*. Boston: Houghton Mifflin Company

Andrews, R. (2006). *Managing the environment, managing ourselves: a history of American environmental history*. Yale University Press.

Aspin, L.. (1999). "Trends in judicial retention elections, 1964–1998." *Judicature* 83, 79.

Associated Press. (1998). "Topless snapshot enrages candidate." National Political, Dateline: Shawnee, Oklahoma.

Associated Press. (1999a). "Man given suspended sentence in kidnapping and torture of common-law wife." State and Regional, Dateline: Woodward, Oklahoma.

Associated Press. (1999b). "Tide turning against judicial Elections." State and Regional, Dateline: Oklahoma City.

Associated Press. (2000a). "Appeals court disqualifies judge from case." State and Regional, Dateline: Oklahoma City.

Associated Press. (2000b). "Judicial retention bill fails in legislative committee." State and Regional, Dateline: Oklahoma City.

Association of County Commissioners of Oklahoma. (2005). Responsibilities of county commissioners. Retrieved from www.oklacco.com.

Aynesworth, H. (2006). "That sucking sound would be the whole town going under." *The Washington Times*. Retrieved March 2007 from *The Washington Times* Website: http://washingtontimes.com/national/20060220-121016-2913r.htm.

Baird, D. & Goble, D. (1990). *The story of Oklahoma*. Norman, OK: University of Oklahoma Press.

Bality, A., Caneday, L., Fite III, E., Wikle, T., & Yuan, M. (1998). *IRB management plan 1999*. Oklahoma Scenic Rivers Commission: Tahlequah, Oklahoma, 1998, 1–94.

Bibliography

Barrett, Edith J. (1995). "The policy priorities of African American women in state legislators." *Legislative Studies Quarterly*, 20: 223–248.

Barrett, K., Greene, R., Mariani, M. & Sostek, A.. (2003). "The way we tax." *Governing*, 16.5, 20–31.

Baum, L.. (2004). *The American courts*. Boston, MA: Houghton Mifflin.

Baum, L.& Kemper, M.. (1994) (Eds). "The Ohio judiciary." In *Ohio Politics* (Chap. 13). Kent, Ohio: Kent State University Press.

Bellmon, H.. (1992). *The life and times of Henry Bellmon*. Tulsa, OK: Council Oak Books.

Benjamin, G.& Malbin, M. J. (1992). "Term limits for lawmakers: How to start thinking about a proposal in process." In G. Benjamin & M. J. Malbin (Eds.), *Limiting Legislative Terms* (Chap. 1). Washington, DC: Congressional Quarterly Press.

Bowman, A. O'M.& Kearney, R. C. (2002). *State and local government* (5th edn). Boston, MA: Houghton Mifflin Company.

Boyd, D. J. (2006)."State budgets: Recent trends and outlook" in *The Book of the States: 2005 Edition*. (401–7) Lexington, KY: The Council of State Governments.

Brace, P. & Butler, K. S.. (2001). "New perspectives for the comparative study on the judiciary: The state supreme court project." *The Justice System Journal*, 22, 243–262.

Brooks, H. E. & Doswell III, C. A. (2001). "Deaths in the 3 May 1999 Oklahoma City tornado from a historical perspective." *American Meteorological Society*, 2002; 17: Issue 3, 354–361.

Brus, B.. (2007, May 25). "OKC's MAPS3 survey shows strong support for mass transit." *The Journal Record*.

Busch, A. E. (1996). "Early voting: Convenient, but . . .?" *State Legislatures*, 22.8, 25–27.

Button, J. & Hedge, D.. (1996). "Legislative life in the 1990s: A comparison of black and white state legislators." *Legislative Studies Quarterly*, 21, 199–218.

Caldeira, G. A. (1983). "On the reputation of state supreme courts." *Political Behavior*, 5, 83–108.

Canon, B. C. & Baum, L. (1981). "Patterns of adoption of tort law innovations: An application of diffusion theory to judicial doctrines." *The American Political Science Review*, 75, 975–987.

Carp, R. A., Stidham, R.& Manning, K. L. (2004). *Judicial process in America*. Washington, D.C.: Congressional Quarterly Press.

Carson, J. (2006). "Oklahoma agriculture: The first 100 years." Oklahoma Department of Agriculture. Monograph.

City of Oklahoma City. (2004). Who's who on the horseshoe? Retrieved from www.okc.gov

Clark, W. (1988). "Constitutional reform and economic development in Oklahoma." *State Policy and Economic Development in Oklahoma: 1988*. Oklahoma City, OK: Oklahoma 2000 Inc.

Claunch, F.t. (2002). "Con: Is the lottery a good gamble for Oklahoma? Not by a clear measure." *Oklahoma Policy Studies Review*, 3.1, 3, 6–7.

Cobb, R. B. & Elder, C. D. (1972). *Participation in American politics: The dynamics of agenda-building*. Baltimore: Johns Hopkins University Press.

Coleman, B. (2006). "Oklahoma Lobbyists' Job Salary." Received from http://sw2.salary.com/salarywizard/layouthtmls/ok/sw21_compresult_state_okcm02000070.html on August 17, 2006.

Bibliography

Constitution Revision Study Commission. (1991). *The constitution of the state of Oklahoma: Recommendations for revision, final report.* Oklahoma City, OK: Author.

Cooper, M.S., Dahlgren, J., Barnes, D., Fram, M., West, R. & Smolen. M. (1994). *How do we improve water quality in the Illinois River Basin?* A report by the Oklahoma Cooperative Extension Service, Oklahoma State University.

Copeland, G. W. & Rausch, J. D.. (1993). "Sendin' em home early: Oklahoma legislative term limitations." *Oklahoma Politics, 2.1,* 33–50.

Council of State Governments (CSG). (1996). *Book of the states.* Lexington, KY: Council of State Governments.

Council of State Governments (CSG). (2003). *Book of the states.* Lexington, KY: Council of State Governments.

Crutcher, M. M. D. (2005). Make tattoos legal—and safe. *The Daily Oklahoman,* p. 25A.

Dauffenbach, R. C. (1994). *State government finance in Oklahoma after SQ 640.* Oklahoma City, OK: Oklahoma 2000 Inc.

Dauffenbach, R. C. (2005). "Economy watch—Focus on oil and gas" *Oklahoma Business Bulletin* (April), 1–8.

Dauffenbach, R. C. (2006a). "Business highlights" *Oklahoma Business Bulletin* (April), 1–7.

Dauffenbach, R. C. (2006b). "The skinny on Oklahoma's personal income" in *State Policy and Economic Development in Oklahoma: 2006* (1–20). Oklahoma City, OK: Oklahoma 21st Century, Inc.

Davis, J. A., Metla, S. & Helan, J. 2006. "Profiles & stereotypes of lobbyists in Oklahoma." Oklahoma Politics, 15:1–18.

Debo, A. (1985). *Prairie city: The story of an American community.* Tulsa, OK: Council Oaks Books, Ltd.

Debo, A. (1987).*Oklahoma: Foot-loose and fancy-free.* Norman, OK: University of Oklahoma Press.

Delcour, J.. (2004). "Bottom-of-the-barrel pay." *Tulsa World,* p. G1.

Demillo, A. (2006). "Supreme Court denies Arkansas permission to sue Oklahoma in dispute over water pollution." *Associated Press.* 2–22.

Dolan, K. & Ford, L.. (1995). "Women in the state legislatures: Feminist identity and legislative behaviors." *American Politics Quarterly, 23,* 96–108.

Dresang, D. & Gosling, J. J. (1996). *Politics and policy in American states and communities.* Boston, MA: Allyn and Bacon.

Durocher's OKC Business. (2004). Istook introduced bill to simplify taxes. Retrieved from www.okcbusiness.com.news.

Dye, T.. (1997). *Politics in states and communities* (9th edn). Upper Saddle River, NJ: Prentice Hall.

Edmondson, D. (2005). AG sues poultry industry for polluting Oklahoma waters. Press Release. Retrieved March 2007 from the Oklahoma Attorney General's Website: http://www.oag.state.ok.us/oagweb.nsf/0/2448aafc29ac39668625701f0067edbe?OpenDocument.

Economics of high technology in Oklahoma. (1985). Stillwater, OK: Office of Business and Economic Research, College of Business Administration, Oklahoma State University.

Egan, T. (2006). *The worst hard time: The untold story of those who survived the Great American Dust Bowl.* New York, NY: Houghton Mifflin Company.

Elazar, D.. (1966). *American federalism: A view from the states*. New York: Thomas Y. Crowell Co.

Elazar, D.. (1982). "The principles and traditions underlying state constitutions." *Publius: The Journal of Federalism, 12*, 11–25.

Ellis, R.. (2004). Ballot issues meet voter's approval. *The Daily* Oklahoman, p. 14A.

Emerson, A. R. (2002). *Legislator's guide to Oklahoma taxes*. Oklahoma City, OK: Oklahoma House of Representatives, Research Division.

Epstein, L., Segal, J. A., Spaeth, H. J.& Walker, T. G. (2003). *The Supreme Court compendium: Data, decisions & developments*. Washington, D.C.: CQ Press.

Eulau, H., Wahlke, J. C., Buchanan, W.& Ferguson, L. C. (1959). "The role of the representative: Some empirical observations on the theory of Edmund Burke." *American Political Science Review*, 53.3, 742–756.

Federal funds information for states. (2004) *State Policy Reports, 22*. Washington, D.C.: Author.

Ferguson, L. R. (1989). *Oklahoma legislative process—A training manual* (5th edn.). Oklahoma City, OK: Minority Leader of the Oklahoma House of Representatives.

Fischer, L. H. (1981). *Oklahoma governors 1907–1929: Turbulent politics*. Oklahoma City, OK: Oklahoma Historical Society.

Focht, W. (2004). "A research and education agenda." In The Oklahoma Academy 2004 Town Hall—*Oklahoma's environment: pursuing a responsible balance*, 7-9–12.

Focht, W. & Hull, J. (2004). "Framing policy solutions in a conflicted policy environment: An application of Q methodology to a Superfund cleanup. *klahoma Policy Studies Review*. Spring/Summer. 1, 30–37.

Fowler, L. L. (1992). "A comment on competition and careers." In G. Benjamin and J. Michael Malbin (Eds.), *Limiting legislative terms* (Chap. 9.) Washington, DC: Congressional Quarterly.

Fox, W. F. & LeAnn L. (2006). "State tax collections: eroding tax bases" In *The book of the states: 2005 Edition* (411–16) Lexington, KY: The Council of State Governments.

Friedrich, C. (1963). *Man and his government*. New York: McGraw-Hill.

Galanter, M. (1974). "Why the 'Haves' Come Out Ahead: Speculations on the Limits of Legal Change." *Law and Society Review, 9*, 95–160.

Gerschenkron, A. (1962). *Economic backwardness in historical perspective*. Cambridge, MA: The Belknap Press.

Gibson, A. M. (1981). *Oklahoma: A history of five centuries*. Norman, OK: University of Oklahoma Press.

Gillham, O. (2006). "Picher relief: Hometown exodus." *TheTulsa World*. Retrieved March 2007 from *The Tulsa World* Website: http://www.leadagency.org/modules.php?op=modload&name=News&file=article&sid=211&POSTNUKESID=da814c37235aab63aa27e02e2878c3f2.

Githens, M., Norris, P. & Lovenduski. J. 1994. *Different roles, different voices: Women and politics in the United States and Europe*. New York: Harper Collins College Publishers.

Glick, H. R. (1991). "Policy making and state supreme courts." In John B. Gates & C. A. Johnson (Eds.), *The American courts*. Washington, DC: Congressional Quarterly Press.

Glick, H. & Emmert, C. (1987). "Selection systems and judicial characteristics." *Judicature 70*, 230.

Bibliography

Goble, D. (1980). *Progressive Oklahoma, the making of a new kind of state*. Norman, OK: University of Oklahoma Press.

Goble, D. & Scales, J.R. Jr. (1983). "Depression politics: Personality and the problem of relief." In K., Jr. (Ed.), *Hard times in Oklahoma: The Depression years* (pp. 3–21). Oklahoma City, OK: Oklahoma Historical Society.

Goodsell, C. T. (1994). *The case for bureaucracy: A public administration polemic* (3rd edn.). Chatham, NJ: Chatham House.

Governing's State and local sourcebook 2006. "Environmental spending." Data from p. 21. Retrieved March 2007 from: http://www.census.gov/govs/www/estimate04.html.

Gray, V. & Eisinger, P. 1997. *American states and cities*. 2nd edn. New York: Longman.

Greater Oklahoma City Chamber of Commerce. (2005). MAPS for kids background. Retrieved from www.okcchamber.com

Greiner, J. (2003). "State cuts near bone, Group says." *The Daily Oklahoman*, p. 1-A.

Hale, D. (1982). "The people of Oklahoma: Economics and social change." In Anne Hodges Morgan, and H. Wayne (Eds.), *Oklahoma: The views of the forty-sixth state*. Norman, OK: University of Oklahoma Press.

Hamilton, A. (Ed.). (2003). *Oklahoma almanac 2003–2004*. Oklahoma City, OK: Oklahoma Department of Libraries.

Hamilton, A. (2000). Artist-senator prepares his statue of an American Indian to stand atop Oklahoma's new Capitol dome. *The Dallas Morning News*, p. 41A.

Hamm, K. E. & Hedlund, R. D. (1990). "Accounting for change in the number of committee positions." *Legislative Studies Quarterly, 15.2*, 201–226.

Hanson, R. (1996). "Intergovernmental relations." In V. Gray & H. Jacob (Eds.), *Politics in the American states*. Washington, DC: Congressional Quarterly Press.

Hardy, R. J., Dohns, R. R. & Leuthold, D.. (1995). *Missouri government and politics*. Columbia, MO: University of Missouri Press.

Harrigan, J. J. & Nice, D. C.. 2004. *Politics and policy in states and communities*. 8th edn. New York: Pearson Longman.

Hedlund, R. D. (1992). "Accommodating members' requests in committee assignments: Individual level explanations." In G. F. Moncrief & J. A. Thompson (Eds.), *Changing Patterns in State Legislative Careers* (pp. 149–174). Ann Arbor, MI: University of Michigan Press.

Heidler, D. S. and Heidler, J. T. (2007). *Indian removal*. New York: Norton.

Henschen, B. M., Moog, R. & Davis, S. (1990). "Judicial nominating commissioners: A national profile." *Judicature, 73*, 329–333.

Hepner, M. (2004) "Corporate tax shelters cost Oklahoma $69 million." *Oklahoma Policy Digest, 2.1*, 7–8.

Hibbing, J. R. (1991). *Congressional careers: Contours of life in the U.S. House of Representatives*. Chapel Hill, NC: University of North Carolina Press.

Hicks, J. D. (1931). *The populist revolt*. Minneapolis, MN: University of Minnesota Press.

Hinton, M. (1997). "Task force mulls messy problem of chicken waste." *The Daily Oklahoman*. Retrieved March 2007: http://www.newsok.com/theoklahoman/archives/.

Holloway, H. & Myers, F. S. (1993). *Bad times for good ol' boys: The Oklahoma County Commissioner Scandal*. Norman, OK: University of Oklahoma Press.

Holmes, A. (Ed.). (2004). "A Lottery for Oklahoma?" In *State policy and economic development in Oklahoma: 2004* (pp. 53–64). Oklahoma City, OK: Oklahoma 21st Century, Inc.

Hovey, K. & Hovey, H. A. (Eds.). (2004). *Congressional Quarterly state fact finder 2004.* Washington, D.C.: Congressional Quarterly Press.

Hovey, K. A. & Hovey, H. A. (2006). *Congressional Quarterly's fact finder 2006.* Washington, D.C. CQ Press.

Howard, W. W. (1889). "The rush to Oklahoma." *Harper's Weekly* 33. 391–94. Retrieved March 2007: http://www.library.cornell.edu/Reps/DOCS/landrush.htm.

Imperial Refining Company-National Priorities List. (2007). Environmental protection agency. Retrieved: http://www.epa.gov/earth1r6/6sf/pdffiles/0605091.pdf.

Inhofe, J. (2003). "Inhofe: Tar Creek memorandum is real progress." Retrieved March 2007: http://inhofe.senate.gov/pressapp/record.cfm?id=203429.

Inhofe, J. (2006). "Inhofe-Henry-Boren announce Tar Creek buyout." Press Release of Senator Inhofe.

Retrieved March 2007: http://inhofe.senate.gov/pressapp/record.cfm?id=255524.

Ireland, T. C., Snead, M. C., Steven R. M. (2006). "Oklahoma: If we aren't high-tech, where are our competitive advantages?" *Oklahoma Business Bulletin* (January), 11–20.

Jadlow, J. W. & Lage, G. M. (Eds.).(1992). "Oklahoma in the global economy." In *Oklahoma Economic Outlook* (pp. 66–19). Stillwater, OK: Oklahoma State University Press.

Janda, K., Berry, J. M., & Goldman, J. (1997). *The challenge of democracy: Government in America* (5th edn.). Boston, MA: Houghton Mifflin Co.

Jewell, M. E. & Olson, D. M. (1982). *American state political parties and elections.* Homewood, IL: Dorsey Press.

Jewell, M. (1982). *Representation in state legislatures.* Lexington, KY: University of Kentucky Press.

Jones, R.W. & McClure, N. (1997). *How much spending money do Oklahoma consumers really have available?* Retrieved September 1997 from the Oklahoma Council for Public Affairs Web site: http://www.ocpathink.org.

Jones, S. (1974). *Oklahoma politics in a state and nation.* Enid, OK: The Haymaker Press.

Kagan, R., Cartwright, B., Friedman, L. M. & Wheeler, S. (1977). "The business of state supreme courts, 1870–1970." *Stanford Law Review, 30,* 121–156.

Kathlene, L. (1995). "Alternative views of crime: Legislative policymaking in gendered terms." *Journal of Politics, 57,* 696–723.

Keefe, W. J. & Morris S. O. 1997. *The American legislative process: Congress and the states.* Upper Saddle River, NJ: Prentice Hall.

Keller, M. (1987). "The politics of state constitution revision, 1820–1930." In K. L. Hall, H. M. Hyman & L. V. Sigal, *The constitutional convention as an amending device* (pp. 67–111). Washington, DC: American Historical Association and American Political Science Association.

Kelly, K.. (2007). Personal Interview. Tourism Director for the Tahlequah Chamber of Commerce.

Kersch, K. (1997). "Full faith and credit for same-sex marriages." *Political Science Quarterly, 112.1,* 117–136.

Bibliography

Kershen, D. (1997). "An Oklahoma slant to environmental protection and the politics of property rights." *Oklahoma Law Review.* 50: 391–398.

Killian, J. H. (Ed.). (1987). In *The constitution of the United States of America: Analysis and interpretation.* Washington, DC: U.S. Government Printing Office.

Killman, C., Hinton, M. & Hoberock, B. (2007). "Report lists gifts to lawmakers" *Tulsa World.*

Kincaid, J. (Ed.). (1982). In *Political culture: Public policy and the American states.* Philadelphia, PA: Institute for the Study of Human Issues.

Kirkpatrick, S. A. (1978). *The legislative process in Oklahoma: Policy making, people, and politics.* Norman, OK: University of Oklahoma Press.

Kirksey, J. F. & Wright, III, D. E. (1992). "Black women in state legislatures: The view from Oklahoma." *Oklahoma Politics, 1,* 67–80.

Klein, J. (1963). *The Oklahoma economy.* Stillwater, OK: Oklahoma State University Press.

Klos, J. J. (1965). *Public welfare in Oklahoma.* Stillwater, OK: Oklahoma State University Press.

Kraft, M. (2004). *Environmental policy and politics.* 3rd edn. Pearson/Longman.

Kraft, M. E. & Furlong, S.R. (2004). *Public policy: Politics, analysis, and alternatives.* Washington, DC: CQ Press.

Krehbiel, R. (2003). "State workforce is up." *Tulsa World,* A23.

Krehbiel, R (2006). "Tax breaks increased along with state's revenues" *Tulsa World* October 15, A-19.

Lackmeyer, S. (2003). 10 years later: Projects put city on MAPS. *The Daily Oklahoman,* 1A.

Lage, G. M. (1996). "Restructuring of the Oklahoma economy." *Oklahoma Business Bulletin, 64.3,* 6–12.

Lage, G. M.. Moomaw, R. L. & Warner, L. (1977). *A profile of Oklahoma economic development: 1950–75.* Oklahoma City, OK: Frontiers of Science Foundation.

"Legislative candidates listed." (1992). *The Daily Oklahoman,* p. 18.

Lawler, J. J. &. Spurrier, R. L. Jr. (1991). "The judicial system." In D. R. Morgan, R. E. England & G. Humphreys (Eds.), *Oklahoma politics and policies* (Chap. 8). Lincoln, Nebraska: University of Nebraska Press.

League of Women Voters of Oklahoma, (1994). *A resource guide to Oklahoma courts.* Oklahoma City, OK: Author.

Leavitt, N (2004). "Is Oklahoma a new human rights hot spot? Why the state's judges and governor were right to stop an execution that nearly violated international law." *Findlaw's Legal Commentary.* Retrieved November 11, 2004 from http://writ.findlaw.com/commentary/20040524_leavitt.html.

Lester, J. P. & Stewart, J. (2000). *Public policy—An evolutionary approach.* CA: Wadsworth/Thompson Learning.

Lorch, R. S. (2001). *State and local politics: The great entanglement.* Upper Saddle River, NJ: Prentice-Hall.

McCormick, R. (Ed.). (1986). "Progressivism: A contemporary reassessment." In *The party period and public policy* (pp. 263–288). Oxford, UK: Oxford University Press.

Melone, A. P. & Karnes, A. (2003). *The American legal system: Foundations, processes, and norms.* Los Angeles: Roxbury Publishing Co.

Mock, J. (2006). Capitol: Legislation heads to full House. Bill legalizing tattooing draws panel's approval. *The Daily Oklahoman,* p. 1A.

Moncrief, G. F. & Thompson, J. A. (Eds.). (1992). *Changing patterns in state legislative careers.* Ann Arbor, MI: University of Michigan Press.

Money, J. (2002). "Scenic Rivers' water quality brings debate." *The Oklahoman*, 1. Retrieved March 2007 from the Oklahoma Scenic River's Commission Website: http://www.oklahomascenicrivers.net/News/Illinois_debate.doc.

Money, J. (1996). "Independent movement growing." *The Daily Oklahoman.*

Monies, P. (2003). "Work force push a priority issue under state plan." *The Daily Oklahoman*, p. 3D.

Moomaw, R. L. (Ed.). (2006)."Education reform in Oklahoma: A state at risk?" in *State policy and economic development in Oklahoma: 2006* (pp. 63–78). Oklahoma City, OK: Oklahoma 21st Century, Inc.

Morgan, D. R., England, R. E.& Humphreys, G. G. (1991). *Oklahoma Politics and Policies: Governing the Sooner State.* Lincoln, NE: University of Nebraska Press.

Morgan, D. R. (1991). "State and local spending in Oklahoma: Comparing actual expenditures to service needs." *Oklahoma Business Bulletin, 59.3*, 13–17.

Morgan, H. W. & Morgan, A. H. (1977). *Oklahoma: A history.* New York: W.W. Norton & Company, Inc.

Morgan, K.L. & Morgan, S (Eds.). (2002) In *State rankings 2002* Lawrence, KS: Morgan Quitno Press.

Mulva, J. J. (Ed.). (2004). "Sustainability: Good business and good sense." In The Oklahoma Academy 2004 Town Hall—*Oklahoma's Environment: Pursuing a Responsible Balance*, 5-26–28.

Mundende, D. C. (2004). "Saving the land: soil and water conservation in Oklahoma." *Chronicles of Oklahoma. 82,* 4–31.

Murry, D. A. (Ed.). (1988). "The legislative development efforts and economic diversification." In *State Policy and Economic Development in Oklahoma* (pp. 23–26). Oklahoma City, OK: Oklahoma 2000 Inc.

Murry, D. A., Olson, K. W., Holmes, A., Warner, L., Dauffenbach, R. C.& Gade, M. (1996). *In search of smaller government: The case of state finance in Oklahoma.* Oklahoma City, OK: Oklahoma 2000 Inc.

Myers, J. (2003). "Inhofe still firm on Tar Creek." *The Tulsa World*, 1. Retrieved March 2007:http://www.leadagency.org/modules.php?op=modload&name=News&file= article&sid=36.

Myers, J. (1996). "Group violated law in state races, FEC claims," *Tulsa World Online*, http://www.tulsaworld.com.

Nascenzi, N. (1999). Seminar teaches tattoo techniques. *Tulsa World*, p. 10.

National Conference of State Legislatures. (2007). Received from http://www.ncsl.org on August 10, 2006.

National Priorities List Sites in the United States. (2007). EPA. Retrieved March 2007 from: http://www.epa.gov/superfund/sites/npl/npl.htm

Nathan, R. P. (1996). "The role of the states in American federalism." In C.E. Van Horn (Ed.), *The state of the states* (pp. 13–32). Washington, DC: Congressional Quarterly Press.

NewsOK.com. (2005). Quick poll. *The Daily Oklahoman.*

O'Connor, K. & Sabato, L.J. (1997). *American government: Continuity and change.* Boston, MA: Allyn & Bacon.

O'Connor, K. & L. Sabato. (2006). *American government: Continuity and change* (2006 edn.). New York: Pearson Education, Inc.

Bibliography

Oklahoma Academy for State Goals. (1985). *Oklahoma revenue: Sources and uses, final report.* Oklahoma City, OK: Author

Oklahoma 2000, Inc. (1996). *In search of smaller government: The case of state finance in Oklahoma.* Norman, OK: University of Oklahoma Printing Services.

Oklahoma Center for the Advancement of Science and Technology, (2004) *Meeting challenges in the new economy: Recommendations to improve Oklahoma's position in technology-based economic cevelopment.* Oklahoma City, OK: Author.

Oklahoma Center for the Advancement of Science and Technology (2007). *2007 Impact report.* Oklahoma City, OK: Author.

Oklahoma Conservation Commission. (1998). *Riparian area management handbook. Oklahoma Cooperative Extension Service Division of Agricultural Sciences and Natural Resources.* E-952. Oklahoma State University.

Oklahoma Department of Commerce. (2004). *Improving your community: Community county profiles.* Oklahoma City: Author.

Oklahoma Department of Commerce (2006a). "Oklahoma oil & gas briefing". January 23.

Oklahoma Department of Commerce (2006b). "High technology report". May 19.

Oklahoma Department of Commerce (2006). "Oklahoma Economic Briefing". July 10.

Oklahoma Department of Commerce (2007a). *Oklahoma business incentives and tax guide 2007.*

Oklahoma Department of Commerce (2007b). *Oklahoma Quality Jobs Program 2007 Guidelines.*

Oklahoma Department of Libraries. (1997). *The Oklahoma almanac.* Oklahoma City: Author.

Oklahoma Department of Libraries. (2004). *The Oklahoma almanac.* Oklahoma City: Author.

Oklahoma economic outlook. (2003). Stillwater, OK: College of Business Administration, Oklahoma State University.

Oklahoma Ethics Commission. (1997). "Oklahoma registered lobbyists, 1997–1998." Oklahoma City, OK: Author.

Oklahoma Office of Personnel Management. (2003a). *FY2004 Annual compensation report.* Oklahoma City, OK: Author.

Oklahoma Office of Personnel Management. (2003b). *Fiscal year 2003 annual report.* Oklahoma City, OK: Author.

Oklahoma Office of Personnel Management. (2006). *2006 Annual compensation report.* Oklahoma City, OK: Author.

Oklahoma Office of Personnel Management. (2007). *Oklahoma state government equal employment opportunity/affirmative action status report.* Oklahoma City, OK: Author.

Oklahoma State Courts Network. (2004). Oklahoma statutes citationalized. Retrieved from www.oscn.net.

Oklahoma Sustainability Network. (2007). Retrieved March 2007: http://www.oksustainability.org/index.php.

Oklahoma Tax Commission. (2004) *Annual report FY 2003.* Oklahoma City, OK: Author.

Oklahoma Tax Commission. (2006). *Tax expenditure report* 2005–2006.

Oklahoma Territory Census of 1890. Retrieved March 2007: http://web.archive.org/web/20060206034927/http://www.ok-history.mus.ok.us/lib/1890/1890index.htm

Oklahoman, The. (2004). "Court upholds cockfighting ban." p. 1A.

Olson, K. (1984). *Oklahoma state and local taxes: Structure, issues, and reforms: A report to the Kerr Foundation.* Stillwater, OK: Oklahoma State University Press.

Olson, K. (2003). "The Oklahoma state budget crisis: Lessons from the past, policies for the future." In *State policy and economic development in Oklahoma: 2003* (pp. 1–20). Oklahoma City, OK: Oklahoma 21st Century, Inc.

Osborne, D. & Gaebler, T. (1992). *Reinventing government: How the entrepreneurial spirit is transforming the public sector.* New York: Penguin Books.

Osborne, D. & Hutchinson, P. (2004). *The price of government: Getting the results we need in an age of permanent fiscal crisis.* New York: Basic Books.

Peters, T. J. & Waterman, R. H. Jr. (1982). *In search of excellence: Lessons from America's best-run companies.* New York: Harper & Row.

Padgett, J. F. (1985). "The emergent organization of plea bargaining," *The American Journal of Sociology, 90.4,* 753–800.

Palmer, T. (1994). *Lifelines: The case for river conservation.* Covelo, CA: Island Press.

Penn D. (1990). "Measures of diversification." In *State policy and economic development in Oklahoma: 1990, A report to Oklahoma 2000 Inc.* (pp. 33–38). Oklahoma City, OK: Oklahoma 2000 Inc.

Phillips, D. & Harrison, M. (2004). *Out of the dust: The history of conservation in Oklahoma in the 20th Century.* Oklahoma Association of Conservation Districts, Oklahoma Conservation Commission, and USDA Natural Resources Conservation Service.

Porto, B. L. (2001). *May it please the court: Judicial processes and politics in America.* New York: Longman.

Price, M. (1998). "Report ranks Oklahoma's tax burden." *The Journal Record.*

Rafool, M. & Warnock, K. (1996). "Let the voters decide." *State Legislatures, 22.8,* 33–50.

Rainmondo, H.J. (1996). "State budgeting: Problems, choices and money." In C. E. Van Horn (Ed.), *The State of the States* (pp. 33–50). Washington, DC: Congressional Quarterly Press.

Rainey, H. G. & Steinbauer, P. (1999). "Galloping elephants: Developing elements of a theory of effective government organizations." *Journal of Public Administration Research and Theory, 9.1,* 1–32.

Rawls, W. (2005). "Hired guns: Ratio of lobbyists to legislators 2004." Retrieved from http://www.hillnews.com/news/022304/ss_gelak.aspx= on August 10, 2006.

Reingold, B. (1992). "Concepts of representation among female and male state legislators." *Legislative Studies Quarterly, 17*: 509–537.

Richardson, J. (2001). Archives of the West from 1877–1887. Indian policy reform extract from President Chester Arthur's First Annual Message to Congress December 6, 1881. Retrieved March 2007: http://www.pbs.org/weta/thewest/resources/archives/seven/indpol.htm.

Richardson, L. Jr. & Freeman, P. (1995). "Gender differences in constituency service among state legislators." *Political Research Quarterly, 48,* 169–179.

Schafer, S. (2002). "Blood sport's fans, foes take aim," *Tulsa World,* p. A1.

Shafritz, J. (2005). *Introducing public administration.* New York: Pearson Education, Inc.

Simpson, P. M., (2000). "The judicial system of Oklahoma." In C. L. Markwood (Ed.), *Oklahoma government & politics* (pp. 119–138). Dubuque, Iowa: Kendall/Hunt Publishing Co.

Snead, M. C. & Ireland, T. C. (2002). "Oklahoma regional and county output trends: 1980–1999." *Oklahoma Business Bulletin, 70,* 7–18.

Snead, M. (2007). *The Oklahoma economy. 2007 Economic outlook.* Stillwater, OK: Center for Applied Economic Research, Oklahoma State University.

Smith, C. E. (1999). *Courts, politics and the judicial process* (2nd edn.). Chicago: Nelson-Hall Publishing Co.

"State of the states: Assessing the capacity of states to achieve sustainable development through green planning." (2001). San Francisco, CA: Resource Renewal Institute.

State Rankings. (1999). A report by the Environmental Defense Fund. Retrieved March 2007: http://www.environmentaldefense.org/article.cfm?ConentID=1560

Stephens, M. (1997). "Oklahoma legal changes in animal waste

management precipitated by citizens' concern." Public Policy Director, Kerr Center for Sustainable Agriculture, Inc. Retrieved March 2007 from the Kerr Center Website: http://www.p2pays.org/ref/21/20034.htm.

State v. Walker 568 P.2d 286 (1977).

"Steady Climb: Legislative staff growth makes sense." (2004). *Daily Oklahoman,* p. 12A.

Stogsdill, S. (2007). "Tar Creek residents await buyout offers." *The Joplin Globe.* March 06. Retrieved March 2007 from *The Joplin Globe* Website: http://www.joplinglobe.com/neo_sek/local_story_065011922.html.

Strain, J., Reherman, C. F. & Crozier, L. (1990). *An outline of Oklahoma government.* Oklahoma City, OK: Americanism Commission, American Legion Department of Oklahoma.

Strain, J. L., Crozier, L. & Reherman, C. F. (1997). *An outline of Oklahoma government.* Edmond, OK: Department of Political Science, University of Central Oklahoma.

Stumpf, H. P. (1998). *American judicial politics* (2nd edn.). Upper Saddle River, NJ: Prentice-Hall Inc.

Sturm, A. L. (1982). "The development of American state constitutions." *Publius: The Journal of Federalism, 12,* 57–98.

Thomas, C. S. & Hrebenar, R. J. (1990). "Interest groups in the state." In V. Gray, H. Jacob & R. Albritton (Eds.)., *Politics in the American states: A comparative analysis* (5th edn.). Glenview, IL: Scott, Foresman/Little, Brown.

Thornton, A.. (2004). 3 tribes help fund lottery campaign. *The Daily, Oklahoman,* p. 1A.

Tolbert, M. (2004). "This generation's problem." In The *Oklahoma Academy 2004 Town Hall—Oklahoma's environment: Pursuing a responsible balance,* 6,24–25.

Turpen, M.. (2007). "Turpen's top seven: Why being a lawyer is the greatest job in the world." *Oklahoma Bar Journal.* Retrieved from http://www.okbar.org/obj/ backpage/090404.htm

UCO College of Business Administration. (2001). Sales tax on services. Retrieved from: http://busn.ucok.edu/ole.

U.S. Bureau of the Census. (2000). Population statistics for towns and cities in Oklahoma. Retrieved from www.us-news-watch.com/population/Oklahoma-pop.html.

U. S. Bureau of Economic Analysis. (2004). *2004 survey of current business, 84.* Washington, DC: Author.

Bibliography

U.S. Bureau of Economic Analysis (2007). *Survey of current business* (April).

U.S. Bureau of Labor Statistics. (2006). *Career guide to industries, 2006–2007*. Washington, DC: Department of Labor.

U.S. Department of Justice, (2004) "Civil cases and verdicts in large counties, 2001," *NCJ 202803*: April 2004. Washington, DC: Author.

Valenti, M. (1999). "Double Wrapped." The American Society of Mechanical Engineers. Retrieved March 2007: http://www.memagazine.org/backissues/membersonly/january99/features/doublewrap/doublewrap.html.

Walton, R. (2004). Motorcycle club revs up over tattoos. *Tulsa World*, p. A26.

Warner, L. (1990). "Oklahoma constitutional revision 1988–89." In *State Policy and Economic Development in Oklahoma: 1990*. Oklahoma City, OK: Oklahoma 2000 Inc.

Warner, L. (1995a). "An overview of Oklahoma's economic history: Part I." *Oklahoma Business Bulletin, 63.9*, 5–21.

Warner, L. (1995b). "An overview of Oklahoma's economic history: Part II" *Oklahoma Business Bulletin, 63.12*, 5–13.

Warner, L. (2002) "A note on new administrative organization of Oklahoma economic cevelopment." *Oklahoma Business Bulletin, 70 (July)*, 5–10.

Warner, L. & dauffenbach, R.C.. (2002). "Increasing Oklahoma's competitiveness in the new/global economy: An Assessment." *Oklahoma Business Bulletin, 70 (April)*, 7–20.

Warner, L. & Dauffenbach, R.C. (2004a) "Two Oklahoma incentives for economic development: Introduction to ad valorem tax exemption and Quality Jobs Act." In *State Policy and Economic Development in Oklahoma: 2004* (pp. 1–12). Oklahoma City, OK: Oklahoma 21st Century, Inc.

Warner, L. & Dauffenbach, R.C. (2004b) "Oklahoma's ad valorem tax exemption and the Quality Jobs Act: Analysis of economic impacts and tests for differential frowth" *State Policy and Economic Development in Oklahoma: 2004*. Oklahoma City, OK: Oklahoma 21st Century, Inc., pp. 13–28.

Warner, L. & Dauffenbach, R. C. (2006). "State policy and Oklahoma high-tech economic cevelopment" In *State Policy and Economic Development in Oklahoma: 2006* (49–62). Oklahoma City, OK: Oklahoma 21st Century, Inc.

Watson, R. A. & Downing, R. G. (1969). *The politics of the bench and the bar*. New York: Wiley.

Watson, Richard A., Rondal G. Downing, and Frederick C. Spiegel. (1967). "Bar politics, judicial selection and the representation of social interests." *The American Political Science Review, 61.1*, 54–71.

Wayne, Stephen J. (1997). *The road to the White House—The politics of presidential elections*. New York: St. Martin's Press.

Western Ecological Region, Corvallis, Oregon. (2007). Retrieved March 2007: http://www.epa.gov/wed/pages/ecoregions/ok_eco.htm.

Winters, R. P. (1996). "The politics of taxing and spending." In V. Gray & H. Jacob (Eds.), *Politics in the American states*. Washington, DC: Congressional Quarterly Press.

World's Editorial Writers. (2005). Tattoos. *Tulsa World*, p. A12.

Zizzo, D.. (200). "State voters favor tobacco trust fund," *The Daily Oklahoman*, p. 6.